To Advance the Race

To Advance the Race

Black Women's Higher Education from the Antebellum Era to the 1960s

LINDA M. PERKINS

© 2024 by the Board of Trustees
of the University of Illinois
All rights reserved
1 2 3 4 5 C P 5 4 3 2 1
♾ This book is printed on acid-free paper.

Library of Congress Cataloging-in-Publication Data
Names: Perkins, Linda Marie, author.
Title: To advance the race : Black women's higher education
   from the antebellum era to the 1960s / Linda Perkins.
 Description: Urbana, Chicago : University of Illinois Press,
   [2024] | Includes bibliographical references and index.
 Identifiers: LCCN 2023045665 (print) | LCCN 2023045666
   (ebook) | ISBN 9780252045738 (hardcover) | ISBN
 9780252087837 (paperback) | ISBN 9780252056598 (ebook)
Subjects: LCSH: African American women in higher
   education—History. | African American girls—
   Education—History. | Historically Black colleges and
   universities—History. | Educational anthropology—United
   States. | Education and social justice—United States—
   History. | Racism in education—United States—History. |
   Sexism in education—United States—History.
Classification: LCC LC2781 .P43 2024 (print) | LCC LC2781
   (ebook) | DDC 378.1/982996073—dc23/eng/20231011
LC record available at https://lccn.loc.gov/2023045665
LC ebook record available at https://lccn.loc.gov/2023045666

"To the Females of Colour": In any enterprise for the improvement of our people, either moral or mental, our hands would be palsied without women's influence . . . let our beloved female friends, then, rouse up, and exert all their power, in encouraging, and sustaining this effort [education] which we have made to disabuse the public mind of the misrepresentations made of our character and to show the world, that there is virtue among us, though concealed; talent, though buried; intelligence, though overlooked."

—*The Weekly Advocate* (January 7, 1837)

Contents

Acknowledgments   ix

Introduction   1

PART ONE

1 Education for "Race Uplift": History of Black Education in the North Prior to the Civil War   17

2 Abolitionist Colleges   30

PART TWO

3 College-Bred Black Women at Predominantly White Institutions in the Post–Civil War Era   63

4 Major Public Universities and Black Women in the Heartland   106

PART THREE

5 Black Women and Historically Black Colleges   127

6 The Emergence of the Deans of Women at HBCUs: Lucy Diggs Slowe—The First Black Woman Dean   145

7 Deans of Women at HBCUs after Slowe: Tuskegee Institute and Bennett College   180

PART FOUR

8 The Beginning of the Black Female Professoriate   233
9 Education and Marginality: The Conclusion   283

   Notes   313
   Bibliography   345
   Index   361

Acknowledgments

This book has been many years in the making, and I am indebted to many people. The genesis was in graduate school at the University of Illinois Urbana-Champaign in the 1970s. Dr. James D. Anderson introduced and opened my eyes to the history of Black higher education and was my doctoral advisor. Dr. V. P. Franklin was also on the faculty and noted a dearth of research on Black women in higher education and suggested I pursue a topic in that field. These Black male scholars launched my lifelong research interest in Black women's educational history. While on the University of Illinois–Urbana-Champaign faculty in the early 1990s, outstanding graduate students assisted me. They included Drs. Deirdre Cobb Roberts and Stephanie Tatum, both of whom have become senior scholars. I'm grateful to the late Mrs. Dorothy Porter-Wesley who was curator of the Moorland-Spingarn Research Center at Howard University, who encouraged my research and urged me to apply for a postdoctoral fellowship at the Mary Ingraham Bunting Institute at Radcliffe College in the late 1970s. This two-year award afforded me the opportunity to work with educational historian Dr. Patricia Albjerg Graham at Harvard University to continue and expand my research on Black women in higher education. I am forever in her debt. We continued our relationship decades after my years at Radcliffe, and she read the draft of my entire manuscript.

The Black Women's Oral History Project at Radcliffe (of which Dr. Porter-Wesley was on the board) afforded me the opportunity to meet with some of the women in the project. This manuscript includes oral histories of many Black women relevant to this study (all of whom are deceased) who were not included in the Radcliffe project but are certainly worthy. They were college graduates from the 1930s–1950s, and their experiences and reflections are the backbone of this study. I am deeply grateful for their generosity of time and enthusiasm for this book. Their histories allowed me to discuss the first generation of Black women graduate students and college faculty members. I'm particularly indebted to Jean Fairfax, whom I interviewed as one of the earliest Deans of Women at Tuskegee. She counseled me that it would be a mistake to only focus on Black women at HBCUs. She was a 1941 graduate of the University of Michigan and noted that Black women were in colleges and universities throughout the country. Following this advice (and adding another decade to my research), I began researching Black women in the Seven Sisters colleges, major public institutions, and important locations like Hunter College in New York City.

I have had outstanding research assistance from current and former graduate students at Claremont Graduate University, where I have taught for the last twenty years. Among them is the late Dr. Edward Robinson, who helped organize all my oral histories and primary sources and kept my files in order. I regret that his untimely death did not allow him to see the fruits of his labor. I am also indebted to Dr. Elizabeth Craigg Walker, who worked with me for years on this project and is now an outstanding educational historian and professor. Dr. Tiffani Smith has also worked with me for numerous years on this book, and my most recent research assistant Monica Perkins (no relation) has provided outstanding assistance. Her careful fact-checking, proofreading, and timely responses to inquiries have made her a joy to work with. Elisa Slee proofread my final manuscript and provided invaluable assistance in a short period of time. I'm deeply indebted to her. I would also like to thank Delores Combs for transcribing many oral interviews and histories of the women in the study. Her interest in the project made working with her an enjoyable experience.

I am also indebted to my colleagues in the history of women's higher education with whom I have served on untold numbers of panels with, published with, and received their feedback on my work. They include Kabia Baumgartner, Linda Eisenmann, Karen Graves, Margaret Nash, Kelly Santorius, Sally Schawager, and Cally Waite. The late Patricia Palmieri did not live to see the completion of this book. She and I discussed our mutual manuscripts for years as we did research on our respective projects. Her friendship and encouragement are deeply appreciated.

Thanks to my former Claremont Graduate University colleague Dr. Daryl Smith who constantly asked me when my book would be finished. I was pleased to announce to her when it was finally completed. I am also indebted to the funding sources that made this research possible, including the Mary Ingraham Bunting Institute at Radcliffe College, two Spencer Foundation grants, the National Endowment for the Humanities Travel to Collection Fund, the University of Illinois, and the Claremont Graduate University faculty research funds. And I am grateful to Dean DeLacy Ganley of the School of Educational Studies at Claremont Graduate School for supporting this manuscript.

I am appreciative of the many archivists who have helped me along the way. I particularly want to thank the late William Bigglestone, archivist at Oberlin College who directed me to the invaluable sources on Fanny Jackson Coppin and other Black students at Oberlin during the Civil War years; the late Beth Howse at the Special Collection at Fisk University who helped me for years with information on Black women students and faculty at Fisk as well as the Rosenwald Fellowship Papers; the former archivist and curators of the Moorland Spingarn Research Center at Howard University: University Archivist Dr. Clifford Muse, Assistant Curator of Manuscripts Dr. Ida Jones, and Curator of Manuscripts Ms. Joe Ellen El Bashir. I am indebted to the archivists and their staff at the Seven Sisters colleges and at Hunter College.

My greatest debt goes to my parents: Marion and Minerva Perkins who instilled in their children the value and love of education. Their sacrifices to help us obtain our goals is beyond words. I also want to thank my sister, Kathy Perkins, a scholar of Black women playwrights, who was a great source of support. Being able to discuss our overlapping research was very gratifying. Finally, I want to thank my daughter Lauren Perkins Wimbush for her support and encouragement. I don't think she can remember when I wasn't working on this book. I began working on this book before she was born. By the time she was in college, she had accompanied me to the Moorland Springarn Archives and Special Collections to help me research early Black women faculty at Howard University.

I am thankful to the two anonymous reviewers of this manuscript whose very constructive comments helped me with revisions. Finally, I would like to thank the editorial and production staff of the University of Illinois for their excellent work in seeing this project to its completion.

To Advance the Race

Introduction

In 1837 New York, the quote from an article within a Black newspaper urged African American women to seek an education during the antebellum period.[1] During the era of slavery, and afterward, African Americans viewed education as synonymous with freedom. By Emancipation, in 1863, every southern state prohibited the education of enslaved Africans, and in some cases, free Blacks as well.[2] There had been scattered opportunities for free Blacks and selected enslaved Africans to become literate. However, David Walker's 1829 incendiary publication brought all teaching of enslaved Africans to an immediate halt. *An Appeal to the Coloured Citizens of the World* by Boston Black abolitionist David Walker encouraged enslaved Africans to violently resist the unjust institution. The Black abolitionist in Boston[3] stated "coloured people to acquire learning in this country makes tyrants quake and tremble on their sandy foundation.... the bare name of educating the coloured."[4] This document was widely distributed throughout the free Black communities of the North and in parts of the South.

Literate and formerly enslaved Africans participated in a series of rebellions served to reinforce the notion among southern whites that educated Blacks were dangerous. Blacksmith Gabriel Prosser in Virginia (1800), carpenter Denmark Vesey (1822) in South Carolina, and Nat Turner (1831) in Virginia were all Black-led slave rebellions. Due to events like these, the fear of educated Blacks became so great that as noted earlier, educating Blacks in the South was forbidden and forced underground. Thus, it is in this context that African American women were encouraged to become active agents for "race uplift" and Black advancement. While education within the white community was historically viewed as a male prerogative, to enslaved and free Blacks, education was viewed as essential for the entire race. In the above 1829 Boston appeal, Walker emphasized that education was essential for all "coloured people."

This book explores the nineteenth-century notion by enslaved and formerly enslaved Africans that education was essential for their freedom and their advancement and how this belief impacted the education of Black women and girls from the antebellum era through the mid-1960s. The mid-1960s was the watershed moment marked with the passage of the 1964 Civil Rights Act, the 1965 Higher Education Act, and the assassination of Reverend Martin Luther King Jr. in 1968. These events, coupled with the Johnson Administration's Great Society legislation, such as affirmative action and TRIO programs (Upward Bound, Educational Opportunity Programs, Student Services Programs) enhanced the educational access of poor and Black students. The instituting of these programs led to the conscious recruitment of African American students into predominantly white institutions of higher education. This study discusses and explores the efforts and value of African American families to educate their daughters, as well as their sons, from the earliest years of this nation. During this period, African Americans overwhelmingly viewed education as benefiting the entire race and not merely the individual. Throughout the nineteenth and twentieth centuries, the educational accomplishments of Black women and men were highly celebrated within African American communities. Antislavery newspapers highlighted these accomplishments, and Black newspapers and other publications, especially *The Crisis* magazine, published by the National Association of Colored People (NAACP) starting in 1910, consistently published photos and noted the educational accomplishments of Black women as often as it did about the men. Any educational achievement of a Black person during this period was viewed as an accomplishment for the race. Black women outside the antebellum South sporadically attended female seminaries, academies, and later, normal schools from the 1830s throughout the nineteenth century, in New England and throughout the North. From the early nineteenth century, African American women's opportunities to obtain secondary and collegiate education on a continuous basis came through three abolitionist founded institutions— New York Central College (NYCC) in McGrawville, New York; Oberlin College in Ohio; and Berea College in Kentucky. While Oberlin College is the oldest, and still survives, NYCC lasted for slightly over a decade (1849–1860). African Americans attended Berea College from 1855 to 1904, until the Kentucky legislature outlawed integrated education. Many northern educated Black women from these institutions or colleges, as well as other predominantly white institutions from the late nineteenth and early twentieth centuries, moved south to teach in order to meet the demand for teachers for Black youth. They also became some of the first female faculty members at historically Black colleges and universities. Although the call for African Americans to pursue an education was articulated through the philosophy of "race uplift," the reality of gender was also an issue. This study will discuss the intersection of race, gender, social class, and geographical location as the decades unfold and African American women attended a variety of institutions of higher education in the nation. While the contributions of Black women were sorely needed, their race emerged out of enslavement and sought to build their own institutions, their roles were overwhelmingly seen as teachers.

The early history of Black women in higher education has received very little scholarly attention. Black women and girls desired to have an education from the moment it was available to them, an important aspect of African American history. Gender issues and records have been discussed in some of the classic literature on Black higher education. A recent study of Black women's education in the antebellum period, *In Pursuit of Knowledge: Black Women and Educational Activism in Antebellum America* by Kabria Baumgartner is the most extensive research on this era.[5] Some scholars whose works provided visibility for Black women through their works include W. E. B. Du Bois' early research on Black college students in 1900 and 1910. His studies included a discussion of women. He continued his inclusion of women in *The Crisis* magazine by chronicling Black women college students and graduates each year in the August Education issue. Sociologist Charles S. Johnson published a sociological study in 1938 entitled the *Negro College Graduate,* in which he provided statistical and narrative information on African American women.[6] Harry Washington Greene's *Holders of Doctorates among American Negroes* published in 1946 includes Black women and their dissertation topics and the degree awarding institutions.[7]

In the 1940s and 1950s, Black women scholars wrote four relevant dissertations exploring the views, concerns, curricula, and interests of Black women college students and graduates. Many of these students and graduates expressed ambivalence about the purposes of their education and the social consequences of their academic and professional success.[8] As Black men struggled to obtain "manhood" rights, the achievements of many Black women (and the larger number of Black women college students) were viewed by many as negative for the race during the 1940s, after World War II. What was once viewed as the strength of the collective efforts began to be rolled back due to the larger societal belief that men should dominate and be leaders, while women should take their rightful place as supportive "helpmates." In 1940, Pauli Murray, who became an activist lawyer and Episcopal priest and founder of the National Organization of Women, coined the sexism of Black men as "Jane Crow."[9]

Studies, such as Darlene Clark Hine's study of African American women nurses, Paula Giddings' history of Delta Sigma Theta, Cynthia Neverdon-Morton's study of African American women of the South and their desire to "advance" the race, Stephanie Shaw on Black professional women workers during the Jim Crow era, and Stephanie Y. Evans and Brittany Cooper's work on the intellectual history of Black college women are important sources in the field.[10]

Two recent institutional histories discuss early Black women students: *Scarlet and Black, Volume Two: Constructing Race and Gender at Rutgers, 1865–1945* and Andrea Walton's collection of essays, *Women at Indiana University.*[11] These works, as well as this book, provide evidence that there is not a single narrative when it comes to the education and the experiences of Black women's higher education.

In most instances, because Black women were not perceived as equal to white women, they were not afforded the genteel respect and chivalry inherent in what was considered "true womanhood" in the nineteenth century.[12] Sojourner Truth in her famous question in 1851 "Ain't I a Woman?" reminded her audience that she was also a woman although she had not experienced the respect that most white women were afforded.[13]

With the passing of the Fifteenth Amendment in 1870, Black men were granted the right to vote, signaling the first time Black men were granted citizenship rights that Black women were denied. White women had always been denied suffrage, but this change in status for Black men ironically put Black women and white women on an equal basis being denied voting rights. By 1900, twenty-two Black men had served in the United States Congress and scores had held state and local government positions. These newly acquired rights for Black men were short-lived with the end of Reconstruction. In *Plessy v. Ferguson* (1896), the Supreme Court legitimized racial segregation and led to untold violence and brutality against African Americans.[14] Jim Crow laws sanctioned discrimination in employment, public education, public accommodations, transportation, serving on juries, and other areas.[15] Despite whites' retrenchment of rights for Blacks, Black men's notions of patriarchy increased. While Black men were oppressed by the same system as Black women, many of them embraced patriarchal views of gender. Sexism and misogyny are explored throughout this volume. How these views negatively impacted Black women's advancement in Black institutions and organizations, as well as personal relationships, will be discussed. The stringent nineteenth century Victorian notions of sexual propriety, acceptable dress codes (including appropriate colors for Black women to wear), and prescribed social and cultural norms defined respectability for women, and most Historically Black Colleges and Universities (HBCUs) adopted these practices. In addition, these institutions and the communities these women came from stressed conservative religious doctrines. White missionaries as well as Black religious denominations established earlier colleges with a focus on moral and religious training. Recent scholars have written in great depth concerning the negative consequences of the concept of "race uplift" by means of "the politics of responsibility."[16] These strategies for helping the race were being analyzed through the lens of classism and elitism. While it is clear that many of the women in the nineteenth century did embrace some aspects of Victorian womanhood, these women were far from accepting the established gender norms that society expected of them. They traveled widely as speakers, kept their birth names when they married and added their husband's last name (e.g., Mary Church Terrell, Fanny Jackson Coppin, Fanny Barrier Williams, Ida B. Wells Barnett, etc.), and worked when they were not expected to or needed to for financial reasons. Recent biographies of Lucy Diggs Slowe, Fanny Barrier Williams, Anna Julia Cooper and Ida B. Wells Barnett, Pauli Murray, and Constance Baker Motley detail these women's lives and activities within the Black communities they led and the dual issues of race and gender that they confronted.[17] These were not traditional women. However, to be sure, there were also women who were more traditional than the above women, who had national and international visibility. While these women were all religious (and Pauli Murray became an Episcopal priest), with the exception of Fanny Jackson Coppin, who is the oldest of all of these women and constantly made religious references in her letters and reports, most of these women's work was not full of religious references. Religious denominations and geographical location dictated their beliefs and actions.

This book will also discuss the tremendous impact traditional gender ideologies played in the lives of African American women. In 1903, W. E. B. Du Bois used the phrase "the talented tenth" to identify the leaders of the race who were college educated.[18] While the phrase is most associated with Du Bois, northern white philanthropist Henry Morehouse coined the actual concept in 1896.[19] The early generations of Black women college students (1850s–1880s) consistently stated that their desire for higher education was motivated by their desire to help their race. As the nineteenth century ended, attitudes toward Black women's educational aspirations and leadership roles shifted toward more patriarchal views of womanhood, with many race uplift activities becoming gender stratified (e.g., the formation in 1896 of the National Association of Colored Women followed by the all-male American Negro Academy, a Black intellectual organization in 1897). While Black women were expected to "uplift the race," many prescribed this work within the confines of domesticity, being public and private school teachers of Black youth. They were expected to be nurturers and supporters rather than leaders within the race. By the 1920s, as Black women began earning PhDs and serving as college professors in Black colleges in the South, they found themselves indispensable, yet they were not expected to assume leadership outside of perceived female designated disciplines (education, home economics, nursing, and physical education). The majority of Black women were enrolled in state teacher's colleges throughout the twentieth century because college educated and certified teachers were in great demand and would ensure employment in the increasingly growing public schools of the South. Many Black women were instilled with deep religious orientation from their communities, and especially from HBCUs, resulting in them not voicing opposition to being underpaid or passed over for positions in Black institutions. In their oral histories, many would often note "money wasn't important" but the work and contributions they were making to their communities and students were their rewards; many also believed that a discussion of money was unseemly. This was not universally true; for example, at Howard University, where there was a cadre of distinguished women faculty, they did band together and sought as a group more equitable salaries and promotions on the campus beginning in the early 1950s.[20] For other Black women academics—their struggle for equitable pay was a solo effort.

By the mid-1920s to the early 1950s, there was increased concern among some Black women about the nature and purposes of higher education and the suggestion that Black women and girls were receiving negative messages about their roles in society. Several important figures and organizations emerged during this period. Prominent among them was the first woman dean at Howard University (1923), Lucy Diggs Slowe; she was one of the founders in 1924 of the National Association of College Women (NACW) and the National Association of Women's Deans and Advisors of Women in Colored Schools (NAWDACS) in 1929. The organizations Slowe founded and affiliated with became the vocal advocates for the rights of Black women college students on Black campuses—demanding that these young women be counseled beyond teacher education and other perceived female-dominated professions. The documents of these organizations provide an extensive view of the lives of women students in HBCUs. Both NACW and NAWDACS organizations urged that Black women students be taken seriously as potential leaders of their communities beyond the female spheres.[21]

As such, this book includes a discussion of the early graduate education of African American women, as well as including the role of the Julius Rosenwald Foundation and the General Education Board of the Rockefeller Foundation in providing fellowship funds for enrollments in master and doctoral programs during the 1930s and 1940s. The applications and final reports to these foundations provide detailed information of Black women's work and experiences in HBCUs. While much of the literature of Black women educators examines their significant role as teachers and school founders, this study encompasses the first generation of Black women in the professoriate on Black college campuses.[22]

In the discussion of Black women's higher education as students, professors, and administrators, this study will discuss their experiences in a variety of educational and geographical settings. While most Black women attended Black colleges in the South after Emancipation, Black women have matriculated in a wide array of institutions of higher education. The earliest Black women college students attended predominantly white institutions outside of the South, most notably Oberlin College in Ohio. They also attended, in limited numbers, elite women's colleges in the East (known as the Seven Sisters colleges), as well as other select private white institutions outside the South that occasionally admitted them. Many Black women attended large public institutions but also attended large private ones as well (such as the University of Chicago, Cornell, Syracuse, University of Pennsylvania, and others). Black women educated at elite colleges in the North in the late-nineteenth and early twentieth centuries were often middle class and studied abroad and had experiences that distanced them socially from most of the African Americans they would ultimately teach in southern Black schools and colleges. But, in their desire to advance the race, they brought their experiences to the students they taught, mentored, and influenced. Black women also attended predominantly white land-grant and other public institutions in the "heartland" and the Midwest and in California beginning at the turn of the twentieth century. According to Barbara Solomon, historian of women's higher education, Oberlin, Kansas State, and Hunter College in New York City had admitted more Black women by the 1930s other than HBCUs.[23] Like those women in the small liberal arts colleges, Black women at large public universities had to confront discrimination in housing and on campus activities until the 1940s, and in many instances, even later. Discussed further in the following chapters, African American women have attended a vast array of educational institutions resulting in varied experiences.

While this book discusses Black women's education and race, the issue of gender becomes pronounced after World War II. The GI Bill, which provided funds for housing, education, and other benefits for veterans after the war, resulted in working-class white men obtaining higher education from some of the top institutions in the country. This had the reverse impact on Black men who overwhelmingly did not have high school diplomas due to the absence of public high schools for Blacks in the South until after World War II. As the number of white men college graduates grew, and white women retreated in large numbers to the home as homemakers after WWII, the reverse was the case with the Black community. White collar jobs soared for white men; by the mid-1950s, white collar jobs outnumbered blue collar jobs, and for the first time in the country, 60 percent of the country was defined as middle class by the government.[24] In 1953, men were 64 percent of white students in college. For the same year, women were 59.1 percent of Black college students. The number who earned bachelor's degrees in 1953 at HBCUs were 36 percent men and 64 percent women.[25] The racism of white veteran counselors resulted in Black men who were able to attend college often being referred to industrial programs. In addition, Black veterans were not able to obtain the zero interest loans to move into the new suburban homes that exploded throughout the country. In 1946, the Association of American Colleges and Universities noted only 5 percent of HBCUs were accredited.[26] Hence, the higher education options for Black veterans were limited.

As college-educated white women became full-time homemakers or worked part-time, if at all, in the late '40s and throughout the '50s, Black women persisted in college attendance and the workforce by necessity and desire. The gender imbalance in educational attainment of the Black and white races brought enormous conflict between Black men and college-educated women. Black men were shut out of jobs and saw white men earning great wages, buying homes with stay-at-home wives; therefore, some Black men began to resent Black women for their accomplishments and employment. Also, while 80 percent of Black college women graduates were married in the mid-1930s, only 14 percent were full-time homemakers. Only 9.8 percent of white women college graduates were employed at this time.[27] By the mid-1950s, 75 percent of Black women who were college graduates married; however, 50 percent noted they were married to men who were of a lower education or socioeconomic status.[28] This trend persisted through the end of this study. Being married is not the mark of success—yet society, and constant articles and studies in the Black popular press and by academics, monitored Black women's marital status after the 1940s. As Black women's educational accomplishments outpaced those of Black men, these women were made to feel guilty because of their degrees.

The Black community historically encouraged Black youth to pursue an education to help the race. From the antebellum era through the 1950s and 1960s, Black women and girls were prominent in major lawsuits to integrate both public schools and universities. At no point in the push for educational equity and advancement were Black women and girls absent from these activities. The response to their efforts by the Black community, especially men by the mid-1960s, will conclude the study.

Chapter One, "Education for 'Race Uplift,'" will discuss the philosophy of "race uplift" in the nineteenth century and the early roots of education for women in general and Blacks, in particular, until the end of the Civil War in 1865. While education, up until this point, was historically believed to be unsuited for women, by the 1840s there became a view of "female education" whose curriculum specifically focused upon women's "separate sphere" and the notion of "true womanhood."[29] This thesis was not universally true and has been challenged by the revisionist research of Margaret Nash, which during the antebellum period, indicates that there were far more opportunities for women's education than previously reported.[30] Black women were not perceived as women by the larger society, and assumptions made during this period regarding women's gentility and fragileness were not applied to them. The notion of Black women being gendered was highly contested because they were reduced to people without a gender, and their struggle was foremost and always about race. Women banded together with Black men in the monumental effort to help their enslaved and later Emancipated brothers and sisters. A formal education was central to this mission. While white individuals and organizations established schools for African Americans during this period, the earliest efforts for Blacks were by Blacks themselves. V. P. Franklin's research on Black determination is the framework for this book.[31]

Chapter Two, "Abolitionist Colleges," will discuss the importance of abolitionist colleges (NYCC in McGrawville, New York; Oberlin College in Ohio; and Berea College in Kentucky), the earliest institutions of higher education to admit Black men and women on a continuous basis without regard to race or gender. White abolitionists established all three colleges. NYCC, for example, was located in upstate New York and founded by antislavery Baptists. The earliest Black woman college graduate, Grace Mapps, is believed to have been awarded a degree at NYCC in the 1850s.

The town of Oberlin, Ohio, was a stop on the Underground Railroad. Formal education was so important to many free Blacks that they relocated to Oberlin in order for their children—boys and girls—to attend the primary, high school, and college. The earliest Black women graduated from Oberlin in 1850 with certificates in the Ladies Department. By 1865, three Black women had obtained baccalaureate degrees in the college division. By 1910, more than four hundred African American women had attended Oberlin. Sixty-one had earned degrees from the Ladies Department, the college's Music Conservatory, or the college. Berea College in Kentucky was the only white college in the South prior to Emancipation that admitted both Black men and women with white students. Historian John Frederick Bell's recent book, *Degrees of Equality: Abolitionist Colleges and the Politics of Race* discusses all three of these institutions and their importance in the education of previously enslaved Africans and free Blacks.[32]

Chapter Three, "College-Bred Black Women at Predominantly White Institutions in the Post–Civil War Era," discusses the small, but important number of African American women who studied at elite white private institutions (the Seven Sisters colleges), and other private white schools in the nineteenth and early twentieth century outside the South. There were only two accredited Black colleges that were of collegiate level prior to 1935. As a result, Blacks in the North had a substantial educational advantage over their southern kin in attending accredited liberal arts colleges. As late as 1910, there was not a single rural eighth grade public school nor was there a public high school in the entire South for Black residents.[33] Hence, like most white colleges had in their early years, many Black colleges had preparatory departments to provide a high school diploma because of the lack of high schools throughout the South. The educated Blacks (men and women) from the white institutions from the North staffed many of the HBCUs, as these institutions sought collegiate status and accreditation. Many of these women had studied abroad. In the 1920s, Alpha Kappa Alpha, the oldest Black women's sorority, began offering fellowships for their members to study abroad. Beginning in the mid-1920s, Black women studied at the Sorbonne, the University of Berlin, Oxford, and other European institutions.

Chapter Four, "Major Public Universities and Black Women in the Heartland," discusses education in the Midwest. Due to migration of African Americans from southern states to the mid- and far west, Black women who moved from these southern states attended public land-grant (and some private) institutions throughout the Midwest (Iowa, Illinois, Michigan, Indiana, Ohio, Kansas, Nebraska, Minnesota, etc.). In addition, Black women from neighboring states that barred Black students from attending their colleges (Oklahoma and Texas) also matriculated at colleges in these states. They also attended colleges in the West like the University of Southern California, University of California, University of the Redlands, and the University of Nevada. This chapter discusses the women in these institutions and the important role their membership in Black sororities played as students. These organizations were central to the women's camaraderie and mutual support.

Chapter Five, "Black Women and Historically Black Colleges," discusses the growth of Black colleges, both public and private. These institutions were established before the Civil War and afterward by white missionaries, Black religious denominations, and the federal government. Public colleges were established through the Second Morrill Act (1890). Because of the hardening of legal segregation following Reconstruction, this Act provided federal funds for border and southern states that barred Blacks from attending the white state schools established through the first Morrill Act of 1862. This Act provided land and funds for nineteen separate Black public colleges resulting in a dual-segregated public education system.

Because public education for Black students did not exist in the South except in major cities until the 1940s, the Black land-grant institutions provided preparatory and high school classes well into the first four decades of the twentieth century. Prominent women educators started private preparatory schools in the South—Lucy Laney founded Haines Institute in Savannah, Georgia, Mary McLeod Bethune designed the Institute in Daytona Beach, Florida, and Charlotte Hawkins Brown established Palmer Memorial Institute in Sedalia, North Carolina that prepared students for these and other institutions of higher education. Two HBCUs were established in the 1850s in Ohio and Pennsylvania by religious denominations. African Methodist Episcopal Church founded Wilberforce College, a coeducational institution, and Presbyterians founded Ashmum Institute, (later named Lincoln University) for Black men in Pennsylvania. In this chapter, I will discuss Black women's student's gendered experiences within the various HBCUs. Particular attention will be focused on curricula and extracurricular opportunities.

Chapter Six, "The Emergence of the Deans of Women at HBCUs," discusses the appointment of Lucy Diggs Slowe, the first Black woman dean at Howard University and her impact and importance in developing deans of women's departments and appointments at HBCUs. A 1908 alumna of Howard University with a master's degree from Teachers College at Columbia in Student Affairs (1915), Slowe was the leading Black authority on student personnel and current issues on college women. A feminist, Slowe was a proponent and advocate for Black women students. She was a charter member of the National Association of College Women (NACW)—an organization established in 1923 for Black women who were graduates of accredited colleges. Because of this restriction, the only women eligible to become members were graduates of white colleges and Howard and Fisk universities, the only two accredited HBCUs at that time. This group was in the vanguard of monitoring the conditions of Black women students in Black colleges. After Slowe became dean at Howard in 1922, in 1929 Slowe established another group for women who worked as deans and advisors of women in HBCUs, the National Association of Women and Advisors of Women in Colored Schools (NAWDACS). The activities of these two groups with Slowe's leadership will be discussed.

Chapter Seven, "Deans of Women at HBCUs after Slowe," discusses the activities of the NACW and the NAWDACS after the unexpected death of Lucy Diggs Slowe in 1937. By then, other women whom Slowe mentored had emerged and could continue her work on behalf of Black women students. The two groups continued their conferences as well as discussed issues related to the well-being of women students at HBCUs. Bennett and Spelman Colleges, the women's colleges, sponsored conferences to discuss Black women's higher education.

Chapter Eight, "The Beginning of the Black Female Professoriate," discusses the increase in the number of Black women in graduate and professional schools from the 1920s through the early 1960s. The first Black woman to earn a medical degree was in 1864, and the first with a law degree was in 1872. By 1921, three Black women earned PhDs from the University of Chicago, Radcliffe College (Harvard University), and the University of Pennsylvania. Beginning in the 1940s, the Julius Rosenwald and the Rockefeller Foundations offered graduate and professional school fellowships to promising Black scholars and artists, primarily to increase the number of PhDs on the faculties at HBCUs, as many sought full accreditation. Before these funding opportunities, many Black women graduate students, primarily teachers, paid their own tuition to attend summer school to pursue their graduate degrees for years. These fellowships were a godsend for the women who won these awards. Unlike their white women counterparts who often faced gender discrimination in employment in higher education except in perceived female-dominated fields like home economics and physical education, Black women with graduate degrees were readily employed by HBCUs and public and private secondary schools. While Black women were the majority in undergraduate programs at HBCUs by the 1940s, Black men dominated graduate and professional school enrollment during this period. Because most Black women undergraduates, particularly those who attended HBCUs, were in teacher education or were enrolled in state teacher's colleges, the curriculum for those programs did not include many requisite college courses resulting in disqualifying these women for graduate programs without taking additional undergraduate courses (usually an additional year of undergraduate classes). Hence, most of the earliest Black women graduate and professional students were graduates of white institutions of higher education or Fisk and Howard universities, the first two Black colleges to be fully accredited.

Chapter Nine, "Education and Marginality: The Conclusion," focuses on the change in attitudes in the African American community about gender roles. The chapter's title comes from one of the four major dissertations published during the 1940s that highlighted the dilemmas facing Black women college students. The study noted these women's "marginality" within the Black community. Each study was a doctoral dissertation that addressed the problems, needs, and challenges of college-educated Black women and those enrolled in college. Sexism was rampant on Black college campuses even though Black women were the majority at most of the campuses, and Black women served on the faculties of these institutions, including the all-male Morehouse College. Black women were paid significantly less than male colleagues with the same (and often less) education and experience and were rarely promoted to positions of leadership that were not in fields that were stereotypically female—primarily home economics and women's physical education. These college-educated Black women who were primarily on the campuses of Fisk and Howard Universities organized the NACW in 1924 and the NAWDACS in 1929. Both organizations became the voice and conscience of Black women students and faculty in their quest for gender equity on these campuses. This chapter discusses how these organizations kept the issue of gender equity visible in journal and newspaper editorials and articles in the Black press. Black women were active in sororities and other national Black women's organizations with overlapping memberships, and they collaborated with one another on these issues. Three of the dissertations on the Black woman college student were completed at Teachers College, Columbia University in 1942, 1948, and 1956; the fourth one was written at the University of Southern California in 1948. The authors surveyed and interviewed Black women undergraduates from selected HBCUs during the Second World War and postwar era during a period when the National Association for the

Advancement of Colored People had commenced numerous lawsuits challenging segregation of southern graduate and professional schools. Black women students were prominent in this litigation.

The Conclusion assesses the significance of the evidence documenting the historical difference in the purposes and support of education for African American women and girls within the Black community during the first one hundred years of their formal education. Bound together, as Fanny Jackson Coppin noted in 1863, by a "common sorrow," all African Americans were expected to help one another with the purpose of "helping the race" as the primary reason given why women, particularly in the nineteenth century, pursued an education. As the decades proceeded, Black women added economic improvement and elevated social status as additional reasons for pursuing higher education. The earliest formally educated Black women were overwhelmingly educators—due to the dramatic need and the fact that this was the only field they were guaranteed employment in. Women were grossly underpaid and often similar to missionaries when one reviews their selfless efforts and many contributions with extremely low compensation.

The present and historical gap between Black men and women's achievements in higher educational attainment and the impact on the Black community is explained by the racial and gender history of this nation. By 1952, nearly 65 percent of the college degrees from Black colleges went to women. Initially educated to "help the race," men and women in the nineteenth century were encouraged to pursue an education. However, overwhelmingly Black women's degrees were in education, while most Black male college students majored in fields that led to graduate and professional school. The early literature on the higher education of white women revealed they were frequently discouraged from obtaining a higher education in the early nineteenth century and told there was "no utility" for their degrees. However, as Black colleges and Black communities developed, Black women were readily employed within them. College-educated Black women combined career with family—even those who did not have to work for financial reasons. These women believed their talents and skills were needed in their communities and the world. Despite the civil rights campaign rhetoric emphasis on Black "manhood," Black women and girls were key factors in the social movement. Black girls were prominent in the NAACP lawsuits, such as the 1954 *Brown v. Board of Education* Supreme Court case with Linda Brown of Topeka, Kansas, being the lead plaintiff. The six-year-old Ruby Bridges integrated the all-white Frantz Public School in New Orleans in 1960 escorted by federal marshals. When the nation witnessed the integration of Central High School in Little Rock, Arkansas, in 1957, six of the nine Black students to integrate the school were young women. Similarly, as the all-white major institutions of higher education were integrated in the South,

Black women were prominent in these endeavors as well—Charlayne Hunter at the University of Georgia with Hamilton Holmes in 1961; and Vivian Malone along with James Hood at the University of Alabama in 1963. The book concludes with the 1964 Civil Rights Act, which banned discrimination based on race, religion, gender, or national origin, marking a fitting conclusion to this book. By the 1960s, African American women had witnessed a backlash regarding their efforts—from both outside and within the Black community since the early twentieth century (reflected in the findings of the four dissertations discussed in the previous chapter). When sociologist Daniel Patrick Moynihan issued his report on the Black family in 1965, which erroneously characterized it as pathological and "matriarchal," the editor, in a special issue of the Black publication *Ebony* magazine agreed with the study noting significant contributions to the race that can be traced to the educational and professional gains of Black women. However, the editorial, while noting Black women, in spite of their historical contributions in helping the Black community and their families, stated, Black people should "put the past behind us." It continued that Black women's educational success has come "at the expense of the psychological health of the Negro male." Black women were advised to take a subordinate role in the family and focus on homemaking and volunteer work in the community.[34]

This study concludes in the mid-1960s as the modern Civil Rights Movement with the Great Society programs of President Lyndon B. Johnson that instituted affirmative action programs including the recruitment of Black men and women, as well as other students of color in predominantly white institutions. By this period, many more opportunities existed for Black youth—male and female—in terms of education and occupations. Black women college graduates were no longer locked into the field of education and had a larger array of college choices. This study will use the terms Black and African American interchangeably.

PART ONE

CHAPTER 1

Education for "Race Uplift"
History of Black Education in the North Prior to the Civil War

> I would crawl on my hands and knees through mud and mire, to the feet of a learned man, where I would sit and humbly supplicate him to instill into me, that which devils nor tyrants could remove, only with my life—for coloured people to acquire learning in this country, make tyrants quake and tremble on their sandy foundation . . . The bare name of educating the coloured people, scares our cruel oppressors almost to death.
> —David Walker, *Appeal*, 96.

African Americans have always viewed education as paramount to their liberation in this nation. In 1829, the above plea by the literate free Black, David Walker, expressed the urgency that education would bring to his enslaved race in the south. Between 1777 and 1804, every state north of the Mason-Dixon line had passed antislavery legislation, and 75 percent of all formerly enslaved Africans in the North were free by 1810. Slavery was completely eradicated in the North by 1830. Despite legal freedom, free formerly enslaved Africans in most places experienced enormous economic, political, educational, and social discrimination. By 1840, 93 percent of formerly enslaved Africans in the North were not allowed to vote. They were forbidden from carrying mail, testifying in court, marrying outside of their race, and carrying firearms. They were segregated in public transportation and in schools, if that option existed for them at all.[1] Gender distinctions were few in the treatment of formerly enslaved Africans. Men and women were equally disenfranchised. The men were not afforded "manhood rights" and the women were not afforded recognition as women or the title of respect as "ladies." Both groups were relegated to primarily menial and domestic occupations. As a result, they established private schools, independent newspapers, and self-help organizations for self-reliance and mutual support.

As more and more enslaved Africans escaped to the free states of the North in the 1840s, assisted by abolitionists on the Underground Railroad, the United States Congress passed the Fugitive Slave Act in 1850. This Act required residents of free states to return runaway enslaved Africans from southern states back to their owners. Persons found harboring or feeding fugitives were liable to up to six months' imprisonment and a $1,000 fine. Because enslaved Africans could not utilize the courts on their behalf, free Blacks were often seized and sent into bondage.[2] This was the case of the infamous Solomon Northup, born a free Black man in New York. He was kidnapped in 1841 when he was tricked into going to Washington, DC, a slave territory, on the pretense of a job for an event as a violinist. Northup was sold into slavery in the Deep South. He was enslaved in several locations in Louisiana.[3] Walker's *Appeal* urged slaves to take physical violence against their oppressors. Uprisings led by literate Blacks, such as Gabriel Prosser, Denmark Vesey, and Nat Turner occurred from 1800 to 1831. Enslaved women as well as men were involved in uprisings and were resistant to slavery in other ways. For example, Harriett Tubman began helping enslaved Africans escape to the North on the Underground Railroad in 1849, leading over three hundred slaves to freedom. It was in the shared oppression of slavery and discrimination experienced by enslaved and formerly enslaved Africans that men and women forged a bond of racial solidarity. The connection between literacy, slave uprisings, and other forms of resistance was clear. After the revolt of Gabriel Prosser and his wife, Nancy, and others in 1800, one white slaveholder remarked, "every year adds to the number of those [enslaved Africans] who can read and write." This increase of knowledge is the principal agent in evoking the spirit we have to *fear* (emphasis added).[4] By the 1830s, the fear of educated Blacks resulted in all educational efforts for them being prohibited in southern states.

While Blacks in all southern states were barred from any education before Emancipation, a few Blacks in the northern states had experienced formal education in some locations for over a century. Elias Neau, a French Huguenot who fled to New York in the late 1600s to escape religious persecution, joined the Episcopal Trinity Church where he served for fifteen years as a catechist preparing formerly enslaved Africans and Native Americans for baptism. He subsequently opened a school for enslaved Africans in 1704, and later had his life threatened when there was an enslaved African uprising in New York in 1712. Many outraged New Yorkers believed that educating enslaved Africans fueled discontent and uprisings. The view that education for Blacks was dangerous was a consistent theme in African American history. Neau's school continued until his death in 1722.[5] In addition, Anthony Benezet was a French Huguenot, who also fled to an English Colony for religious freedom and settled in Philadelphia, Pennsylvania, in 1731. Benezet became a member of the Society of Friends, known as the Quakers. He felt strongly that slavery was against the tenets of Christianity and became an abolitionist, establishing the first antislavery society in the United States, the Society for Relief of Free Negroes Unlawfully Held in Bondage. Progressive in his views, Benezet started the first public school for girls in the country in 1754. With the increasing number of free Blacks settling in Philadelphia, he opened an evening school for them in 1770.[6] These schools were followed by the opening and closing of other private schools for Black students by various religious organizations and abolitionist societies. These schools opened and closed sporadically, due to insufficient funding, and they generally offered the same courses that academies of the period offered. Given the Puritan nature of the period, education emphasized religion.

It was not uncommon for Blacks to be teachers as well. For example, in 1793, "the Committee for the Improving the Condition of Free Blacks in Pennsylvania" opened a school and recommended a Black woman as the teacher. Because Blacks in the North were overwhelmingly excluded from white schools, they established their own. Prince Hall, a literate, free Black abolitionist in Boston, petitioned the state legislature of Massachusetts in 1787 to establish an "African" school. After the petition was tabled, a Black chaplain opened a school that was closed within a year. Two years later, Hall's son Primus started a school in his home. Both Black and white teachers were employed to teach in the school, including students from Harvard College. By 1800, George Middleton and sixty-six members of the self-help African Benevolent Society petitioned the town of Boston for an African school. The tone of the petition was tempered and reflected the religiosity of the time. It read in part: "the people of color with deepest humility" request that the "guardians and patrons of early education" consider their request for a school for their children. The petition noted the fear whites expressed regarding the education of Black students, acknowledging many believed such was "impolitic and dangerous . . . as nature designed them to be merely menials." Yet the men argued education would make Blacks better citizens with improved morals. The petition also noted, "Knowledge forms the basis of a Republican government" and would render their community members "good and peaceable members of society." They requested a school for their children to learn to read, write, and learn arithmetic. These skills, they argued, would enhance the lives of those even "in the poorest occupations and correct the morals and insure more orderly behavior." Clearly, the petition was conciliatory and non-threatening given the purpose was one to help those in "low" positions and to help improve their obviously low morals. Throughout the century, however, this modest plea resulted in the town of Boston agreeing only to pay for a teacher if the Black community provided their own space for the school.

Hillary Moss's book, *Schooling Citizens: The Struggle for African American Education in Antebellum America* details whites' efforts to deny education to Blacks in the North. Moss notes that having an education was tantamount to citizenship in the eyes of whites and a privilege Black residents should not be granted.[7] Both Black men and women were equally discriminated against in their desire for schooling. However, it was Black women and girls that experienced significant contempt, particularly if the curriculum they sought was not vocational and domestic. The example below is a case in point. Attempts for Blacks to obtain any type of education indicating their thirst to grow and develop as human beings often resulted in violence. For example, in 1835, angry citizens destroyed Noyes Academy, a boarding school in New Canaan, New Hampshire, that enrolled both Black and white students. The rage against the education of Black women of many of the white citizens was vicious. In 1832, Prudence Crandall, a white Quaker opened a boarding and day school in Canterbury, Connecticut, for the "higher branches" of education that went beyond the rudimentary classes in public district schools. Black families were anxious for their daughters, as well as their sons, to obtain the best education available. As would be the case for many other Black families during this period, a Black farmer whose family name was Harris was enthusiastic for his seventeen-year-old daughter Sarah to enroll in the Canterbury School. According to abolitionist Samuel J. May, Sarah had excelled at the district school but was

> hungering and thirsting for more education. This she desired not only for her sake, but that she might go forth [sic] qualified to be a teacher of the colored people of our country, to whose wrongs and oppression she had become very sensitive. Her father encouraged her, and gladly offered to defray the expense of the advantages she might be able to obtain (by attending the Canterbury School).[8]

In what would become routine arguments on behalf of certain Blacks for privileges believed reserved for whites, Blacks were described in terms of their "respectability," their appearance and how they presented themselves. This issue, which was noted by historian Evelyn Higginbotham as the "politics of respectability," was entrenched in "race uplift" philosophy. Two centuries later, some scholars provide a harsh critique of this concept as assimilationist and futile. However, these critiques overlooked the degrading manner in which Blacks were described throughout the nineteenth century. References to Black women as "nigger wenches" were commonplace—however, Blacks would eventually realize that it wasn't their "respectability" that was an issue but their race, which is the argument that contemporary scholars of this concept emphasize.[9]

May noted of Sarah:

> She was a young lady of pleasing appearance and manners, well known to many of Miss Crandall's pupils, having been their classmate in the district school. Moreover, she was described as a virtuous, pious girl, and had been for some time a member of the church of Canterbury.[10]

Despite Sarah's "excellent character and lady-like deportment" and the fact that she attended the same church as the white students, there was overwhelming opposition to Sarah Harris attending the school. May noted that the townspeople viewed Harris as a member of a "proscribed, despised class" who should not be admitted into this elite private school with their daughters. They would not have their daughters attend a school with a "nigger girl." But May noted, "no objection could be made of her admission to the school, excepting only her dark (and not very dark) complexion."[11] The use of the racial epithet was commonplace and openly used to describe Black people.

Crandall was given the ultimatum that if she did not dismiss Sarah, the parents of the white students would withdraw their daughters. The recognition of Black women as "ladies" and women who sought advanced learning was offensive to many whites. As will be discussed later, the struggle for Black girls and women to attend white female institutions was as difficult as it was for Black men to enter all male schools. The issue was white supremacy and the refusal to acknowledge Blacks as humans.

Crandall closed her school and reopened it as a school exclusively "for young ladies and little misses of color." Her subsequent posting of an advertisement for the school in the abolitionist newspaper, *The Liberator*, was a bold and radical act, and the reference to Black girls as "ladies and little misses" was highly inflammatory because the references were reserved for white women and girls only. Despite the opposition of the townspeople, Crandall reopened her school enrolling between fifteen and twenty young Black women from Philadelphia, Boston, New York, and Providence.[12] Within a month, an obsolete vagrant law, which allowed the selectman to order an inhabitant not of the state to leave, was used on one of the students. The number of young women from these cities speaks to the importance Black parents placed on the advanced education of their daughters. Crandall was arrested and jailed. Her trial in 1833 resulted in a hung jury, but she was scheduled for a retrial months later. In the interim, vandalism to the school, the refusal of the townspeople to do any type of business with Crandall, and the violent threats to her and the students resulted in her abandoning the school and the girls leaving as well. While the names of the Black girls and professions of their parents are not known, these young women braved the hostility of the protesters and showed up for the opportunity to advance their knowledge. This was one of the most violent examples of the threat that an advanced education to Black girls presented. This was in an era when women had virtually no rights; hence, the hysteria over their education was equal to and in many ways worse than that of the Black men. Samuel J. May, who served as Crandall's attorney lamented:

> Twenty harmless, well-behaved girls, whose only offense against the peace of the Community was that they had come together there to obtain useful knowledge and moral culture, were to be told that they better go away, because forsooth, the house in which they dwelt would not be protected by the guardians of the town, the conservators of the peace, the officers of the justice, the men of influence in the village where it was situated. The words almost blistered my lips. My bosom glowed with indignation. I felt ashamed for Canterbury, ashamed for Connecticut, ashamed of my country, ashamed of my color.[13]

As educational opportunities presented themselves to Blacks, male and female, those who could made significant sacrifices for their children to attend these schools. Three Black men, Alexander Crummell, Thomas Sidney, and Henry Highland Garnet traveled more than four hundred miles to attend the aforementioned Noyes Academy in New Hampshire that was destroyed. Throughout Connecticut, and elsewhere in the North, when free Blacks attempted to attend schools with whites or in separate academies that offered advanced education in the 1830s, they were met with violent resistance as in the case of the Canterbury School. For example, in 1833, white students at Wesleyan University in Middletown threatened to physically remove two Black male students if they didn't withdraw from the college. In 1835, white residents of Norwich attacked an academy for "Negroes," and four years later whites raided a school in Brookfield for admitting one Black student.[14]

The struggle for education, as noted by historian V. P. Franklin, as "both formal and informal, was judged to be the main thoroughfare by which Blacks could leave 'Babylon' and reach 'Canaan-land.'"[15] This view was embraced by African American women. They were imbued with a sense of urgency to become educated for use within the Black communities of the nation.

Efforts of free Blacks to seek greater educational opportunities in the North in the 1830s and 1840s paralleled the founding of seminaries for white women. As noted earlier, revisionist history has debunked the previous notion of "true womanhood" that was described by historian Barbara Welter.[16] This concept emphasized innocence, modesty, piety, purity, submissiveness, and domesticity. Women were to be educated for "ideal womanhood," which ensured they would become loving wives and good mothers. This view of womanhood was not accepted by all white women. Several studies have noted that there was a minority of women who desired not to marry and preferred to live independent lives. Lee Virginia Chambers-Schiller's study of single women during the antebellum era noted that there was a sizable number of women who remained single not because of the shortage of men but because they desired to be independent. Margaret Nash's research also reveals a more expanded view of the lives and educational opportunities for women of this era. Women were able to live with other women or relatives and worked as teachers and in factories during this period. Patricia Palmieri's work on the all-women faculty at Wellesley College later in the century was defined by one of them as "Adamless Eden." And the author also refuted this thesis of "true womanhood" as well when it came to Black women.[17]

Blacks believed, nearly unanimously, that if they proved to society they were capable of learning and of good moral character, discrimination would cease. Of course, this was a fallacy they would repeatedly discover over decades and centuries. Yet, this theme permeated the writings and speeches within the Black community of the period. For example, in 1829, Samuel Cornish, the editor of the New York Black-owned newspaper, *The Rights of All*, noted that all Blacks had to do was exhibit their intellect to society. By doing so, the nation would be rid of prejudice. Again, the answer was education. He said, "Knowledge is power" and told his readers when Black youth are educated, "merit will form the character and respectability. The term Africa will no longer be synonymous with degradation."[18] Conscious of the belief that Blacks were vulgar and ignorant, Black women incorporated the word "ladies" into the names of their educational, civic, and religious self-help organizations. Regardless of whites' opinions of them, Blacks defined themselves.

As noted above, free Black women of the North were anxious to avail themselves of educational opportunities. In a study of the history of Black women's schools in the United States from 1827 to 1863, Beatrice B. Butcher notes that sporadic attempts to offer classes to Black girls and women were recorded in abolitionist and other New England newspapers. She stated, however, that most of the schools established emphasized the most rudimentary of education and handwork.[19]

Blacks, however, were interested in more than basic education, and they were also interested in self-determination. The viewpoint on education of Black women held by their families and communities was for the larger goal of benefiting and helping other Black people. It was not simply to make contributions as wives and mothers. As Blacks found the means to obtain more than a domestic education, they established their own schools. By 1838, ten private schools existed in Philadelphia, the home of the largest population of Blacks in the North. Black teachers operated all of the schools.[20] Unlike whites who overwhelmingly established separate private schools for boys and girls because they were being educated for different purposes, Blacks, eager for the education of their sons and daughters, opened coeducational schools. A perusal of advertisements in Black newspapers of the period reflected this trend. Ads for schools such as "B. H. Hughes School for Coloured Children of Both Sexes" and "Evening School for People of Color of Both Sexes" were common. The largest Black literary society of New York, the Phoenix, organized in 1833, provided lectures, evening schools, a high school available to their members of both genders, and employed both Black male and female teachers.[21]

Free Black women organized for self-education through literary and educational societies, with Philadelphia spearheading such organizations. In 1831, a group of Black women organized the Female Literary Association of Philadelphia. The group viewed its efforts not only for self-improvement but also as race improvement. In the Preamble of the group's constitution, the women stated that they believed it was their

> duty . . . as daughters of a despised race, to use our utmost endeavors to enlighten the understanding, to cultivate the talents entrusted to our keeping, that by so doing, we may in a great measure, break down the strong barrier of prejudice, and raise ourselves to an equality with those of our fellow beings, who differ from us in complexion.[22]

Poems, essays, and short stories were submitted unsigned for members of the group to critique. The abolitionist newspaper *The Liberator* often published samples of these literary works to demonstrate the artistic and literary capabilities of Black women to the larger society. The women also noted in their statement their desire to prove that they were "equal" to the majority society. So, despite the views of the larger society toward the education of Black women, the women themselves took their development into their own hands. William Lloyd Garrison, the white editor of *The Liberator*, commented on the high quality of the work of these women stating, "If the traducers of the colored race could be acquainted with the moral worth, just refinement and large intelligence of this association, their mouths would hereafter be dumb."[23]

In Boston, the Afro-American Female Intelligence Society appeared a year later after the Philadelphia group was established. This was both a literary and a charitable organization. Funds from this group were utilized to purchase books and newspapers and to rent a meeting room. The society provided a dollar a week to any member who became ill "in case of unforeseen and afflictive event" stating, "it shall be the duty of the Society to aid them as far as in their power."[24]

This group of women in Boston sponsored the first public lecture to be given by an American female, an African American. The deeply religious Maria W. Stewart, with less than six weeks of education, urged Black women to improve their education and aid in the struggle for racial "uplift." She told her audience:

> Oh, daughters of Africa, awake! Arise! Show forth the world that ye are endowed with noble and exalted faculties . . . let us promote ourselves and improve our own talents.[25]

Stewart expressed the importance of higher education and academies for Black women and suggested women pool their resources to establish a high school. She told her listeners, "knowledge is power." Stewart gave four lectures in Boston from 1832–1833 and continued to impress upon her Black audience their duty and obligation to the race. She moved to New York City in the 1830s and was educated through memberships with the Black women's literary societies and subsequently became a teacher.[26]

The outspoken Stewart demonstrated the important role that Black women played in the advancement of their communities. Unafraid, they took to the public platform and pleaded for the rights of their race. Although clearly race conscious, these women were also very clear and outspoken about issues of gender. Matilda, for example, is the pseudonym of a Black woman who voiced her opinion on the importance of education for Black women. Months after the first Black-owned newspaper, *Freedom's Journal*, was published, Matilda wrote a letter to the editor in which she criticized the circumstances surrounding the education of Black women. She said she felt there was too little emphasis placed on the education of the women of the race. She wrote:

> There are difficulties, and great difficulties, in the way of our [black women] advancement; but that should only stir us to greater efforts. We possess not the advantages with those of our sex, whose skins are not coloured like our own, but we can improve what little we have, and make our one talent produce two-fold. The influence that we have over the male sex demands, that our minds should be instructed and improved with the principles of education and religion, in order that this influence can be properly directed. Ignorant ourselves, how can we be expected to form the minds of our youth and conduct them in the paths of knowledge? I would address myself to all mothers, and say to them, that while it is necessary to possess a knowledge of cookery, and the various mysteries of pudding-making, something more is required. It is their bounden duty to store their daughters' minds with useful learning. They should be made to devote their leisure time to reading books, whence they would derive valuable information, which could never be taken from them.[27]

Wherever Blacks were located, education was a primary goal. And, as Matilda indicated, many Black women were not content to simply learn domestic science in order to become good mothers and wives, instead, they wanted to obtain an education that would assist in their critical thinking and leadership within their communities.

Viewing education as a vehicle for self-reliance and self-improvement, Black women established formal schools, as well as educational organizations, and saw themselves as a vital link in the obtainment of knowledge and race values to their youth and community. The literary societies established by Black women prior to the Civil War performed great services within the Black communities by providing lectures, libraries, and reading rooms as well as instruction.[28]

Secondary education for Black women and girls, as well as Black men and boys, was difficult to obtain prior to the Civil War since these institutions were still in their infancy. Thus, the 1829 founding of the St. Frances Academy for Colored Girls boarding school in Baltimore was an important event for the race. The institution was established by a group of French-educated Black nuns (the Oblate Order) who had migrated to Baltimore from Saint-Domingue, Haiti.

Most of the women were from prosperous families. Elizabeth Lange, who became the first Superior of the Order and head of the school, had operated a free school for poor Black children in her home prior to the opening of St. Frances. Lange taught her classes in both French and Spanish. Because the St. Frances Academy was the only institution available to Black females that offered courses above the primary level, the school was well known among Black families with girls coming from southern states and Canada to study. To preserve their native languages, the Sisters conducted classes at the Academy on alternate days completely in French. In 1865, the school became coeducational and changed its name to St. Frances Academy.[29] The Academy maintained an outstanding academic reputation and was featured in the 1871 "Special Report of the Commissioner of Education on the Improvement of Public Schools in the District of Columbia" for its academic excellence:

> From the first [the St. Frances Academy for Colored Girls] has been through all its years, almost forty in number, a well-appointed female seminary, amply supplied with cultivated and capable teachers, who have given good training in all the branches of a refined and useful education, including all that is usually taught in well-regulated female seminaries.[30]

Another renowned private high school for Black students was the Institute for Colored Youth in Philadelphia. Established in 1852 by the Society of Friends, it was the country's first co-ed classical high school. The school always had an all-Black faculty comprised of the most highly educated Black scholars of that era.[31]

Segregated public schools for Black students opened in Massachusetts in 1820, and by Emancipation, most New England states provided public education for them.[32] In Beatrice Butcher's study of the history of separate schools for Black women from prior to the Civil War, she noted that white women who established schools or classes for Black girls overwhelmingly offered instruction in handiwork (needlepoint, sewing, and knitting) with little academic substance. Since these classes were within what was viewed as the "female" sphere and non-threatening to the white communities, they caused no outrage or upset. As white women's antislavery organizations were established, these classes continued.

For example, an announcement of the *Portland Courier* (Maine) in May of 1837 read:

> Portland Female Anti-Slavery Society—A Committee of ladies have volunteered their services to meet twice a week for the purpose of instructing the female-colored population in knitting, mending and various kinds of needle work. We trust their efforts in this or any other way, to elevate the character of an unjustly degraded race, may be blessed with abundant success.[33]

Butcher's research revealed that the single-sex schools established for Black girls by white female abolitionists were based on the model for white females that stressed "female education" and reinforced women's subservient role in society. Their motivation for educating Black women and girls was based on a spirit of helping a "downtrodden race of women, to teach handwork and rudiments of an English education, to teach vocational skills (sewing, knitting, embroidery, and ornamental handworks and courses that were perceived as unique to the education of women)."[34]

Myrtilla Miner, a white abolitionist from upstate New York, opened a school for "colored girls" in Washington, DC, in 1851. Although there were more than ten thousand free Blacks living in Washington at the time, there were no public schools and very few private ones for Black students. As with other attempts to establish schools for Black students, male or female, there was hostility and opposition. Slavery still existed in the District although the slave trade ended in 1850. There was a general fear that a school offering advanced courses would result in free Blacks from other areas migrating into the city because access to education was always a primary attraction for formerly enslaved African men and women. As will be discussed later, Black families frequently relocated to areas where educational opportunities were available to their children. Indeed, all Blacks whether free or enslaved in the states of Maryland and Virginia were forbidden from any type of education. There was also a concern Black women would be given an education beyond their social status. The proposed school was to focus primarily on teaching training since there was such a great demand for teachers. The school's promotional literature read, "this school embraces boarding, domestic economy, normal teachers, and primary departments."[35] The tuition-based school planned to accommodate 150 students. The school opened with six students in the home of a Black male resident who rented Miner a room. As was the norm, Miner and the students were harassed and verbally abused. One white male protester referred to the women students as "impudent hussies" and stated Miner was running a *nigger* school.[36] Black women experienced continuous hatred and insults in their attempt to simply improve their lives as well as contribute to society. The school grew to approximately forty students for the first two years and primarily attracted daughters of the Black elite that were overwhelmingly distinguished by their light-skinned complexion—referred to as mulattos, quadroons, octoroons, etc. Historian Dorothy Sterling noted that Miner as an educator had high standards for her students and provided a rich curriculum that included scientific studies as well as the traditional "female" courses. She took her students to museums and other places of interest in the city. Well-known white persons visited the school and reports were given in various abolitionist newspapers for fundraising purposes to reinforce the notion that Black people were salvageable. Of these displays, Miner stated:

> Visitors . . . from all parts of the country . . . many of them entertaining the idea that the colored race is capable of receiving a high order of mental and moral cultivation, will, with this example before them, be constrained to admit that these people can be elevated by proper education and kind Treatment; and many will return to their homes more disposed to aid in a movement calculated to relieve our country from a vast increasing evil.[37]

Most missionary and private schools put Black students on display to the public to demonstrate their academic accomplishments to show that they were educable. Sterling noted this was a common flaw with many white abolitionists as well as some Black teachers later. Sterling wrote, "Miner let her pupils know she looked down on them because she was determined to bring them up to her level." She also noted that Miner had contempt for Black people: "some pupils dropped out [of the school] but others, spurred on by her criticisms, worked to win her approval."[38] Miner was not unlike many white missionaries and abolitionists who held stereotypical and racist notions about Blacks. These white saviors believed they could civilize downtrodden former slaves and descendants of slaves. And as noted, Miner devoted her attention to racially mixed Black girls, whom she believed more capable than their darker sisters.

Below is a very painful letter that reinforces Sterling's observation by one of Miner's students who wrote her expressing her gratefulness for Miner's deciding to work with what the educator characterized as ignorant, uncultured Black people:

> I know that you could have taught cultivated schools elsewhere and have been surrounded by congenial friends, but you turned to us ignorant and uncultivated as we were. And how have you been repaid? for having taught us contumely [sic] and reproach were heaped upon you by your enemies and ours—enemies that you never have made but for us. Yet still you falter not, but continue your labors for us, regardless of failing health, regardless of ingratitude and bitter enemies. Why is it that with all this you still toil nobly on?[39]

These "enemies" referred to in the above statement include Blacks who criticized Miner for only admitting light-skinned young women to her schools. In

28   CHAPTER 1

response to this charge, she confirmed that her students were overwhelmingly light skinned but consisted of "the better class of colored" students, the ones she was preparing to teach other Blacks.[40] Miner believed that Black young women, who in her view "lack refinement," dropped out due to her harsh criticism of Black young women. The notion of white moral and cultural superiority was a negative reality of the cost Blacks paid to obtain an education.

Some years after this young woman studied at Oberlin College in the Literary Department, she noted her desire to return to her home of Washington, DC, and teach at Miner's school. She was encouraged to do so by Emily Howland, one of the white teachers who replaced Miner after the latter became ill and left the school. However, the student, Emma V. Brown candidly stated her conflicted feelings toward Miner:

> I have thought of your suggestion about my applying to the trustees for Miss Miner's school. I do not like or Respect Miss M. I know this is wrong, but I cannot help Feeling so, or explain my feelings. Yet, I owe her an eternal debt of gratitude. I should not have been here [Oberlin], and might have remained in ignorance forever if it had not been for her instrumentality.[41]

Brown noted she would contact the trustees to inquire if Miner was not returning to the school as the principal. She stated, "if this was true, I shall apply for it [teaching position]." She was emphatic in her disdain of Miner and wrote, "I shall never teach there while she has anything to do with it. I suppose there will be openings elsewhere."[42] Brown became a prominent educator and taught in prestigious Black high schools. The first was the private Quaker-founded Institute for Colored Youth in Philadelphia, which was mentioned earlier. She later served as principal of the prominent Preparatory School in Washington, DC, that became M Street School and later renamed Dunbar High School. Brown's mother was a widow, prominent dressmaker, and owned a huge brick home in Georgetown. In a reference for a teaching position, one of Brown's Oberlin professors wrote that she was "a light quadroon, a superior scholar, a good singer, a faithful Christian, and a genteel lady."[43] It was rare that a Black person's phenotype was not described when whites gave references or made testimonies about their abilities. Such distinctions were a reality for Blacks.

Miner left the School for Colored Girls in 1855 for medical reasons. The school later closed by 1861 due to the Civil War. Despite Miner's departure, the school was successful in producing well-trained Black women teachers. By 1858, six of her students were conducting their own schools. In 1879, the school reopened and became a part of the Washington, DC, public schools.[44]

CHAPTER 2

Abolitionist Colleges

This chapter explores the opportunities and experiences of Black women students in abolitionist colleges during the antebellum era. As noted earlier, most Black women desired the opportunity to earn the same type of education as men. In McGrawville, New York, there was the short-lived New York Central College (NYCC), founded in 1849 by antislavery Baptists. The college provided an opportunity for Black men and women to achieve an equal education with whites of both genders. This group of Baptists split off from Southern Baptists and Northern Baptists, who condoned slavery and formed the American Baptist Free Mission Society. Based on Oberlin College in Ohio's model of coeducation and the inclusion of Black students, NYCC had a classical curriculum as well as one in agricultural science.[1] Unlike Oberlin, which did not have Black faculty until the mid-twentieth century, New York Central College had an integrated faculty from the beginning. Three Black men served on the faculty including George Vashon, the first Black man to earn a bachelor's degree from Oberlin in 1844. Vashon served as professor of belles lettres and mathematics at the college from 1854–57. The other Black professors were Charles Reason, the first to join the faculty in 1849 as a professor of belles lettres, Greek, Latin, and French, as well as mathematics. William Grant Allen, who followed him in 1850, was also a professor of belles lettres, Greek, and Latin. Although the college closed in 1860, one of its graduates in the 1850s was Grace A. Mapp from Philadelphia, making her one of the first Black women to get a college degree.[2] Because very little has survived the college after its closing, Mapps is rarely noted for her educational accomplishments and her degree.

Mapps and Charles Reason left NYCC for the Quaker-founded Institute for Colored Youth in Philadelphia (ICY) in the mid-1850s. Reason became the principal and Mapps became the head of the School's Ladies Department.

Grace Mapps was born into a staunch Quaker family, and she is often confused with Sarah Mapps Douglass, her aunt, who was an educator also teaching at the Institute for Colored Youth. Sarah Mapps Douglass was the elder and came from a prominent Black Philadelphia family. She was educated by private tutors, and a school she ran merged in 1854 with the ICY. Sarah [later Douglass] became the principal and teacher of girls in the preparatory department, and Grace Mapps was the principal and teacher of the female department of the high school.[3]

When NYCC closed in 1860, approximately 1,500 students of various racial backgrounds had attended the institution including the primary and collegiate divisions. Because there are few surviving records of the college, historian Catherine M. Hanchett conducted extensive research on NYCC and estimated a third of the students were persons of color.[4] However, based on the biographical records of the students that she could find, she could only guess that roughly one hundred of these students were Black or had African origins.[5] Hence, the number of Black women students and graduates is inconclusive.

Hanchett, attempted to discover through her research the backgrounds of students at NYCC. In a roster that she put together, sixteen Black women appeared on her list. Seven were from the local area and the others were from Pittsburgh, Philadelphia, Washington, DC, and Brooklyn, New York. Numerous Black women students from the institution transferred to Oberlin College. Yet, like Grace Mapps, many of these women gained prominence. Among these students were Mary Edmonia Lewis, who later became a sculptress of international acclaim, and Emma and Emily Edmonson.[6] These last three students transferred to Oberlin College.

The Edmonson sisters were renowned former enslaved persons, who were a part of an unsuccessful attempt of seventy-seven people to escape slavery on the schooner *Pearl* sailing from Georgetown (early DC) to New Jersey in 1848. They were from a family of fourteen children. Their father, Paul Edmonson, was set free by his owner's will upon his death. However, their mother was an enslaved woman. Hence, slave laws mandated that the children's status followed that of the mother. While four of the oldest Edmonson daughters were purchased out of slavery by their husbands and friends, the master forbade the younger children to be purchased, thus the desperate attempt to escape in 1848.[7]

As mentioned earlier, phenotype was a major element in how African American women were perceived by white sympathizers. Described as "two respectable young women of light complexion," after an unsuccessful attempt to sell them in New Orleans to men who were looking for mistresses or "fancy" women, they were returned to Alexandria to negotiate with their slave trader. Abolitionists appealed to Blacks and whites to raise money to purchase the freedom of the sisters. White ministers, who were attempting to raise money for the young women, were outraged with the enslaver who sought $2,250 for the two young women. However, because of their light-skin appearance, their owner believed he could garner a higher bid. Again, the beauty and appearance of the women were described in appeals for funds. Expressing alarm at the fate that these women, whom he described as "of elegant form and very fine faces" and "nearly as white as their master," were destined to be sold into prostitution if they were not rescued.[8] Reverend Henry Ward Beecher, recently appointed minister of the Congregationalist Plymouth Church in Brooklyn, urged his congregation to help raise funds to save the Edmonson sisters from being sold in New Orleans. It was stressed that these young women were *Christians,* and the parishioners were asked to think of how they would feel if their daughters were in the same position. When he retold the expected fate of the women being sold into prostitution, one observer reported, "the people in the pews were visibly shaken, and in response men emptied their pockets while women tore off jewelry to contribute to the cause."[9] When the money was raised to secure the young women's freedom, appeals were also made to raise money for these young women's education. Ironically, appealing to fund their education did not result in the same results as appeals to purchase their freedom. It's unclear if people were less interested in educating these women than keeping them from being sold. The young women ended up attending a homeschool of a white abolitionist, W. R. Smith in Macedon, Wayne County, New York, in 1849. Macedon was the most northern stop on the way to Canada. Myrtilla Miner, mentioned earlier, was one of the teachers in Smith's school but left to establish her own school in Washington, DC, in 1851. That year, the Edmonson sisters left and enrolled in the recently founded NYCC nearby. When they arrived, the enrollment was over one hundred students. Students were able to work to help defray their expenses. Male students were paid five cents an hour while women students were paid three cents an hour for their work.[10] It's unclear if the salary discrepancy was due to sexism or because the tasks of women differed from men and were considered less. The Edmonson sisters did domestic work.

While women students earned less than male students, male students paid more for housing than women students. Male students were charged one dollar a week for board and five dollars a year, while women students were charged three dollars a year. Despite the opportunities to work at the school, the sisters always suffered financial problems. Frederick Douglass in his Paper, the *North Star,* placed an article requesting $40 to help pay for the well-known sisters' education at NYCC but there were no responses. The young women had to stop their classes for months at a time in order to work and raise money.[11] By 1852, the renowned writer Catherine Beecher Stowe, the sister of Reverend Henry Ward Beecher and celebrated author of the famous *Uncle Tom's Cabin*, had also written a nonfiction piece on the failed escape attempt of the Edmonson sisters. With funds from her writings, Stowe offered to send the young women to Oberlin

College in Ohio. NYCC was financially unstable while Oberlin was thriving. Stowe believed that the young women would receive "a thorough solid education calculated to strengthen and develop their reasoning and powers and judgment" at Oberlin.[12] Stowe provided rave reviews to the Oberlin administrators in seeking their admissions. She noted that the young women were Christians and "from excellent stock." As a result of such glowing recommendations, Emily and Mary enrolled in the fall of 1852 in the preparatory department.

Stowe paid the young women's expenses, in addition to seeking funding from various church groups for their support. While the experience at Oberlin was positive, Mary Edmonson fell ill, and in 1853 she died of tuberculosis at the age of twenty. Emily did not want to remain in Oberlin without her sister, so she returned to Washington, DC, to continue her studies with Myrtilla Miner and to work with her as her assistant. Emily remained in Washington, DC, the rest of her life.

Oberlin College

Although single-sex private seminaries for women emerged during the 1820s, in New England and the North, most of these institutions barred Black women from attendance. Founded in 1833, Oberlin College in Ohio is widely known for being the first educational institution that afforded Black students the opportunity to attend an educational institution with whites without regard to race or gender. Founded by Congregationalists, the profoundly religious college was referred to as "God's college." The institution was in the Midwestern agricultural community of Oberlin, Ohio. The campus, as well as the town, was very active in the antislavery movement and served as an important stop on the Underground Railroad.

While the abolitionist colleges discussed enrolling Black students, members of the faculty and students on these campuses did not often welcome their presence. Although there were many antislavery activities throughout the nation, particularly in New England and the North, religious denominations split over the issue of slavery.

The Presbyterian Church founded Lane Seminary in Cincinnati in 1829 to educate ministers. Lyman Beecher from Massachusetts, the father of Henry Ward Beecher and Harriett Beecher Stowe, became the first president in 1832. In 1834, there was a split at Lane on the topic of the emancipation versus colonization of enslaved Blacks. The seminary held nine debates over an eighteen-day period on the question of slavery. When it was over, many of the participants concluded slavery was sinful and the mission of the American Colonization Society to send slaves back to Africa was immoral. A group of forty students and faculty, who became known as "the rebels," were invited to join the newly founded Oberlin Collegiate Institute. The institution needed revenue from the students as well as the faculty to help build the institution. Asa Mahan, the only Lane Trustee who denounced slavery, was invited to become Oberlin's first president. Mahan informed the Oberlin founder, John Jay Shipherd, that he would come if he could bring the other Lane faculty member, John Morgan, also dismissed due to his antislavery stance. In addition, Mahan requested that Reverend Charles G. Finney be hired to head the college's first theological department. However, the absolute deal breaker for Mahan was his insistence that on the first meeting of the Trustees they resolve that "students shall be received into this Institution irrespective of color." Mahan continued that "this should be passed because this is the *right principle; and God* will bless us in doing right." He also indicated his lack of desire to work at an institution unaccepting of Blacks, stating, "if our Board, would violate right, so as to reject youth of talent and piety, because they are *black*, I should have *no heart* to labor for the up building of our Seminary, believing that the curse of God would come upon us as it has upon Lane Seminary, for its unchristian abuse of the poor Slave."[13]

Hence, it was the men from Lane who broached the topic of Oberlin becoming an interracial institution. Oberlin already admitted white women. When the founder, Shipherd, introduced the topic of admitting Black students to Oberlin, he was surprised at the opposition to the proposal. Opponents expressed "panic and despair," and the entire college was panic-stricken. There was fear that the college would become a "negro college" and "hundreds of Negroes" would flood the institution. The students were polled through a questionnaire "as to the practicability of admitting persons of color." The results were surprising when one looks at the gender response. Only six female students voted to admit Black students whereas fifteen women voted to keep them out. On the other hand, the male students were more open to the idea. Twenty men voted to include Black students in the college versus seventeen who voted to exclude them.[14] The attitude of the white female students toward race is instructive and will occur throughout this study. This negative view on the part of white women students and administrators toward integration and Black women emerged in other settings. Despite the opposition of many, Oberlin agreed to admit Black students. During the presidencies of Mahan (1835–1850) and Charles G. Finney (1851–1866), two radical antislavery advocates, the tone of the college was very supportive of Black students. However, that changed with their departures and after Reconstruction, when the rights that Blacks experienced after Emancipation were short lived and in 1896 the landmark *Plessy v. Ferguson*—separate but equal Supreme Court decision—became the law of the land.

Antislavery activities at Oberlin dominated the pre–Civil War years of the college of the aforementioned presidents, and according to the college's historian

Robert Fletcher, "few of the nine thousand [students] who matriculated before the firing on Fort Sumter escaped complete conversion to the cause."[15] Faculty members commonly gave antislavery lectures at the college, and in 1846, an economic boycott of products made by enslaved persons was instituted. The college viewed Independence Day as one of "cruel mockery" and instead commemorated the emancipation of slavery in the British West Indies on August 1st.[16]

Available housing and educational opportunities for formerly enslaved Africans resulted in many free Blacks and fugitive Blacks migrating to the town of Oberlin. According to one Oberlin historian, by 1860, 20 percent of the town's 2,250 citizens were Black, including 422 free Blacks and "mulattoes" and fugitive Blacks who came through on the Underground Railroad.[17] Blacks who could afford to relocate were particularly drawn to the town not only because of its liberal and antislavery stance but also because of the opportunities at Oberlin College. Now, the college had a preparatory school, a music conservatory, a ladies department, and a classical college. However, the lack of public schools at the time resulted in most of the students of all races enrolled in the preparatory department. It was not until 1916 that the preparatory school was no longer necessary as a result in the growth of public schools. Preparatory schools were routine in colleges of the period, and many continued well into the twentieth century. The majority of Black college students attended historically Black colleges and universities (HBCUs) until recent decades, and all but three HBCUs were founded in the South after the Civil War.[18] The lack of elementary and high schools for formerly enslaved Blacks in that region resulted in preparatory schools on many of those campuses until the 1940s.

As seminaries for white women throughout the country continued to discriminate against Black women, many found their way to Oberlin. For example, when Blanche V. Harris was barred from entering a white female seminary in Michigan in the 1850s, where her mother worked as a domestic and her father as a cook, her entire family moved to Oberlin. Similarly, Mary Jane Patterson, Oberlin class of 1862, was the first Black woman to earn a collegiate degree from the institution. She moved in the 1850s with her entire family from North Carolina to attend Oberlin. Three Patterson daughters and one son graduated from Oberlin.[19] The Pattersons relocated with several other Black families from North Carolina (the Copelands and the Comptons) after a school for free Black children was burned to the ground on three separate occasions. Deciding to not rebuild the school, the families moved to Oberlin. As persecution of free Blacks intensified throughout the nation, Oberlin became a haven. Black women students enrolled in Oberlin beginning in the 1840s. It's often very difficult to discuss with accuracy the number of Blacks in college during this period and throughout the nineteenth century because many Blacks who were racially mixed chose not to identify themselves as Blacks. For instance, prior to Oberlin

FIGURE 1. Mary Jane Patterson, Class of 1862, Oberlin College. Courtesy of the Oberlin College Archives.

admitting Black students, Black men attended and earned college degrees from white male colleges in New England. Until recently, it was reported that the first Black men to graduate from college did so in 1826—Edward Jones graduated from Amherst College in Massachusetts and John Russwurm graduated from Bowdoin College in Maine.[20] However, recent research reports that Alexander Lucius Twilight earned a degree from Middlebury College in 1823. During his years at Middlebury, Twilight was never identified as a Black man and was thought to be white. He was born in 1795 to a free mulatto father, and his mother was considered a "quadroon"—one quarter Black. The family was listed as white in the Vermont census starting in 1810. Middlebury College historian Bill Hart found no evidence that Twilight ever identified as a Black man.[21] Given the impossibility of knowing how many Black students who had Black heritage and did not identify as Black, this study will only discuss those students who self-identified as Black.

Between 1840 and 1860, the Black student population of Oberlin was between 4 and 5 percent. According to a study of Black students at Oberlin prior to the Civil War, Lawson and Merrill reported that of the one hundred Black students attending during this period in the ladies and collegiate departments half were born free, primarily from the North where slavery had been abolished and the other half from the South where slavery still existed but were free like the aforementioned Pattersons, Copelands, and Comptons whose families migrated from North Carolina. Of this group, thirty of the students came from thirteen families. Unlike the majority of white students at Oberlin who came from rural communities, the Black students were largely from cities such as New York, Pittsburgh, Cincinnati, Washington, DC, Cleveland, and Louisville, as well as areas from upstate New York and smaller communities in Ohio. Less than ten of the students were born in slavery.[22] Ironically, the Black students in many instances were far more affluent than their white student counterparts.

According to Oberlin College's historian Robert Fletcher, approximately 11,000 students had attended Oberlin by 1866. He noted that 6,500 were male and a little over 4,800 were females and "were almost all farmers' sons and daughters with pious intentions, poor preparation and little money."[23] One white female student in 1858 wrote a letter home to her parents in Massachusetts confirming the vast mulatto Black student population, and her perception that they were more privileged than the white students. She lamented that the "niggars" didn't look like "niggars" stating most of them looked white and there were no more than six "pure niggars" at the school. She also said that they dressed "a great deal better than the rest of the students."[24] However, the "pure niggars" she was referring to were Africans no doubt. The American Missionary Association who established missions in Africa selected students to send to Oberlin to convert and civilize their fellow tribesmen. One such student was Margu Kinson (later known as Sarah), an African student who was enslaved and held captive on the infamous Amistad slave ship where the enslaved persons rebelled in 1839 off the coast of Cuba. The mutineers were brought to the United States for trial. The case became a huge cause for members of the antislavery movement, and in 1841 the Supreme Court ruled in favor of the Africans and set them free. The committee that worked to help them became the American Missionary Association (incorporated in 1846).

Margu was ten years old and one of four children taken to Farmington, Connecticut, to live in an abolitionist community while funds were raised to return them to Sierra Leone. They were given anglicized names with hers becoming Sarah. Upon arrival, she continued to live with the missionaries instead of being returned to her family. Sarah converted to Christianity and was sent by the Oberlin graduates to their alma mater as a way of assisting her in establishing a school for girls when she returned to Sierra Leone. She arrived at Oberlin in

1846 and began in the preparatory department studying arithmetic, geography, penmanship, and recitation, and then advanced to the literary department. Sarah lived in the ladies dormitory and worked doing laundry to cover the expenses of her room and board. She left Oberlin in November 1849 and returned to Sierra Leone to become headmistress of a girl's school. In an effort to emphasize that Black students were educated, their accomplishments and academic successes were widely publicized. Hence, Sarah's success was publicized throughout the abolitionists' publications and one white benefactor who paid for clothing for Sarah while at Oberlin boasted at how the African student's education at Oberlin had resulted in her becoming "an intelligent, useful, Christian, laboring to elevate her countryman." *The American Missionary* reprinted this story and noted that Sarah was further proof that educating Africans was assisting a "debased and heathen people by Christianity and education."[25] The indoctrination of white supremacy to Black students as "heathens" emerged a century later in the Black Power movement efforts to undo the psychological damage done in the name of benevolent education.

The tuition of $25 per year during this period was paid through multiple means. Many of the Black students' parents were middle- and upper-class artisans and businessmen (barbers, carpenters, coopers, and masons) and paid their tuition. One-third of the Black Oberlin graduates by 1865 were children of artisans. Southern white planter fathers with Black children frequently sent them to Oberlin as well. Fletcher noted numerous instances of this. He wrote that as early as 1837, a wealthy Louisiana planter sent his four "colored" children (two boys and two girls) to Oberlin and to freedom. Many other examples followed this: in 1851, a Mississippi planter sent his two sons to Oberlin. Another planter in 1854 from Kentucky sent his daughters to be educated at Oberlin—the person who contacted the college on this man's behalf noted the circumstances and wrote: "Their father lives in Washington, Kentucky, has kept his daughters at a school in Ohio for some years, most of the time. He is a man of wealth and White and owns Slaves, but his daughters are nearly White. Their mother is not living." A slaveholder in 1855 sent his quadroon son and daughter to be educated as well. While it's clear the overwhelming number of early Black students at Oberlin were racially mixed or very light-skinned, there were others who were not. Many Black students, as did the white students, worked while they were at Oberlin. The school had a manual program that paid women students $1.50 a month to wash, iron, and sew the clothes of the students. In addition, white abolitionist Reverend Charles Avery of Pittsburgh established a special scholarship fund in 1849 for Black students. The fund's first scholarship recipient was a Black female student—Amelia Freeman from Pittsburgh who enrolled in the ladies department. When Avery died in 1858, his will indicated that he left Oberlin funds for scholarships for fifty Black students. These funds were available to both Black male and female students. Many Black students supplemented their funds by working their way through as well.

The support for Black women students by their families was apparent by the large numbers who enrolled. While men of both races had advantages not afforded to women in terms of opportunities for education at advanced levels, these opportunities were extremely rare for Black women. Fully, two-thirds of the Black students at Oberlin prior to Emancipation were women and girls. In addition, Black women students tended to be more financially well off than their overwhelmingly rural white female counterparts. The majority matriculated in the ladies department, also referred to as the literary department, because the curriculum was more in keeping with society's notion of appropriate education for women and girls—literature and the fine arts—and did not include advanced mathematics, Greek, and Latin, which was thought to be the purview of men and beyond the grasp or utility for women. Furthermore, most Black females would not have access to such subjects. The women who matriculated and graduated from the literary department are important figures and should not be thought of as accomplishing less than those few who decided to pursue the "gentlemen's" collegiate degree. According to the catalog of 1835, the literary department was the equivalent of the leading female seminaries of the period. Women in this department were also allowed to take courses in the collegiate department. The requirements as stated in the catalog were:

> Young ladies of good minds, unblemished morals, and respectable attainments are received into this department, and placed under the superintendence of a judicious lady, whose duty it is to correct their habits and mold female character.[26]

Acknowledging that Black women and girls could have "unblemished morals and be respectable" shaped the behavior and became a guiding principle of virtually all their life's work. The "respectability" curse that always plagued black women throughout their lives was one that resulted in their socialization throughout the nineteenth and twentieth centuries to ensure that Black girls learn the necessity of how they present and comport themselves in society.

The first Black woman graduate of the ladies department was Lucy Stanton in 1850. She was from Cleveland and the stepdaughter of a wealthy Black businessman and abolitionist, John Brown. Brown was an active member of the Underground Railroad and used his home to harbor persons seeking freedom on their way further north. Lucy Stanton was born in 1831 and her biological father died before she was born. As Black students were barred from attending the public schools of Cleveland during her childhood, Brown established the first private school for Blacks in the city. After attending this school, Stanton entered Oberlin in 1846, where she was an extremely active student and elected president of the prestigious Ladies Literary Society (LLS), the women's debate club of the college. Lucy Stone, another Oberlin student, became a prominent women's rights activist and founded the LLS in 1835. The male students at Oberlin were required to debate one and a half hours a week for their rhetoric class, while the women students were reduced to serving as an audience to the male students. Outraged by the sexism of the administration that women should keep "silent" as the scriptures of the Apostle Paul mandated, Stone organized a secret group of women who were willing to defy this notion.[27] The group initially met in the woods near the college similar to the way many enslaved persons did to secretly learn how to read and write. When the weather turned inclement, they met at the home of a Black woman who lived on the outskirts of Oberlin. At the opening meeting, Stone told her fellow women classmates:

> We shall leave this college with the reputation of a thorough collegiate course, yet not one of us has received any rhetorical or elocutionary training. Not one of us could state a question or argue it in successful debate. For this reason, I have proposed the formation of this association. (60–61)

The LLS is considered the oldest women's literary club in the country. Stanton was the first Black member of the organization. The LLS debated many burning questions of the period such as antislavery, temperance, women's rights, marriage, and religion. In addition to debates, the LLS held programs that included the reading of poems, essays, and prepared orations. The largest of these programs took place during the week of commencement and were open to the public. For this occasion, at her 1850 commencement, Stanton gave a rousing antislavery oration, "A Plea for the Oppressed," which was published in its entirely in the *Oberlin Evangelist*, the religion publication of the college.

It cannot be emphasized enough how radical and exhilarating it was for a Black woman to lead an intellectual and feminist organization that was predominately white, and for her to have the opportunity to study and be treated with respect and dignity in the 1840s—something Black women were still fighting for a century later. In addition, Black women participating in activities with white women in which they were referred to as "ladies"—even though the term today would make feminists cringe—in the 1850s this was nothing short of revolutionary. These events were encouraging to Blacks everywhere. By the end of the Civil War in 1865, twelve Black women had graduated from the literary department at Oberlin and three had earned bachelor's degrees. Georgiana Mitchem from Peoria, Illinois was the first Black woman to enter the collegiate department in 1856. She remained for two years without graduating. It's unknown why she left. The demand for teachers was so great among Black communities that students often left to begin teaching without finishing their degrees. Mary Jane Patterson who graduated in 1862 and historically has been acknowledged as the first Black woman to earn a college degree followed Mitchem, although it is believed that

Grace Mapp, mentioned earlier, graduated from New York Central College in the 1850s.

By 1865, two other Black women earned bachelor's degrees—Fanny Jackson of Washington, DC, and Frances J. Norris of Rome, Georgia. A fifth Black woman, Elizabeth Evans from North Carolina, also enrolled in the collegiate department in 1862 and stayed for two years. In addition to these women who earned degrees, there were fifty African American women who were candidates for the literary degree at Oberlin in 1865. By this year, fifteen Black women had earned degrees from Oberlin from both the literary and collegiate department and seventeen Black men had earned collegiate and professional degrees. The near equal number of degrees by both genders demonstrated the desire on the part of both groups to prepare themselves for the challenge of helping to improve the status of their race.

According to Henle and Merrill, most of the Black students in the collegiate department were products of private Black schools that offered Latin and Greek, which were prerequisites for entering the collegiate department.

Fanny Jackson, who attended Oberlin during the Civil War years and was a member of the class of 1865, provides us with some insight into life at the institution for Black students during that era.

Fanny Jackson Coppin and Oberlin College (1860–1865)

Fanny Jackson (later known as Coppin) entered Oberlin College in 1860. She is one of the two students who recalled their experience at Oberlin in print during this period. Jackson was born into slavery in Washington, DC, but obtained her freedom when her aunt, who was free, purchased her. The aunt worked for nearly twelve years to purchase Fanny's freedom. In 1850, because of the Fugitive Slave Law and because of better educational opportunities, Fanny moved to New Bedford, Massachusetts, to live with another aunt and uncle. She secured a job as a domestic worker, and as a result of her long work hours, she was unable to attend school on a regular basis. The next year, Fanny and her guardians moved to Newport, Rhode Island, again seeking better educational options for her. Not wanting to be a financial burden on her family, Fanny secured a job as a live-in servant in the home of a prominent author, George Henry Calvert, great-grandson of Lord Baltimore, settler of Maryland. Calvert's wife, Mary Stuart, was a descendant of Mary, Queen of Scots. Fanny's aunt and uncle discouraged her from taking this position, and Fanny recalled:

> So, I went into service. Oh, the hue and cry there was when I went out to live! Even my aunt spoke of it; she had a home to offer me; but the 'slavish' element was so strong in me *that I must make myself a servant.* Ah, how those things cut me then! But I knew I was right, and I kept straight on.[28]

FIGURE 2. Fanny Jackson (Coppin), Class of 1865, Oberlin College. Courtesy of the Oberlin College Archives.

Fanny Jackson recalled her opportunity to take advantage of the literary exposure she had while working at the Calvert's and recalled the environment as one of "refinement and culture." In addition to the exposure she received from living in the household, she was able to use her earnings to hire a private tutor for one hour, three days a week. She worked for the Calverts for six years. While living with the Calverts, without their knowledge, Fanny learned how to play the piano and guitar, and was the organist for the Colored Union Church of Newport, the second oldest Black church in the state. She secretly learned to play the piano by renting a piano and kept it at her aunt's home to prevent the Calverts from realizing she had aspirations beyond being a servant. They had no idea she had a tutor, took music lessons, or played the organ for her church. When Mrs. Calvert asked her about her absences from the house, she told her but believed she would be "terribly scolded." Because the Calverts were childless, Fanny Jackson stated her relationship with them was one of a daughter. However, when Jackson informed the Calverts of her desire to continue her education, they offered to increase her salary if she remained their servant. There was no encouragement of her educational pursuits, and she did not mention any encouragement or support from the Calverts in assisting her with a transition to the normal school. Of the offer to remain in their employment for a larger salary, she said:

> The deep-seated purpose to get an education and to become a teacher to my people, yielded to no inducement of comfort or temporary gain.[29]

Fanny Jackson enrolled in the Rhode Island State Normal School, probably in 1859. Always anxious to learn more than what was offered in segregated public schools, as before, Jackson employed a tutor to supplement her education to study French. Had Harvard admitted Blacks and women, Fanny noted she would have aspired to attend that institution. Learning that the curriculum of Oberlin College in Ohio was the same as Harvard and that it accepted Blacks and women, she set her sights on attending the Ohio college. Enter Bishop Daniel Payne of the African Methodist Episcopal Church (AME), the Black denomination founded in 1816 as a result of the racism Blacks experienced in the white George Methodist Church in Philadelphia. Payne was the sixth Bishop of the AME church and a staunch supporter of education. When he heard of Fanny Jackson's desire to attend Oberlin, although she was not a member of the AME church but a young Black woman with a passion for education, he provided her with a scholarship from the church. With these funds, along with support from an aunt, Fanny Jackson enrolled in Oberlin College in 1860. Jackson later received a scholarship from Oberlin through the Avery funds for Black students as well. The enthusiasm and support that Black families, and the larger community, provided Black women with, encouraged and provided an affirmation that they were necessary and valued members of their race.

During the period that Fanny Jackson attended Oberlin (1860–1865), few distinctions were made among students. There were no course grades, no prizes or honors, and students recited in alphabetical order. Secret societies or similar organizations were strictly prohibited and viewed by the college administration as "undemocratic." During this period at Oberlin, there was a strong feeling of community and purpose. In 1860, Jackson initially enrolled in the ladies department. However, she really wanted to achieve the highest level of academic success and passed the examination to enter the collegiate department in 1861. She became 1 of only 119 students in the collegiate department out of 1,311 total students at the college.

When one considers that Blacks and women were perceived as intellectually inferior to white men and adds the multiple barriers to both groups for education beyond a rudimentary level, the importance of Oberlin to Black women cannot be overstated. On this point, historian Eleanor Flexner noted:

> If a white woman was supposed to be mentally incapable of receiving the same education as a man, and Negroes were Inferior to whites, it followed that the Negro girl had the least possible potential for mental growth.[30]

To enter the collegiate department at Oberlin, one had to be examined in Andrews's, *Latin Grammar and Reader;* Nepos; Cicero's *Select Orations;* Virgil; Latin prose composition; Crosby's *Greek Grammar and Lesson;* three books of Xenophon's *Anabasis;* and the Gospels of the New Testament; algebra to equations of the second degree; and Weber's *General History*.[31] While the collegiate department (although commonly referred to as the gentleman's department) was open to women in principle, Fanny Jackson noted, the Oberlin administration didn't "advise it" for their female students. Jackson wrote, despite this view, she "took a long breath and prepared for a delightful contest."[32] She entered a class of forty men and thirteen women.

While quite conscious of the view that women were not capable of advanced classes in higher mathematics, Greek, Latin, and other classical courses, it was Jackson's consciousness about race that was foremost in her mind. She noted that the belief in Black intellectual inferiority was universal and commented:

> I never rose to recite in my classes at Oberlin [without feeling] that I had the honor of the whole African race upon my shoulders. I felt that, should I fail, it would be ascribed to the fact that I was colored.[33]

As Jackson noted, it was only her identification as a Black person that she thought was relevant at Oberlin. She felt it important to show the capabilities of Black people. Far from failing, Jackson attained an impressive academic record and involved herself in nearly all aspects of life at Oberlin. This alone was extremely significant since most Black students on white campuses had very limited opportunities to participate in extra-curricular activities, to live on campus, or do much beyond the classroom. Because French was not a part of the Oberlin curriculum, Jackson, in addition to her regular courses, studied French privately. Jackson sang in the First Church Choir of Oberlin and was a member of the Musical Union at the College. To supplement her income, she taught piano lessons to sixteen children of Oberlin faculty.[34]

Like Stanton a decade before, Jackson was also a member of the Ladies Literary Society and frequently appeared on their programs. In 1862, she composed a poem, "The Mystery of Life," and in 1864, gave an oration titled, the "Hero of Gettysburg," and appeared in a colloquy, in which she depicted the continent of Africa. In her senior year, she gave another oration titled, "Lorain News—August 30, 1895." Unfortunately, no copies of these works have survived.[35]

In addition to the experience the LLS afforded Jackson in public speaking and literary creativity and as a member of the collegiate department, she was responsible for "compositions, declamation, and extemporaneous discussions weekly; and public original declamation, monthly." These combined experiences provided the foundation in public speaking, which enabled her to become an elocutionist of prominence throughout her life. As noted earlier, public speaking for women was perceived by society as unladylike and daring. During an era when the notion of separate "spheres" of men and women dominated the public's view, the women at Oberlin who participated in the LLS challenged this assumption. However, Black women were not bound by such conventions since a

Black woman, Maria Stewart, who was a journalist, women's right's activist, and abolitionist, had given four public speeches between 1832–1833 to racially integrated audiences of men and women in Boston on these topics. Also, Sojourner Truth's famous "Ain't I a Woman?" speech further confirmed that Black women were not concerned about convention but expressing their concern over racial and gender inequality. Truth gave dozens of lectures throughout her life. Black women, whether formally educated or not, were very vocal in public settings on issues of inequality throughout the nineteenth and twentieth centuries.[36]

The years that Fanny Jackson attended Oberlin were historic not only for her and the college but for the nation as well—the Civil War years. The town of Oberlin, as noted earlier, had a strong abolitionist tradition. When the call came in 1861 for volunteer troops, the issue of slavery prompted Oberliners to respond in large numbers. Jackson's class gave a party to bid the student soldiers their best wishes and offered their prayers as the men marched down Main Street to the railroad station. The women students were equally as enthusiastic, and many organized to knit clothing for the soldiers while others petitioned the college to attend meetings concerning the war. The feminist LLS debated the question whether "ladies should organize themselves into Military Companies and drill." Throughout the war years, no less than 850 students enlisted in the army. In 1862, enrollment at Oberlin had dropped 35 percent, and by 1864, women constituted a majority of the student population.[37]

Oberlin had a profound impact on Jackson's life as it did for other Black students. They were impressed by their fellow classmates' earnestness and dedication to the abolition of slavery, but also by the opportunity to obtain a first-rate education that was the same as their white peers. Oberlin also allowed Jackson to fulfill her life's goal—"to get an education, to help my people." When the freedmen and freedwomen began to pour into the town of Oberlin, Jackson established a free school for them. The school offered classes four evenings a week on Oberlin's campus. Although the class was open to Blacks of all ages, she noted that most of the students were adults who came to class after working all day. She taught them basic reading and writing. Of this experience, she recalled years later:

> It was deeply touching to me to see old men painfully following the simple words of spelling; so intensely eager to learn. I felt that for such people to have been kept in the darkness of ignorance was an unpardonable sin, and I rejoiced that even then I could enter measurably upon the course of life which I had long ago chosen.[38]

Despite her academic demands and large number of music pupils, Jackson was extremely conscientious with her evening class and often conducted public exhibitions to display the work of these students. Throughout her career as an educator, Jackson always put on display the talents of Black students (as well as her own) to publicly demonstrate Black intelligence to doubters and to inspire Blacks to see how important education was to race progress. The evening school of formerly enslaved Blacks drew many visitors and the local newspaper carried accounts of its progress. For example, on February 4, 1863, the *Lorain County News* reported that:

> Coming along College Street the other evening we heard a John Brown song ringing out in a full chorus from twenty-five or thirty voices in the rooms of the evening school at Elmore Block . . . all the exercises are entered into with as much heartiness and interest as the closing song of the evening in question. The school consists entirely of adults of both sexes, who were deprived of school privileges in early life and whose days are now given to labor.[39]

The following year, the newspaper reported again on the school:

> We had the pleasure last Friday night of making the evening Colored School, taught in Colonial Hall this winter . . . This school is opened to all the Colored people of Oberlin, both young and old, who desire to receive instruction in the elementary branches, reading, writing, spelling grammar, etc., and is most ably conducted by Miss F.M. Jackson, a young lady of rare accomplishments and devotion to the work. On the evening of our call the exercises were most interesting. The pupils were mostly adults, who, after a hard day's labor embracing the opportunity afforded them for self-improvement, bent their minds to the tasks before them with an earnestness and concentration that were truly gratifying. Miss Jackson has the knack of being at once interesting and instructing, a fact evidently well appreciated by her scholars who appeared to enter with great enthusiasm into all her novel plans for their improvement.[40]

The success and the publicity of Jackson's evening class resulted in her being selected to teach in the preparatory department at Oberlin. It was customary for the college to hire forty juniors and seniors to teach in the preparatory school but no Black student prior to Jackson had ever been offered this opportunity. Jackson's appointment in the preparatory department meant that she was not solely the teacher of her race, but of the white students as well. While this was another "first" in the history of Oberlin and the list of achievements for Blacks, it was clear that a Black student had to be superior for the same position many white students had received as a matter of course. It was common knowledge at Oberlin that mediocre and even inferior student teachers were chosen throughout the years due to matters of the economy rather than brilliance.[41] Yet, Jackson's appointment was done with great trepidation. She was told if any white student objected to being taught by her, the college would have to rescind their offer. While Oberlin was clearly more progressive than the country on issues of race, there were limits to their vision of progress. Officials at the college defined progress as preparing religious and moral Black students to help their race, not for Blacks to be viewed as authority figures or experts with whites. Despite this obviously racist condition Jackson was given, she saw this as another opportunity to prove that Blacks were competent in the eyes of whites. Rather than condemn Oberlin for its hypocrisy on "brotherhood" and humanity, she praised them for their courage to appoint her. On the matter, she stated:

> It took a little moral courage on the part of the faculty to put me in my place against the old custom of giving classes only to white students.[42]

While it would have been ungracious for Jackson to state otherwise in 1864 when such a historic appointment was made, the lack of outrage is perplexing to contemporary readers. However, Jackson was sincere in her belief that the college was courageous in her appointment. In reality, not to appoint her would have been a glaring omission on Oberlin's part, considering the constant publicity concerning Jackson's talents as an effective teacher. When she met her class for the first time, she said there were some stunned and surprised faces, and one male student said he was "insulted" to have not only a woman teacher but a *Black* woman teacher. However, somehow Jackson stated she was able to win him over after his first recitation, and in the end, he proclaimed his preference for her over any other teacher. She was highly successful in this teaching position and her class grew from forty to one hundred students, requiring her to establish two sections. Again, Jackson was very conscious of proving Black competence when this was never such a burden for white students. News of the class was reported widely in various newspapers and visitors constantly came by to observe her teaching. Although Jackson's class became a virtual tourist attraction, and she was deemed a huge success (and clearly a credit to her race), Oberlin did not attempt to hire Jackson permanently for the preparatory department as was customary with other successful graduates. It may have been thought Jackson's sole purpose, as she had repeatedly stated, was to obtain an education so that she could teach her own people, but Oberlin had no Black faculty while the other two abolitionist colleges, New York Central College and Berea College that are discussed later in this chapter did.

The Oberlin Black community, while appreciative of the many opportunities afforded to them by the college, was also quite aware of the glaring contradictions regarding complete racial equality as well. As early as 1852, a group of Oberlin residents petitioned the college to hire Black faculty members. This request was counter-petitioned by a group of white Oberlin residents who opposed the request. Finally, in 1853, after a year of no response to the petition, the Trustees issued a statement which read: "In the choice of Professors and teachers of all grades, we are governed by intrinsic merit irrespective of color."[43] This statement served as an insult to the college's Black students and graduates. In 1852, seven Blacks had graduated from Oberlin, and by 1865, the year of Fanny Jackson's commencement, no less than nineteen men and women of "intrinsic merit" had earned Oberlin degrees. All of the above graduates became prominent educators, college presidents, and professionals. Even President Fairchild, the president of Oberlin in 1883, commenting on the sixty Black graduates of Oberlin by that year noted that many of these graduates were "brilliant scholars" and had received "distinction" in their various professions since their years at the college. However, it was not until 1948, nearly a century after the petition of Black students for Black faculty members, that a Black person was employed full-time by the college.[44] Indeed, while education was clearly the route to Black self-determination and progress, it did not erase the long-held notions, even by those believed the most liberal and progressive, that it was a "risk" to include even the highest achieving Black persons in positions of equality with whites. Nevertheless, many educated Black persons, such as Jackson, held firm to the belief that proving one's worth and being outstanding would erode racism and move Blacks forward.

The first year at Oberlin, Jackson lived on campus in Ladies Hall. The following four years at Oberlin, she lived with two prominent white Oberlin College families—the Pecks and the Churchills. Jackson recalled that both families accepted her as an "honored member of the family." Henry Peck was a professor of sacred rhetoric and moral philosophy and was a staunch abolitionist. Of the entire Oberlin faculty, Peck was considered the most liberal and described even as a radical when it came to abolitionist issues.

Directly across the street from the Pecks lived a Black attorney and early Oberlin graduate, John Mercer Langston. Born free in Virginia in 1829 of a mixed-race mother and white planter, his father provided funds for him and his two older brothers, Charles and Gideon, to attend Oberlin. In 1835, Charles and Gideon were the first Black students to enroll at Oberlin, entering the preparatory department. John entered the preparatory department several years later when he was old enough and graduated from the collegiate department in 1849. After earning a degree in theology from Oberlin in 1852, Langston then studied law and was admitted to the Ohio bar in 1854. He clerked for Oberlin township, as well as being a member of the town council. Langston was an active abolitionist who housed runaways on the Underground Railroad. Jackson recalled that Langston's home was always cordially opened to Black students at Oberlin, and she recalled it to be opened to anyone else "who cared to share his hospitality."[45]

Jackson lived with the Pecks for four years. When Peck was appointed United States Minister to Haiti in 1865, she lived her remaining six months in the home of Charles Henry Churchill, professor of mathematics and physics. In addition to being a scientist, Churchill was an accomplished musician and a leader of the college's Musical Union. Jackson maintained a lifetime relationship with both families and always stayed with the Churchills whenever she returned to Oberlin over the years.

At Jackson's commencement in 1865, she rejoiced not only at her significant accomplishment of graduating with a bachelor's degree—one that clearly demonstrated the superior intellect of a Black person who was also a woman, but also at the end of the Civil War. Graduating in a class of twenty-two men and thirteen women, Jackson was elected the Class Poet. Her poem, "The Grandeur of Our Triumph" celebrated the war and the victory of the Union.

> Unto God belongs the praises
> His right arm the vengeance deals;
> In the whirlwind of the battle
> We have heard his chariot wheels.
> We have heard his mighty trumpet;
> We have seen his flaming sword,
> And, the grandeur of our triumph,
> Is the Glory of the Lord.[46]
>
> Fanny Jackson
> "The Grandeur of Our Triumph"

Fanny Jackson had experienced a life at Oberlin rare to Blacks and women of her era. Regardless of the racial slights affecting her at Oberlin College, Jackson excelled and was a star student. Throughout her life, she was a staunch supporter of Oberlin and came to its defense whenever there were allegations of racism towards Black students. When Richard T. Greener, a Black student in the preparatory department in 1864, accused the college of racism, news of this spread to newspapers across the country with articles titled "prejudice at Oberlin!" Jackson published a lengthy letter in Oberlin's defense in an antislavery newspaper—the *National Antislavery Standard*, in which she passionately stated:

> A student here, whether he is white or black is judged according to his character and scholarship, and not according to any intrinsic circumstances. With the members of the Faculty, as with all persons of culture, "the *mind* is the measure of the man." The colored as well as the white students are treated with uniform respect and kindness.[47]

Jackson stated that bigotry was not found among Oberlin's faculty or administration, all of whom she described as being "high toned and [possessing] upright character." Throughout her lifetime, Jackson believed that racism was something that only uneducated and uncultured people possessed. She also attributed whatever prejudice—the word less stinging than racism—was a result of southern students at Oberlin. Furthermore, she wrote:

> Prejudice in Oberlin is preached against, prayed against, sung against, and lived against ... They [the faculty and administration] regard a colored man as a *man* and do not consider that they are conferring a favor upon him by so doing.[48]

All Black students did not feel as passionately about Oberlin as Fanny Jackson did and recalled different experiences. One Black woman student, Emma Brown, who was in the literary department, wrote in her diary on May 22, 1860 "there is considerable prejudice here which I did not at first perceive." She again noted in May 27th of that same year:

> There are 200 lady students. Quite a number . . . There are quite a few colored students . . . that is comparatively speaking . . . There is one colored girl [Mary Jane Patterson] taking the Classical Course. I have been told that she is a pretty good scholar.[49]

The Oberlin of the pre–Civil War years did not survive, and more pronounced racial events emerged after this period. However, Jackson's experiences at Oberlin during the period prior to the war were free of racial discord by her perspective. With few exceptions, she had been treated as an individual, equal to others both as a Black person but also as a woman. All evidence from her records during her Oberlin years reflects she was highly regarded by the faculty, administrators, students, and the community. While the number of men in her class dropped from the entering number of forty to twenty-two by commencement, she was still in a male-dominated class. Hence, her selection to be Class Poet reflected genuine respect for her talents. Jackson was a superstar at Oberlin and continued to be so after she left. There was another Black woman in Jackson's class, Frances J. Norris, from Rome, Georgia. She was born to an enslaved mother and a white planter who paid for her education at Oberlin. Norris was light-skinned enough to pass for white but was known and identified as a Black woman. Her father never married, and when he died, he left his sizable estate to her. She returned to Georgia and became a businesswoman specializing in real estate and catering.[50] Norris is rarely mentioned in the Oberlin records, but she was a good student and graduated in the classical program earning a baccalaureate degree. Most Black students who attended or graduated from Oberlin in the first thirty years of the institution's history maintained a lifelong connection with the institution. Norris did not, however, and apparently severed all ties with Oberlin after she graduated.

Mary Jane Patterson who was the first Black woman to earn a collegiate degree from Oberlin also was less visible on campus than Jackson. Patterson's family lived in Oberlin, and unlike Jackson she did not need to live in the dormitory or with faculty members. Furthermore, because she resided in the town of Oberlin, she was perhaps less likely to desire participating in campus activities. Patterson graduated in a class of twenty-eight students in 1862. On this occasion, the *Oberlin Evangelist* reported of this class: "In the College Graduating Class of 28 [students], including six young ladies, the colored race has had one representative of each sex. Both appeared well on the stage, their places not below the average of the class." It is indeed curious that the editor, Professor Henry Cowles, a founding member of the theology department at Oberlin, abolitionist, and Yale College graduate, had to single out the presentations of the two Black graduates and to assure the readers that their work was "not below the average of the class." These paternalistic statements—now defined by racial theorists as racial microaggressions—were pervasive in observations regarding Black people. Cowles also made specific mention of the women graduates—although Mary Jane Patterson was evaluated based on her race and not her gender. Of the white women graduates, he wrote, "all but two read essays—all brief, of course, but long enough to give their numerous friends pleasing evidence of their culture, intellectual and moral, and of their preparation for usefulness as educated women."[51] There was no assessment of the white male graduates' presentations. Mary Jane Patterson's commencement essay was titled "The Hero of Italy" in reference to politician Garibaldi.

Fanny Jackson's utopian view of Oberlin was not unique but represented the views of most Black students who attended during the antislavery era. In a study of Black students at Oberlin from 1835 to1865, Juanita Fletcher found that these students maintained lifelong friendships with their white classmates and generally held positive feelings toward the institution. In 1844, one such student wrote that there was no place in the United States where a Black [man] could receive an education "as cheap as he can at Oberlin, and at the same time, be respected as a man." He recalled that the college had expelled an affluent white student for referring to a Black student as a "black nigger."[52] Fanny Jackson recalled her classmates were determined that she would take "from Oberlin nothing but the most pleasant memories of my life there."[53] Fletcher notes that because of the many acts of kindness that Black students experienced at Oberlin, and indeed the educational opportunities that were virtually nonexistent elsewhere on a continuous basis, most Black students in the early years at Oberlin accepted the minimal acts of racism at the college. Obvious racial slights, such as the refusal to hire a Black to student teach in the preparatory department until Fanny Jackson's appointment in 1863 and the refusal to hire a Black faculty member until the mid-twentieth century, usually went unchallenged. Of this refusal of Blacks at Oberlin during this period to raise objections to racist acts, Fletcher noted:

> Unable to achieve group support in evaluating white behavior objectively because of their small number and urgently needing white approval, Negro students fully accepted accommodations made by whites to cultural taboos at Oberlin, happily judging such behavior as indicative of good-will.[54]

These student's behavior must be kept in historical context—what institution could a Black woman attend where she could not only join an organization with the term "ladies" in the title, let alone become the president? Black women students were elected as class poets, held offices in college organizations, lived on campus, ate in the dining hall with other students, and participated fully in campus activities. They were fully integrated within the facets of the school. Black women knew hundreds of their white classmates located throughout the nation and world engaging in missionary work. The American Missionary Association (AMA), established in 1846 by primarily Oberlin students, was responsible for establishing many of the leading Black liberal arts colleges in the South, including Fisk University and Talladega and Tougaloo Colleges. The AMA was a mixed blessing by offering a classical education to formerly enslaved persons while limiting Blacks the opportunity to teach and have leadership positions in these institutions until the 1940s.[55] This reality exposed the profound contradiction of many white liberals.

Nevertheless, the decades prior to the end of the Civil War afforded a small group of Black men and women a tremendous head start in their task towards bringing justice and knowledge to members of their race. Carter G. Woodson, in his *History of Black Education Prior to 1861* wrote: "This school [Oberlin] did so much for the education of Negroes before the Civil War that it was often spoken of as an institution for the education of the people of color."[56] In his study of Black college students in 1910, W. E. B. Du Bois noted that Oberlin was the "great pioneer" in the work of blotting out the color-line in colleges and said, "It had graduated more Negroes than any other institution of its kind."[57] Blacks who had the opportunity to attend Oberlin as well as other institutions that admitted them through this era were ready as soldiers to go out and battle the nation on behalf of their race.

Berea College

The third of the abolitionist colleges founded prior to Emancipation was Berea College in Kentucky by southern abolitionist minister John G. Fee, the AMA, and the wealthy antislavery Kentucky politician Cassius M. Clay. The school was originally planned to be established in northern Kentucky in 1853 in Bracken County; however, Clay offered Fee ten acres of land to establish an antislavery school and church located at the foothills of the Cumberland mountains, thirty-five miles south of Lexington in Madison County. Fee named the area Berea after a biblical town found in the book of Acts.[58] The AMA was founded in 1846 from four missionary societies. The organization was an antislavery abolitionist organization with memberships consisting almost exclusively of graduates from Oberlin College.[59]

While both Fee and Clay were abolitionists, they clashed over the issues of immediate versus gradual emancipation as well as whether the school should be integrated. Fee, like Clay, was from Kentucky. However, Fee was openly against slavery and refused to allow any slaveholders to attend his church.[60] A graduate of Lane Seminary in Cincinnati, Fee wanted Berea to be to Kentucky what Oberlin College was to Ohio, "antislavery, anti-caste, anti-rum, anti-sin."[61] These radical views were antithetical to the residents of this slave-holding state, and Fee was both physically and verbally attacked because of them. The Ku Klux Klan frequently harassed him. Clay withdrew his support for the school when Fee indicated that it would have to be an interracial school. To execute this change in 1858, Fee rewrote the school's constitution to make it interracially inclusive. Clay refused to serve on the board, and three other prominent Kentuckians also declined to serve. Parents who heard that Fee was planning to integrate the primary school, withdrew their children from Berea Institute, the primary school that served as a forerunner to the college.[62]

After the 1859 armed insurrection by enslaved persons in Harpers Ferry, Virginia, fear mounted in the slave-holding South and resulted in more opposition toward Fee and other faculty he had recruited to Berea. They were forced out of town and considered "exiles." While in "exile," Fee spent his time during the Civil War years teaching and preaching among Black soldiers, formerly enslaved persons, and their families in Camp Nelson in Kentucky. Fee, true to his belief that God was no respecter of race or gender, had the AMA hire African American teachers for the freedmen and women. When Fee invited an African American woman teacher, Belle Mitchell, to sit with him at dinner at Camp Nelson, twenty miles south of Lexington where the school was located, the white AMA officers and missionaries were shocked at this expression of "social equality," left the dining hall, and requested that Mitchell be removed from the building. As noted repeatedly, however, being antislavery did not mean being pro-Black and certainly did not include any notions of equality by even whites who considered themselves "friends of the race." Defending the Black woman teacher, Fee told the AMA members, "the young woman is fitted for her position; she is modest and discreet; she is a Christian, and as such, Christ's representative."[63] Throughout their lives, African American women constantly felt the need to have their honor and virtue defended.

While the AMA, as mentioned earlier, was supposedly composed of antislavery members, African American teachers and students experienced profoundly racist and condescending treatment from most of these members. While many white AMA members went south to teach and open schools (and later colleges) for the recently emancipated Blacks, many African American women also went south to aid in the massive effort to educate them as well. Many of these Black women were former students and graduates of Oberlin College. They were constantly denied teaching positions by the AMA and complained when the organization hired them to be sent to remote and difficult locations that white teachers would not go to. When Black and white teachers taught in the same location, they were segregated in housing and meals. These Black AMA teachers constantly wrote letters of complaints to the AMA superintendent in the 1860s about "prejudice against complexion" by the AMA staff in the South. They noted that the white AMA teachers constantly alleged the inferiority of Black students and their parents and treated Blacks with "sharp" social distinctions.[64]

Keep in mind, as one of the initial sponsors of Berea, the AMA was thought to be one of the most open and liberal institutions for African Americans. Like most schools that closed during the war, the Kentucky school reopened in January of 1866 as Berea Institute. Fee and his coworker, Reverend J. A. R. Rogers, a graduate of Oberlin College and the Theological Seminary, newly elected trustees, established a new constitution and acquired more land to build new buildings. The school was divided into two departments (the primary and the elementary division) and also an academic department for the secondary students. Fee recruited forty to fifty black families from Camp Nelson he had met during the war. The camp was twenty miles from Berea. Like the Black families that relocated to Oberlin because of the opportunities for their children, these Black families were able to purchase land in Berea.

The first Black students enrolled in the school in March of 1866. In cringeworthy language, Rogers, who served as principal of the school from 1858–1869, told white students in morning prayers before classes started that it was their role to treat those of "less culture," meaning the Black students, with kindness and noted that those who have more privilege were obligated to treat others with "noblesse oblige." He further reminded them of the importance of Christian love and noted that some of the best colleges in the country now admitted Black students. After his sermon to the white student body, four young Black girls entered the primary class, and more than twice that many enrolled in the secondary course along with Black male students. While there was no disruption in the primary class, the response of the secondary class was one of outrage with half the students of that level leaving their classes in protest. Rogers, in a history of Berea, explained the walkout of the white students and explained that "lifelong habits and prejudices were deep and not easily overcome."[65] The irony of the walkouts was that Berea Institute attracted poor whites from the Appalachian region. And, even though these poor whites were as desperately in need of an education as were the recently emancipated Black students, their notions of white racial superiority colored their judgment. Rogers recounted a story when one of the white students, whom he felt he had reached by his talk about Christian behavior, walked out. He stated that the student returned and confided in him: "I decided to return to school. I met great opposition from companions and relatives. An uncle offered to defray my expenses if I would leave Berea and go to some other [segregated] institution, but God has helped me, and I have got along some way, I hardly know how."[66]

Rogers continued that many of his "warmest friends of the college" who were eager for the college to open (the Berea Institute became a college in 1869) would interfere with the "best progress and discipline, but this fear was not realized." Throughout his condescending history book, Rogers pointed out that Berea had the "best colored people in the country" and that they were self-respecting and eager to "deport" themselves in an "unexceptional manner."[67] Rogers was self-congratulatory in the fact that Berea College and the town not only welcomed Black residents and students, but they sought Black residents and students out. He found Blacks coming to Berea as "phenomenal." He continued, "from the pickaninny to the old granny in the chimney corner . . . Berea was the land of promise, and to each it, with all they had on their backs, or at best in a rickety old cart, was the fulfillment of their hopes."[68]

Unlike the Black students who attended Oberlin and tended to be overwhelmingly mixed race, of some financial means, and came from a variety of geographical locations, Berea Black students were the opposite. They tended to be poor and newly emancipated and eager to build a life as free people with their families. Despite the racist and paternalistic comments of Rogers, Berea sought a balanced number of Black students in the first 25 years of the institution.

While many white students left Berea in 1866 upon the enrollment of Black students, within months, other white students began to enroll. Education was necessary for the poor Appalachian whites in the area as well as Blacks. Berea was affordable, and virtually all the students worked at the school as well as took jobs in the summer to teach throughout the rural areas of the South. Fee made it clear to white students that the school would be integrated and none of them should attend if they were not willing to accept attending a school with Black students. Since most of the white students were from the local Appalachian region, this was a dilemma for them.

Over the years, Berea had multiple names for their various departments: primary, grammar, intermediate, ladies' department, preparatory department, normal, and college. The primary, grammar, and immediate departments covered reading, writing, and arithmetic, and the preparatory department covered advanced work that included Greek, Latin, mathematics, science, philosophy, history, and English. The normal department was for the preparation of teachers, and the ladies' department, like at Oberlin College, was a three-year classical curriculum for women that only included English, French, Latin, algebra, logic, and philosophy but excluded Greek. During this historical period, when women and men were perceived to have different roles in life, the college course—which had been referred to as the "gentlemen's" course—was not perceived as necessary for "ladies" who were going to be wives, mothers, and schoolteachers.

However, Fee's views on the education of women were as advanced for the period as his views on the education of Blacks. He wrote, "the true civilization, is to elevate [women] to make her man's intellectual, social and moral equal—as God designed her."[69]

In 1869, when the college department was added, Reverend E. Henry Fairchild was recruited as president. Fairchild was a New Englander and graduated with two degrees from Oberlin College theological department. Fairchild was a staunch supporter of Black- and co-education and served as president until his death in 1889. In the 1870s, Fairchild expanded the campus with the establishment of two large dormitories—one for men and the other for women. A chapel followed, and by the 1880s a large classroom building was erected. By 1891, Berea had nine buildings and the faculty consisted of men and women. Many of them were products of Oberlin College.

Early Berea ensured that Blacks and whites of both genders were appointed to the faculty. In Rogers's memoirs, he recalled that of the fifteen teachers during the early years of his principalship, at least ten were Oberlin graduates and of this group nine were women. In addition, three Black alums served on the faculty from the 1870s through 1904 including one Black woman. Julia Britton (later known as Hooks) was born the daughter of free parents in 1852 in Frankfort, Kentucky, and raised in Lexington. She attended a school for Black students in Louisville and took piano lessons privately with an English woman. The women faculty taught primarily in the lower grades at Berea. Britten enrolled at Berea in 1869 to study music and graduated in 1874, the second Black woman to graduate

FIGURE 3. Julia Britton Hooks—first Black professor at Berea College, 1870. Berea College Special Collections and Archives.

from the upper school. She was hired to teach music at Berea, which she did for several years prior to her marriage and moving south to teach in Mississippi.

By the end of the 1866 school year, there were ninety-six Black students and ninety-one white students enrolled at Berea. In 1867–68, the student body grew to 307 with only one-third of the students being white.[70] During the four years from 1866 to 1870, approximately fifty-five Black girls and young women attended Berea in all levels of classes. While the school did not keep or mention the race of the students during this period, scholars in the twentieth century have gone through class books, school, and community records in an attempt to identify the Black students. Former Berea professor Richard Sears compiled a list of Berea students by race and year of attendance by painstakingly consulting marriage records and deeds, census data, newspaper records of students (the Black press), cemetery records, and published materials on family histories. In addition, he listed the forty Black families that moved to Berea after the opening of the school to Black students. This constitutes the best records of the student population available. His list shows more than seven hundred Black women and

FIGURE 4. Black women students 1897, Berea College. Berea College Special Collections and Archives.

Abolitionist Colleges   57

girls attended Berea from 1866 to 1904 when the school closed admissions to Black students. While many were at the primary levels, others came prepared for the intermediate, normal, and collegiate levels. For example, Fannie Miller, from Danville, Kentucky, had earned a high school diploma from Allegheny Academy in Meadville, Pennsylvania, when she arrived at Berea in 1871.[71] Almost all but a handful of Black students were from Berea or neighboring counties. A perusal of the roster compiled by a former faculty member at the college shows that there were 117 Black women students during the decade of 1870, of this number, two were Black women students from nearby Cincinnati, Ohio, and one from St. Louis, Missouri.[72] For the decade of the 1880s, with 161 Black women students—there were two from Mississippi and one from Georgia. And in the remaining two decades when Black students could attend, there were a few from Ohio, Indiana, Mississippi, and Florida.

Life at Berea was strict for students with stringent rules regarding mandatory attendance at the many religious events. Male students could visit women

FIGURE 5. Black women students in front of a cottage, Berea College. Berea College Special Collections and Archives.

students in the parlor of Ladies Hall twice a week with a chaperone present. In addition to the living quarters on campus, students lived at home or with faculty members in Berea. Almost all Berea students worked throughout their tenure to defray school fees and costs. Again, unlike the Black students at Oberlin, finances of Black Berea students were a constant problem. Many stopped and started their studies over a period of years to earn funding to continue their education. The need for teachers was so great with the development of schools in the South that many Black students often left to teach. The state of Kentucky did not require a college degree, hence many Berea students attended part-time for more than a decade. For example, the previously mentioned Fannie Miller, attended Berea during the years 1871–1887.[73]

While in theory, Berea sought to maintain its pledge to make "no distinction on account of color," the issue of interracial dating became a cause of great debate when a white male student sought to date an African American woman in 1871. The acting lady principal refused to allow the young man to socialize or see the Black woman due to "grounds of color." Students immediately protested that what they saw was a blatant affront to Berea's "anti-caste" mission. The faculty met with the trustees and approved interracial dating of students. Throughout the 1870 and 1880s, students dated and attended social events across racial lines.[74]

The era of President Fairchild (1869–1889) was considered the "golden age" of Berea when Black students, men and women, were fully integrated into the school—including housing, classes, student organizations, extra-curricular activities, and work assignments. Black and white students belonged to and served as officers of literary and other clubs on campus.[75] This all changed when Fairchild died and William G. Frost, a professor of Greek from Oberlin, became president in 1892. For two years prior to his appointment, the president was William Stewart. However, the trustees were against him (who was Fee's choice) and replaced him with Frost. Just like Oberlin of this time period, the treatment of Black students changed dramatically. The period of Reconstruction, which brought with it a rollback of racial progress, enveloped Berea. Frost, who held a PhD from Harvard, believed in the intellectual and social inferiority of Black people. During his presidency, he focused on the education of the white Appalachian students and significantly increased their numbers. When he became president in 1889, there were 184 Black students out of a student body of 384. In 1903, the student body had grown to 961 students with Black enrollment remaining at 184. Frost reinstituted restrictions on interracial dating, imposed segregated housing, eating arrangements, sports, and segregated the band. One of the Black faculty still employed when Frost became president was James S. Hathaway, class of 1884. Hathaway taught Latin and mathematics for ten years before being denied a promotion by Frost, whereupon he resigned and accepted a professorship (and later a presidency) at the Kentucky State Institute for Negroes in Frankfort (now Kentucky State University). After Hathaway left, Black alum John H. Jackson, also class of 1874, held a professorship of pedagogics for one year, becoming the college's last Black faculty hired before the 1904 segregation.

Fee, who died in 1901, fought to keep Berea true to its original roots—but he was old and outnumbered. Not only Berea but also the entire state of Kentucky had rescinded educational equity to Black students. In 1891, the state of Kentucky passed a constitutional amendment barring integrated education in public schools. With Berea being the only integrated private school in the state, it was only a matter of time before they were required to cease such an arrangement as well. In 1904, the Kentucky Legislature passed the Day Law, named after Breathitt Countian Carl Day, who introduced the bill in the Kentucky House of Representatives. The bill also stipulated that the same school could not operate separate Black and white branches within 25 miles of each other. This ended Black students attending Berea College. Frost attempted to fight the legislation by saying Blacks were already fully segregated on campus. However, that wasn't enough. Blacks were moved off campus in 1904 and forbidden from attending Berea until 1954 when the Supreme Court passed the *Brown v. Board of Education* case that outlawed segregation in education. The Black community asked why Frost and the trustees decided to eliminate Black students instead of the white students. Frost responded that the white Appalachian students would have no other options while Black students could attend the now existing Black colleges, such as Tuskegee or Fisk. However, he neglected to note that other colleges existed for white students as well. The removal of Black students from Berea resulted in Black women losing the opportunity to attend this coeducational institution for a half century.

… PART TWO

CHAPTER 3

College-Bred Black Women at Predominantly White Institutions in the Post–Civil War Era

As the nation moved into the mid-nineteenth century with the Civil War ending, this chapter discusses the educational opportunities and challenges of both freed and formerly enslaved Black women. I explore Black women's educational experiences in white women's schools and colleges and those established exclusively for Black women and girls. Disrespect and constant attacks on the character of Black women continued, as greater educational opportunities grew for white women after the Civil War with the growth of female seminaries and later colleges.

While Oberlin was the primary institution for Black women to obtain a collegiate level education prior to Emancipation, post–Civil War there were other institutions in limited numbers available to them. Black women attended the elite Seven Sisters colleges in New England and the North in small numbers. They also sporadically attended other institutions throughout the North. For example, Mary Annette Anderson from Shoreham, Vermont, was the daughter of a former slave who moved north after the Civil War and purchased a farm there. Her mother was French Canadian and Native American. Anderson attended Northfield Seminary in Massachusetts where she excelled as a student. She entered Middlebury College in Vermont at age 21 in 1895, where she graduated valedictorian of her coed class in 1899. Founded as an all-male college in 1800, Middlebury became coed in 1883. An extraordinary student, Anderson also became the first Black woman to be inducted into Phi Beta Kappa in the nation, the highest academic honor society for undergraduate colleges. She delivered the commencement address for her class, "The Crown of Culture," and was the first woman to address guests at the "corporation dinner" that included the president, trustees, alumni, professors, and distinguished guests. She also wrote the class poem for Class Day.

FIGURE 6. Mary Annette Anderson, Class of 1899, Middlebury College. Middlebury College Special Collections.

Despite the liberalism of Middlebury, Anderson did not escape racism outside of the college. Unlike other (women) classmates who graduated and were offered teaching positions in Massachusetts, she did not receive an offer because the state did not employ Black teachers.

With the growth of schools and colleges for African Americans throughout the South, educated Black women were in great demand as teachers at all levels of education. Hence, a year after graduation from Middlebury, Anderson found employment at Straight University in New Orleans—a Black college founded by the American Missionary Association (which later became Dillard University). She taught there for one year and then moved due to multiple job offers at other Black institutions, including an invitation from Booker T. Washington to join the faculty at Tuskegee Institute in Alabama. She decided, however, to accept a faculty position at Howard University in Washington, DC.[1]

Her decision to accept Howard over Tuskegee is not hard to understand. Tuskegee was still of high school grade and stressed industrial education. Anderson, the product of a strong New England liberal arts college, was much better suited for Howard, which boasted university status and was in the nation's capital rather than the rural deep South. In contrast, Washington, DC, while segregated, was vibrant. Anderson taught English and rhetoric until 1907, when she married Walter Lucius Smith, a 1902 graduate of Howard from Metropolis, Illinois. He was a teacher and later principal of M Street High School, which later became the renowned college preparatory Dunbar High School. Howard's rule at the time required married women to give up their jobs. While in Washington, Anderson was very active in the College Alumnae Club—an organization of Black women college graduates of primarily white colleges headed by Oberlin

College graduate Mary Church Terrell. This group worked to assist young Black women who planned to attend college.[2]

Other types of higher education institutions emerged that afforded African American women in small numbers to attend outside the South in the nineteenth century.

Hunter College

Hunter College, the public, all-female city college in New York City, was founded in 1869 as the Female Normal and High School but was soon renamed the Normal College in 1870. In 1914, it was renamed Hunter College.[3] Entrance to Hunter was based on competitive academic examinations, was tuition free, and open to any woman in New York City who could make at least 85 on the examination. It was a commuter campus, which allowed Black women students not to concern themselves with housing discrimination. In 1873, eight African American women were admitted to the Normal College. Hunter prepared students for teaching (although Black women could not teach in the city). By 1890, fifty-six Black women attended Hunter. The socioeconomic backgrounds of the Black women mirrored those of their white counterparts. The occupations of their parents listed on their registration records noted janitor, laundress, seamstress, waiter, clerk, teacher, cook, coachman, caterer, steward, merchant, sexton, and rector.[4]

As more opportunities for Black women in other public institutions increased, the number of Black women at Hunter declined by 1891. Moreover, the difficulty of gaining teaching positions in New York resulted in many Black women attending historically Black colleges, where the preparation of teachers was one of their primary missions, and the need for Black teachers in the South was dire; therefore, Black women reduced their attendance at Hunter. In the South, teachers found jobs within the region without diplomas or degrees. Black women, with even one year of normal training, were employable in southern segregated schools. Often, the Hunter College registrar's records noted that African American students left school "to teach."[5]

Black women were welcomed in dining areas and other aspects of campus life at Hunter. Women's historian Barbara Miller Solomon noted that after Oberlin College, Hunter College and the University of Kansas enrolled more Black women before 1950 than any other university that was not a historically Black college.[6] After becoming a full-fledged liberal arts college in 1914, Hunter's excellent academic reputation and free tuition resulted in it becoming the largest women's college in the world by the 1930s. It had more than five thousand students and enrolled more than fifteen thousand students when summer and extension courses were included.[7]

Unlike the elite private women's colleges, Hunter College was largely a college for poor and overwhelmingly immigrant women who sought degrees for vocational reasons and not to obtain the expected MRS degree that many women who attended more elite schools sought. In the 1886 *Annual Report,* it was reported:

> We have Jews and Gentiles and the children of almost every European nationality, dark-skinned Negroes sitting beside fair-haired Scandinavians, and almost every breed under the sun is represented. This is the true democratic mingling of the classes which could only exist in a Republican country like the United States.[8]

The historian of Hunter College noted why many of the Hunter women, unlike the women in private women's colleges, attended college:

> For some it was the path out of poverty and menial work. For others, it was a place of refuge when all other doors were closed. From 1920 through World War II, Hunter students were united by their ethnicity, their poverty, their immigrant status—by their anger, and eagerness, and desperate aloneness—by their sense of exclusion—far more than by common links to undergraduate women elsewhere.[9]

This perspective was reflected in the autobiography of African American Pauli Murray who moved to New York City from North Carolina in the 1920s. Murray attended Hunter from 1928 to1933. She grew up in the segregated schools of Durham, North Carolina where her schoolteacher aunt raised her. Murray was determined to attend an integrated school in the North and declined a scholarship to the historically Black Wilberforce College in Ohio. The rejection of Wilberforce was also due to financial reasons since her scholarship offer was not substantial enough to get her through the first year. Inspired by a teacher who wore a sweater with the letter C on it, which she told Murray stood for Columbia University, Pauli decided she wanted to follow in this teacher's footsteps and attend the institution. She, however, was not aware the teacher had attended Teachers College at Columbia University and not the all-male Columbia College of the University. When she and her aunt took her high school transcript to Columbia College, the admissions office informed them of this and advised them that Hunter College was a free women's college in the city that admitted students based on examination scores. Murray said:

> Neither of us [she or her aunt] had heard of Hunter College but if it had free tuition, it might solve our problem.[10]

Murray noted she was disappointed that Hunter was a commuter campus and a single-sex college. She commented, "to go to Hunter, it seemed to me, would be to swap segregation by race for segregation by sex." She also noted, however, that she was unaware of the high academic reputation of Hunter. Murray recalled, "In my naiveté, I did not know that it was the largest women's college in the world" and that it was also considered "the poor girl's Radcliffe."

The admissions officer was gracious and encouraging. Murray recalled:

> Despite these barriers, however, the admissions people at Hunter did not turn us away without hope; They sat down with Aunt Pauline and worked out a curriculum of the courses I would need for admissions provided she could resolve the problem of residence. They recommended that I try to complete my education in a New York City high school and receive a diploma which would be accepted automatically by Hunter College.[11]

Murray needed another year of English, Latin, French, and a list of courses she had never taken. Living with relatives in Queens, Murray enrolled in Richmond High School and was the lone Black student in a high school of four thousand. Her relatives in Queens, as well as her Aunt Pauline in North Carolina, were very fair-skinned and were not identifiably Black. While Murray's Aunt Pauline was a fiercely proud Black woman, Murray noted that her New York relatives were believed to be foreign, and she suspected they were passing for white.

She remembered:

> It was an ambiguous situation in which their denial of their racial origins was more a matter of silence than of a contrary assertion.[12]

Hence the situation was more of a don't ask, don't tell one.

Murray did exceptionally well academically, passed the New York Regents high school exam, and was admitted to Hunter in the fall of 1928. She graduated from Hunter in January 1933, one of four Black women in a class of 247. Her desire to become a lawyer resulted in her facing the reality of racism and sexism. She was rejected from the University of North Carolina Law School in 1938 because of her race and from Harvard Law School because of her gender. Instead, Murray went to the historically Black Howard University Law School and graduated in 1944. She earned a master's in law from Boalt Hall in Berkeley, California, funded by a Julius Rosenwald Fellowship. She graduated from law school and passed the California Bar in 1945. Twenty years later in 1965, she became the first Black person to earn a Doctorate in Juris Science from Yale Law School at the age of 62. An activist lawyer and writer, Murray also became an Episcopal priest obtaining a theological degree from General Theological Seminary in 1978.[13]

The welcoming experience of Murray at Hunter was extraordinary considering the many difficulties Black women found in attempting to enroll in predominantly white institutions of higher education—particularly women's

FIGURE 7. Mary Huff Diggs, first Black faculty member of Hunter College, 1947. Courtesy of Hunter College Archives.

colleges. While the number of Black women until the 1960s was steady but small, Hunter was unique in its diversity and openness to students without regard to religious, racial, or socioeconomic status.

As early as 1900, Black scholar W. E. B. Du Bois noted in his study of Black college students that it was easier for an African American man to gain entrance into a white male college than for a Black woman to gain entrance to a white women's college. Du Bois noted white women's colleges were "unyielding" in their opposition to enrolling Black women students.[14] This remark was directed toward several of the elite Seven Sisters colleges. He monitored the admissions of Black students in white institutions and annually polled them on their policies and numbers of Black students. He polled a series of women's colleges about their policies of admitting Black women. An administrator of Vassar responded to Du Bois' query in 1900, "We have never had but one colored girl among our students, and no one knew during her course that she was a Negro, the feeling of respect and affection that she won during her college course has not been changed on the part of those who knew her here. There is no rule of the college that would forbid our admitting a colored girl, but the conditions of life here are such that we should hesitate for the sake of the candidate to admit her and in fact should strongly advise her for her own sake not to come."[15] As we shall see, the statement regarding the Black student who was not known to be Black until her senior year created a major scandal and she was far from accepted by her peers once her race was discovered. Barnard College, the sister college to Columbia, responded: "No one of Negro descent has ever received our degree, and I cannot say whether such a person would be admitted to Barnard as the question has never been raised, but there is nothing in our regulations that excludes anyone of nationality or race." However, it was evident that despite

FIGURE 8. Pauli Murray, Class of 1933, Hunter College. Courtesy of Hunter College Archives.

a lack of written regulations, it was well known that Black women were not accepted or wanted. Du Bois received similar responses from Wells College and Elmira College in New York stating they had never had Black women students and did not know what the trustees would do if one applied.

And of course, southern women's colleges such as Randolph-Macon Women's College in Virginia said they believed that Blacks and whites should be educated

FIGURE 9. Toussaint's L'Ouverture Club, 1939, Hunter College. Courtesy of Hunter College Archives.

separately. Mills College in Oakland, California, honestly stated they did admit Black women. Du Bois noted that Wellesley, Smith, and Radcliffe did admit Black women.[16]

The College of New Jersey for Women (later named Douglass College) was the women's college of Rutgers College (later University), one of the original colleges that was founded in 1766. By 1864, it became a land-grant college. Although Rutgers admitted the first Black male in 1888, the women's college of the university was established in 1918. Just like with other Black women who were not known to be Black until they arrived at the college, this was the situation with the first African American woman student at the New Jersey College for Women (NJC). In 1934, Julia Baxter, the daughter of a veterinarian from Bernardsville, New Jersey, was the first Black woman student. Assuming she was white, the school administrators encouraged her to withdraw once they discovered her race. Baxter declined but like Black women at other white institutions during this period was not allowed to live on campus. Despite this discrimination, the very light-skinned middle-class Baxter appeared to have had a positive experience at NJC. She was a product of a white community and had been the only Black student in her high school, so attending college with white women was a continuation of her earlier education. Like the women who attended other women colleges, they tended to be fair-skinned and bi- or multiracial. A few other Black women attended and graduated during the decades of the '40s. Carey and Walker's chapter on Black women at Douglass College noted: "The Black women who graduated from NFC between 1938 and 1945 came from relatively diverse socioeconomic backgrounds which set them apart from Black women who attended the Seven Sister Colleges." Due to the activism of the NAACP and the National Urban League, Black women were allowed to live in the dormitories in 1946. Unlike Black women in many other white colleges, the women at NJC reported a positive experience at the college.[17] The experiences of Black women students at the elite Seven Sisters colleges discussed in the next section provides insight into the struggles and successes of these highly talented women.

The Seven Sisters Colleges

The seven private elite New England and northern women's colleges—Mount Holyoke, Vassar, Wellesley, Smith, Radcliffe, Bryn Mawr, and Barnard—commonly known as the Seven Sisters colleges, were founded in the nineteenth century as a response to the exclusion of women from the leading private elite male colleges in the same geographical regions. They were considered the "sister" colleges to the all-male Ivy League colleges of the period. By 1890, these women's colleges became known for their academic excellence as well as the predominantly wealthy student body. Only Mount Holyoke was originally founded for middle-class women. By the turn of the century, Mount Holyoke along with the other six women's colleges became known as the campuses for the wealthy white Anglo-Saxon Protestant of the middle and upper classes.

Despite Du Bois' observations regarding the difficulty of Black women gaining entrance into these institutions, a small number of African American women did gain admittance in the late nineteenth century. Because photographs were not required for admissions during the early eras of college admission (photos became required later—primarily to exclude Jewish students, who often changed their names to avoid being eliminated because of their religious background), often these colleges did not knowingly accept Black women. Many of the earliest Black women were light-skinned enough to be mistaken for a white person. Hence, many of the earliest Black women students at these institutions were indistinguishable from white women and presumably passed for white. This discussion, however, will concentrate on those women who identified as or were later discovered to be Black. The admission and treatment of Black women in these colleges varied. Until the 1960s, most of these institutions accepted Black women in token numbers and their numbers were rarely more than two per class. The archives of Smith, Radcliffe, Wellesley, and Mount Holyoke are rich with biographical data, enrollment information, and oral histories. Barnard, Vassar, and Bryn Mawr, the last of the Seven Sisters to admit Black women, did not maintain historical records of Black women during the period being discussed. The Black women who attended these institutions, as well as the other predominantly white institutions in the nineteenth and early twentieth centuries, were pioneers, as well as privileged to pursue and obtain baccalaureates and later graduate degrees decades before such advantages would be available to their southern Black sisters.

As noted earlier, all Blacks in the South suffered from legal segregation due to the 1896 *Plessy v. Ferguson* Supreme Court decision, which established the "separate but equal doctrine." This ruling impacted schools, housing, public accommodations, and all aspects of life for Blacks in the region. This is why Pauli Murray left North Carolina for New York City to avoid attending a segregated college. While Black women outside the South had access to various types of high schools and colleges, those in the South did not. According to educational historian James D. Anderson in his study of the history of Blacks in the South, public high schools did not exist for Black citizens there until the mid-1930s. He wrote, until that time: "Almost all of the southern rural communities with significantly large Afro-American populations and more than half of the major southern cities failed to provide any public high schools for Black youth."[18]

By the late 1890s, most African Americans resided in the South. Many of the earliest Black women in the Seven Sisters colleges were daughters of the Black middle- and upper-class descendants of free Black families, and were biracial, multiracial, and very light-skinned. These young women frequently were well traveled and spent their summers in such vacation locations as Martha's Vineyard, Saratoga Springs, and Newport, Rhode Island.[19] According to Willard B. Gatewood's study of the Black upper class from 1880 to 1920, higher education was central to their identity: "No matter how significant family background, complexion, and church affiliation might be as stratifiers, they were singly and collectively less important than the disciplined, cultivated mind produced by higher education."[20] These institutions were ones of choice for many prominent Black families prior to the 1960s. The Seven Sisters colleges are important to Black women's higher education because these institutions offered women students the equivalent education of the top male institutions. Although the number of Black women who attended these institutions prior to the 1960s was small (around five hundred), their influence within the African American community and beyond was significant. They became members of the faculties of African American colleges, as well as prominent lawyers, judges, physicians, scientists, and leaders in other fields.

Wellesley College

Wellesley College in Wellesley, Massachusetts, and Smith College in Northampton, Massachusetts, were both founded in 1875. Radcliffe College (formerly known as the Harvard Annex) was founded in 1879. Although these three institutions are not the oldest of the Seven Sisters colleges, they do have the longest and most continuous history of Black women students and graduates. African American women began attending these three institutions in the mid-1880s in token yet steady numbers. Both Mount Holyoke, founded in 1837 as a women's seminary (it attained collegiate status in 1881), and Vassar, founded in 1865, had African American women students in the late nineteenth century, but these students were not known to be African American until after they arrived on campus. Neither Barnard, founded in 1889, nor Bryn Mawr, founded in 1884, admitted Black students until well into the twentieth century.

The first African American to graduate from Wellesley College was Harriett Alleynce Rice of Newport, Rhode Island. Rice, the daughter of a steward on the steamship, *The Pilgrim*, lived on campus in a single room, according to the campus directory.[21] After graduating in 1887, Rice earned a medical degree in 1893 from the Women's Medical School of the New York Infirmary. From all indications, Rice's experience at Wellesley was positive. She kept in touch with the college and returned in 1920 to lecture on her experiences as a medical assistant in France during the First World War. She noted that the American Red Cross had refused her services due to her race, and she worked instead for the French government.[22] In an alumnae questionnaire she was asked, "Do you have any handicap, physical or other, which has been a determining factor in your [professional] activity?" Rice replied, "Yes! I am colored which is worse than any crime in this God *blessed Christian* country! My country (100%) tis of thee!"[23]

The credentials of African American women who attended these elite colleges did not exempt them from the racial barriers that all Blacks experienced. While it appears that the African American women who attended Wellesley in the first two decades of the twentieth century did not express any overt instances of discrimination at the institution, Jane Bolin, class of 1928 did. Bolin's lineage stems from an old line of a free Black family, who were politically and civilly active and could trace their lineage in the Poughkeepsie, New York, area since the late 1790s. Her grandfather was active in the Black convention movement of the nineteenth century and she was the daughter of a prominent lawyer, Gaius Charles Bolin, who was the first African American to attend and graduate from Williams College (1889), the elite male college in western Massachusetts.[24]

While Bolin lived two blocks from the elite Vassar College, the college had never knowingly accepted a Black student. Although Bolin was biracial (white British mother) and fair-skinned, she identified as Black and had no desire to test the racially discriminatory admissions policies at Vassar. She reported that Wellesley was the only college she applied to. She noted she entered at age sixteen "sensitive and idealistic."[25] Her biographer noted that Bolin's enthusiasm for Wellesley was "dashed upon enrollment—which set the stage for her four years at Wellesley."[26]

Bolin recalled that she and Ruth Brown, the only other Black women admitted as first-year students in 1924, were assigned to room together in an apartment off campus. Although Black women were allowed to eat in the dining hall, southern students refused to sit with them. In a skit, Brown was asked to play Aunt Jemima, and although Bolin was an honor student, she was rejected from a sorority that stated it was concerned with social problems. She recalled her rejection letter was put under her door unsigned. Despite these events, Bolin said the "sharpest and ugliest" memory of Wellesley occurred during her senior year in a conference with a counselor while discussing her life after Wellesley. Bolin told the counselor she planned to apply to law school. The counselor "threw up her hands in disbelief and told me there was little opportunity in law for women and absolutely none for a 'colored' one. Surely, I should consider teaching."[27] Responding to an invitation to write reflections of her memories of Wellesley for a 1974 alumnae volume, Bolin candidly recounted the many slights she experienced both as a student and as an alumna. She noted that despite her discouragement, she was admitted to Yale Law School after she graduated Wellesley—and while she did not mention it—she was the first African

American woman to be admitted and to graduate from Yale Law School. Mayor Fiorello LaGuardia in New York City appointed Bolin to a judgeship when she was thirty-one years old in 1939. Bolin noted this was a historic appointment and she received enormous publicity and congratulations that poured in from all over the world. She recalled the list of those wishing her congratulations included, "my law school, high school and even grade school teachers, but not a single note from teacher, president, dean, house mother, or anyone (except a few classmates) who were at Wellesley during my four years."[28] In closing Bolin stated:

> There were a few sincere friendships developed in that beautiful, Idyllic setting of the college but, on the whole, I was ignored outside the classroom. I am saddened and maddened even nearly a half a century later to recall many of my Wellesley experiences but my college days for the most part evoke sad and lonely personal memories. These experiences perhaps were partly responsible for my lifelong interest in the social problems, poverty and racial discrimination rampant in our country. I thank you very much for inviting me to submit a memoir for Wellesley's Centennial. You will understand that I report my memories honestly because this racism too is part of Wellesley's history and should be recorded fully, if only as a benighted pattern to which determinedly it will never return and, also, as a measure of its progress.[29]

Bolin's treatment wasn't unique, and Black women at Wellesley were required to live in a single room or share one with another Black woman if one was in their class until the 1960s. Bolin, who came from an activist family, refused to

FIGURE 10. Jane Bolin, Class of 1928, Wellesley College. Courtesy of Wellesley College Archives.

accept this treatment without comment or pretending to be grateful for her admission to Wellesley. She put her feelings on the record in the college's Centennial publication.

W. E. B. Du Bois began keeping data on Black students in white institutions and reported their accomplishments as well as their challenges in his studies titled the College-Bred Negro. As editor-in-chief of *The Crisis* magazine, Du Bois, chronicled the educational progress and discrimination of Blacks in higher education.[30]

Radcliffe College

Radcliffe College, originally known as the Harvard Annex, was founded in 1879 in Cambridge, Massachusetts, by the Society for the Collegiate Instruction of Women. The women applicants had to meet the same admissions requirements as men bound for Harvard and were taught by Harvard's faculty. Their degrees and honors were provided on the same basis as Harvard's.[31]

Radcliffe enrolled African American women continuously from the 1890s. Though barred from campus housing, the women participated in all other aspects of campus life and extracurricular activities. The first Black graduate of Radcliffe was Alberta Scott of Cambridge. Born in Richmond, Virginia, she moved with her parents to Cambridge when she was six years old. Her father

FIGURE 11. Alberta Scott, Class of 1888. Schlesinger Library. Harvard Radcliffe Institute.

FIGURE 12. Eva Dykes, Class of 1917, Radcliffe College. Schlesinger Library, Harvard Radcliffe Institute.

was a boiler tender and stationary engineer. Scott graduated with distinction from Cambridge Latin High School and entered Radcliffe in 1894. At Radcliffe, Scott was active in the Idler, a dramatic club, as well as the German Club. She was also involved in music while in college. After graduating in 1898, Scott went south to teach at Tuskegee Institute in Alabama, the college founded by educator Booker T. Washington. Tragically, Scott became ill in 1900 and returned to Cambridge, where she died in 1902 at the young age of 27.[32]

Due to the housing issue, most of Radcliffe's earliest Black women students were from Cambridge and the greater Boston area. Students from outside the area had to find accommodations with members of Cambridge's Black community (this was the same for Black men who attended Harvard as well).

As with all these institutions, Black women had varying opinions regarding the discrimination they experienced. Margaret Perea McCane, who graduated from Radcliffe in 1927 and whose college years overlapped with Bolin's attendance at Wellesley, recalled:

> It was fortunate that all of us lived at home, because in those days Black students could not live in the dormitories at Harvard or Radcliffe. It wasn't until my junior year in college that a Black girl was admitted to the dormitory at Radcliffe and it was a few years later that Black boys at Harvard could live at college.[33]

But, McCane rationalized:

> Those were some of the things that one took in one's stride then. I do not say that it was fair and that we should have been able to accept it. It was a situation [in] which one dealt with the problems that one had, with the handicaps that one met, and one did not let those things stand in the way of one's getting an education, a good education for that was why you were there. And you recognized the fact that your contacts and what you did and the record you made were going to influence other young black people who followed you. I think that always stood as a goal before all of us.[34]

Thus, for many Black students, not being able to stay on campus, and frequently being barred from organizations and activities, was a small price to pay for the prestige of the degree. Their views on this matter faced head on the long-debated issue within the Black community of whether or not they should protest or accommodate discrimination to obtain a larger goal. When it came to housing discrimination, McCane believed obtaining a degree equivalent to one at Harvard was worth it. Mary Gibson Huntley, a 1918 graduate of Radcliffe from Washington, DC, agreed. Although she was denied housing on campus as well as financial aid, she said, "the prestige of my degree brought contacts in emergency, when professional or racial problems arose."[35] Charlotte Leverett Smith Brown, a 1920 graduate of Radcliffe, agreed as well. She was the first Black student to graduate with a degree in chemistry from the institution. She stated, "I have always been and always will be proud that I am a Radcliffe graduate, and find that when questioned the mention of Radcliffe seems to settle all arguments and discussions."[36] Despite these positive reflections, not all Black alumnae from that era shared these sentiments. For example, when one of Radcliffe's early graduates was asked to reflect on her years at the college, the interviewer observed, "[Although] she had an interesting career . . . she is very, very bitter about Radcliffe because of her experience there. And, she deeply resents Radcliffe's failure to recognize its early Black graduates and their accomplishments."[37]

As we shall see, the housing issue remained the number one issue for Black students who attended white institutions of higher education.

A member of the Radcliffe Board, John F. Moors, apologized to the president of Radcliffe in 1925 for missing a board meeting where this topic was on the agenda. He wrote:

> I wish I could hear in particular the discussion of the new Negro problem. I can, perhaps, contribute a little information and my own opinion.
>
> I have never had any doubt that students of all races, intellectually and morally qualified, should be admitted to our higher institutions of learning; but when some years ago two Negroes were excluded from the Freshmen Dormitories of Harvard, the exclusion at first seemed to me justified because residence in those dormitories was compulsory. In other words, while Harvard should give these Negroes every intellectual opportunity it seemed to me at first, it was not obliged to enforce distasteful social relationships. Moreover, the disappointment to two Negro boys seemed to be a minor incident compared with the whole tragedy of the 10,000,000 Negroes in this country.
>
> Later, when the controversy over this exclusion became acute, I was impressed by the fact that what was at issue was not the suffering of two boys but a stigma on a race. With this new conception in mind, I voted confidently for the final solution reached.
>
> I have not heard the exact phrasing of that solution. In substance, it was that no race should be excluded from the dormitories and yet no student should be forced into a race relationship, which he did not like. In other words, students of any race are admitted now to the Freshmen Dormitories, but any boy who objects to a Negro resident in one dormitory has the right to be transferred to another.[38]

Moors said that one of the suggestions regarding the housing ban for Black men was to have a special dorm for them. He said this was decided against because the dorm would have been referred to as "coon hall" and the stigma of race would remain. He said, "as long as an inch of Harvard property is debarred to one student because of his race but open to all others, the stigma remains."[39] Moors said it was rare that a Black student sought housing in the dormitories.

But he continued that the difference in the situations between Radcliffe and Harvard was that Radcliffe doesn't require its students to live in the dormitories. Moors noted the impact that living on campus had on students and said living on campus played a huge role in the social life of students. Yet, having to interact across racial lines may cause "embarrassment" on social occasions.[40]

Moor ended his letter by advising:

> I am strongly of the opinion that the example of Harvard offers the best solution for Radcliffe now in sight. No solution is going to make everyone happy ever afterwards.

He noted that this issue could become one that would receive nationwide news coverage:

> If the young woman who makes the present demand is excluded, a new country-wide controversy is liable to arise involving not only Radcliffe but her big sister and applications, will, I think, be numerous and disagreeable. If, however, the College accepts this young woman into one of its dormitories with fair notice to the others who will be residents there, my impression is that the Negroes themselves will soon become partners in not forcing the issue unduly.[41]

Finally, he concluded, "the likelihood of interracial marriage was remote among students and felt at that point in history such an event was unlikely."[42]

Beginning in 1926, Black women were allowed to live on campus at Radcliffe. Radcliffe's African American graduates contributed greatly to the education of their race at both historically Black colleges and Black public high schools. Beginning with the first Black graduate, Alberta Scott, who taught at Tuskegee Institute in Alabama, all but one of Radcliffe's Black graduates during the first decade of the twentieth century taught at some point at a Black educational institution.[43]

By the second decade of the twentieth century, Radcliffe graduated more than one Black woman each year. By 1920, four Black women graduated in the same class. These statistics were unheard of at the other Seven Sisters colleges, where such numbers would not be achieved until the 1940s and 1950s. By 1950, Radcliffe had graduated fifty-six African American undergraduates and thirty-seven Black women graduate students. It was by far the leader in the number of Black women graduates among the Seven Sisters colleges.

Smith College

A wealthy single woman, Sophia Smith, endowed Smith College in Northampton, Massachusetts, in 1868. A devoutly religious woman, Smith sought to

FIGURE 13. Otelia Cromwell, Class of 1900, Smith College. Smith College Special Collections.

FIGURE 14. Carrie Lee, Class of 1917, Smith College. Smith College Special Collections.

establish a college where women could have an education equal to that of the leading men's colleges. But, she also wanted the college to be "pervaded by the spirit of evangelical Christian religion." Like its sister institutions of Wellesley and Mount Holyoke, religion was central to the life and mission of the college.

The first African American woman to graduate from Smith was Otelia Cromwell of Washington, DC, who graduated in 1900. Her father, John Wesley Cromwell, was a prominent educator, and, after earning a law degree, a chief examiner of the United States Post Office. Otelia Cromwell was a product of the segregated schools of Washington. She transferred to Smith College in her junior year after attending Miner's Teachers College, a Black institution in her hometown. As was the tradition at most white women's colleges, Cromwell was not allowed to live on campus and was housed at the home of a Smith College Professor of Greek, Julia Caverno. Despite this unexpected situation, Cromwell enjoyed her stay at Smith and wrote to her father her first year there, "I am having a very happy time of it this year." After graduating from Smith, Cromwell spent a year in Germany and obtained a master's degree from Columbia University in 1910 and a PhD in Elizabethan literature from Yale University in 1926, the first African American woman to earn a doctorate from that institution. Cromwell spent her professional career teaching at Miner's Teacher's College in Washington, DC.

In 1913, Smith College faced an embarrassing situation that forced them to confront the housing policy of Black students having the right to live on campus.

The issue came to a head when Carrie Lee, the daughter of a letter carrier from New Bedford, Massachusetts, was admitted to the college. Unlike Cromwell, who came from a known Black high school, college officials were not aware that Lee was African American, since she attended a predominantly white high school. She had been assigned a dormitory room with a white student from Tennessee. When the white student protested, Smith officials told Lee she could not live on campus and would need to find other accommodations from the college's approved Northampton housing list. The only housing left was a situation where Lee would be required to be a servant and not use the house's main entrance.

Lee's outraged parents immediately contacted the NAACP to report the treatment of their daughter. According to NAACP Board meeting minutes on this event, Dr. Joel E. Spingarn, one of the organization's founders who served as chairman, treasurer, and president, met with the President of Smith College, Marion Burton, to discuss the matter. He told the school's dean that he would "unloose the dogs of war at Smith" if the situation was not resolved favorably."[44] The college found Lee living accommodations in the home of Professor of Greek, Julia Caverno, the same person who allowed Otelia Cromwell to live with her.

Du Bois reported this incident at length in *The Crisis*. He wrote that a "refined young girl of cultured parents here who had won a scholarship 'to one the nation's prestigious colleges had been denied housing.'" He wrote that after a white woman from Nashville complained of having Lee as a roommate:

> The colored girl was asked to leave and was unable to secure a room on the campus or anywhere in the college town. One of the teachers, a staunch friend, took her in but was unable to solve more than the room problem. Then began the wary search for a board which was finally only secured on the condition that the young lady would act as waitress. Though she had never done work of this kind she pluckily determined to stay on the ground and fight out her battle. Meantime, the Association [NAACP] was working hard to reach the proper authorities. Fortunately, a friend of the colored people on the board of trustees of the college became interested and succeeded in getting the girl on the campus in a delightful room where she is entitled to all the privileges of the college, including, of course, the dining room. Best of all, she is becoming popular with her classmates and through her charming personality is winning friends for her race.[45]

Members of the NAACP board played a pivotal role in changing Smith's housing policy. Moorfield Storey, a successful Boston lawyer and chairman of the NAACP Board of Trustees, wrote Smith's president, the Reverend Mario Burton, that if the story about Lee's housing dilemma was true, "I think it is the very greatest discredit to Smith College." Story continued:

> For a Massachusetts College to so far forget the principles which have made Massachusetts what it is, and to weakly abandon the rights of colored people

in order to conciliate Southern prejudice is to the last degree weak and discreditable. I sincerely hope that this statement I have received is not true, or that if it is true, the policy will be abandoned. Otherwise, I hope the facts will be published throughout the breadth and length of this state in order that the citizens of Massachusetts may understand how little regard the trustees of Smith College have for the principles of justice.[46]

Ruth Baldwin, an NAACP board member, Smith alumna, and the first woman to serve as a Smith College board member, used her influence to have Smith's housing policy changed.[47] After investigating college policies, Baldwin discovered that there was no official policy regarding Black students living on campus. This discriminatory practice was based on decisions of the individual college officials. Baldwin believed that since Wellesley now allowed Black women to live on campus (although in separate rooms from white students), this fact would perhaps help influence sympathetic board members. She was successful in having the matter resolved in October 1913 when the trustees affirmed the rights of African American women to live in Smith housing.[48]

The NAACP's influence at Smith widened with the appointment of William Allan Neilson as the college's third president in 1917. Neilson was a member of the national board of the NAACP. Walter White, the African American general secretary of the NAACP, recalled that Neilson "devoted a great portion of his extracurricular activity to service as a member of the board of directors of the NAACP."[49]

White recalled:

Thanks to Dr. Neilson and to others on the Smith faculty, the College maintained leadership among American educational institutions in ignoring artificial lines of demarcation based on race, social position, wealth, or place of birth. Few colleges I have known have been more free from hypocrisy or more ready to examine new ideas than Smith.[50]

White sent his daughter, Jane, to Smith in the 1940s because of his relationship with Neilson and White's positive views of the college.

After Otelia Cromwell was admitted in 1898, Smith consistently admitted African American women, usually one per year. Black women in these colleges had to adjust to be the one and only for years. It was not until 1925 that two Black women graduated in the same class. This was repeated in 1926, and then not again until 1934. By 1964, sixty-nine Black women (including a few African women) had attended or graduated from Smith.[51]

Mount Holyoke College

Mount Holyoke in South Hadley, Massachusetts, is the oldest of the Seven Sisters. Mary Lyon, an iconic figure in the history of women's higher education, founded it as a women's seminary in 1837. Its mission was to train teachers, missionaries, and wives of missionaries, but Mount Holyoke did not achieve collegiate status until the 1890s.

In 1845, Mount Holyoke trustees voted not to admit Black women. After the vote, Mary Lyon received a long letter from a white male resident of nearby Springfield. He protested the college's discriminatory admissions policy and said it was hypocritical for the school to profess Christian principles espoused by the school. He wrote that public sentiment was undergoing a rapid change, and that the events at Prudence Crandall's Canterbury Female Boarding School would not be repeated. He noted that Dartmouth College had recently decided to admit colored students and concluded by stating, "I hope that the religious influence that goes out of the Mount Holyoke Seminary will no longer be contaminated with this hatred or that it will not deliberately decide to reject colored applicants."[52]

The college's earliest Black women students, like Carrie Lee at Smith, were not known to be African American when the college accepted them. Hortense Parker in the Class of 1883 of Ripley, Ohio, was the first known Black student.[53] She was followed by Martha Ralston of Worcester, Massachusetts, who became the first Black woman to earn a college degree from Mount Holyoke in the class of 1898. In both instances, these Black women were viewed as an unexpected surprise. All students were required to live on campus at Mount Holyoke. Although college records for the Parker years are missing in the archives, subsequent records indicate that Black women who were enrolled in the early years lived in single rooms in the Seminary Building.

Alumnae records indicate that Ralston's father was an Englishman and that her home was located in one of the wealthiest sections of Worcester.[54] A patron financed Ralston's education. She had planned to study in Europe; however, the patron died during her senior year, preventing her from going abroad.[55] From all indications, Ralston had a positive experience while at Mount Holyoke. A white classmate wrote her mother upon Ralston's arrival and said, "There is a colored girl here in the freshman class. She comes from Worcester, Mass, and the other girls who come from that place like her very much and say that she is of a very good family."[56]

In 1913, when the Carrie Lee incident occurred at Smith College, other women's colleges were contacted regarding their admissions and housing policies for Black women. Florence Purington, the dean at Mount Holyoke College, responded to Smith's dean Ada Comstock:

> We do not intend to receive negro students at Mount Holyoke. It has happened once or twice that they have appeared, color unannounced, among the regularly accepted students. In those cases, they have had rooms in our College dormitories. The two colored students whom I recall were not

very dark-skinned and were personally quite attractive. They were cordially received by the other students. If a negro student were to present herself now, I hardly know what course would seem best, as we have a much larger percentage of Southern girls than was the case a few years ago.[57]

Since college applications at this time did not ask a student's race, the "surprise" Black students who showed up at those institutions were not welcomed. While the dean noted that the previously unknown Black students had been "cordially" received and did well academically, it's curious that these facts did not provide a change in the views of the administration regarding their admissions.

As noted earlier, there were numerous biracial/multiracial affluent and middle-class Black women in New England and the northern states who aspired to attain the best college education available for women during their era. However, a few of the Black women students came from prominent Black families that were not from the region. For example, the first African American graduate in the twentieth century at Mount Holyoke was Frances Williams of St. Louis, Missouri. Until her death in 1992, Williams was the school's oldest living Black alumna. Like Otelia Cromwell, the first Black graduate of Smith College, Williams was also the product of an outstanding segregated Black high school, Sumner High School. Like Cromwell, Williams came from an educated family. Both her parents were college graduates, as were her three siblings. Her father was principal of the well-known Charles Sumner High School, a Black public school in St. Louis with high academic standards and a stellar faculty of highly educated Black teachers. After graduating valedictorian from Sumner, Williams attended the University of Cincinnati for one year. She found the campus too large and impersonal and decided to transfer to another institution. Her mother sent Williams's transcript to Mount Holyoke in 1916, never indicating that her daughter was African American. After Williams received a letter of acceptance, her mother wrote to the college informing them that her daughter was Black. Despite Dean Purington's comment about not knowing what she would do if a Black student applied, Williams's application forced the institution to confront the issue. Williams's mother received a response from college officials stating that they did not believe her daughter would be happy there. In response, Williams's mother responded that she was sending her to earn an education, not to be happy.

Williams, a light-complexioned woman, recalled that many fellow students would not sit with her at meals, but she also recalled other students who found no problem with her race. She had a double major in chemistry and economics and graduated Phi Beta Kappa in 1919. Her parents paid her tuition and college expenses while at Mount Holyoke. After graduation, she received a fellowship to attend the New York School of Social Work where she earned a certificate. She subsequently earned a master's degree in political science from the University of Chicago. She spent her professional career focusing on race relations for the Young Women's Christian Association (YWCA) and other civil rights organizations.[58]

More than any other Seven Sisters college, Mount Holyoke attracted African American women from Black high schools and the South, including several from Atlanta, Georgia. There was one Black graduate in the Mount Holyoke class of 1926 from Wilmington, Delaware; the next five Black students at the school were from Atlanta and Washington, DC. Of this group, two were graduates of the prestigious all-Black Dunbar High School in Washington, which had a long history of sending its graduates to elite New England colleges. The other three were transfer students, two from the Black female Spelman College in Atlanta, and one from Atlanta University.[59] The president of Spelman, Florence Read, was a prominent white alumna of Mount Holyoke, and Spelman, founded in 1881, was modeled in part after Mount Holyoke.[60]

Few African American women graduated from Mount Holyoke prior to the mid-1960s; by 1964, only thirty-nine had graduated since Hortense Parker in 1883. One African American graduated from Mount Holyoke during the 1920s, six during the 1930s, twelve during the 1940s (due to increased pressure from religious and civil rights groups), twelve during the 1950s, and five from 1960–64.[61]

Despite their small numbers, African American women at Mount Holyoke participated fully in campus organizations and events. They noted the institution nurtured them intellectually and spiritually. The Black women who attended Mount Holyoke prior to the 1960s all said they would attend the college again.[62]

Bryn Mawr College

Orthodox Quakers founded Bryn Mawr College in Bryn Mawr, Pennsylvania, in 1885, "for the advanced education and care of young women, or girls of the higher classes of society."[63] Bryn Mawr's mission, as interpreted by the institution's president, M. Carey Thomas, whose presidency spanned from 1893 to 1922, excluded Black women. Although Thomas explained the absence of Black students as being due to the "difficulty of the admissions examination and the fact that we do not admit on certificates of high school graduates," in reality, it was her deeply held belief in the inferiority of African Americans that kept them out. Her bigotry, according to Thomas's biographer, Helen Horowitz, was rooted in her Baltimore upbringing, in which her only interactions with Black people was with servants.[64] When Du Bois polled white women colleges on their admission policies for Black women, Thomas sent an insulting and condescending response stating, "no person of Negro descent has ever applied for admission to Bryn Mawr college, probably because the standard of the entrance examinations is very high and students are admitted on certificate."[65]

In 1903, Jessie Fauset, an African American woman from Philadelphia, graduated at the top of her class from the prestigious Girl's High in the city. It was customary that the school's top student would be awarded a scholarship to Bryn Mawr. When Thomas discovered that Fauset was an African American, she raised money for a scholarship for Fauset to attend Cornell University (Thomas's alma mater) to assure that no Black woman attended Bryn Mawr. Thomas received an inquiry in 1906 from Georgiana Simpson, a teacher at the prestigious Black M Street high school (later named Dunbar High School) in Washington, DC, to inquire whether Bryn Mawr would consider an African American applicant (since it was widely known among educated Blacks that Jessie Fauset was not allowed to enroll). Thomas responded that the question of enrolling a Black student had never come up at the college and "it is the policy of the college not to decide a general question until a special case is presented." However, Thomas did indicate that there was no probability that a Black student would be admitted. She wrote:

> As I believe that a great part of the benefit of a college education is derived from intimate association with other students of the same age interested in the same intellectual pursuits, I should be inclined to advise such a student to seek admission to a college in one of the New England states where she would not be so apt to be deprived of this intellectual companionship because of the different composition of the student body. At Bryn Mawr college we have a large number of students coming from the Middle and Southern states so that condition here would be much more unfavorable.[66]

Simpson had a bachelor's and master's degree from the University of Chicago and in 1921 became one of three Black women in the country to earn a PhD. Simpson's doctorate was also from the University of Chicago in Germanic Languages. The notion that a student from M Street High School would not have the same "intellectual pursuits" due to race was ridiculous and offensive. While Thomas was viewed as a champion of women's higher education, her interest in women's higher education was restricted to a narrow elite group of white women. She made this clear in an address in 1916 at the opening of school to the student body. Thomas noted the superiority of the Anglo-Saxon race:

> If the present intellectual supremacy of the White races is maintained, as I hope it will be because they are the only races that that have seriously begun to educate their women . . . One thing we know beyond doubt and that is that certain races have never yet in the history of the world manifested any continuous mental activity nor any continuous power of government. Such are the pure Negroes of Africa, the Indians, the Esquimaux, the South Sea Islanders, the Turks, etc. . . . These facts must be faced by a country like the United States which is fast becoming, if it hasn't already become, the melting

pot of nations into which are cast at the rate of a million a year the backward people of Europe like the Czechs, the Slavs, and the south Italians. If the laws of heredity mean anything whatsoever, we are jeopardizing the intellectual heritage of the American people by this headlong intermixture of races . . . If we tarnish our inheritance of racial power at the source, our nation will never again be the same. . . . Our early American stock is still very influential, but this cannot continue indefinitely. For example, each year I ask each freshman class to tell me what countries their parents originally came from and for how many generations back their families have been on American soil. It is clear to me that almost all of our student body are early Americans, that their ancestors have been here for generations, and that they are overwhelmingly English, Scotch, Irish, Welsh, and other that of admixtures, French, German, Dutch largely predominate. All other strains are negligible. Our Bryn Mawr college students are therefore as a whole seem to belong by heredity to the dominant races. You, then, students of Bryn Mawr, have the best intellectual inheritance the world affords.[67]

Thomas retired as president of Bryn Mawr in 1922, but Thomas remained as a director and member of the Board of Trustees until her death in 1935. Marion Edwards Park, a former dean of Radcliffe College, succeeded her as president. Soon after Park became president, an African American student from New England enrolled at Bryn Mawr. The experience became so negative that she left after one week. The circumstances of her departure are unknown and have been erased from the institutional record. The former student requested that her name not appear on anything related to Bryn Mawr.

The Jewish and Black Question

Thomas insisted, throughout her presidency, that Bryn Mawr never enroll an African American and ensure the college remained a bastion of Anglo-Saxons and daughters of "old families" in the country. This impacted the admissions of other women who also were not white Anglo-Saxon Protestants (WASPS). For example, in 1926, Marion Park received an inquiry regarding the college's admissions practice of Jewish women from an alumna. The author was very aware that Jewish students were also discriminated against in admissions to many elite colleges. She wrote:

> As an alumna of Bryn Mawr (1906), I am venturing to write you about a young candidate for Bryn Mawr, Sophia Teller, whose father wrote you on December 27th, 1925. Mr. and Mrs. Teller are Jewish friends of mine whom I have come to admire and respect very deeply. Of course, there is considerable time ahead before the daughter will be ready for college—three years from next September, but it is not too early for the application. Mr. Teller is

Head of Stuyvesant Neighborhood House which, as you perhaps know, is a successful settlement run by both Jews and Gentiles. He is himself a graduate of Haverford. Mrs. Teller is a sister of Dr. Judah L. Magnes. They are both liberal in their religious views and are more apt to attend the Community Church than synagogues. I am wondering what is the present custom at Bryn Mawr on the matter of race discrimination? Will you tell me? In my day, it must have been on a quota basis, I think. Since there were always a few Jewish girls, but not many. Is it a quota basis now? And does the "personality test" of which I hear from friends who are teaching in Bryn Mawr preparatory schools, means that race is taken into consideration? Of course, you will see from my questions that I hope there is no discrimination now, and that the daughter of my friends may be admitted as readily as if she is a Gentile, if she passes the usual examinations. You will not mind my writing so frankly. Sincerely, Grace Hutchins[68]

Park assured Hutchins that there was no quota regarding Jewish women:

Thank you for your letter about Sophia Teller. There is absolutely no restriction on the number of Jewish students either by establishing a quota or by weighing the nationality in the various siftings that go in the admission committee. The number of Jewish students remains about the same from year to year because, I think, about the same number try to enter and out of them a fairly regular proportion are successful. A Jewish applicant is entirely on par with a Gentile. Sincerely, yours, ME Parks[69]

Park, as mentioned earlier, came to Bryn Mawr from Radcliffe, whose first African American student entered in 1894. There had been a small but continuous number of Black women at the institution since that time, although they were not allowed to live on campus. In 1927, the Bryn Mawr board of directors, after much discussion, voted to authorize Park to respond to requests regarding the admissions of African Americans with the proviso that she make clear that such students would be considered only as "non-residential students." As a board member, Thomas was steadfast in her opposition of Black students being admitted. The first Black woman to enter Bryn Mawr was Enid Cook, from the prestigious Dunbar High School in Washington, DC. She transferred after attending one year at Howard University, where she was a straight-A student. She majored in chemistry and biology and graduated in 1931. Cook lived with a Bryn Mawr faculty member her first year, and the remaining years with Black families in Bryn Mawr. She continued as a graduate student at the University of Chicago and graduated with a PhD in bacteriology in 1937. Unlike the earlier Seven Sisters colleges that had allowed African American women admissions to their institutions since the nineteenth century, Bryn Mawr, Vassar, and Barnard were the last holdouts. The issue of admitting African American women and where to house them was viewed as a "problem."

As mentioned earlier, M. Carey Thomas, while no longer president of Bryn Mawr after 1922, remained a trustee. Her biographer noted that Thomas "kept her hand in Bryn Mawr," even to the point of interference.[70] In 1930, a discussion on racial restrictions on housing reemerged at Bryn Mawr as a result of the reluctant admission of the second African American student, Lillian Russell, from the Boston area. Thomas wrote to Virginia Gildersleeves, dean of Barnard College, to inquire as to Barnard's policy on allowing Blacks to stay in the dormitories. Thomas confided that she was concerned with so many Blacks living close by in Philadelphia, because she anticipated that continuous inquiries would arise from this population. She stated four African American women had been allowed to stay on campus during a summer school program and that a "solid block of negro men" from neighboring Bryn Mawr came over to social events as guests of these women. In alarm, Thomas said the number had been as many as "twenty-five to thirty." Clearly, the fear of Black men on campus as guests of Black women students was an additional concern of the Bryn Mawr administration.[71]

Park's opinion on the topic was quite different, but she was reluctant to go against the tide. As early as 1926, she had appeals from an alumna about whether Enid Cook—who did enroll in 1927—would be considered. As with all the appeals on behalf of Black (and Jewish students) the institutions were assured that these were the right kind of students. Cook's father was a Howard University professor, and she was said to be a straight-A student. Since Cook would be coming from Washington, DC, there was the question of housing. On this matter, Park wrote:

> There are, however, enough southerners and enough Philadelphians (and in Philadelphia there is a great deal of prejudice) to make me feel there would be great opposition to a student in residence. . . . My own feeling in the matter is completely neutral as is that of most New Englanders. I believe, however, that the experiment would be impossible if, as you suggested, it was done occasionally, and it would probably be a very unhappy one for a pioneer. I think Bryn Mawr will work its way in time towards acceptance of colored students and I think a non-resident student is a better entering wedge than a student in residence. . . . When I was Dean at Radcliffe, there were four colored students there and I know from experience how extremely difficult a situation it is even in a New England college. The girls are very much isolated and became in one case very aggressive and disagreeable and in the others, so self-distrustful and timid that everyone was in distress about them. There was one colored student at Simmons when I was there who finally left the [residence] hall and lived in the family of a colored lawyer in Cambridge. The problem is much easier in theory than in practice.[72]

The solution wasn't to take the moral high ground and insist that the college would accept students regardless of race, creed, or religion—as Oberlin College had done in the 1830s—but rather to continue to tell African American students to "wait" until it was time. And it should be noted other institutions did not universally uphold the constant excuse that the college did not want to "offend" their alumna or current students. For example, Virginia Foster Durr, a white southerner who grew up in a prominent Birmingham, Alabama, family and attended Wellesley from 1920–23 recalled the college being very accommodating to Black women. Although Black women were assigned separate rooms, they did live on campus.

In her first day in the dormitory, she recalled:

> I went to the dining room and a Negro girl was sitting at my table. My God, I nearly fell over dead. I couldn't believe it. I just absolutely couldn't believe it. She wasn't very Black, sort of pale, but she was sitting there eating at the table with me in college. I promptly got up, marched out of the room, went upstairs and waited for the head of the house to come. She was a tall, thin, New England Spinster. She wore glasses on her nose, and she would cast her head down and look over them at us. I told her that I couldn't possibly eat at the table with a Negro girl. I was from Alabama and my father would have a fit. He came from Union Springs, Bullock County, and the idea of my eating with a Negro girl—Well, he would die. I couldn't do it. She would have to move me immediately.[73]

Foster recalled the house mother emphasizing that Wellesley had rules, and that students had to eat at the table to which they had been assigned for a month, after that time Foster could change tables. The house mother informed her that if she could not comply, then Foster was free to withdraw from the college without any penalty to her academic record. The thought of leaving Wellesley and her social life resulted in Foster remaining at Wellesley. She attributes this incident in the dining hall at Wellesley as a morally transformative experience. She later became a leading civil rights leader. When she and her husband, attorney Clifford Durr, moved to Montgomery in the 1950s, Rosa Parks, who later became renowned for her refusal to sit at the back of the bus in Montgomery, became her part-time seamstress. When Parks triggered the historic 1955 Montgomery Bus boycott upon her arrest for refusing to give her seat to a white man, Durr and her husband along with Black civil rights leader E. D. Nixon went to bail her out of jail.[74]

In a history of southern white women at the Seven Sisters colleges from 1875 to 1915, Joan Marie Johnson noted that while some administrators at these colleges that barred Black women from admission or housing often gave the excuse that it was because they did not want to offend their southern students. These women were not monolithic in their views concerning Black students. Johnson states that some northern women were equally as racist as southern women, while others were relatively liberal. Some (particularly those in the decades after the Civil War) could not imagine having social interactions with Black students, while others like the above Virginia Foster Durr adjusted and became very progressive on racial issues once they left college. Johnson observed that those who were extremely racist would never have attended a college that admitted Black students. When the southern women returned home, many supported women's suffrage, founded women's clubs, were social activists and, according to Johnson, "disproportionately directed women into the social welfare branch of Progressive Era reform" in the South. Attending these colleges outside the South had a profound impact on them.[75]

Ironically, southern white women, like African American women, had to contend with stereotypes northern students held toward them. Southern women were thought to be less intellectual, fragile southern belles, and primarily interested in beauty, marriage, and frivolity.[76] In addition, there were profound cultural differences between southern women and women from the North. Just like students of color, who a generation later, established Black Student Unions and other ethnic clubs, southern women banded together and established Southern Clubs. Regarding the clubs, Johnson noted:

> The Southern Clubs primarily offered an organized opportunity for Southern students to locate each other and socialize without having to rely on chance meetings. The club provided a place where southerners were free to be themselves without judgment from northerners; they established a formal community among southern exiles.[77]

Southern white women who attended colleges outside the South, knew that there were African American women and Jewish students on these campuses, although not in great numbers.

The Housing Issue

The issue of housing was paramount for African American students in predominantly white campuses. And, as Du Bois noted in 1900, many white women were "unrelenting" in their racism toward African American women. Despite the leaders of women's colleges being viewed as feminist icons, M. Carey Thomas among them, their views on race and religion were frequently profoundly and unapologetically racist and anti-Semitic.

The organization of the elite women's colleges (called the Five College Conference in the 1930s before they included Radcliffe and Barnard in 1952)—met annually to discuss various issues—curricular, governance, their admissions requirements, and standards, as well as the type of students they desired. At the group's 1936 meeting at Mount Holyoke, the presidents discussed racial quotas. President Neilson at Smith reported that the question of quotas had been broached at the college. He said there was a policy in housing for Jewish students in which no more than two or three could live in the same house (the term Smith used for dormitories). He stated the alumnae had often expressed a desire to cap the number of Jewish students between 11 and 13 percent. According to Neilson, although the number of Jewish students was increasing, the Board was not willing to establish a quota.[78]

President Marion Park from Bryn Mawr noted that there had never been a quota because Philadelphia had very few Jews, hence there was not a need for one. She stated there were usually no more than 7 percent Jewish students. However, Bryn Mawr, like all these institutions, kept a tally of the students who were thought to be Jewish. Their admissions office reported in 1926 that Jewish students made up 2 percent, 8 percent in 1927, a drop to 3 percent in 1928, 6 percent for 1929 and 1930, and a drop to 1 percent in 1931; the highest year was 8 percent in 1932 followed by a drop to 2 percent in 1936 followed by 6 percent in 1937, the year of the report. There was a note on the report that said: "these figures represent only the students who admit being Jewish." Many of the students who are Jewish register "no affiliation."[79] Just as some Black students who could pass for white did not volunteer their Black heritage, likewise, for Jews who could "pass" for WASPS, they often did. This report was in response to a confidential inquiry from the dean of the all-women's Simmons College in Boston regarding Jewish quotas (Park had served as Interim Dean at Simmons prior to serving at Radcliffe):

> I am very much in need of some information which I make bold to ask you to give me confidentially. Does Bryn Mawr limit in any way the number of Jewish students admitted to the College? If it does, by what means is the quota established—by Trustee vote, faculty action or administrative rule? Anything that you can tell me will be very helpful.[80]

Park noted as she had in the Five College Conferences that Bryn Mawr did not have Jewish quotas. She also reiterated what was reported in her data on Jewish students—they often did not admit they were Jewish but said they were "Christian Scientists, Unitarians, etc. rather than Orthodox Jews." Park did note, however, "I don't know what I should do if the number rose rapidly or if the less good type of Jewish girl came in larger numbers. We do seem to have a very high standard of Jewish students and they take their place in the college and in the Alumnae Association easily and naturally."[81] In other words, Bryn Mawr attracted "good Jews."

Like many African American students who did not volunteer their race, the same was true of Jewish students, who realized many institutions kept their numbers to a minimum or had a quota. It's unclear what the Jewish population was at Bryn Mawr during Thomas' presidency—the inquiry from the alumna from the class of 1906 clearly remembered the absence of Jewish students. And in 1926, only 2 percent were Jewish students.

President Mary Emma Woolley from Mount Holyoke also reported that having Jewish students had not been a problem because their numbers had been small. She said that year the freshman class had eighteen Jewish students—more than any other year. She noted that five or six of the women had come from Fieldston in New York (an elite private day school).[82]

Dean Mary Lowell Coolidge of Wellesley stated that the college had approximately 10 percent Jewish enrollment. However, she noted that the college frequently received complaints from alumnae that the number was too high. She also expressed Wellesley's desire not to increase the number of Jews. She indicated the college would keep the top students and discourage the others. Coolidge also reported that most Jewish students were non-residential which would also keep the number of Jewish students down. She noted in the past Wellesley had 12 percent Jewish students. Vassar reported that they did not have a quota and had only 5 to 8 percent Jewish students. She believed Vassar's location reduced the number of Jewish students since she believed most Jewish students preferred to be close to cities.[83]

The presidents and deans of these colleges also noted that Jewish students were the most "conspicuous" among the radical students on their campuses and "alumnae sometimes complained" about this as well. In their discussion of Black students ("negroes"), President Park noted that Bryn Mawr only accepted Black applicants as non-residential students. Smith reported that there were two to three Black students in the dorm; Mount Holyoke reported the same; Wellesley had anywhere from one to four; and Vassar reported one African American dormitory resident.[84]

The following year when the group met at Smith College they returned to the same discussion. In previous years, the number of Jewish applicants received at Smith were small, but Mount Holyoke noted a sudden increase in the number of Jewish applicants that year. They had only received a small number in the past. Smith reiterated that its board had no desire to establish a Jewish quota. Wellesley reported it received the bulk of its Jewish applicants from Brookline (a Boston suburb) and New York City. They planned to only accept 10 percent of the Jewish applicants from those areas because of the large number of Jewish applicants. Bryn Mawr reported no Jewish quota. Vassar reported that while they did not accept many Jewish applicants, the largest number of Jewish applicants came from New York City and noted the Committee on Admissions was "unfavorable to accepting too large a number of the [Jewish] applicants who apply."[85]

Although a couple of Black women graduate students were granted permission to live on campus during the 1930s and early 1940s, it wasn't until 1942 that the restriction barring Black women from living on campus was rescinded. The first Black woman moved into unrestricted campus housing in 1946. Although the first African American women were admitted in 1927, because of Bryn Mawr's long history of discrimination and negative attitudes towards them, this was not a college of choice for most highly academically talented Black women and few sought admissions. By 1960, only nine Black women had graduated from Bryn Mawr: two in the 1930s, one in 1948, and one each year from 1954 to 1960. There were no graduates in 1956.

Vassar College

Vassar was founded in Poughkeepsie, New York, in 1865, with an endowment from a wealthy brewer, Matthew Vassar, and was the first full-fledged college for women designed to offer a liberal arts curriculum from its inception. It was also the last of the Seven Sisters colleges to knowingly admit African American women, and one of the most resistant. This was due primarily to its wealthy and elite white female student body and their desire not to have Black women classmates. The first known African American student at Vassar was Anita Florence Hemmings from Boston. She enrolled in 1893 and graduated in 1897. Florence was of extremely light-skinned complexion and believed to be white until a scandal erupted a few weeks prior to her graduation when it was discovered that she had "negro" blood. This discovery created a huge racial dilemma for Vassar, which prided itself on its white elite student body. Local and national newspapers carried the story widely, with one headline reporting "Negro Girl at Vassar: The Handsomest Girl There." Yale and Harvard men were among those who sought favor with the "brunette beauty."[86] Another article read: "Vassar girls are agitated over the report that one of the students in the senior class of '97 is of Negro parentage."[87] It continued, "Vassar is noted for its exclusiveness, and every official of the college refuses to say aught regarding this girl graduate." The faculty and administrator debated whether they would allow her to graduate since commencement was imminent. Whether the college would set a precedent and allow a Negro to receive a Vassar degree, the article stated: "Never had a colored girl been a student at aristocratic Vassar, and professors were at a loss to foresee the effect upon the future if this one were allowed to be graduated."[88]

In the end, Hemmings did graduate, with the faculty reasoning she would soon be gone, and the matter would be forgotten. Hemmings married a physician, and their daughter, Ellen Park Love, graduated from Vassar in 1927. Love identified as white and marked her nationality as English and French on her application.

W. E. B. Du Bois, editor of *The Crisis* magazine of the NAACP, polled white institutions annually to determine if they had any Black students or graduates.

He wrote to the college president, Henry MacCracken, in 1930 regarding the absence of Black women students. He wrote:

> For many years, *The Crisis* magazine has secured annually information concerning colored students in northern institutions. The answer from Vassar has always been that you have no colored students. I write to ask you if there has been any change in this rule recently. Are there any colored students at Vassar College today? If a properly equipped colored woman should apply, would you admit her?[89]

MacCracken sent a curt two-sentence response informing Du Bois to refer to the Vassar catalog that stated: "No rules other than those stated govern the admissions of all students." Despite this statement African American women were neither admitted nor welcomed at Vassar. In 1931, Du Bois angrily wrote in *The Crisis*:

> Vassar is the only first grade women's college in the North which still refuses to admit Negroes. Bryn Mawr and Mount Holyoke held out long but finally surrendered, although Bryn Mawr still keeps its dorms lily white.[90]

By the 1930s, the NAACP began to dismantle the *Plessy* "separate but equal doctrine." Lawsuits were initiated against select southern public university law schools. In addition, Du Bois contacted private institutions to inquire if they admitted African American students—if so, he asked that they supply their numbers and their accomplishments.

A prominent African American minister from Harlem, the Reverend James Robinson, gave a lecture at Vassar in the late 1930s at a conference co-sponsored by the college and the YWCA. In his lecture, he challenged the Vassar women to open the doors of the college to Black women. When they replied they did not know any Black women, Robinson stated he would find good African American candidates.[91]

Robinson recommended an outstanding candidate from his congregation, Beatrix McCleary, the daughter of a physician. Extremely light-skinned, McCleary could have easily passed for white. "Beatty," as she was known, entered Vassar in the fall of 1940. McCleary was a brilliant student and excelled at Vassar; she was elected to Phi Beta Kappa, obtained the highest honors in zoology and was the first African American elected to the Daisy Chain—a group of women who are honored, and chosen, as "daisies" based on their leadership skills, class spirit, and passion for volunteering at college. This group carried a chain of daisies on commencement.[92] The first two years at Vassar, McCleary was put in a single room. Her third year, she combined her room with three other students who had singles: a Chinese student, a Jewish student, and one Anglo-Saxon student. She shared a three-room suite her senior year with a white student.[93]

Six years after McCleary enrolled at Vassar, six additional Black women were admitted to the college, resulting in seven Black women graduating during the 1940s. Even with their proven success, all of them were required to live in separate dormitory rooms. Du Bois, with little patience for the excruciatingly slow pace of the admission of Black women at the institution, spoke there in 1942 and informed the audience that instead of a token number of African American women being admitted to the twelve hundred student college, Vassar should accept one hundred Black women. Du Bois made it clear that many Black women were more than qualified to attend Vassar.[94] For the next twenty-five years, no more than three African American women were admitted per class. Some years, no Black women were admitted. By 1960, only twenty-three African American women had graduated from Vassar. These women were all solidly middle to upper class and the daughters of Black professionals. They were also products of integrated high schools of New York and New England, or the renowned Dunbar High School of Washington, DC. These women excelled at Vassar and continued on to graduate and professional school. McCleary, the first acknowledged Black graduate, as well as June Jackson Christmas, the second Black woman (entered in 1941) both became medical doctors. Although these women had broken the color barrier at Vassar, Jackson Christmas noted it was done at a great price:

> For the Black woman who entered Vassar during these early years, the lone Black student entered to live the demanding life of being the "one and only," a life many remember as lonely as an atmosphere which was unaccepting and, at times, hostile. Administrators and faculty who might have provided support and guidance or served as role models were lacking. For most of those early students, the college community did not provide a sense of being valued or belonging.[95]

Barnard College

Barnard was founded in 1889 as the "sister" institution to the all-male Columbia College in New York City. Given Barnard's location, it should have been most accessible and available to African American women. However, this was not the case. The Black community believed that Barnard discouraged applications from them and instituted quotas once the college began accepting Black women in 1925. The first African American to enter Barnard was the famed Harlem Renaissance writer Zora Neale Hurston. Hurston was the personal secretary of the writer Fanny Hurst. After receiving a scholarship from one of the college's founders, Annie Nathan Meyer, Hurston, who had attended two historically Black colleges, transferred to Barnard. Hurston spent only three semesters at Barnard and graduated in 1928. Hurston said it was a privilege for white students to know her, not the other way around. In her autobiography, *Dust Tracks on a Road*, she wrote:

> I have no lurid tales to tell of race discrimination at Barnard. I made a few friends in the first few days. The Social Register crowd at Barnard soon took me up, and I soon became Barnard's sacred Black cow.[96]

Hurston defied the early stereotype of Black women students at elite women's colleges. They tended to be light-skinned and from professional families—usually from outside the South. Hurston was a southerner from the all-Black town of Eatonville in Florida. She championed Black folklore and idioms. Her attitude was very cavalier, and she displayed none of the anxiety of proving that Black people were just as smart as whites; nor did she seem to worry about adhering to any type of respectability images that plagued the behavior of middle-class Blacks. Hurston clearly understood race and the benefits of having Barnard credentials.

> I felt that I was highly privileged and determined to make the most of it. I did not resolve to be a grind, however, to show White folks that I had brains. I took it for granted that I knew that. Why else was I at Barnard? So, I set out to maintain a good average, take part in whatever went on, and just be a part of the college like everybody else. I graduated with a B record, and I'm entirely satisfied.[97]

Belle Tobias and Vera Joseph enrolled the year after Hurston graduated. Tobias was a botany major and Joseph was a chemistry major—both products of the New York public schools. Belle was the daughter of prominent civil rights and religious leader Channing Tobias, who was secretary of the Colored Department of the National Council of the Young Men's Christian Association, the first African American to serve as director of the Phelps-Stokes fund, and a member of the board of the national NAACP. Belle graduated Phi Beta Kappa in the class of 1931 and earned a master's degree the following year at Wellesley.

Vera Joseph, an immigrant from Jamaica, was inspired to attend Barnard by one of her teachers who recognized her brilliance. She excelled while at Barnard and graduated Phi Beta Kappa. Joseph's studies were financed through a Barnard scholarship and an award by Black businessmen and educators in Harlem. She continued her education at Columbia Medical School in 1932, graduated, and became a physician.

Barnard also denied Black students the opportunity to live on campus while Joseph was at the institution. Despite this discrimination, Joseph commented that she was excited about her classes and not unhappy at Barnard. Although after commencement, she noted that she was not invited to join the New York Barnard Club in New York. Like virtually every Black woman student at the Seven Sisters colleges, Joseph expected to professionally utilize her degree.

Joseph noted, "After graduation I recognized that I was being discriminated against and resented it. But, more important things than admission to a social club were happening in my life; I was going to medical school."[98]

Jeanne Blackwell transferred to Barnard in 1934 after spending three years at the University of Michigan. In 1931, Blackwell graduated as valedictorian of her class from the segregated Douglass High School in Baltimore. There, she had wanted to attend one of the Seven Sisters colleges. However, her family could not afford the tuition. Due to her financial circumstances, she enrolled in the University of Michigan, a distinguished public university. Blackwell also aspired to be a physician and studied pre-med at Michigan. However, she spent her three years at Michigan battling to live on campus, which was a primary and recurrent concern for Black students at white campuses. Her mother was concerned that Blackwell was devoting too much time on the housing issue and suggested she transfer to another institution. Barnard accepted her but was not aware that she was African American. Blackwell assumed, erroneously, that her housing situation would be different than at Michigan. As was the case at Michigan, she was refused campus housing once she arrived at Barnard. In 1935, Blackwell graduated after one year at Barnard and earned a second BS from the Columbia School of Library Science the following year. She later became a prominent authority on Black literary and scholarly collections. In 1955, Blackwell was appointed curator of the renowned repository of African American collections, the Schomburg Center for Research in Black Culture of the New York Public Library.[99]

Throughout the 1930s and 1940s, the NAACP waged legal battles against discrimination of Blacks in public higher education—bringing lawsuits to public universities and pressuring private ones by constantly inquiring as to their admissions policies and treatment of Black students. The Seven Sisters colleges were the pinnacle of elite women's higher education, similar to Black men attending the Ivy League and small elite men's colleges such as Amherst and Williams. The elite men's colleges graduated Black men as early as 1826 (Amherst and Bowdoin Colleges). In contrast, the elite women's colleges were extremely slow to admit Black women, and when they did, only in token numbers.

In 1943, Reverend James Robinson gave an address at an interfaith conference in the Teacher's College at Columbia University. Robinson singled out Vassar and Barnard as examples of institutions that established quotas for Black women. Virginia Gildersleeves, Dean of Barnard, immediately issued a written response refuting this assertion.

> Dear Mr. Robinson:
> It has been reported to me that you stated in an address at the Teacher's College Chapel yesterday that Barnard discriminated against Negro students and admitted a Negro student every two years. This is quite untrue. We have

no Negro quota. We never received many applications for admission from Negroes. If we are going to have a Quota, we certainly would not have such a foolish one as that reported in the strange rumor which seems to have reached you.

We always have some Negro students in Barnard. This year our most valuable graduate fellowship is held by a Negro, and one of our most distinguished alumnae is a Negro, of whom we are very proud. I am anxious to do anything I can to further the solution of this serious race problem, and I shall be glad to discuss it with you, if you would like to call and see me. I regret that you have such a bad opinion of us.[100]

An editorial in the same issue of the *Barnard Bulletin* responded that while the institution may not have quotas, much more should be done to attract Black students. In addition, the editorial noted that although Black women could attend Black colleges, there were other Black women, who "are willing to sacrifice personal happiness" in return for the opportunity of "proving themselves in the North."[101] The editorial recommended that a certain number of scholarships should be earmarked for Black women at Barnard. Despite the good intentions of the editorial, the notion that African American women would have to "prove themselves" was the burden that they had to endure. Women should not have to consider attending Barnard or one of the other Seven Sisters colleges to "prove" themselves in contrast to a historical Black college, where it was assumed they did not have to "prove" themselves. In addition, the view that Black women would have to sacrifice "personal happiness" was a frequent comment by segregated white institutions who often used this as a reason why Black students shouldn't attend. These colleges believed that prospective Black students should expect segregationist policies in various aspects of college life—such as housing, exclusion from membership in certain organizations, and generally being marginalized on campus.

The reality was Barnard *did* have quotas. Dorothy Height, who became a prominent Civil Rights and Women's Rights icon, noted in her autobiography that after she won a four-year college scholarship from the National Elks, she applied and was accepted to Barnard in 1929. When she arrived on campus, as was the case with Jean Blackwell whom the college didn't know was African American, they told Height although they had accepted her, the admissions office had no idea she was an African American and they had already enrolled their quota of two Black students for the year. Shocked, Height, who had grown up in an interracial, primarily immigrant community outside of Pittsburgh and had won a national scholarship in which she competed with white girls and boys, wrote:

> It took me a while to realize that their decision was a racial matter: Barnard had a quota of two Negro students per year, and two others had already taken the spots.[102]

Height was told by the Barnard dean, "You are young enough to wait for next year." Height noted she pleaded with the dean, but she was adamant the college had their two Black students for the class of 1933 and rules are rules. Belle Tobias and Vera Joseph mentioned earlier were the two Black women for that class. Height said she was "crushed and confused," and she took her transcript and references and gained entrance to New York University. She was immediately accepted and said from that day on, "I have loved every brick in that University."[103]

The NAACP and Reverend Robinson's efforts paid off. Charlotte Hanley was the immediate beneficiary of the attempt to increase the number of Black women at Barnard. Hanley graduated from Yonkers High School, a suburb of New York City, in 1942, and planned to move to the city to live with her maternal grandmother while attending the tuition-free Hunter College. Both Hanley's aunt and grandmother had attended Hunter, but shortly after Reverend Robinson's lecture and the subsequent reaction of the Barnard dean, a friend of Hanley's family informed them that Barnard was willing to offer a full tuition fellowship to a deserving Black student. Hanley had not considered Barnard because it was expensive and believed the college was only for the daughters of the affluent. She and her mother met with Reverend Robinson to discuss the opportunity and he encouraged her to apply. Her application for admission was accepted, and she entered Barnard in 1943, receiving a full scholarship for the four years of her studies except for $50. She lived in Harlem with her godparents the first year but commuted an hour each way the remaining years from her home in Yonkers. She worked at the community center of Reverend Robinson's church to earn money for books and living expenses.[104]

Hanley, who graduated in 1947, recalled a positive experience at Barnard. Although she initially majored in mathematics, a renowned economics professor, Raymond J. Saulnier, who was the Director of the Department of Financial Research for the National Bureau of Economic Research and later economic advisor to President Dwight Eisenhower, encouraged her to change her major to economics. Hanley stated that her professional success was due to Saulnier who offered her a job as a researcher at the Department of Financial Research in the summers and during her senior year at Barnard. After graduating, she became the first African American to be hired as an economist at the Federal Reserve Bank in Chicago, where she was subsequently appointed assistant vice president.[105] Hanley's encouragement by a white male professor was a story repeated by numerous Black women who were in non-traditional fields for women.

Despite the Seven Sisters colleges enrolling a predominately elite and affluent student body, the colleges were not monolithic. As previously shown, some admitted African American women in the late nineteenth century while others, grudgingly, and under great pressure, admitted them decades later in the twentieth century. The issue of campus housing was universal at each institution as well as other white colleges and universities.

The number of Black women students remained small. In both the written and oral histories of these women, there was a universal belief of an unwritten, and unspoken, quota for Black women of never more than one or two a year being admitted. Francis Monroe King, a 1942 graduate of Mount Holyoke College, recalled:

> When I was a freshman, the only other Negro was a senior. By my sophomore year there were two in the freshman class, thus shattering a long-standing unwritten quota among the Seven Sister colleges of "only two at a time on campus." When I was a senior, two more Negroes were freshmen, bringing our total to five![106]

Charlotte Hanley Scott, Barnard class of 1947, also recalled that there were usually two women per year during her years at Barnard. By the 1950s, more Black women were being admitted. An article on Black students at Barnard noted that by the 1950s, three Black women were admitted per class and were referred to as the "Holy Twelve" because there were never more than twelve Black women enrolled at one time.[107]

The early Black women graduates of the Seven Sisters colleges were very much aware of their privilege, singularly and as a group. Although they faced discrimination in housing and elsewhere, their purpose was to obtain the education afforded by the colleges. Unlike their southern Black sisters, where public high schools were not available outside of major cities like Atlanta, New Orleans, or Birmingham and many historically Black colleges were not accredited or of collegiate status until the 1930s and '40s, these northern and New England–educated Black women were able to study fields once denied to women and African Americans elsewhere. Being enrolled in a women's college provided students with the opportunity to study science and fields like economics that were not readily available to them in coeducational institutions. This exemplary group of women became a series of firsts and leaders in their professions. Among them: Harriet Rice, Wellesley's first Black graduate in 1887, became a physician (Women's Medical College of New York); Otelia Cromwell, Smith's first graduate in 1900, earned a PhD in Elizabethan literature from Yale in 1926, becoming Yale's first African American woman graduate; Jane Bolin, Wellesley class of 1928, became the first Black woman to graduate from Yale Law School in 1931 and became the first African American woman judge in the nation (1939, New York city); Eunice Hunter Carter, from Smith's Class of 1921, became the first African American graduate of Fordham University Law School (1933) and also the first African American woman district attorney in the state of New York; Vera Joseph, Barnard Class of 1932, became a physician (Columbia Medical School); Bryn

Mawr's first Black graduate, Enid Cook '31, earned a PhD in bacteriology from the University of Chicago in 1937; Vassar's first Black graduate, Beatrix McCleary '44, became the first Black woman graduate of Yale's Medical School in 1948; Evelyn Boyd, Smith '45, became the first African American woman to earn a PhD in mathematics (Yale, 1950). Many of the Black women at Mount Holyoke became physicians or research scientists, and in a 1988 study, fourteen of the twenty-eight living Black alumnae were recognized for becoming prominent physicians or research scientists.[108]

The increased number of Black women in the Seven Sisters colleges, and other private institutions after the mid- and late 1940s, resulted from the growth of interracial student coalitions, the protest efforts of the NAACP, individual efforts by people like Reverend James Robinson, and the establishment of the first Black talent identification program, the National Scholarship Service and Fund for Negro Students (NSSFNS). The Black women who attended the all-women's colleges were able to excel and take full advantage of fields that women, regardless of race, often had little to no access to such as the hard sciences, economics, and mathematics, which made them competitive to attend the top graduate and professional schools and to becoming leaders in their fields.

National Scholarship Service and Fund for Negro Students

Du Bois' inquiries to white institutions of higher education, regarding the number of Black students enrolled, or the institution's admissions policy regarding race, was often met with a response denying that the institutions ever received Black applicants. Felice Nierenberg Schwartz, a wealthy white Smith College student from New York City who attended college during the World War II years, was very concerned that only six of the two thousand women within the student body were Black students when she attended. Ralph Harlow, the head of Smith's religion department, challenged his students to not just study religion but put their beliefs to action. She recalled that Harlow came to class "dripping with [newspaper] clippings" of moral and ethical issues of the day. As a project, she began a letter writing campaign to white colleges to inquire if they had African American students. And, if not, why not, and would they admit qualified Black students if some were identified. This was the same strategy that Du Bois utilized annually for *The Crisis*. The responses were the same as given to him—most colleges replied that they never or rarely received applications from Black students. After Schwartz graduated from Smith in 1945, she returned to New York to establish her recruiting organization and was determined to flood white colleges with Black applications. She was given office space at the national office of the NAACP, but after nine months, she moved into an office of

Reverend James Robinson at the Church of the Masters in Harlem. Robinson, as mentioned earlier, had already been very active in attempting to integrate white colleges as well as white hospitals and summer camps.[109] By 1947, the National Scholarship Service and Fund for Negro Students (NSSFNS) was established to recruit "talented Negro students" to attend previously all or predominately white institutions of higher education. These were almost exclusively private institutions, and in the 1930s, the NAACP began lawsuits to challenge segregation in public institutions of higher education. Schwartz put together a very distinguished, racially and gender diverse, board consisting of social justice advocates for the organization including Harry Carman, Dean of Columbia University; Henry Van Dusen, President of Union Theological Seminary; Attorney Susan Brandeis, daughter of Supreme Court Justice Louis Brandeis; Frank Bowles, Director of the College Entrance Examination Board (CEEB); John Monro, Director of Financial Aid for Harvard College; Henry C. Luce, influential Editor-in-Chief of Time, Inc.; and Lyle Spencer, the head of the Science Research Associates and an authority on educational tests and guidance. Among the African Americans to serve on the board were: Robert C. Weaver, a labor and housing specialist and officer of the John Jay Whitney Foundation, and later, the first African American Secretary of Housing and Urban Development (HUD); Kenneth B. Clark, the distinguished African American psychologist whose research on the impact of the segregation of Black children was later cited in the landmark *Brown v. Board of Education* Supreme Court case of 1954; Jane Bolin, Wellesley '28, as noted earlier, the first Black woman to graduate from Yale Law School '31, the first Black woman to be admitted to the New York Bar, and in 1939, the first Black woman appointed as judge in the United States; and Channing Tobias, Chairman of the NAACP.

Schwartz used her own funds and volunteers to run NSSFNS the first two years of the organization's history. With her influential board and enormous contacts, within two years, Schwartz had a paid staff and three sources of scholarships: The Sister Funds, which provided monies for Black women to attend one of the Seven Sisters colleges; the Embree Memorial Scholarship; and the Jean Tennyson Fund that provided financial assistance for students to attend male and coeducational colleges, such as Dartmouth, Hamilton, Harvard, Oberlin, Swarthmore, and Yale. These funds benefited African American women, as well as men seeking admittance to white institutions. In the organization's October 1951 newsletter, the publication highlighted Mary Esther White of Smithtown Branch, New York, as one of ten women selected for a scholarship to one of the Seven Sisters colleges. She was on her way to Barnard College.[110] The following year, two of the three highlighted scholarship recipients were women: Derosette Hendricks from Rutherford, New Jersey, who was headed to Wheaton College in Massachusetts; and Ollie Mae Stanley from Greensboro, North Carolina, who was going to Oberlin College.[111]

NSSFNS was extremely successful. The organization hired college counselors to ensure that the students applied to colleges compatible with their interests and helped them navigate the application process. The organization received additional funding from other foundations including the Ford Foundation that funded a project to recruit talented Black students from the South to attend white institutions. The Southern Project was established in 1950 and co-directed by two Black male professors from HBCUs, Paul F. Lawrence from Howard University and Donald Wyatt from Fisk University. Lawrence and Wyatt visited seventy-eight Black high schools in forty-five southern cities and towns. Despite their excitement and enthusiasm in this endeavor, they ran into political problems with the presidents of HBCUs. The United Negro College Fund (UNCF) was founded in 1944, as the fundraising arm of private Black colleges, and presidents of HBCUs felt particularly threatened by the Southern Project. This group represented the top academic liberal arts colleges that included Morehouse, Fisk, Dillard, Spelman, Tuskegee Institute, Lincoln in Pennsylvania, and others. There was alarm on the part of the Black college community that NSSFNS would skim off the top Black students from HBCUs. This was a continuous issue and a confusing one as well. The NAACP was waging lawsuits for Black students to gain entrance into white public institutions, while NSSFNS was also seeking to have Black students admitted into white private institutions. Both Kenneth Clark and Robert Weaver were also on the board of UNCF, and they indicated not seeing a conflict between the two organizations. However, they held a minority opinion and the Black college presidents were able to convince Ford, and other foundations, to cease funding to NSSFNS, and after the two-year grant expired, the project was discontinued. The NSSFNS explained their philosophy on integrated education to the Ford Foundation in 1951 when it revealed that Black colleges officials were challenging their efforts.

> You raised the question of the philosophy behind our program, particularly with relation to the Negro colleges. I will try to answer the question, but I can't pretend the answer will be entirely impartial. This organization was established on the basis of a profound distaste for segregated education and on the theory that our country's educational pattern could be, at least to an extent, altered through a program such as ours. The experience of the past three years has justified these feelings. The educational map is slowly being changed, partly, as a result of our efforts.
>
> There is, however, an even more significant change going on concurrently in the South where, in at least 13 states, court and voluntary decisions have caused some public and private institutions which had heretofore been all white to accept some Negro applicants, mostly, up to this point, on the graduate level. We feel this trend cannot be ignored and the actions we propose to take with respect to the described—on page 4 section d, of the "Chairman's report" entitled "The Proposed Southern Project."

As this trend toward breaking down of segregation in the white schools of the South goes on, we believe that there will be a parallel trend of Negro colleges attracting white students. This Agency proposes, as a feasible and appropriate time, to exert an influence toward the furtherance of both of these ends by referring Negro students to what are now white southern colleges and white students to the now Negro colleges.

It was clear that the members of the board of NSSFNS were adamant about pursuing integrated education for Black students in the country's leading white colleges. Prior to the Southern Project, the organization recruited Black students throughout the northern and western areas of the country (and Washington, DC, because of the renowned college preparatory Dunbar High School) and sought students with strong high school backgrounds. NSSFNS pushed to have "talented Negro students" in what were considered the top academic institutions, including Black women who benefited greatly from this program. In addition to recruiting Black students into colleges, the group started a prep school program to better prepare Black students for top colleges. They were able to place Black students in top boarding and elite day schools like Phillips Exeter, Mount Herman, Northfield School for Girls, The Putney School, and the New Lincoln School. Throughout this venture, Black women and girls were included at every turn. The prep school initiative later became A Better Chance program that still exists to place students of color in selective boarding and day schools.

Although Black college presidents sabotaged the Southern Project, in two years of the program, NSSFNS counseled more than 3,000 Black students in the South. The first year, only 49 percent of the students were considered competitive to apply for northern schools, but by the second year, 59 percent were deemed qualified through their grades and test scores. However, only 33 percent of the eligible students applied. From the two years of effort, 520 Black students from the Southern Project enrolled in a white college. This number represented more students than all the Black students who had enrolled in white colleges in the past ten years in the South. Despite these numbers, the organization's leadership felt disappointed that more students who were deemed qualified didn't apply or take advantage of the opportunities. They believed the reasons were: being hesitant to venture outside of a segregated environment, which had been their lifelong experience; financial concerns; and lack of encouragement from principals, parents, counselors, and teachers (many who were against the program) who were loyal to HBCUs and didn't want to see students abandon them.

Vernon Jordan recalled how his Black teachers responded when he indicated his intention to apply to one of the white colleges he learned about through the Southern Project. Jordan, who later became the president of the UNCF and the National Urban League, reported that until the time he met Professor Lawrence, he and his two best friends were planning to attend Howard. He described Lawrence as a "very tall and imposing man. I remember being quite impressed with him, and what he had to say. His message was something of an eye-opener to me." Although Jordan did apply to Howard as planned, he also applied to the numerous white institutions that NSSFNS had suggested. He said, to his surprise, his teachers were reluctant to write letters of recommendation for him, as he applied to the white colleges. His impression was that his teachers, and other members of the Black community, believed Blacks who desired to attend white schools thought themselves better than other Blacks. Jordan noted they had a mentality of "if Morehouse or Morris Brown Colleges (or other Black colleges) were 'good enough for me'—why aren't they good enough for you?" Jordan wrote, "there was this notion that my decision to apply to a white school was passing judgment of them, and the schools they attended." Jordan accepted an offer from DePauw University in Indiana and graduated in 1957. He continued his education at Howard University Law School, where he graduated in 1960.[112]

Many Black women students took advantage of the Southern Program. In the organization's 1953 newsletter, *Opportunity News*, seven of the highlighted recipients of scholarships were women. Among them were Joretha Langley of Columbia, South Carolina who attended Wilson College in Pennsylvania, and Clarice Dribble of Tuskegee Institute who had first attended the Northfield School for Girls boarding school in Massachusetts headed to college at Sarah Lawrence College in New York. Joan E. Cole, from Baltimore, became the first African American to attend St. John's College in Maryland, and Barbara Jeanne Leece from New Hope, West Virginia, was attending West Virginia Wesleyan.[113]

While the Southern Program provided alternative college opportunities for southern Black students, many presidents of HBCUs viewed the program as a threat to their college enrollments. Years later, in an oral history, Felice Schwartz, the founder of NSSFNS, reflected on the responses of Black college presidents to her efforts. She said she started the organization when she was in her twenties and was very idealistic. "I guess the hard thing was my biggest opposition came from the presidents of Negro colleges. Understandably, when you look at it retrospectively, because if we were successful, we would pull the cream of the Negro population . . . of course, we had to refer the cream of the students, so that we were robbing the Black colleges of some of the really good students, and it was shattering to get letters from these leading Black educators that showed bitterness about this movement. But, as I said, I understand it. I did understand it subsequently, but I didn't at the time."[114]

Alongside this movement to recruit and enroll African American students into private historically white colleges, African American students had been attending white public land grant and other public institutions since the late nineteenth and early twentieth centuries. These institutions provided both great opportunities and significant obstacles to the African American women who attended them. The next chapter will discuss their history and experiences.

CHAPTER 4

Major Public Universities and Black Women in the Heartland

The federal Morrill Act of 1862 instituted the establishment of state land-grant colleges and the growth of other public colleges and universities. While unable to attend these public institutions in the South and border states, African American students began attending many of these institutions—particularly in the Midwest, Plains states, and the far West. Due to Black women representing a double minority—they constantly had to confront being an African American *and* a woman. The University of Michigan, Ann Arbor, was established in 1837, and its first students began matriculating in 1841. While not a land-grant college, it did benefit from earlier federal land grants of 1826 and 1836. It was one of the first major public institutions to admit Blacks and women. It began admitting Black men in 1868 and women of all races in 1870 as a "dangerous experiment."[1] Two Black men entered the first year they were allowed in 1868 without incident or comment from the university's administration. In 1880 Mary Henrietta Graham became the first African American woman to enroll and graduate from the university. Graham was a resident of Ann Arbor and earned a bachelor of philosophy with a degree in literature.[2] In 1882, she married attorney, civil rights activist, and newspaper publisher, Ferdinand Barnett, and moved to Chicago with him to work on his paper, *The Chicago Conservator*. She died of a heart attack at the age of 32 in 1890. In 1895, Attorney Barnett married anti-lynching crusader Ida B. Wells.[3]

Other Black women also attended Michigan in the nineteenth century, and the earliest graduates obtained professional degrees. Canadian Sophia Bethena Jones, in 1885, became the first African American woman to earn a medical degree from Michigan. Unable to earn a medical degree at the University of Toronto due to her gender, Dr. Jones enrolled at the University of Michigan, which did admit women. Her father, James Monroe Jones, was the first Black graduate of Oberlin and was active in abolitionist activities. As was the case with most highly educated Black women, they were immediately employable in Black colleges and schools.[4] Dr. Jones became the first Black faculty member of the all-female Spelman College in Atlanta where she established the college's nurses training program. She subsequently served as resident physician at another HBCU, Wilberforce University in Ohio. Dr. Jones later worked in private practice in St. Louis, Philadelphia, and Kansas City. She retired to southern California in the 1920s with one of her sisters and died there at the age of 75 in 1932.

Ida Gray, born in 1867 in Clarksville, Tennessee, was orphaned as an infant when her mother died, as her unnamed white father was never a part of her life. After the death of her mother, Gray moved to Cincinnati, Ohio, to live with an aunt. While there, she attended the segregated public school and graduated from Gaines High School in 1887. During her high school years, she worked in the dental office of brothers Jonathan and William Taft, who were strong proponents of women becoming dentists. When Jonathan Taft was recruited to the University of Michigan to establish their first dental school, Gray, who had worked in his dental office for three years, passed the entrance examination to the new Michigan School of Dentistry and followed Taft to Ann Arbor. She entered in 1887 and graduated in 1890 with a Doctor of Dental Science (DDS) becoming the first Black woman to graduate in dentistry from Michigan, as well as the country. She returned to Cincinnati and opened a successful practice with clients of all races. Gray's educational and professional accomplishments made her a role model for Black women and girls and were celebrated in the Black press. Gray relocated to Chicago in 1895 when she married James Sanford Nelson, a lawyer originally from Canada. With her success Gray opened a dental practice becoming the first African American dentist in Chicago. As in Cincinnati, she maintained an interracial clientele and served both adult and child patients. After her first husband died in 1926, she remarried in 1929 to William A. Rollins. Gray was very active, and held offices in professional women's clubs, as well as charitable organizations, such as the Phyllis Wheatley Club, a group that maintained a Black women's shelter in Chicago.[5]

Two other Black women graduated in the class of 1896, including Emily Harper Williams, who spent her career teaching in HBCUs. She taught for years at Hampton and Tuskegee Institute and later in Washington, DC. Women who attended Michigan during the nineteenth century were able to take the same classes as men and were present, as mentioned earlier, in the professional schools. It also appears African Americans in the early years at Michigan fared much better on racial issues.

Other Black women attended Michigan in the late nineteenth century without apparent racial animosity or mishaps. Ruth Bordin in her history of women at the University of Michigan noted instances of Black women having positive experiences on campus.[6] These sentiments were reflected in a 1924 survey of 3,000 women who had attended the University of Michigan since their admission in 1870. The purpose of the survey was to get insight and reflections on being among the earliest women to attend a coeducational institution of higher education.[7] In 1924, there were 10,250 women who had attended Michigan since 1870. The survey was part of a fundraising effort to establish and endow a Women's Building to serve as the activity center of undergraduate women, alumnae, and their guests. While none of the Black women who attended the medical or dental schools submitted reflections of their academic or social experiences, the comments of white women students did provide insight into what it was like to be a woman student at Michigan in the early decades.

A white graduate, Julia Stannard '92 stated when she observed what the Medical School was doing on behalf of women currently, she remembered how little was done for women thirty years earlier. She said, "indeed the presence of women studying medicine [during the period she attended] was still one of simple endurance."[8] Stannard recalled that women were pretty much left on their own.[9] An 1899 graduate had warm memories and wrote, "The unfailing courtesy and fair treatment we medical women received from both men students and faculty members." However, a university graduate in the next year (1900) wrote: "It was impressed upon the women of our department that the U of M was a *men's* school and often we had the feeling that we were trying to rob men of a livelihood. The girls had to study harder and make better records to 'pass.' No internships were offered to women or secured on their behalf."[10] The African American women alums found success in their medical and dental professions as previously noted and provided services needed within the Black communities (although Dr. Sophia Jones and Dr. Ida Gray had white patients as well).

A couple of Black women did respond to the survey. Emily Harper (Williams '96) responded positively to her experience at Michigan and was "thrilled" when she met President [James] Angell (the president from 1871–1909 and a renowned figure in higher education), who knew her by name. She said she discovered years later, since she was the only "brown girl" in a group of more than a hundred new students, he had no problem remembering her name. Thirty years after her graduation, she responded to the invitation to her class reunion stating: "I wish my husband had time to go with me. I went with him to his twenty-fifth class reunion at Harvard, and I would like to show him that the Michigan Alumni are just as fine as those of Harvard."[11]

The memories of Katherine Crawford, medical school graduate in 1898, were mixed and less enthusiastic than those of Williams, who graduated from the undergraduate program in 1896. She said she recalled many genuine friendships of members of her class as well as other women at the college. However, she noted, some of her experiences at the university were "exceedingly bitter ... immeasurably so, even as I view them after more than a quarter of a century, but they taught me my capacity for endurance."[12] For most Black women at Michigan, like those elsewhere, their experiences, as Crawford noted, were bittersweet. They accomplished their educational goals but did so often at great personal and emotional expense.

Numerous scholars have studied African American students in various Midwestern state schools in their early attendance years. Richard Melvin Breaux researched these students at the University of Iowa, University of Kansas, University of Minnesota, and the University of Nebraska from 1900–1940. Tamara Lynette Hoff completed a study of African American women at the University of Illinois, Champaign-Urbana from 1901–39 and Deidre Cobb Roberts studied African American women students at the University of Illinois, Champaign-Urbana from 1945 to 1955. These studies and primary documents and interviews provide information on these women's experiences in the first half of the twentieth century at these institutions. What is consistent with African American students in these institutions is their being denied access to student housing and student organizations. While the Black women who were students at the Seven Sisters colleges and some of the other small residential campuses where they attended, were often isolated on their campuses, Black women on large public campuses had other Black classmates. In addition, the Black communities of college towns of major universities provided support and refuge to these women.

Black students at these large state universities did have a community among themselves. The growth of Black Greek organizations played an important role in their social life. As noted earlier, Black communities in these college towns also embraced these students. They provided housing, community activities, barber and beauty salons, as well as psychological and emotional support. Black churches in these communities celebrated these students' successes and provided a home away from home for them.

Many free African American men and women who were educated outside the South prior to the Civil War moved or returned to the South to participate in the massive educational and social movement of "race uplift."[13]

The rise of the Ku Klux Klan, the white supremist group, along with the instituting of restrictive Black Codes (laws that kept African Americans as second-class citizens) segregated them in employment, housing, and education. These events were coupled with vicious and exploitative sharecropping practices, where Black farmers were basically re-enslaved. This resulted in the first massive migration of Blacks out of the South starting in 1879. Described as the "Exoduster Movement" based on the Exodus story from the Bible, Blacks left Mississippi, Louisiana, Arkansas, Tennessee, and Kentucky, and headed to Kansas seeking opportunities to obtain land and freedom. A year before it officially became recognized as a state, Black residents in Kansas can be traced back to 1860, and during this time, around 627 Black people lived in the Kansas Territory. In 1862, Black residents saw motivation in the 1862 Homestead Act that provided settlers of modest means a way to acquire 160 acres of land if they developed it and stayed for five years. Excited by this opportunity, by the end of the 1870s, the Black population of Kansas increased to 26,000.[14] The influx of African Americans resulted in them pursuing land, opportunities, and an education. The University of Kansas played a prominent role in Black Kansans' pursuit of higher education for their youth.

The University of Kansas in Lawrence was established in 1864, and it provided a great opportunity for Black men and women to pursue a secondary and higher education. Lawrence was located between Kansas City and Topeka with African Americans first arriving between 1860 and 1865 primarily from Arkansas and Missouri—the neighboring slave states. There were approximately 1,000 Black residents in 1865. By 1900, their numbers grew to 2,032. However, Lawrence's Black population was not impacted significantly from the Blacks who came during the Exodus.[15] Like many early colleges where opportunities did not exist for students to initially receive a secondary education, the University of Kansas offered preparatory classes from 1866 to 1883 and added college level classes in 1869. According to Du Bois' study, *The College-Bred Negro* in 1910, the first African American student to enroll in the preparatory department of the University of Kansas was a woman in 1870, and in 1873, she entered the college of liberal arts and sciences, making her the first African American to take college level courses. It's unclear what year she left, although she did not earn a degree. From 1870 to 1890, the number of African American students was small—normally four or five per year with ten per class in the early 1900s. The university reported that forty-four Black students were enrolled in 1908–9. By that year, 211 Black students had attended the university. Of that number, sixty-eight were women. Despite the larger number of men in the first forty years of their attendance, the first six Black students at the University prior to 1876 were women. It was only later that Black men enrolled and graduated in larger numbers. According to a study of African American students at the university, from their beginning until 1909, author Larry Peace noted that most students stayed only a few years and usually left by their sophomore year. As previously noted in discussions of Black students in higher education, the demand for teachers was so great in the early years that employment could be obtained without a college degree. In many areas within the South, teachers often had very little education.

By 1909, Black women had matriculated in every department within liberal arts and sciences but had yet to enroll in the professional schools of medicine, law, and engineering except for the School of Pharmacy. This school had two

Black women enroll and one graduating by that year. The study's author commented, in an apparent element of surprise, that Black women at the university had "kept pace with the men not only in number but also in the quality of their work." In comparing the fields and classes that both genders studied, Peace observed, "The women clearly out classed the men, from the standpoint of credits, in the languages and in history, while the men took the lead in biological, physical and social sciences and in mathematics."[16] According to the study, it was clear that Black students of both genders did well academically. Three Black women graduated before 1899; of the three, two graduated in 1895, along with three Black men. One of the three women was Sadie Stone, the middle-class daughter of an early Black resident of Lawrence who owned a restaurant. He financed his daughter's education at Kansas. The other two women graduates were Cassandra "Cassie" Moore and another unnamed woman.[17] Once *The Crisis* magazine was established in 1910, photos and more information were published regarding Black graduates.[18] Although Sadie Stone received financial assistance from her family to support her education, most of the Black students at the university were overwhelmingly self-supporting. Peace's study indicated that while the occupations of working white students listed were mostly clerks, stenographers, and bookkeepers, the positions of the fifty-three out of the sixty Black graduates who worked were table-waiters, janitors, porters, farmers, maids, and laundresses.[19]

Black students could attend classes at Kansas, as well as many other institutions that will be discussed. Yet, as repeatedly noted, they were barred from on campus housing and many extracurricular activities into the 1940s. Once campus housing was permitted for Black students, they were assigned rooms with other Black students. The Peace study noted that while the Black student has been successful in the classroom, "he has taken an insignificant part in university affairs in general." However, this wasn't by choice but because of their exclusion. With rare exception, Black student activities outside the classroom were limited to those in the Black community. They maintained their own single-sex literary associations within the Black community. This was especially true of their involvement in the Black churches in the community. Kansas Black students took the lead in all aspects of organizations within the churches. Peace said, "they held all church offices, from Sunday school teacher and chorister to minister." In addition, "while the colored students do not take any part in the social life of the University, in conjunction with the town people, they provide themselves with all the latest fad and luxuries of social enjoyment. They had their receptions, their banquets, their club dances, and their annual spring parties."[20] Hence, while they had no social life on campus—these students, male and female, had a robust and fulfilling social life within the Black community.

Black Greek Organizations

In 1915, Black women students established a chapter of Alpha Kappa Alpha (AKA), the oldest Black sorority in the nation. Founded in 1908, at Howard University—the subsequent chapters were founded on predominantly white campuses for camaraderie and support. The Delta chapter at the University of Kansas was the fourth chapter of AKA and received publicity in the Black press. The *Topeka Plaindealer* noted the purpose of the sorority was to:

> Study and solve problems as will help the colored woman take her place in the vanguard of civilization; to cultivate and encourage high scholastic and ethical standard[s] among college students and the establishment of unity and friendship among the more efficient college students and to keep alive among the alumnae their interest in college life progressive movements emanating there from for the avowed purpose of improving the social status of the race, raising moral standards and increasing educational efficiency.[21]

The *Ivy Leaf*, the AKA magazine, announced the chapter's founding as well and stated it had been established by one of the nine founding members of AKA, Beulah Burke, who was teaching in Kansas City. She established three undergraduate chapters in major Midwestern universities—the Beta chapter at the University of Chicago (1913), Gamma chapter at the University of Illinois, Champaign-Urbana (1914), and Delta chapter at the University of Kansas (1915).[22] In 1921, the *Ivy Leaf* reported that in the six years of Delta chapter's existence, it had initiated thirty-four members, twelve of whom had graduated and twelve currently enrolled. It noted that two of the former members who were graduates died that year. One was from the class of 1916 and had been a teacher in Wichita, worked for two years at an insurance company, and was teaching in Norfolk, Virginia, when she died. The second member was from the class

FIGURE 15. Alpha Kappa Alpha House, 1947, University of Illinois. Courtesy of the University of Illinois Archives.

of 1920 and was a teacher in Wichita. The article pointed out that the chapter maintained high academic standards and had the respect of the university and the student body. It also reported that the chapter had sponsored events in the university's gymnasium for social events and other public functions. It reported most of their graduates were teaching, as was the case with most Black women college graduates in various parts of the country.[23]

In 1917, the Black male students established the Upsilon chapter of Alpha Phi Alpha, the oldest Black fraternity in the country. Black male students founded its organization in 1906 at Cornell University. In 1925, ten years after a chapter of AKA was founded, the second Black sorority, Delta Sigma Theta, established a chapter in Kansas. The Black fraternity Kappa Alpha Phi also established a chapter. According to historian Richard Breaux's study of Black students at Kansas, he noted that prior to the founding of the Deltas and Kappas on campus, the AKA and the Alphas dated each other and socialized together. The members of these organizations, and other Black students at KU, were a community unto themselves but were also part of a larger, more economically and socially diverse community of Blacks in Lawrence.[24] Black students at other large universities replicated these experiences on their campuses—they had Black Greek letter organizations, lived together, and relied on the Black communities of their campus towns for their support. At the University of Kansas, AKAs and the two Black male fraternities rented houses for Black student housing. In addition, these Greek members were often the student leaders and activists on these campuses.

In the history of Black students' higher education in the heartland, including the University of Kansas, University of Minnesota, the University of Nebraska at Lincoln, and the University of Iowa, Breaux notes that historians of higher

FIGURE 16. Gamma Chapter, Alpha Kappa Alpha, 1947, University of Illinois. Courtesy of the University of Illinois Archives.

Major Public Universities and Black Women in the Heartland

education have overlooked the significant role Black Greek letter organizations played in the academic, social, and emotional support of Black students on white campuses in the early decades of the twentieth century. The Black women who attended private liberal arts colleges were few, and they were often not in areas with African American communities and did not benefit from having this important support system (although city chapters were formed for women who lived in areas where there were multiple colleges in the area, e.g., Chicago, New York, Philadelphia, Boston, Cleveland, Indianapolis, etc.—see charts 1 and 2). The lone Black student had to suffer through segregated housing and often experienced acute isolation. On larger campuses, where the numbers of Black students were sizable (although small compared to the large universities), their numbers could sustain the chapters of these organizations. They filled the void that their exclusion from organizations and activities on campus dictated. In addition, the sororities and fraternities developed leadership skills in the members and resulted in life-long bonds. These chapters were at the forefront in providing and resolving the housing issue for themselves since they were denied campus housing privileges into the 1940s and afterward. The members of the Black organizations took great pride in their academic achievements. And, the Black press as well as the publications of these organizations boasted of their scholastic accomplishments.

According to Breaux, the period of 1905 through 1922 was the "golden age" for Black Greek-letter organizations at these institutions.[25] During this period, nearly every Black athlete at the University of Kansas, University of Minnesota, University of Iowa, and the University of Nebraska–Lincoln were members of a Black fraternity.[26] Although, as mentioned earlier, AKA and Delta were founded at Howard University, their subsequent chapters were established at predominantly large white institutions where the numbers of Black women grew during this period. Membership in these organizations required collegiate status at an accredited institution. Hence, most of the earliest members were students at predominantly white institutions. The names of the chapters followed the Greek alphabet with alpha being the first. As noted above, Delta chapter at KU of AKA was the fourth chapter of the sorority founded in 1915. Beta the second chapter was established in 1913 at the University of Chicago followed by Gamma in 1914 at the University of Illinois, Champaign-Urbana. The growth of the chapters of the Black sororities mirrored the increasing number of Black women attending white institutions. Five AKA chapters were established on white campuses in the teens, twelve in the '20s, eight in the '30s, five in the '40s, eleven in the '50s, and twenty-two in the '60s when there was a massive growth of Black women students in predominantly white campuses. Likewise, historian Paula Giddings notes that after the founding of Delta at Howard in 1913, twenty-seven of the next thirty chapters were established on white campuses.[27]

CHART 1. Alpha Kappa Alpha Undergraduate Chapters at Predominately White Institutions (PWIs) 1913–69

UNIVERSITY	CHAPTER	YEAR CHARTERED
City Chapter - Chicago, IL	Beta	10/13/1913
University of Illinois, Urbana-Champaign Urbana, IL	Gamma	12/1/1914
University of Kansas Lawrence, KS	Delta	11/1/1915
University of Pittsburgh Pittsburgh, PA	Iota	5/8/1918
City Chapter Indianapolis, Indiana	Kappa	2/1/1919
Ohio State University Columbus, OH	Theta	2/1/1919
University of Cincinnati Cincinnati, OH	Omicron	4/1/1921
University of California, Berkeley Berkeley, CA	Rho	8/1/1921
City Chapter New York City, NY	Lambda	4/22/1922
City Chapter Los Angeles, CA	Sigma	7/1/1922
Indiana University Bloomington, IN	Tau	12/1/1922
Boston City-Wide Boston, MA	Epsilon	5/3/1924
City Chapter Cleveland, OH	Omega	11/1/1925
University of California, Los Angeles Los Angeles, CA	Alpha Gamma	12/1/1925
City Chapter - Denver/Boulder Denver, CO	Alpha Kappa	11/1/1928
University of Toledo Toledo, OH	Alpha Lambda	12/1/1928
University of Michigan Ann Arbor, MI	Beta Eta	6/1/1932
University of West Florida Pensacola, FL	Beta Gamma	11/12/1932
University of Washington Seattle, WA	Beta Theta	8/1/1933
City Chapter Louisville, KY	Beta Epsilon	11/6/1933
Wayne State University Detroit, MI	Beta Mu	4/3/1936
Kansas State College Manhattan, KS	Beta Nu	1/1/1937

continued

CHART 1. continued

UNIVERSITY	CHAPTER	YEAR CHARTERED
Ball State University Muncie, IN	Beta Phi	6/1/1938
University of Nebraska Omaha, NE	Gamma Beta	12/7/1940
City Chapter Philadelphia, PA	Gamma Epsilon	6/24/1945
City Chapter Newark, NJ	Gamma Zeta	11/1/1947
City Chapter Buffalo, NY	Gamma Iota	11/1/1948
East Michigan University Ypsilanti, MI	Xi	1/22/1949
University of Arkansas Fayetteville, AR	Alpha Rho	5/19/1951
Southern Illinois University Carbondale, IL	Delta Beta	4/19/1952
Pennsylvania State University University Park, PA	Delta Gamma	3/1/1953
Youngstown State University Youngstown, PA	Delta Delta	5/9/1953
Michigan State University East Lansing, MI	Delta Zeta	2/1/1954
Florida Memorial University Miami Gardens, FL	Delta Eta	11/1/1954
City Chapter Brooklyn, NY	Alpha Mu	3/13/1955
Temple University Philadelphia, PA	Delta Mu	11/5/1955
California State University Fresno Fresno, CA	Alpha Nu	3/21/1959
City Chapter Pittsburgh, PA	Alpha Sigma	5/1/1959
University of Texas at Austin Austin, TX	Delta Xi	5/16/1959
Northern Illinois University DeKalb, IL	Delta Omicron	5/1/1960
University of Akron Akron, OH	Delta Pi	4/1/1961
City Chapter San Antonio, TX	Delta Rho	11/22/1961
University of Central Oklahoma Edmond, OK	Beta Beta	3/31/1962
Ohio University Athens, OH	Delta Phi	1/16/1964

UNIVERSITY	CHAPTER	YEAR CHARTERED
University of Missouri Columbia, MO	Delta Tau	11/1/1964
Western Michigan University Kalamazoo, MI	Delta Chi	12/1/1965
Wichita State University Wichita, KS	Epsilon Alpha	2/18/1967
University of Louisiana at Lafayette Lafayette, LA	Epsilon Beta	12/1/1967
Kent State University Kent, OH	Epsilon Gamma	1/1/1968
University of Wisconsin–Madison Madison, WI	Epsilon Delta	5/18/1968
University of Memphis Memphis, TN	Epsilon Epsilon	9/17/1968
Western Kentucky University Bowling Green, KY	Epsilon Zeta	11/22/1968
Bradley University Peoria, IL	Epsilon Eta	12/14/1968
Northwestern University Evanston, IL	Gamma Chi	3/1/1969
University of Iowa Iowa City, IA	Epsilon Theta	5/10/1969

Source: Marjorie H. Parker, *Past Is Prologue: The History of Alpha Kappa Alpha (1908–1999)*, 1999.

Breaux noted that the Black men and women who attended these institutions tended to be from the middle class—or from families who had middle class aspirations. These students tended to major in classical and liberal arts fields or in a professional field as opposed to a vocational field.[28] These early Black women sought liberal arts degrees, which often weren't available to them at the teacher training institutions that most of the earliest Black women college students attended in the HBCUs in the South. While the access to liberal arts majors was far more available to Black women in predominantly white institutions, with rare exception these early women graduates overwhelmingly became teachers. This was because the demand for teachers was so great for Black schools in the South and there were limited teaching opportunities for Black teachers throughout the country except in all-Black schools (e.g., in cities like St. Louis, Washington, DC, and Indianapolis).

Although Black students at Kansas and other large public universities created an intellectual, social, and religious world outside of their universities and had thriving lives in the Black communities of their institutions, they were not

CHART 2. Delta Sigma Theta Chapters Founded at Predominantly White Institutions (PWIs), 1918–69

NAME OF CHAPTER	NAME OF SCHOOL	YEAR FOUNDED
Gamma	University of Pennsylvania	1918
Delta	University of Iowa	April 4, 1919
Epsilon	Ohio State University	November 19, 1919
Zeta	University of Cincinnati	October 10, 1920
Eta	Syracuse University	1920
Theta	Cornell	1920
Theta*	Duquesne University	January 25, 1946
Iota	Boston City - City Wide	December 29, 1921
Kappa	University of California, Berkeley	February 21, 1921
Lambda	Chicago - City Wide	March 1921
Mu	University of Pittsburgh	November 21, 1921
Nu	University of Michigan	April 7, 1921
Xi	University of Louisville	April 15, 1922
Omicron	University of Nebraska - Lincoln	April 1922
Pi	University of California, Los Angeles	January 23, 1923
Rho	Columbia University	December 7, 1923
Tau	Wayne State University	January 24, 1924
Upsilon	University of Southern California	June 4, 1924
Phi	Iowa State University	December 29, 1923
Chi	Indianapolis - City Wide	March 14, 1925
Psi	University of Kansas	June 25, 1925
Omega	Cleveland - City Wide	1925
Alpha Alpha	Kansas City, Kansas and Kansas City, Missouri	1925
Alpha Nu	University of Illinois at Urbana - Champaign	March 16, 1932
Alpha Omicron	Seattle - City Wide	April 30, 1930
Beta Zeta	Pittsburg State University	1937
Beta Theta	Phoenix - City Wide	1937
Beta Lambda	University of Toledo	1938
Beta Psi	Portland - City Wide	1940
Gamma Beta	Washburn University	1941
Gamma Eta	East St. Louis, Illinois - City Wide	1942
Gamma Theta	Dayton, Ohio - City Wide	1943
Gamma Kappa	Buffalo, New York - City Wide	1943
Gamma Nu	Indiana University	November 8, 1947
Gamma Xi	University of Nebraska	1947
Gamma Pi	Columbia College	1948
Gamma Chi	Claflin University	1948
Delta Beta	Eastern Michigan University	1949

NAME OF CHAPTER	NAME OF SCHOOL	YEAR FOUNDED
Delta Zeta	New Jersey - City Wide	1950
Delta Upsilon	Western Michigan University	May 24, 1953
Delta Phi	Ball State University	August 1, 1953
Delta Psi	University of Detroit - City Wide	1954
Epsilon Beta	University of Texas, Austin	1960
Epsilon Gamma	Pennsylvania State University	May 21, 1960
Epsilon Delta	Temple University	July 24, 1960
Epsilon Epsilon	Michigan State University	April 30, 1961
Epsilon Zeta	California State University, Los Angeles	1962
Epsilon Iota	Ohio University	October 5, 1963
Epsilon Kappa	University of Memphis	1963
Epsilon Mu	Kent State University	1964
Epsilon Nu	San Francisco State - City Wide	June 4, 1964
Epsilon Xi	Southern Illinois University	June 11, 1964
Epsilon Omicron	Bowling Green State University	1965
Epsilon Pi	Brooklyn - City Wide	July 17, 1965
Epsilon Rho	University of Dayton	July 19, 1965
Epsilon Tau	New York - City Wide	July 1965
Epsilon Upsilon	Hartford - City Wide	March 12, 1966
Epsilon Phi	Philadelphia - City Wide	March 27, 1966
Epsilon Psi	University of Missouri at Columbia	May 21, 1966
Zeta Alpha	University of Akron	1967
Zeta Beta	Wichita State University	1967
Zeta Gamma	Youngstown State University	1968
Zeta Zeta	Truman State University	1968
Zeta Eta	University of North Texas	1968
Zeta Theta	Purdue University	November 3, 1968
Zeta Iota	Northern Illinois University	November 11, 1968
Zeta Kappa	Northern Michigan University	1969
Zeta Lambda	University of Central Missouri	1969
Zeta Mu	Miami University	March 29, 1969
Zeta Nu	Indiana State University	1969
Zeta Xi	University of Wisconsin	April 18, 1969
Zeta Pi	Denver, Colorado - City Wide	May 10, 1969
Zeta Upsilon	San Antonio - City Wide	May 10, 1969
Zeta Rho	Ferris State University	1969
Zeta Sigma	University of Houston	May 29, 1969
Zeta Phi	Georgia State University	May 30, 1969
Zeta Chi	Southern Illinois University	1969
Zeta Psi	University of Georgia	1969

happy about nor accepting of their exclusion from campus activities.[29] An article published in *The Crisis* magazine in the annual college issue in August of 1927, by Loren Miller, a former Black student at Kansas, recalled the experiences of Black students on the campus when he was a student. Miller wrote that, while there were one hundred and fifty Black students on campus, the university would "ignore their presence as far as possible." He noted that Black students were excluded from literary and dramatic organizations and glee clubs. He also noted that the two Black fraternities that owned homes for their members were not allowed to be members of the National Panhellenic Council—the governing board of the Greek letter organizations on campus. In addition, he said Black students were barred from attending school parties, proms, and dances, and their organizations were blocked from renting space on campus. Miller pointed out that students in the fine arts were required to attend concerts as a part of their studies and were segregated in the balcony. Although physical education was required, Miller notes the irony of Black students being excused from swimming because they were barred from using the pool. These types of racist restrictions were not unique to Kansas but routine for almost all white institutions, with the rare exception of those perceived as liberal ones.[30]

The above comments appeared at odds with the article in the AKA's *Ivy Leaf* in 1921, which stated they rented the university's student union for their dances and other events. However, both Miller's and the AKA's comments are true. In the early years of Black attendance at Kansas, with their numbers few, they did not experience the blatant and uniform racism of Black students of later decades. In the 1880s and 1890s, Black students at Kansas could use the swimming pool and play intercollegiate and varsity sports (baseball, track, and football). While they were segregated from eating in local restaurants, there was no racial segregation in the student-run restaurant on campus. Despite these privileges, Black students still experienced discrimination on campus. Professors often had Black students sit at the back of the classroom, and they were not allowed to be members of the band, glee, and pep clubs. And nearly universally true on white college campuses, Black students were not allowed to live in the college dormitories or college-approved housing near the university.[31]

In the early 1920s, the University of Kansas began admitting Black students from the neighboring states of Oklahoma, Missouri, and Arkansas. These states barred Black students from attending the white institutions in their states at all degree levels. While the university didn't keep data on the number of Black students who came from out of state, in 1927, there were 123 Black students enrolled. When administrators began to complain about the growing numbers of Black students, increased segregation on the campus ensued. A change in key administrators on campus accounted for the reversal of treatment. For example, a new basketball coach, Forrest Allen was appointed at the end of WWI and served until 1955. In addition, he was also head of the athletic department, where he served from 1919–37. With these appointments, Allen, a native of Missouri, began excluding Black men from all sports teams. The swimming requirement for all students was suddenly exempted for Black students to bar them from using the university's pools. By 1927, the opening of a new student union resulted in the segregation of Black students in the cafeteria. Also in that year, the Big Six athletic league was established, including teams from the segregated states of Missouri and Oklahoma, which had no Black players and refused to play against teams with Black players.[32]

Miller's article in *The Crisis* magazine resulted in Du Bois investigating the allegations and contacting the chancellor, Ernest Lindsay, of the university regarding the segregation of Black students in the union's cafeteria and throughout the university. Chancellor Lindsay responded that in the crowded union cafeteria, Black students "insisted on sitting uninvited" with white students.[33] He told Du Bois that he couldn't risk the failure of the cafeteria if white students refused to sit with Black students. As a compromise, he met with Black students and asked that they voluntarily sit in a segregated part of the cafeteria. Lindsay set aside one-third of the cafeteria for the Black students. Lindsay told Du Bois he sometimes sat with the Black students in their section apparently as a gesture to indicate he wasn't racially biased. He told Du Bois that the racial climate at the University hadn't improved over the years, but it had gotten worse, noting the "widening breach between the negro student and the white student on the campus," particularly in social aspects.[34] The segregation of Black students at KU continued until the 1950s when a new chancellor, Franklin Murphy, was appointed. He had previously served as the dean of the KU School of Medicine in Kansas City. In that position, he integrated the operating rooms and the nurses' dormitories at the school and employed Black technicians. By the 1940s, some changes had been made for Black students at KU. They could live on campus but could only share a room with other Black students unless a white student agreed to room with them. Murphy had the local restaurants, barbershops, and theaters opened to Black students by threatening to have competitive businesses open on campus at cheaper prices. To avoid losing business, most of these places complied.[35] These humiliating experiences were repeated throughout white public universities. At the University of Iowa, during this period, Black students recalled that they were restricted to eating in a corner of the college cafeteria, with an iron chain around the area, accessible by a sliding door with an armed guard to ensure they did not leave their area.[36]

Du Bois, through *The Crisis* magazine, kept close tabs on the progress and treatment of Black students in white institutions, and as noted earlier, there was an annual college issue in July of Black students. Throughout the 1930s–50s, the NAACP filed lawsuits to challenge the 1896 Plessy "separate but equal" doctrine in higher education. These suits sought specifically to address the lack of opportunities for Black students to attend graduate and professional schools in the segregated south and Border States. The success of two lawsuits that challenged the exclusion of Black students from state-funded law schools in the 1930s resulted in southern and border states having to pay for Black students who were denied entrance to segregated white undergraduate, graduate, or professional schools to attend such schools out of state.[37]

Black Women and Sports

The period after World War I witnessed the rise in physical education as an academic major. This field arose after it was recognized that a large number of military men were not physically fit. Prior to 1915, only three states required physical education classes in schools. After the war, the number jumped to twenty-eight, and by 1929, forty-six states required such classes in public schools. Black women began to take advantage of this new field, as well as participating in collegiate sports.[38] They began to participate in sports on white campuses in growing numbers during the decade of the 1920s. Breaux's research on the Black students in the four universities in the "heartland" noted that the 1920s was the "golden age" of women's competitive sports. Black women, as did the men, had varying experiences in their attempt to join athletic teams.

As the number of Black women students in these institutions grew during the mid-teens so did their presence in various sports. For example, at the University of Iowa, Harriette Alexander made the women's field hockey team in 1919. Lorraine Crawford, a native of Des Moines, Iowa, played on the women's volleyball team in 1923. In the same year, her teammate and housemate, Corine Mathis, of Bailey, Oklahoma, played on the women's baseball, volleyball, and basketball team while also running track. A superior athlete, Mathis was the leading scorer of the sophomore volleyball team and, along with three other women, broke the university-wide women's relay record.[39]

Sarah McGhee became a member of the women's baseball team at the University of Illinois in 1923. Majoring in physical education afforded Black women opportunities to be on various sports teams. For example, Alice Sims, from Tulsa, Oklahoma, was on the hockey team and was one of the first Black women to play on a university team. In 1927, Sims received an Emblem by the Women's Athletic Association for scoring six hundred points that year. Another physical education major, Gwendolyn Butler from Kansas City, made the sophomore baseball and hockey teams at the University of Kansas in 1930, making her the only African American student on any athletic team at the institution.[40] Sims continued her work in women's sports in Black communities in Minneapolis and St. Paul. Many other Black women at Kansas followed

Sims and Butler as PE majors in subsequent years and served on the hockey teams.

In addition to serving on various teams as a result of being PE majors, Black women at numerous schools in the heartland and Midwest established their own sports teams. As early as 1922, the *Ivy Leaf* reported that the AKAs at Kansas were organizing their own basketball team. In an issue in 1925, the publication reported that the AKA basketball team had played in several conference games with high schools and colleges. The magazine also reported that the Topeka, Kansas, sorority chapter had organized two basketball teams and participated in an intramural game with eight sororities. It noted that AKA teams played in three of the games. The Black sorority women played against members of white sororities the article noted, saying this was the first time "colored" teams were included in the games. The AKA chapter at the University of Minnesota had established a basketball team and also participated in intramural games. However, various institutions had different attitudes toward including Black women teams. For example, the AKA basketball team at the University of Nebraska had to fight for the right to play against the white sororities on campus. In the December 1930 issue of the *Ivy Leaf*, their chapter reported: "Through persistent efforts of the Intra-racial staff of the YWCA, our sorority has at last gained the privilege of taking part in the intramural athletic contest with the white sororities."[41] After these women were allowed to participate in intramural sports, they competed in basketball, bowling, ping pong, and rifling. The Black women students during this decade participated not only in organizations for racial justice such as the NAACP and the Urban League, but they increasingly participated in interracial organizations, particularly the Young Women's Christian Association (YWCA), which had chapters on college campuses.

Other Black women nationwide in white institutions also broke barriers playing sports. In 1914, Mary Parker set a school record at Simmons College in Boston in the standing and running broad jumps. Some institutions allowed Black women on their basketball teams. In 1917, Phyllis W. Waters became a lettered member of the University of Michigan's women's basketball team and played all four years.[42] However, far more were welcomed on many baseball teams.

On the East Coast, Black women were on the teams of their institutions and not on segregated ones. Inez Robie Patterson at Temple University was considered one of the most renowned and versatile women athletes of all time. Patterson was a native of Philadelphia and entered Temple in 1929. She had the highest average of any athlete in her class of sixty-seven women. She made the All-Collegiate hockey team for four years. In addition, Patterson was in the All-Collegiate teams in tennis, basketball, track, volleyball, and dancing. When she was inducted into the Temple University's Athletic Hall of Fame in

1987, sports experts noted she was probably the "most versatile woman athlete in the history of Pennsylvania."[43] Black women college students increasingly involved themselves in interracial groups for racial harmony. As noted earlier, the YWCA was one important organization. Like many other Black women college graduates, Inez Patterson spent her entire career working for various YWCAs. She trained girls in recreation and physical education at YWCAs in Orange, Newark, and Montclair, New Jersey, and in YWCAs in New York City.[44]

Breaux's research, as well as a 1933 thesis written by Herbert Jenkins on Black students at the University of Iowa, noted that Black women student athletes were permitted to participate in sports that were denied to Black men. Jenkins wrote: "Colored women, unlike the men, are permitted to take part in all intramural sports."[45] He said in interviewing the intramural sports supervisor, he found that Black women didn't experience any discrimination in participating in these competitions. It's unclear why Black women were treated differently in the privilege to play intramural sports. It may have been that the women's teams were intramural, unlike men's teams that competed for championships and had significantly more exposure than women's teams. Most colleges that had Black players did not want to create problems with other teams that did not want to compete with a team with Black male players. As noted, this privilege of including Black women and excluding Black men, didn't come without protest from the women at Nebraska. And although the number of Black women students at Iowa in 1933 was small, only sixteen compared to forty-two Black men, this should not justify the disparate treatment of the two groups.[46]

While Black women at the institutions discussed were allowed to play intramural sports, Black students at Iowa and all other schools were not allowed to swim in the pool with white students. As noted earlier, at the University of Kansas, Black students were exempted from the swimming requirement, and at the University of Iowa, Black women were taught swimming in a separate class from white women. Why were Black women in certain institutions allowed to compete and play on university teams where Black men were not? Women's sports did not attract the crowds as men's sports did, and perhaps these institutions didn't view these women in the same manner they did men's participation. And, again, the white women who were their teammates didn't voice opposition to Black teammates; in some instances white women were vocal in their support of Black women participating on their teams. Nevertheless, the ability of these women to be members of these various teams was no small accomplishment. AKA's *Ivy Leaf* magazine covered the inclusion of women who were in the sorority on the various teams.[47] When we discuss Black women and sports at HBCUs in the next chapter, views about issues of femininity emerged among many within the Black educational community—particularly among the deans of women on these campuses.

PART THREE

CHAPTER 5

Black Women and Historically Black Colleges

After the Civil War, white missionary organizations and religious denominations, both Black and white, began the massive task of educating the recently emancipated Africans. W. E. B. Du Bois noted in his 1901 study, *The Negro Common School,* that two years after Emancipation, nearly 100,000 Black students were in schools in the South. The American Missionary Association (AMA) was the largest group, along with others, which sent thousands of teachers to the South. By 1870, they had 130 common schools in the South. While their contributions were important, Black people also made significant contributions to the education of Blacks in the South. Educated African American women from the North moved South to assist in the education of their race, and some were already teaching in the South.[1]

These women, as well as other educated Black women, not only went South, but organized on behalf of Black women and girls. Organizations, such as the National Association of Colored Women, were founded (1896) to counter the allegations that Black women were "immoral and promiscuous." With chapters throughout the country, this organization helped Black women and girls in educational, social, and employment endeavors on a national level. Mary Church Terrell, an Oberlin graduate of 1884, was the national president. With the motto "Lifting as We Climb"—the educated women organizers reflected the pervasive view of the era that educated Blacks were duty-bound to help the least fortunate of the race and serve as positive role models (later referred to by scholar W. E. B. Du Bois as the "talented tenth" and by historian Kenneth Mack as the "representative man or woman"). These were Blacks who "encapsulated the highest aspiration of his racial or cultural group, in terms of education, professional advancement, and intellectual ability."[2] Despite the contemporary critique condemning the "politics of respectability" of such women and groups, they worked tirelessly and in earnest to help "elevate" the race through their efforts.

These women varied greatly in their socioeconomic backgrounds, educational experiences, and religious backgrounds. The Black South and HBCUs were heavily steeped in conservative religion. The white missionaries that established schools for Black students overemphasized religion, and the morals and behavior of Black women were heavily policed and monitored. But while white institutions of the nation and HBCUs both started out in requiring chapel, HBCUs continued this requirement long after white institutions had ended it. In addition, despite the privileged education, higher socioeconomic status, and world travels of many of these women, they were not immune from racism and Jim Crow laws.

While most institutions of higher education established for Blacks in the South were overwhelmingly coeducational, it was primarily white missionaries that established single-sex schools for Black women and girls. Single-sex institutions were the norm for most of the white founders of the schools and colleges. However, Black parents saw the importance of education for both their sons and daughters and rarely had gender-specific schools. With time, many of the women and girl's schools merged with male schools or became coeducational.

Single-Sex Institutions for Black Women and Girls

Hartshorn Memorial College

Single-sex schools for Black girls overwhelmingly stressed moral and religious development. For example, Hartshorn Memorial College in Richmond, Virginia, was chartered in 1883 for full collegiate status "for the instruction of young women in science, literature and art in the normal, industrial and professional branches and especially in Biblical and Christian learning." Founded by the white American Baptist Home Mission Society, the school had 185 students in 1908 with twelve teachers. Only one Black woman served on the faculty during the school's existence—Rosa Kinckle Jones, a graduate of Howard University and the wife of Joseph Endom Jones, a professor at Virginia Union University. Mrs. Jones taught music on the faculty for nearly forty years, beginning in 1888. Hartshorn was the sister school of the neighboring all-male Virginia Union College. In language that would be replicated in virtually all schools of this type for Black women, the school's history praised its first three graduates ('92) and noted they would be in the vanguard of "moral uplift" within the Black community. In addition, these graduates were described as "educated, refined and Christian models for their husbands and children."[3] More than anything else, educated Black women were expected to be the moral examples and saviors of their families and communities. These beliefs, coupled with the stringent rules and regulations Black women had to endure to obtain an education, spilled over into the "respectability" emphases within the Black community. White missionaries believed that slavery had debased Black women and their communities. These school rules required that students be constantly watched and whereabouts monitored. Daily chapel was the norm at all-Black schools (even decades after they had been abolished or made optional at other colleges). An organization called the White Shield League was established at the school, in which the members wore identical white dresses and pledged themselves to chastity and to abstain from sex until marriage. At Hartshorn, all students had to obey strict dress codes and were taught to dress for health and not for "show."[4] They were forbidden to wear "expensive" clothing, and they could not wear "corsets" because these items were thought to result in ill health and were evil. The women were not allowed to take the streetcars nor date. The women were forbidden to eat pastries or desserts. The reason for this rule was not clear. Hartshorn students were encouraged to participate in temperance activities and organizations so that they could encourage their future husbands and boyfriends to remain sober. The administrators of the school would punish women by public humiliation if they were found not obeying these rules. The names of the women and their violations were noted in their college assemblies. Again, harsh as this treatment was, this was the norm in schools specifically for Black women.

The 1902 catalog noted that while the state could provide a better secular education, the purpose of Hartshorn was to raise up a body of "thoroughly educated Christian women as consecrated workers in the harvest field of the world." Academically, the school offered liberal arts classes, but it also stressed classes in homemaking and manual education for its students. The institution merged with the all-male Virginia Union 1932, thus becoming coeducational.[5]

Scotia Seminary

The white Presbyterian Board of Missions founded the all-female Scotia Seminary in Concord, North Carolina, in 1867. It later became a "seminary" in 1870. The school had a grammar, a normal (teacher education), and an industrial department. The industrial department was restricted to domestic arts, especially sewing and cooking, and the mission of the institution was to train women to be homemakers and teachers and not prepare them for opportunities in the trades. By 1908, the school had 19 teachers and 291 students. By that year over 2,900 girls and women had attended the seminary. Of that number, 604 graduated from the grammar school and 109 from the normal department. The institution became Scotia Women's College in 1916. In 1930, due to the economic depression, Scotia merged with another Presbyterian-founded school, Barber Memorial Seminary, an elementary and secondary school for African American girls located in Anniston, Alabama, that was founded in 1896.[6]

The personal letters of Lois Irvin, a white woman teacher at Barber College, noted her experiences teaching there from 1926–27. She graduated from the Presbyterian College of Emporia in Kansas. She noted that the dean of Barber came to her college to recruit teachers and that she and two of her fellow classmates decided to accept teaching positions at Barber. She said Barber had an integrated faculty and high academic standards. But she noted that the school had strict rules for the faculty and students. She recalled the proselytizing to the students and the requirement that the faculty were required to teach a strict Presbyterian theology. She recalled an extremely talented faculty member dismissed because her teaching and beliefs were not in keeping with orthodox Presbyterianism. Irvin also noted that the religious teaching and style of worship made the students "uncomfortable." They found the style of worship "too sedate." However, this complaint would be replicated throughout white missionary founded schools. As was the norm at the time, the students were required to attend chapel, abide by strict dormitory rules, prohibited from dancing, their uniforms had to be correct, and there were work assignments for the students. Irvin said the students were eager and well behaved. She recalled the school had musicals and dramatic productions, contests, teas, special church services, and her experiences were positive with the students. She stated, however, her desire to leave when she noticed the racist hypocrisy of one of the main leaders of the school. His name was redacted from letters—however, she noted that this man refused to allow students to put the title "Miss" in front of their names in articles in their school newspaper. In addition, she reported that his son made insulting and racist remarks to the kitchen staff, and he "refused to do anything about it." She further wrote, "How can you love God when you hate one of his creatures? You can't."[7] She returned to Kansas to teach.

The elementary and secondary schools at Barber became coeducational and remained open until 1940 in Anniston. Women students could continue to live on campus while the newly admitted male students had to find accommodation elsewhere. In 1930, the seminary merger with the Scotia Women's College resulted in the creation of the Barber-Scotia Junior College for Women. By 1945, Barber-Scotia College became a four-year college and in 1954, a coeducational facility, and received accreditation by the Southern Association of Colleges and Schools. Despite the educational opportunities for Black women and girls, however, the disrespect towards them that was allowed reinforced the belief that it was not necessary to show Black women the same respect as white women.

Atlanta Baptist Female Seminary (Spelman College)

Another all-female seminary for Black women and girls was established in 1881 in Atlanta. Two white Mount Holyoke College graduates and New England missionaries, Sophia B. Packard and Harriet E. Giles, founded Atlanta Baptist Female Seminary. Financially supported by the Women's American Baptist, the school opened in the basement of the African American Friendship Baptist Church with eleven students of various ages. By 1884, the name had been changed to Spelman Seminary and had a high school, normal school, nursing, missionary, industrial, and music departments. The high school graduated its first students in 1887 and a decade later opened a collegiate department and graduated its first student with a baccalaureate degree in 1901. Packard served as president from 1881 to 1891, and Giles was Spelman's second president and served from 1891 until her death in 1909. The sister institution to the all-male Morehouse College emerged as one of the preeminent HBCUs for African American women.

Bennett College

The fourth all-female institution established for Black women was Bennett College in Greensboro, North Carolina. The white Methodist Episcopal Church established the college in 1873 as a coeducational high school and normal school. The school opened with seventy male and female scholars and prepared them for teaching positions. A women's college was viewed as necessary because the Black land-grant college in Greensboro, North Carolina A&T, had been financially starved by the state legislature, which resulted in discontinuing the enrollment for women in 1900. Women students didn't return to the institution until 1924.[8] In the meantime, there was concern that Black women students needed more educational opportunities in the area, and the women of the Methodist Episcopal Church decided to make Bennett a female-only college beginning in 1926. The city of Greensboro now offered two options for higher education for Black women. Bennett and Spelman remain the two colleges for Black women that have survived.

White Christian denominations founded all of the above single-sex institutions; therefore, they were modeled in their custom of single-sex education for women with a stress on religious and moral development.

While only Spelman and Bennett Colleges remained the two single-sex colleges, historian Audrey Thomas McCluskey highlights in her book four prominent and important Black women school founders in South. The women, all devoutly religious, were Lucy Craft Laney, Mary McLeod Bethune, Charlotte Hawkins Brown, and Nannie Helen Burroughs, who established renowned high schools and normal schools. Laney opened the Haines Normal and Industrial School in Augusta, Georgia, in 1866, with the assistance of the Presbyterian Board of Missions. The curriculum of the school included classical, as well as industrial, courses. While the school was coeducational, Laney, as did all of these women, took a special interest in the education of girls. All four women were also prominent members of the National Association of Colored Women's Clubs. Haines was well known for preparing young women for college. The school suffered financially after the Great Depression of the 1930s, which impacted many small private schools, and officially closed in 1949.[9]

Mary McLeod Bethune was a graduate of the all-female Scotia Seminary in North Carolina. She was a practice teacher at Haines Institute, and Laney became her mentor and role model. In 1904, Bethune moved to Daytona, Florida, and opened the Daytona Education and Industrial School for Girls. Although it was technically a school for girls, the school opened with five girls and one boy (Bethune's son). The school stressed domestic science, industrial trades, and religion. The school merged in 1923 with the all-male Cookman Institute in Jacksonville. In 1929, it became Bethune-Cookman College, while still not offering collegiate level courses. By 1935, it was accredited as a junior college, and in 1943 it became an accredited four-year institution.[10]

Charlotte Hawkins Brown opened a boarding school, Palmer Memorial Institute (PMI), in 1902 in rural Sedalia, North Carolina. With financial assistance from the American Missionary Association (AMA), Brown was from Cambridge, Massachusetts, and named the school after President of Wellesley College, Alice Palmer. Unlike the school of Bethune that stressed industrial education, PMI stressed the liberal arts, "high culture," social graces, travel, and attracted children of the Black middle class. The school went from eighth to twelfth grades. Enrollment was kept small, with 240 students being the normal enrollment. The school attracted students not only from the United States but also from Africa, Bermuda, Haiti, Costa Rica, and other places.[11]

Nannie Helen Burroughs of Washington, DC, founded the National Training School for Women and Girls in that city in 1909 through the Women's Convention of the National Baptist Church. A high school and later a junior college, this was the first school founded and run by Black women. The curriculum stressed vocational training and, like Palmer Memorial, the institution attracted students from Africa, the Caribbean, and throughout the United States. Twenty-five years after it was founded, more than two thousand Black women and girls had attended the school. It closed in 1961 when Burroughs died.[12]

All-Male and Coeducational HBCUs

While the above institutions were secondary schools, two Historically Black Colleges and Universities (HBCUs) were founded prior to the Civil War in the 1850s. Wilberforce University was a coeducational college established by the oldest Black religious denomination—the African Methodist Episcopal Church (AME) in 1856. It was a private liberal arts college located in southwest Ohio. The college stressed classical and teacher education to prepare its graduates for the massive task of educating the freedmen after the War. By 1860, Wilberforce had more than two hundred students.[13] Unfortunately, the enrollment data was not broken down by gender. Most of the students were mixed-race from the South whose white fathers sent them and financed their education at Wilberforce. Since these students are the same profile as the Black students who attended Oberlin, it's unclear how parents and guardians who sent these students decided between the two institutions.

The second HBCU founded prior to the Civil War was the all-male Lincoln University that was chartered in 1853 by white Presbyterians for the "scientific, classical and theological education of colored youth of the male sex."[14] Lincoln University became a very important academic institution for the development of Black male leaders and professionals, and it was one of the leading undergraduate institutions for the production of Black PhDs (along with the all-male Morehouse College in Atlanta founded later in 1867 by white Baptists).[15]

Because of the lack of public secondary education throughout the South, except in major cities before 1940, most high school education for Black students was in private schools, primarily in religious denominations and at Black colleges. Many remained high schools until the 1940s.[16] African American and white religious denominations established twenty-four private colleges for African Americans within ten years after the Civil War, most notably the previously mentioned AMA, funded by the Congregational Church (see charts 3 and 4).

In 1890, the federal Second Morrill Act led to the designation of seventeen separate Black land-grant colleges in southern and border states.

This was a result of barring Blacks from attending public colleges and universities established in 1862 by the First Morrill Act, which provided for each state to have land set aside for the establishment of a college for the "sons and daughters of the common man." These colleges were:

> without excluding other scientific and classical studies and including military tactic, to teach such branches of learning as are related to agriculture and the mechanic arts, in such manner as the legislatures of the States may respectively prescribe, to promote the liberal and practical education of the industrial classes in the several pursuits and professions in life.

Hence, while the original purpose was to emphasize the A and M aspects of the colleges, liberal arts were not to be excluded. In the case of the Black land-grant colleges, they were financially starved by the states and, according to an article on the curriculum of these institutions, few offered courses in agricultural and mechanical topics.[17] Historian Raymond Wolters noted that the federal Smith-Lever and Smith-Hughes Acts of 1914 and 1917 were focused upon agricultural and vocational programs and employed county agents to monitor the Black

CHART 3. White Religious Denominations that Founded HBCUs

DENOMINATION	NAME OF UNIVERSITY	STATE	DATE
American Missionary Association Colleges	Fisk University	Tennessee	1866
American Missionary Association Colleges	Talladega College	Alabama	1867
American Missionary Association Colleges	Dillard University	Louisiana	1869
American Missionary Association Colleges	Tougaloo College	Mississippi	1869
Freedmen's Aid Society of the Methodist Church	Bennett College	North Carolina	1873
Freedmen's Aid Society of the Methodist Church	Clark University	Georgia	1887
Freedmen's Aid Society of the Methodist Church	Claflin College	South Carolina	1869
Freedmen's Aid Society of the Methodist Church	Meharry Medical College	Tennessee	1876
Freedmen's Aid Society of the Methodist Church	Morgan College	Maryland	1867
Freedmen's Aid Society of the Methodist Church	Philander Smith College	Arkansas	1877
Freedmen's Aid Society of the Methodist Church	Rust College	Mississippi	1866
Freedmen's Aid Society of the Methodist Church	Wiley College	Texas	1873
American Baptist Home Mission Society	Benedict College	South Carolina	1870
American Baptist Home Mission Society	Bishop College	Texas	1881
American Baptist Home Mission Society	Morehouse College	Georgia	1867
American Baptist Home Mission Society	Shaw University	North Carolina	1865
American Baptist Home Mission Society	Spelman College	Georgia	1881
American Baptist Home Mission Society	Virginia Union	Virginia	1865
Presbyterians Board of Missions	Johnson C. Smith	North Carolina	1867
Presbyterians Board of Missions	Knoxville College	Tennessee	1875
Presbyterians Board of Missions	Stillman College	Alabama	1875
Nondenominational Institutions	Clark Atlanta University *Atlanta University (original name)	Georgia	1867
Nondenominational Institutions	Howard University	Washington, DC	1867
Nondenominational Institutions	Leland University	Louisiana	1870

CHART 4. Colleges Established by Black Denominations

DENOMINATION	NAME OF UNIVERSITY	STATE	DATE
African Methodist Episcopal Church	Allen University	South Carolina	1870
African Methodist Episcopal Church	Morris Brown College	Georgia	1881
African Methodist Episcopal Church	Wilberforce University	Ohio	1856
African Methodist Episcopal Church	Paul Quinn University	Texas	1872
African Methodist Episcopal Church	Edward Waters College	Florida	1866
African Methodist Episcopal Church	Kittrell College	North Carolina	1886
African Methodist Episcopal Church	Shorter College	Arkansas	1886
African Methodist Episcopal Church	Livingstone College	North Carolina	1879
Colored Methodist Episcopal Church	Lane College	Tennessee	1882
Colored Methodist Episcopal Church	Paine College	Alabama	1882
Colored Methodist Episcopal Church	Texas College	Texas	1894
Colored Methodist Episcopal Church	Miles College	Alabama	1898
Black Baptist	Arkansas Baptist College	Arkansas	1884
Black Baptist	Selma University	Alabama	1878
Black Baptist	Virginia University of Lynchburg (formerly known as Virginia College and Seminary)	Virginia	1890

CHART 5. Nineteen Historically Black Universities and Colleges (HBCUs) with Land-Grant Status under the Morrill Act of 1890

NAME OF UNIVERSITY	CITY/TOWN	STATE
Alabama A&M University	Normal/Huntsville	Alabama
Alcorn State University	Lorman	Mississippi
Central State University	Wilberforce	Ohio
Delaware State University	Dover	Delaware
Florida A&M University	Tallahassee	Florida
Fort Valley State University	Fort Valley	Georgia
Kentucky State University	Frankfort	Kentucky
Langston University	Langston	Oklahoma
Lincoln University	Chester County	Pennsylvania
North Carolina A&T State University	Greensboro	North Carolina
Prairie View A&M University	Prairie View	Texas
South Carolina State University	Orangeburg	South Carolina
Southern University System	Baton Rouge	Louisiana
Tennessee State University	Nashville	Tennessee
Tuskegee University	Tuskegee	Alabama
University of Arkansas Pine Bluff	Pine Bluff	Arkansas
University of Maryland Eastern Shore	Princess Anne	Maryland
Virginia State University	Ettrick	Virginia
West Virginia State University	Institute	West Virginia

land-grant colleges. These agents made sure that they didn't "stray from the gospel of vocationalism." Wolters noted that the paternalistic white northern foundations as well as the federal largesse "altered the course of the Black colleges and initiated a second, vocational phase for Black public colleges."[18] These institutions were overwhelmingly normal schools that focused upon training teachers. They primarily enrolled women, and most did not reach collegiate status until the 1930s and 1940s. In addition to the nineteen land-grant colleges (chart 5), seven former Black-founded institutions became state schools. There were two that were major industrial schools. Samuel Chapman Armstrong founded Hampton Normal and Industrial Institute in Virginia in 1868. He was a white son of missionaries and with the assistance from the AMA, Tuskegee Institute in Alabama was founded in 1881 by the well-known Hampton graduate, Booker T. Washington. Hampton emphasized moral and character development, as well as teacher and industrial training. All students at Hampton had to work at the school. In 1881, Washington established Tuskegee Institute in rural Alabama based on the Hampton model. Black students (all students) also worked at the abolitionist college Berea discussed in chapter two. Students working their way through college were not unique to Hampton. At the school, Washington emphasized industrial education and conservative politics, and the requirement that all students work was also a component of their education.

Du Bois, in his 1910 study entitled, *The College-Bred Negro*, noted that there were only eleven HBCUs that were considered of "first grade" based on the number of college-level classes and graduates (chart 6, p. 143). As noted, the female Spelman College was always within the top level of Black colleges.[19] The diversity of these institutions resulted in vastly different experiences with curricular and extra-curricular exposure and opportunities for their students.

Institutional Diversity Among Black Women at HBCUs

Because African American women were overwhelmingly enrolled in state normal schools that were not of collegiate level, only 22 of the 156 college-level graduates of HBCUs were women by 1900. Black women attended these institutions because they prepared them to become teachers, which were in great demand. Also, these schools were not of high academic standards and they were accessible to attend. Since these institutions do not have the archives of the major HBCUs such as Howard, Fisk, Tuskegee, etc., most of the reflections of these institutions are from oral histories and Black educational publications and newspapers. By 1910, the percentage of Black college-level graduates at HBCUs who were women was a low 17.3 percent compared to 82.7 percent who were men. According to a 1916 survey of Black college students, 92 percent of all Black normal school graduates were women. However, regardless of the type of institution, Black women overwhelmingly became teachers due to need and limited career options. There was a desperate need for teachers throughout the South. Fanny Jackson, who headed the Institute for Colored Youth in Philadelphia from 1869 to 1913, noted that many of her students in the school's normal department left prior to graduation for positions in the South because the demand was so great.[20] This was indeed the case for the early Black women students who attended Hunter College in New York City in the last decades of the nineteenth century.

The difference between normal school graduates and college graduates was curricula and future graduate school opportunities. Those students who were not graduates of accredited institutions were unable to transfer to a baccalaureate degree institution or matriculate for a graduate degree without taking additional collegiate level courses. However, in the earliest years of these institutions, producing as many teachers as possible to staff the growing need was paramount.

The collegiate experiences and curricular opportunities for Black women at HBCUs depended upon their backgrounds and what type of institutions they attended. As DuBois' study indicated, Howard and Fisk were by far the most academically competitive among the HBCUs initially. And, this book will discuss women's experiences as students and faculty at these two institutions. Among HBCUs, these two institutions were the first to receive accreditation and were in a class by themselves. The AMA founded Fisk University in 1865 in Nashville, Tennessee. Students took Latin, Greek, mathematics, French, German, world history, astronomy, and other liberal arts classes. In 1930, it became the first Black college accredited by the Southern Association of Colleges and Secondary Schools, making it the premier liberal arts college among HBCUs.

Howard University was founded in 1867 in Washington, DC, by the Freedmen's Bureau with funding from the United States Congress. It was chartered as a private, non-sectarian national university. It was accredited in 1921 by the Middle Atlantic Accreditation Association. It had full university status and boasted ten schools and colleges and, by 1925, enrolled over two thousand college-level students and employed more than 150 professors. It included Schools of Law, Medicine, Dentistry, Pharmacy, Liberal Arts, Fine Arts, Education, Home Economics, Social Work, and Engineering. The university attracted the most highly educated Black scholars in the country.[21] For both institutions, Black women graduates were the most competitive for graduate and professional schools' admissions along with those from the aforementioned predominately white institutions because of their strong liberal arts backgrounds. Decades later, Black women graduates of the private all-female Spelman College would also be very competitive for admissions to top graduate and professional schools as well.

Black women from rural areas (which was the majority) suffered the most in limited educational options due to the lack of high schools. Oral histories of Black women provide insight into the importance their parents placed on education.

For example, Dr. Frankie V. Adams, born in 1902 in rural Kentucky on a farm near Danville, noted her family sent her to board with a woman near Danville, where she could obtain an education in a one-room elementary schoolhouse. She was the youngest of eight children. They subsequently had her live with a prominent Black physician in Danville who had three daughters, one of whom attended Spelman Seminary. Adams's parents were determined that she would get as much education as possible. After completing elementary school in Danville, she went to Knoxville College in Tennessee to attend their high school. She spent eight years there in both high school and college. Adams became active in the Young Women's Christian Association (YWCA) during her college years.[22]

Similarly, Dr. Gladys Forde, born in 1920 in Arkadelphia, Arkansas, and a 1940 graduate of Spelman College, noted her mother Adelaide Fullmighter Forde, who was born in 1895 in Hot Springs, Arkansas, was sent to Spelman Seminary by her parents in seventh grade due to the lack of schools in her rural area. She graduated in 1915. Forde was fortunate to have two college educated parents (her father was a physician). She and her sister, Dorothy, who was a year ahead of her, followed her mother and attended Spelman College. Her sister subsequently attended Meharry Medical School in Nashville, Tennessee, a Black medical school, and became a doctor. However, Forde stated she wanted to attend Fisk since that's where her friends were attending. On this topic, she said, "there was no question in her mother's house, where we [she and her sister] were going." Spelman was it.[23]

These stories are repeated many times by Black women students who grew up in the rural South prior to World War II. Dr. Forde taught at Bennett College in North Carolina in her early career and subsequently earned graduate degrees from the University of Michigan and Carnegie Mellon University. She taught for forty-one years at Fisk University as Professor of Dramatics and Speech.[24] She recalled her experiences as a student at Spelman College, a graduate student, and then a faculty member at various HBCUs. She was a piano major in the music department at Spelman and noted there was a daily required morning chapel, which was common on most campuses, particularly the private HBCUs. She recalled the rules being very strict and that all of the women students were afraid of the dean of students, Ms. Lyons. Forde recalled lights were to be out at 10 p.m. in the dormitory and students were expected to be quiet afterward.

Forde continued on to graduate school after Spelman at the University of Michigan starting in 1940. She lived in what she referred to as the "B" house—an off-campus house for Black women students since they couldn't live on campus. She earned a master's degree in speech and theater and was hired at Bennett College to teach those subjects. She recalled she was also in charge of a weekly radio program and the college's weekly prayer meeting. She was responsible for getting speakers and picking the topics. Forde said President David Jones kept adding more and more duties to her position. She said because this was during World War II, and there was an Army Specialized Training Program at the neighboring state North Carolina A&T, she was asked to establish and run a USO on Bennett's campus. Forde refused to do it and said it was just too much work. She noted this was before she had any knowledge of the American Association of University Professor guidelines about class limits, faculty rights, and rules. However, it's unlikely that it would have mattered because most faculty members at HBCUs had heavy teaching loads and many other duties as well. Forde resigned and went to the University of Iowa to attend summer school. She said while at Iowa, she received a letter offering her a job to teach at Fisk. Unlike white women who often had difficulty obtaining faculty positions in coeducation institutions (except in female dominated fields), African American women (and also the men) with advanced degrees were highly sought after on the faculties of HBCUs. Forde commented that not many Black academics had master's degrees at that point, not to mention PhDs. While on the faculty, she earned a PhD in dramatics and speech from Carnegie Tech (later Carnegie Mellon) University.[25]

Dr. Mildred Barksdale was born in rural east central Mississippi on a farm in the early 1920s in Kentwood County. Her parents sent her away as a young preteen to live with an elderly woman in Meridian, approximately fifteen miles from her home, to attend school. She stated there were no opportunities for education near her home, and she also recalled a dramatic shortage of teachers and that normal institutes were established to quickly have people licensed to teach. Barksdale recalled that a person could earn a teacher's license with a six-week course. She said the quality of preparation for teachers was so poor where she lived that she never had a teacher who had a high school diploma until she was in the eighth grade and had moved to Meridian. After finishing high school, she enrolled in Jackson College in Jackson, Mississippi, in 1940, the first year that the school went from being a Baptist College established by African Americans to a state school. She said Jackson College's primary mission was to train rural elementary school teachers. When she enrolled as a first-year student, the college had only one year, and each year she was there, they added another year until it became a four-year institution by the time she graduated in 1945. Barksdale said while the school was academically weak, she enjoyed being there and having the opportunity to learn. She later earned a PhD in educational psychology from Indiana University. As discussed later, Barksdale had difficulty getting into graduate school without repeating undergraduate classes like all students from unaccredited teacher training institutions. Yet, she knew she wanted an advanced degree. She was accepted to Indiana University in 1950 as a conditional admit for one semester for a master's program. Barksdale was successful in earning her degree and began a career as a college professor at various HBCUs, including Atlanta University and North Carolina Central in Durham, North Carolina. She eventually earned a PhD from Indiana in 1960. She noted she worked her way through graduate school and said Indiana never gave her a penny of financial aid. As a result, Dr. Barksdale lamented that she earned her doctorate at age 37, instead of age 25, because she was self-supporting and funded her own education.[26]

Howard University, Fisk University, and Tuskegee Institute and Women Students

Howard, Fisk, and Tuskegee represent the diverse experiences of Blacks on HBCU campuses. Howard and Fisk were considered the top academic HBCUs—the first two Black institutions to receive academic accreditation. Both were in cities, Washington, DC, and Nashville, Tennessee. Tuskegee was for years an institution that focused on vocational training and was in rural Alabama. The curriculum, location, and leadership of these institutions impacted the experiences and opportunities of Black women students. The women discussed below provide some perspective on these institutions.

Frances Mary Albrier was born in 1898 in Mount Vernon, New York, but raised in Tuskegee, Alabama, from the age of three due to her mother's death. Her oral history provides insight into three major, but different, HBCUs—Tuskegee Institute, Fisk, and Howard University. She and her sister were sent South to be raised by her paternal grandmother. Frances was fortunate to have an educational institution where she resided. She attended elementary and secondary school on the campus of Tuskegee Institute from 1904 until 1916. Like Hampton Institute, students at Tuskegee had to work as well as attend class. According to historian James Anderson, students at Tuskegee were required to work ten hours a day, six days a week, eleven months out of the year as domestic servants, mill hands, or in the fields as farm laborers. Female students received less training than the male students and were required to sew, wash, iron, scrub, and mend.[27] Albrier confirmed this and recalled that in high school students went to class only three days a week and worked the other days including Saturday. She said that Tuskegee only offered the lower levels of math and science and that trades were emphasized. When she went to Fisk for college in 1916, she discovered she didn't have the requisite preparation in science and math for a degree in nursing. After her first semester at Fisk, she transferred to Howard University. She remembered Howard as being very social-class oriented and not like her experiences at Tuskegee or Fisk, where the campuses were smaller and had a sense of community and students felt a part of a family. The faculties at both Tuskegee and Fisk lived on campus among the students and this was not the case at Howard. Albrier stated she disliked the elitism of Howard and felt lonesome there. There were few students from the deep or rural South. She recalled many relationships were based on the prominence and wealth of a student's family. Albrier also felt a clash in values and upbringing. Coming from conservative Tuskegee, she said she admired Booker T. Washington's philosophy of vocational training because it helped Blacks find jobs. She said at Howard, the emphasis was on going into the professions instead of the vocations. Albrier recalled at Howard, women students were encouraged to go into medicine, law, and to become professors. While many would view this as progressive and an example of encouraging Black women not to be pigeonholed into stereotypical careers, to Albrier, this was alien to her background. She believed this type of encouragement and advice to women was not practical. In these professions, she said women would have to be twice as good as a man and they would also face the reality of racism. She noted her objective was to "help her race" and believed Black women's education should help them be better mothers and help raise the standards of their communities and work to help and inspire youth. Still burdened by not having a solid background in science and math, she wasn't able to major in nursing at Howard. Albrier attended Howard during World War I beginning in 1917 and earned a BA in social work in 1920. While she could not pursue nursing, social work was a field she could use to serve her community and race.[28]

Catherine Duncan, who was born three years after Albrier in 1901, grew up in Tuskegee and attended both Tuskegee and Fisk as well. Duncan moved to Tuskegee when she was one year old. Her father was a civil engineer and hired to teach at the school. Duncan said her father was the only civil engineer in the county. He was a graduate of Fisk University, and from childhood, she and her siblings knew that they would attend Fisk, like Gladys Forde, noted earlier, who stated she and her sister were destined to go to Spelman since that was the alma mater of their mother. Educated Black parents produced legacies for these institutions. Duncan stated, while she respected Booker T. Washington and his "dignity of labor" ethos, students at Tuskegee worked hard and only had classes three days a week—as Albrier had noted. All female students were required to make their commencement dresses and hats. She finished high school at Tuskegee in 1917, and as planned, attended Fisk University. Because her secondary education was at Tuskegee where students took classes three days a week and were required to work three days a week learning a trade, Fisk viewed education at Tuskegee "inadequate" and required her to study an extra year. After five years at Fisk, she graduated in 1922. Duncan worked as a teacher of home economics in various high schools in Kentucky, Georgia, at the high school of Southern University in Baton Rouge, Louisiana, and later at Fort Valley State in Georgia where she worked with teachers and became an expert in rural schools.[29]

As noted earlier, Howard was the preeminent Black university, and it attracted the most highly educated Black scholars of the era to the faculty. It also was the birthplace of the first Black sororities—Alpha Kappa Alpha was founded in 1908 and Delta Sigma Theta was founded in 1914. The university attracted many middle- and upper-class students. And, as Albrier noted, there were women faculty and students not only in the College of Arts and Sciences but also in the medical school. The institution produced extraordinary male and female students who continued in professional and graduate programs. And as will be discussed in depth later, women at Howard were found in many of the professional schools of law, medicine, dentistry, pharmacy, as well as the traditional schools of arts and sciences, home economics, social work, and education.

Views of one's college experiences were often based on one's socioeconomic and geographical background. Dr. Thelma Bando, who was born in 1919 in a middle-class family in Philadelphia, attended Howard during the 1930s. The daughter of a physician, her early educational experience, as well as her perception of Howard was vastly different from Albrier's. Bando said all of her teachers were white teachers for her K-12 education in Philadelphia. One of her neighbor's daughters went to Howard and would come home on holidays and boast about how wonderful the university was. Hence, she decided to attend Howard. This was her first experience having Black faculty members. When Bando was at Howard, she was mentored by Lucy Diggs Slowe, the first Black woman dean at Howard and a pioneer in the field of Black women's student personnel. Women's student personnel was a new and growing field, and Slowe was at the forefront of the field. Slowe was one of the founders of Alpha Kappa Alpha, and Bando pledged AKA while at Howard. Bando described the university as "very sophisticated" compared to other HBCUs. Howard had students from all over the United States and the Caribbean islands. She did note that the university attracted many middle-class students. Although Bando attended Howard a decade and a half later than Albrier, she also noted the social class distinctions among students. She said middle-class students looked down upon students who worked their way through Howard. She commented, "working students at Howard were in a different category."[30] Issues of social class distinctions will be revisited when we discuss campus climates and the role of deans of women.

Fisk and Howard were founded one year apart. White organizations founded both institutions—the AMA and the Freedmen's Bureau—with funding from the United States government; both were headed in their early histories by white presidents with predominantly white faculties. African American men always headed Tuskegee Institute with an overwhelmingly Black faculty and staff. While Black women were hired on the faculties of all of these institutions, when Howard and Fisk hired Black presidents—Mordecai Johnson at Howard in 1926 and Charles S. Johnson at Fisk twenty years later in 1946 (no relation)—with their appointments, the number of Black women faculty increased dramatically. Both schools hired leading Black women to serve as deans of women and ones who sought to encourage leadership in women students.

Women always had a presence at Howard University. When the university opened in 1867 among the departments established was the normal and preparatory department to prepare students for the desperately needed teachers of Black youth. The graduates of these departments were all females. They were also in the collegiate, medical, theology, and law departments. The first woman to graduate from the collegiate department was Matilda Adams Nichols. She was one of two graduates in the collegiate class of 1874 to earn an AB degree. She was also in the first class of students in the normal and preparatory department in 1867.[31] Josephine Turpin in 1886 and Julia S. Caldwell in 1888 also earned the collegiate degree. Caldwell spent her professional career teaching in the South—at Morris Brown College in Atlanta, and for twenty-five years teaching at Booker T. Washington High School in Dallas, Texas, where she served for ten years as head of the Latin department and subsequently principal of the school. Black women graduated from both the law and medical departments in the nineteenth century as well. Charlotte Ray was the first to earn a law degree in 1872, and other Black women followed throughout the late nineteenth century.

As one can see, not all African American women desired to become teachers. In institutions like Howard, where they had curricular options, they often sought professional degrees, even when society restricted opportunities for women in these fields.[32]

While women were admitted to all of the departments (later "schools") of the university, their treatment in male-dominated fields was often unpleasant. Two women students at the medical school wrote a letter of complaint in 1873

CHART 6. First Grade Colored Colleges (1910)
(Fourteen or more units of entrance requirements and more than twenty students of college rank)

NAME	NUMBER OF STUDENTS
Howard University	238
Fisk University	117
Atlanta University	78
Wiley College	50
Leland (Dillard)	43
Virginia Union	36
Clark	35
Knoxville University	29
Spelman University	27
Claflin University	23
Atlanta Baptist University (Morehouse)	22

From Dill, Augustus Granville and Du Bois, W. E. B. *The College-Bred Negro American*. (Atlanta, GA: Atlanta University Press, 1910).

of their negative treatment by male classmates, a faculty member, and another employee of the department. As a result, the Howard Medical School Alumni Association passed a resolution against discrimination against women and asked that the Secretary of the Medical faculty read it to the students of the medical department.[33] The issue of sexism at Howard in the professional schools, as well as on the faculty, emerged repeatedly throughout the decades.

Pauli Murray, mentioned earlier, attended Howard Law School from 1941–44. She recalled the sexism she experienced as a student. Murray noted because she had attended a women's college, she was accustomed to seeing women in prominent professional and leadership positions. Howard Law School was different. It was the leading law school in the nation to prepare for civil rights and had on its faculty the men who won landmark Supreme Court victories in this area in the 1940s and 1950s. Murray stated many of the briefs for these cases were done in the Howard Law library with talented law students working with their professors. Excited to work in this field, she was not prepared for her treatment as a woman. She was the only woman in her class; even if she raised her hand, she was seldom called upon to speak. The school had a male legal fraternity and held smokers that she was excluded from.[34]

Murray reflected on this experience in her autobiography:

> Ironically, if Howard Law School equipped me for effective struggle against Jim Crow, it was also the place where I first became conscious of the twin evil of discriminatory sex bias, which I quickly labeled Jane Crow. In my preoccupation with the brutalities of racism, I had failed until now to recognize the subtler, more ambiguous expressions of sexism . . . Now, however the racial factor was removed in the intimate environment of a Negro law school dominated by men, and the factor of gender was fully exposed.[35]

Prior to that time, most of the faculty were white men, and occasionally, Black men. Rayford Logan, in his history of Howard, noted that there were three women on the faculty of the normal department, although their race was not given. The first known Black woman faculty member noted by Logan was Harriett Shadd who taught English for one year, 1905–6, when she left to teach at the renowned M Street high school (later Dunbar High School) until 1923. In the early years of Howard, women faculty and students' needs were not a consideration. In 1913, the then President Stephen Newman recommended to the board that, "any female teacher who thereafter married while teaching at the university would be considered as having resigned in her position." Hence, only single women could serve on the faculty of Howard. In addition, Newman rejected a petition from thirty-three women students that he should hire a dean of women for their general supervision.[36] This request was sent to him each year throughout his presidency, and he rejected it each year.

CHAPTER 6

The Emergence of the Deans of Women at HBCUs

Lucy Diggs Slowe—The First Black Woman Dean

When a new president, J. Stanley Durkee, was appointed at Howard in 1918, he approached Lucy Diggs Slowe, a Howard alumna and offered her the position of Dean of Women in 1922. This appointment was not only significant for Black women at Howard, but for Black women and higher education in the nation. Slowe was from Baltimore, Maryland, and had attended Howard on a full scholarship. She was an older student who graduated from high school at twenty-one and completed Howard at age twenty-five in 1908. During the years at Howard, because she was older, Slowe was employed to chaperone women students to shop and for other activities. Prior to coming to Howard in 1922, she was principal of a junior high school in Baltimore. Slowe graduated at the top of her class at Howard and was a staunch and outspoken feminist. She established a tradition of outspoken women at Howard on behalf of gender equity for the women on campus and society in general. She carefully negotiated the conditions of her position. She requested faculty status of full professor, a full-time clerk to work solely for her, a suite of rooms for her office, that she NOT be required to live on campus (which was the norm for deans of women), and all women charged with working with women students (dorm directors, etc.) report directly to her and all policies pertaining to women at the university would come out of her office with the approval of the president. She asked for a salary of $4,000. She was extremely savvy and throughout her life demanded that women be treated with the same respect and salary as men. Everything was approved except the salary and the faculty rank. She was offered the rank of Associate Professor of English. She compromised and stated she requested a salary of $3,500 and would accept nothing less than $3,200.[1] Her outspokenness and directness for what she expected to accept the position was amazing. She stated when considering moving to a new position, "opportunity for financial advancement and for larger service" were her primary considerations. These

FIGURE 17. Lucy Diggs Slowe, first woman dean at Howard University, 1930. Moorland-Spingarn Research Center, Howard University.

comments were instructive because so many Black women, who were hired to teach or work at HBCUs or other Black institutions or organizations, were reluctant to mention money since being of service was their primary concern. Money was indeed important to these women; however, it was a topic that they often felt that they should not bring up since it would tend to negate their devotion to the work that needed to be done on behalf of the race. Slowe had succeeded in becoming the first Black woman dean at the top HBCU in the country. With this appointment, she became the model in which other deans of women at HBCUs were established; she created an organization of deans of Black colleges, and tried to be a voice for Black women in HBCUs throughout the country. During the years of Durkee's presidency, Howard's last white president, Slowe maintained a cordial relationship with him.

Among HBCUs, Howard was perceived as more liberal in student freedoms than others (although as we shall see, this is all relative when it comes to rules for women students). The year that Slowe was appointed, compulsory chapel was discontinued after students protested the expulsion of several students who had exceeded the eight absences allowed. Learning of the expulsion, more than seventy male students in architecture and engineering threatened to withdraw from the university if this requirement was continued. The students prevailed, and from that point on chapel attendance was voluntary and students were free to worship at churches off campus if they wished. Since faculty members were also expected to attend daily chapel, this change liberated them as well.[2]

Howard was unique in not having to rely on missionary funding like most of the earliest HBCUs that emphasized religion and conservative values. Hence, women students did not have dress requirement restrictions or required study hours that were the norm at most other institutions, particularly religiously founded ones. Students at Howard had a vibrant social life. By the 1920s, there were seven Greek letter organizations that sponsored many events. There were strong sports teams and a classic Thanksgiving football game between Howard and all-male Lincoln University (Pennsylvania) that drew a large crowd.[3] There was a brand-new movie theater, the Lincoln Theater, that opened in 1922 close to campus. In addition, there was the Lincoln Colonnade behind the theater that held public events. Slowe arrived at Howard during the Roaring Twenties when there were various halls that had the "battle of the bands" and dances. The Charleston, the Black bottom, and the shimmy were all popular, and noted performers like Bessie Smith and other blues singers performed locally.[4] Students during the '20s were outspoken and defiant. In addition, this was the era of the Harlem Renaissance where both literature and music were more provocative and unapologetically Black. An article in the student newspaper, the *Hilltop* in 1925, noted the "typical" Howard student spent their time, "theater-going, card-playing, [attending] dances, and all night parties."[5] The campus was not all play for the students but offered them significant academic experiences. There were two student publications: the student newspaper (the *Hilltop*) and the monthly *Journal*. There was a debating team and a vibrant student council. There was a literary magazine, the *Stylus*, a renowned theater company, The Howard Players, and numerous musical organizations, and as mentioned earlier, many athletic teams. The institution had a renowned and world-class faculty including Alain Locke, the first Black Rhodes scholar. It was indeed the "capstone" of Black higher education. Students had a lot of agency on campus through these groups. This was the campus climate Slowe entered when she arrived in 1922.

Slowe established a presence on the campus immediately. In addition, she traveled to visit alumni clubs across the country. As would be the case with Black women professionals—how they dressed and presented themselves were noted and commented upon. Her style of dress was described as unassuming and elegant in style and quality with her hair pulled back in a bun. When she spoke to the Cleveland Alumnae club in 1929, a newspaper article of the visit noted that she was "very attractive, wearing a Black velvet dress with V line collar of ecru lace—a large ecru flower on the left shoulder, a large Black velvet hat with the brim caught back with a fold flower and pull well down over the eyes, Black slippers and gunmetal hose completed the costume." Looking poised and elegant was a signature feature of Slowe and her women students. She was said to never have left campus without a hat.[6]

The campus greeted Slowe cordially and the *Howard Record,* a monthly publication of the faculty and students, noted that Slowe would bring culture and refinement to the college women. Her goal was to shape the "New Howard Woman." As more institutions hired deans of women or women to oversee the growing number of college women who were living on campuses, the women appointed were often not trained in student personnel but simply more like a matron. Slowe viewed herself as a student personnel professional and joined the all-white National Association of Deans of Women so that she could learn the best practices in the field. This organization also afforded her the opportunity to network with leading women in the field. In addition, Slowe wanted Black women college students to be exposed to and benefit from the growing literature and research on college women. She also wanted the women students at Howard to be self-confident and ambitious. By the 1920s, white women were attending college in growing numbers; by this decade, they comprised 47 percent of the country's undergraduate population.[7] African American women were also attending college in greater numbers and their photos and accomplishments were celebrated in *The Crisis* magazine and Black newspapers. By the 1940s, the number of Black women in college exceeded those of Black men. However, the women were overwhelmingly in land-grant colleges and preparing to be teachers.

As a result of growth in coeducation, these institutions began hiring deans of women to handle issues for the women students, such as housing, self-government, etiquette training, leadership training, and intercollegiate athletics. The first dean of women in the country was Alice Freeman Palmer who was appointed into this position in 1892 at the University of Chicago. Palmer was an 1876 graduate of the University of Michigan and former president of Wellesley College. With the growth of such positions in higher education, Teacher's College (TC) at Columbia University established a graduate program to train deans of women in 1916.[8]

Slowe enrolled in the program at TC and studied student personnel courses in the summers of 1930 and 1931. She was also admitted into their doctoral program in student personnel administration. As a result of this training, Slowe became *the* authority and leading Black woman dean of women in the country. She sought to merge theory with practice. Slowe established a mentor's program and trained seniors to work in student affairs. This program was based on a similar one at one of the leading programs at University of Pittsburgh. Her emphasis was on women's student leadership and self-governance. Slowe noted that for a Howard woman student, being selected as a mentor was the "the highest honor that is given to a woman student during her senior year and was a coveted honor." Each spring sophomores and senior women students voted on the students they believed worthy of these positions. The mentors were selected based on specific criteria, and Slowe said in most instances, she felt the choices were sound. The mentors were assigned books to read over the summer and provided counseling on the attributes of a good advisor and mentor. Each mentor was assigned four or five first-year women students to mentor. The school year started with a Greek-like ceremony of the mentees' hands being placed in those of their mentors.[9]

This program mirrored that of the philosophy of the early and leading programs of deans of women in white institutions that developed at coeducational institutions from 1890 through 1945.[10] Numerous Slowe students who participated in this program became prominent deans of women and reflected on their experiences with her. Hilda Davis, from Washington, DC, who attended Howard on a full scholarship, was a sophomore when Slowe arrived as dean and was one of the first students selected as a mentor. Davis, an English and Latin major, exhibited the type of leadership that Slowe encouraged and sought in Black women students. Davis was class secretary for several years; served on the student council; was a member of the editorial staff of the student newspaper; and served as treasurer, and later president, of the Delta Sigma Theta chapter at Howard; and was a member of the Kappa Mu Honor Society. Davis graduated in 1925 and began an illustrious career in student affairs serving as dean of women at numerous Black institutions. She earned a master's degree from Radcliffe in 1931 and a PhD from the University of Chicago in 1953.[11]

Another of Slowe's student mentees was Thelma Preyer Bando, mentioned earlier, who also became a prominent student affairs professional and dean of women. Bando was at Howard a decade after Davis and graduated in 1935. Like Davis, Bando was involved in numerous leadership roles on campus. She was a member of Alpha Kappa Alpha, the sorority of which Slowe was a charter member and founder. Bando was the president of the University's YWCA chapter. The YWCA operated the university's snack shop called the Canteen. Bando was responsible for scheduling the women's work hours, opening up on time, ordering the goods and assessing the stock, balancing the financial statements, depositing the money, etc. Slowe was so impressed with Bando's skills that she took her under her wing.[12] Both Davis and Bando recalled that Slowe had the leading white deans of women scholars in the field come to campus to speak to the women students, and they escorted them around campus during their stay. They included Esther Lloyd-Jones, Harriet Hayes, and Sarah W. Sturtevant of Teachers College and Thrysa Amos of the University of Pittsburgh.[13] These scholars emphasized that residential housing shouldn't just be places for women students to live but would develop the "total" and "whole" student and develop their leadership abilities. Housing for women students was Slowe's number one priority. When she arrived at Howard, there were not enough dormitory rooms for women, with more than 150 women living off campus. Slowe felt that the university had no control over women if they lived off campus. She was successful in having a "female" campus established when three women's dorms were opened in 1932. Slowe sought to make living on campus mandatory except for the women who were DC residents. Having all women on campus was important in her effort to mold character and develop a sense of community, fellowship, leadership, and independence in the women. Within this women's community, Slowe was able to mold and shape the women's talents and leadership abilities. Her goal was to demonstrate that Black women students could be independent and self-governing. An August 1932 article entitled, "Howard Women Run Themselves in New Dorms" in the Washington newspaper *The Afro-American*, highlighted the unique feature of self-governance of the women's dormitories. The article stated the student's house government association planned all the dormitories.[14]

This was a major accomplishment for Slowe and a philosophy of education that she hoped would be instituted in other HBCUs as they developed. She wrote an article after the opening of the women's campus entitled, "The Dormitory—A Cultural Influence," in which she stated the dormitories were homes and not prisons. She sought to have the women's dorms modeled after Harvard and Yale, where they had a faculty member live with the students called a "master." She established that each director of the residence halls taught one class every day. Slowe's model for women's higher education was that of elite white women. She advocated dining rooms that served food family style instead of cafeterias. She believed cafeterias were not conducive to developing social graces. Meals that were served resulted in the women learning correct place settings and other aspects of formal dining.

Slowe was far ahead of her time in advocating the development of Black women students' leadership and advocated more respect for Black women students. For example, she had the name of the "Discipline Committee" in the residence halls of the women changed to "house government association" to erase the punitive sound of the committee. "Chaperones" were now referred to as "mentors." Despite these changes, both former mentees Davis and Bando recalled that while students respected Slowe, they thought she was very strict. All Black campuses kept a strict accounting of the women students with sign-out and sign-in sheets when they left and returned from their dormitories. And they had to have permission to leave campus. Bando recalled that riding in a car with someone without permission was a "sending home offense." She said students who were from DC and wanted to invite a classmate to their homes had to seek permission from Slowe's office, and she would determine whether that person could ride in a car with the host. Bando stated that one of her mother's good friends from Philadelphia was living in DC while she was a student at Howard. The woman's husband taught on the faculty of Howard's Medical School. Bando said this couple had known her since she was a child, and they used to live a few doors from her parents when she was growing up. While at Howard, they invited her to their home to have dinner with them on Friday evenings. She said Dean Slowe knew the faculty member but still had to officially clear him each week to drive Bando to his home when he got out of class. Slowe made no exception for her: the rules were the rules. In retrospect, Bando stated, the institution was "really looking out for your [the student's] safety," and indeed this was the 1930s, and Slowe didn't want to show favoritism.[15]

Bando noted other rules. Women students were not allowed to date any of the men who worked on the campus in servant positions—like cooks, custodians, etc. She said there were a lot of young men who worked at Howard who were the same age as the students and often attempted to date the women students. She said it was a "sending home offense" if Howard women dated any of these men. While such a rule in today's eyes is seen as unreal and a complete infringement on a women's personal life, Bando said that Slowe felt that Howard women should have higher standards in men than to date servants. In discussing this view with both Davis and Bando—looking back at that period in history at Howard, they both stated that there was such pressure on women to find husbands and to be married, Slowe was concerned that these women would date anyone. Davis said Slowe wanted Howard women to select men "on their level"—meaning their educational and intellectual equal. Davis noted it was often difficult for highly educated Black women to find mates; as a result, many women would drop out of college if they had the opportunity to marry. Bando pointed out that because of the many professional and graduate programs, in addition to the undergraduate college, men significantly outnumbered the women at Howard during this period. This exacerbated the overprotective nature Slowe had over the women. But this constant policing of women was the norm at every HBCU. Male students were not required to report their whereabouts or have permission to leave campus or to ride in cars. Women educators and activists of Slowe's generation believed the morality of the race depended upon the behavior of the women.[16] She told the women: "Each Howard woman should remember that on entrance to Howard . . . she becomes subject to the ideals of the University . . . Women set the standards. . . . Our aim here at Howard is to set for ourselves high standards and through our own conduct to impress these standards on others."[17]

Bando recalled that students were required to change their clothes for dinner, and women students often changed their clothes multiple times during the day. She said Slowe informed them that well-bred people never had dinner in the same clothes they had on all day. In the aforementioned student newspaper article on the typical Howard student, it indicated that because women were required to change clothes so often and participate in a myriad of events that "no girl should think of coming to Howard without a wardrobe costing $455 at a minimum."[18] Bando stated that Howard was a training school for social etiquette for its students. The women students sponsored teas at 4 p.m. on Sunday, and they could invite a guest. They were taught how to serve tea and fancy finger foods. Bando also stated the women students "were supposed to be dressed appropriately in pretty afternoon dresses." She said this was important because when Howard students went downtown to shop, they had to wear hats and gloves. The rationale for this dress requirement was the belief that they would be treated with respect because of their respectable and middle-class presentation. In other words, being dressed in a certain manner would afford you a level of respect as a Black person that other Blacks would not receive. These beliefs and the social orientation were drilled into these women that Bando said were being trained for "finer womanhood." Bando stated that Howard did have a severe social class orientation and bias. She often used the term "sophisticated" to describe the students. She said there was an air about the students that set them apart from those at other HBCUs. She recalled a female classmate wearing white knit gloves to class. She said this student "used to wear the most beautiful white knit gloves and wrote her notes with them on. Well today, that to me seems very silly, but at Howard, nobody took exception to that. I mean it was just a normal style of dress."[19]

This was the era of the "New" woman—a phrase that educated white women coined that stressed women's personal development and independence. Slowe wanted to prepare Black women students for the "modern" world, a term also in great use by white women educators and feminists of the period.[20] Although there had been a history of African American women who were independent and personally developed, Slowe brought this philosophy to Howard as if it were a new concept. While she was very progressive in counseling Black women students to seek leadership positions and not be pigeonholed into stereotypical positions as schoolteachers and other traditional female positions, she was extremely Victorian in her views regarding decorum, how one presented oneself, and moral issues. She had a virtual obsession over Black women carrying themselves in what she viewed as a dignified manner.

In her first few months as dean at Howard, she expelled multiple women students. One expelled student she described as "insolent" to a dorm matron (Slowe said it was the student's third offense). The student council protested Slowe's decision. This group was established in 1920 prior to Slowe's arrival, and as noted earlier, students had agency on campus and felt comfortable and within their rights to challenge administrative decisions. The Academic Council—composed of the president, vice-president, academic deans, and registrar—supported her decision and gave her full authority to determine who should be suspended or expelled. Her decision prevailed. Slowe opposed women students participating in pep rallies because she believed their cheering was loud and amounted to "yelling" and was not ladylike. The students were rarely afraid to challenge her views, protested, and wrote in the *Hilltop*: "The opinion of the Dean of Women is wholly illogical and without basis. Because women's voices are naturally high pitched and weaker than those of men, there is no reason why a larger proportion of our women students who love their Alma Mater, should not prove their love as best they can."[21] Ignoring Slowe, the women at Howard continued to "yell" at sports events.

There were many other rules that another one of her former mentees from the 1920s noted were numerous and "silly." Slowe was concerned when she arrived at Howard that women students spent most of their leisure time attending movies and dances with live bands off campus. She wanted them to have what she viewed as more intellectual and elevated social events. However, as noted, this was not the period for such events. For example, in 1924, during the holiday season, Slowe attended a fundraiser for the Phyllis Wheatley YWCA, which was the prominent Black Y in DC. The program was a cabaret that was held at the Lincoln Theater near Howard. The event included a couple of dance routines, one was an Apache dance, the other was a Hula (Hawaiian) dance, a child sang a ragtime song, and there was a comedian that told sexually suggestive jokes. Slowe was outraged at the event, particularly since teachers and other supposedly educated people sponsored it. She wrote a letter of protest to the executive secretary of the YWCA contacted the Assistant Superintendent of the DC Public Schools as well, because there were teachers who were participants in the programming. He responded that his office had nothing to do with what the teachers did outside of the schools. This response incensed Slowe even more, and she started a crusade to expose what she believed was an indecent program that involved public school teachers. The Black newspapers in DC and also the *Chicago Defender* ran articles on the event and Slowe's letters. The DC paper supported Slowe's concerns and her "aristocratic instincts." However, the *Chicago Defender* was satirical and made fun of the elitist and alarmist nature of Slowe's letter:

> Dean Lucy Slowe of Howard University viewed the cabaret scene and the Hula dancing that she deemed was obscene. The review caused a fluttering among the Washington, DC, society folks and the church people are all eyes and ears regarding the outcome of what is rumored to be a very embarrassing situation as many school teachers took active part in the revue, which was recently given for the benefit of the YWCA.[22]

The above incident provides a vivid example of the depths of Slowe's views on decorum and decency. But she was far from alone—Slowe brought in aforementioned educator Charlotte Hawkins Brown, the principal of Palmer Memorial Institute, an elite private boarding school in Sedalia, North Carolina, to be a keynote speaker to the women at Howard the first year she was dean. Palmer was Slowe's age and a friend. They both held the same prudish and Victorian notions of womanhood. Brown applauded Slowe for her contributions to shaping ideal Negro womanhood not only at Howard but also throughout the country. She referred to the women students at Howard as the "flower of womanhood for a struggling race."[23] Again, in this era, many educated African Americans believed that deportment along with education would reduce racism as well as "advance the race." Historian Evelyn Brooks Higginbotham has written in detail about the "politics of respectability" that was entrenched in the ethos of most "race women" like Slowe and Brown.[24] While they were absolutely devoted to improving race conditions within Black communities and fostering better interracial relationships (for example Palmer was on the National Board of the YWCA and Slowe was active in the white organization of deans of women), their views were steeped in social class biases and Christian beliefs. Higginbotham's work discussed these views from the standpoint of Black Baptist women. Betty Collier Thomas's book, *Jesus, Jobs and Justice: African American Women and Religion* provides an exhaustive study of Black women across religious denominations and their activism and work on behalf of the race.[25] Religion was central to the work they did. Hilda Davis, after she graduated from Howard in 1925, went to work with Brown at Palmer Institute in North Carolina. Founded in 1902, Palmer Institute was still in its infancy. Partially funded by the American Missionary Association, the school had a deeply religious orientation. Davis was hired to teach Latin and English, to be the director of activities for girls (based on the skills she learned from Slowe at Howard), serve as registrar, and help develop the junior college curriculum of the school. She earned $65 a month and room and board. Davis recalled Brown prayed over virtually every issue. All meetings started with prayer, and Brown was very strict with students. Davis worked there for five years before leaving to earn a master's degree at Radcliffe in English, which she earned in 1931.[26]

Among the organizations Slowe was active in was the National Association of College Women (NACW)—an organization of educated Black women liberal arts college graduates founded in 1910 in Washington, DC. Originally named the College Alumnae Club, the group was based loosely on the white Association of Collegiate Alumnae (later the American Association of University Women). Washington, DC, had the largest group of college-educated Black women. Headed by Oberlin graduate, Mary Church Terrell, the group's original purpose was to assist Black school children with reading clubs and other activities, but it transitioned into helping Black high school girls to apply to college. In 1919, they had a scholarship program to provide financial aid to needy Black girls. By 1923, the group had grown to eighty members and became national and changed its name to National Association of College Women. They held their first national conference that year, and with Slowe's historic appointment at Howard, she was elected the first national president of NACW. She made clear the purpose of the organization—it would not be social nor political but focus primarily on raising the standards of the colleges where Black women attended, improve the condition of Black women faculty at HBCUs, encourage advanced scholarship and foreign study abroad. In her address to the body, she told them:

> An important task of the National Association of College Women is that of educational standards to meet those of the very best institutions of our land. If a college accepts women students and employs women faculty, it should give them the same status as it gives male students and male teachers, respectively.[27]

The organization had stringent membership requirements (which later brought charges of elitism and exclusivity). To be considered for membership, one had to be a graduate of an institution recognized by the American Council of Education (ACE) and the American Association of University Women (AAUW). This limited membership to graduates of white institutions, Howard, and Fisk. In defense of this policy, Slowe remarked, "as a first step toward improvement in college standards, the sponsors of this organization have set an educational standard as high as that of the best organizations of college women, and it is their policy to accept as members of this organization graduates of those colleges that live up to the standards of the best educational groups in the United States."[28] The members were very distinguished and were graduates of the Seven Sisters colleges, Oberlin, the University of Chicago, Boston University, University of Pennsylvania, University of Michigan, Western Reserve University, Cornell University, University of Minnesota, Ohio State University, Stanford University, Dickinson College, and Howard and Fisk Universities.

Slowe told the group that they were to be an important part of the leadership of the race, noting "the public has a right to expect higher things for the trained woman than the untrained woman."[29] This view was in keeping with the times that it was the educated elite of the race who would be the leadership and spokesperson for the less educated and poor members of the race. While we are aware today of the massive number of grassroots efforts of Black women who made substantial contributions to racial "uplift," until recently little had been written about them. However, that has changed. The literature on the contributions of the non-elite women of the race has grown. Many organizations existed to aid the Black community and Black women in particular. In fact, the other organization had the same acronym the National Association of Colored Women established in 1896 and had as its first national president

Oberlin College graduate ('84) Mary Church Terrell, one of the founders of the NACW. The National Association of Colored Women included women regardless of their educational backgrounds unlike the NACW. Nineteenth century Black people overwhelmingly believed that it was the duty and obligation of every Black person to contribute to the "uplift" of the race. By the turn of the century, increasingly the belief had changed to one that the "best" would help the rest. In many ways, highly educated African Americans in their zeal to "elevate" the race, replaced the white missionaries who were also condescending in their attitudes toward assisting the newly emancipated enslaved Africans. Nevertheless, to Slowe the membership standards were important to their legitimacy, and she declared, "this organization has set an educational standard as high as that of the best organizations of college women, and it is their policy to accept as members of this organization graduates of those colleges that live to the standards of the best educational groups in the United States."[30]

The members of NACW were all graduates of the most competitive schools in the nation. They had competed with white women—and in many instances, white men as well. They were often the first in many academic fields and categories and graduated with honors. The women graduates of Howard and Fisk with liberal arts degrees were also viewed as highly accomplished. The goal of these women was to make the opportunities of Black women in HBCUs the same as those of the men—whether they were on the faculty or a student. In addition, they were very interested in the academic standards of these institutions. The number of Black women graduates rose throughout the '20s. By 1921, three African American women had earned PhDs. Sadie Tanner Mossell (later Alexander) earned a PhD in economics from the University of Pennsylvania, Eva Dykes earned a PhD from Radcliffe in philology (the study of linguistics and language), and Georgiana Simpson earned a PhD from the University of Chicago in Germanic languages. All graduated from the leading Black public high school in the nation—Dunbar High School in DC. Dunbar produced a who's who of distinguished students who graduated from the top institutions in the country. The undergraduate degrees of these women were the University of Pennsylvania, Howard University, and the University of Chicago. The membership was indeed the crème de la crème of educated Black women.

Upon graduation, all three of these women were offered faculty positions at HBCUs. A PhD was not required for most colleges at that point, and unlike white women who often had significant difficulty finding positions that were not in traditional female fields like education, home economics, etc., this was not the case for Black women with academic credentials. Both Eva Dykes and Georgiana Simpson accepted positions at Howard, and Mossell never became an academic. While it's well known that Howard attracted the leading Black male scholars and intellectuals, it also had the leading Black women academics on its faculty as well. Unable to find a position in economics, Sadie Mossell

Alexander returned to the University of Pennsylvania to law school and earned a JD, becoming the first Black woman to earn a degree from that institution, as well as the first Black woman to pass the Pennsylvania bar. She went into law practice with her husband, Raymond Pace Alexander, whom she married in 1923. Mossell Alexander became the first national president of Delta Sigma Theta Sorority. She was the Vice President of the NACW, and at its first national conference she gave an address on the importance of women in business. She reviewed the role of women in the nation's economic growth since the Industrial Revolution, and noted during World War I, the careers opened up for white women as confidential secretaries, clerks, saleswomen, and buyers at department stores. She said with men going to war, women replaced men as heads of departments, and they gained opportunities on Wall Street and financial establishments at the [Chicago] Loop. She said now that the war was over, there were articles with titles such as "Women on Wall Street to Stay" and "Western Firm Prefers to Keep Women Department Heads."[31] She said [white] women have now entered commerce and business to stay. However, she noted that Black women were handicapped "by the impregnable color line." She said the only positions in industry Black women could find were elevator operators, dishwashers, and in rare instances, operators in hosiery mills in the South. However, she said no executive positions were available to them. However, she noted the successful Black women who were in business all worked in Black-oriented enterprises that were all in the Deep South, primarily in banking and insurance companies. She noted these women were both college-educated and also self-made. In fact, the most successful Black woman in business was the self-made Madame C. J. Walker. She was the first Black woman millionaire who earned her fortune from developing Black hair care products. Born in rural Louisiana after the Emancipation in 1867, she was orphaned by the age of ten, and she worked as a domestic worker until she developed her hair products. Alexander concluded by impressing upon the women of the group that there were growing opportunities for Black women in business, and she presented examples as evidence. She challenged the women that they should encourage "fifty college women to be persuaded to equip themselves with a thorough knowledge of one or more of the business sciences . . . to aid in the economic development of the race, which has gained headway in the South and the Southwest."[32] She admonished the women that she thought Black women in the East were more concerned about social status and events, while Black women in other regions were making a greater contribution to the economic development of the race. She told them "in these parts of the country, opportunities for actual service in freeing the race, burdened by economic oppression are awaiting you, even if a few social privileges are denied." While there were indeed self-made successful businesspeople (both Black and white), Alexander wanted Black women to prepare themselves for the expanding world of business and industry in the country. She said Black women should be trained as stenographers (which was a booming field for white women) and could manage a firm's business. Alexander, like Slowe, wanted to encourage Black women to think broadly about their educational choices and their career outlooks. However, as we shall see, there remained serious limitations to the types of curricula offerings for Black women throughout the South for decades. Most HBCUs prepared Black women to be teachers, a field that most in the race viewed as honorable and important. Well-trained teachers were desperately needed in private elementary and high schools in Black colleges and in rural schools. However, Slowe and the above members viewed steering Black women exclusively into teaching as limiting. In the South, teachers were needed, and jobs were plentiful and respectable, although not well paying.

The NACW was interested in researching Black women's status at HBCUs. In 1916, a study was done on HBCUs by the Phelps-Stokes Fund that suggested most Black colleges should be closed and offer vocational education since only 3 percent of students in these institutions were of college level. By the second national conference in 1924, the group established a committee on standards and made unofficial visits to select HBCUs (ones with at least one hundred students in the collegiate department). They selected the top eleven Black HBCUs—two were all-male colleges, so they were eliminated. Eight of the nine colleges had the requisite one hundred college-level students and had an A, or close to an A, rating from accreditation associations. Howard and Fisk, of course, rose to the top in the study. Howard had 1,029 college students, and more than half of the students at Fisk were in the College department. The committee reported that the high schools in these schools stressed Bible, music, and industrial training at the expense of college preparatory classes. They noted that athletic facilities for women students were meager. They also noted the poor preparation of the faculty at these institutions. Of the nine colleges only sixteen faculty members had a PhD, and eleven of them taught at Howard.[33] While this was not unusual considering this was 1923, graduate degrees among Black people were rare. There were still at this point few public high schools for Blacks in the South—and most HBCUs were private high schools. Again, it has to be underscored that Howard was in a league of its own since their funding came from the federal government. They decided to work first with the nine colleges.

Slowe and the other women members were astute enough to know that as graduates of white and "elite" colleges, and not products of the Deep South, they would have to tread lightly in approaching the male presidents of these institutions. They decided that they should first work informally and try to influence alumni as well as individuals who work within the institutions instead of being accused as outsiders who were imposing their opinions on the administrations of these colleges.

With Slowe at the helm, the organization composed a questionnaire and sent them to the colleges above. The questions were pointed and focused upon the

CHART 7. HBCU with 100+ Students at the Collegiate Level Surveyed by the Committee on Standards, National Association of College Women (1923)

NAME OF UNIVERSITY	STATE
Howard University	Washington, D.C.
Fisk University	Nashville, Tennessee
Wilberforce University	Wilberforce, Ohio
Shaw University	Raleigh, NC
Virginia Union	Richmond, VA
Atlanta University	Atlanta, GA
Wiley College	Marshall, Texas
Talladega College	Talladega, AL

status of women students, faculty, and administrators. This was an extremely important study. It asked boldly: "Does the administration offer the same opportunities to women as men?" They asked for the salaries of women and men in the same positions and the rate of promotions by gender. They also asked whether there was a dean of women on campus. Slowe and the NACW membership believed that a dean of women should be the product of a liberal college education and preferably have faculty status. She stated in her presidential address in 1923: "A Dean of Women of unquestionable character, of thorough intellectual training, and of refined manners should be employed by every coeducational college to centralize and supervise the interests of the women students."[34] The college presidents responded positively to the recommendation to establish deans of women positions; however, most of them interpreted the position as one of a matron or chaperone to oversee the moral behavior of female students. Despite the statements of Slowe's former students about her strictness, her writings expressed the opposite. She was opposed to "chaperones" for women students. In an invited lecture at Teachers College in 1931, Slowe stated: "When a college woman cannot be trusted without a chaperone, she is not likely to develop powers of leadership."[35] Throughout Slowe's tenure as dean and in all of her writings and lectures, her emphases were on Black women in higher education institutions developing leadership skills since Black students in Black communities were told that they were expected to use their education for the good of the race. She wanted Black women to be treated with respect and compensated and advanced professionally the same as men.

During her tenure at Howard, she sought to eradicate what she perceived as demeaning rules. She reported the changes she would make at Howard:

> Rules have been reduced to a minimum and personal honor and responsibility increased to a maximum. The directors and student officers emphasize the fact that every resident has in her keeping the good name of the group

of which she is a part. The development of personal responsibility for good government is a valuable social characteristic both in and out of college; hence much attention is paid to the question of self-government.[36]

In 1926, Howard hired its first African American president, Mordecai Johnson, an ordained Baptist minister. He had traditional and conservative views on the role of women. However, during his presidency, he hired many Black women to the faculty, although they were underpaid and were slow to move up the faculty ranks.[37] His view of how women students should be treated was based on his view of the strident rules that women at Spelman, the women's college across from Morehouse, his alma mater, were treated. By the time Johnson arrived at Howard, Slowe had established herself as an authority on Black women's higher education, and especially, student personnel. She was the head of the major organization on this topic and had leading white women in student personnel and deans as regular visitors at Howard. She wanted Black women students to benefit from the opportunities that white women students at what she deemed the "leading" institutions were afforded. Her liberal and feminist views for women students resulted in her being at odds with Johnson throughout the period she worked with him. She was vocal and opposed what she viewed as the conservative religious indoctrination of Black women. She stated:

> Much of the religious philosophy upon which Negro women have been nurtured has tended toward suppressing in them their own powers. Many of them have been brought up on the antiquated philosophy of Saint Paul in reference to women's place in the scheme of things, and all too frequently have been influenced by the patient waiting, rather than the philosophy of developing their talents to their fullest extent.[38]

These comments did not endear Slowe to Johnson. However, Slowe wasn't the only person who believed the emphasis of religion in most Black colleges was negative. While Howard was the preeminent institution of higher education with a distinguished faculty and a solid liberal arts curriculum, a large number of HBCUs did not. Several faculty members of Howard commented on the emphasis on industrial education and religion in other HBCUs. Sociologist E. Franklin Frazier said, too many HBCUs "provided too much inspiration and not enough information." Another Howard professor agreed and wrote in an article in *The Crisis* magazine, that HBCUs needed "less preaching and more teaching."[39]

Slowe wanted the curriculum of HBCUs to provide fields and courses to prepare Black women for the "modern" world. She believed they needed to have courses in political science, economics, psychology, sociology, and they needed vocational guidance. Slowe often recounted the story of an unnamed Black college president (obviously Mordecai Johnson): when asked to offer more courses in the social sciences for women students, he replied, "He wanted the women of his institution to be trained to be good wives and mothers, therefore, he was not concerned about their taking courses in such 'male subjects' as economics, political science and sociology."[40]

Johnson was appalled by Slowe's liberal views. In addition to her recommendation for curricula changes for Black women students, she said most HBCUs treated the women students as infants. Throughout her years at Howard under Johnson's presidency, they maintained an extremely adversarial relationship.

The Race Issue

In 1929, with the growing number of women appointed to serve as advisors or deans of women at HBCUs, Slowe organized this group. She convened the women at Howard and became the National Association of Women's Deans and Advisors of Colored Schools (NAWDAC). This group began to meet at the same time as NACW since some of the membership overlapped and also because many of the women from NACW were speakers for the newly formed dean's group. In addition to hoping to impact the programs for women students at HBCUs, at the 1928 conference of NACW, there were concerns about the treatment and challenges of Black women on white campuses. Since a large percentage of the membership were graduates of predominantly white institutions, they knew firsthand of the issues, many discussed in the previous chapters. Interracial relations were one of the missions of NACW as well.[41] Most of the membership was involved in some interracial organization—primarily the YWCA, but there were others, and the organization had an interracial committee. The NAACP, the interracial civil rights organization, kept data on the treatment and admission of Black students in white colleges, as these women sought to be included in white professional organizations. They also monitored the treatment of Black women at HBCUs who attempted to participate in white conferences and organizations. While Slowe was a member of the white National Association of the Deans of Women, attending their conferences in places that segregated African Americans was an issue. When the dean of women at Hampton wrote the president of the southern region of the organization, Annie Bailey Cook, at the State Teachers College in Harrisonburg, Virginia, about sending a representative from Hampton to the upcoming regional conference in 1936, she responded:

> Your letter has just reached my desk and I hasten to give you the desired information.
> Although we affiliate with the Negro dean of women in our National Association we cannot afford to do so in our Regional for reasons that I believe you can understand and appreciate—even though you might not approve. We have to trust the good judgment [sic] and the good taste of these deans

in not attending the annual meetings as they are always held at colleges and universities within our southern regions.

I feel sure that your Miss Thomas will understand this for last year when we met at the College of William and Mary she did not try to attend and thereby subject herself, the association, and the college to any embarrassment.

I am indeed glad that you find it possible to attend our meeting at which time I hope to have the pleasure of meeting you and of expressing my great appreciation of the work that you and your coworkers are doing at Hampton Institute.

Since Dean Slowe of Howard University has never attended any of our Regional meetings I feel sure she does not plan to do so this year.

Sincerely, Annie Bailey Cook, President of Regional Association[42]

As noted earlier, Slowe was the first Black member of the NADW—she joined immediately after accepting the position at Howard. As the first Black woman dean in the country at the preeminent HBCU, she understood this organization to be most relevant to the goals she sought in her new position. Her biographer noted that Slowe knew that being the lone Black member—she had to "represent" the race. She wrote: "She [Slowe] had to be punctual, clean, and dress impeccably; she had to speak properly and be courteous."[43] Attending all of the national conferences, Slowe was embraced by the leaders of the organization. She addressed the conference and was invited to lecture at Teachers College, one of the leading programs in student personnel. In an attempt to foster greater understanding, cooperation, and sensitivity, in 1925, she lectured on the topic: "How College Women Can Help to Eliminate Race Prejudice." She was also invited to lecture to graduate students in student personnel at the University of Pittsburgh, where she continued her attempt to impact the white women who were future deans of women. She gave two lectures also in 1925: "The College Women's Responsibility to Race Relations" and "The Responsibility of College Women to Their Community." It is unclear how her lectures were received. However, Thyrsa Amos, the dean of women at the University of Pittsburgh, was a prominent NADW member and a leading student personnel authority. She held Slowe in high esteem and frequently visited Howard to observe Slowe's programs with the women. Amos had addressed the women at Howard the year after Slowe was hired at Howard. She gave three presentations—one to women in the two sororities entitled, "Howard First, Your Sorority—Second." She addressed the entire women student body on the topic, "Vocations for College Women," and finally, a lecture on "Being Somebody."[44]

These were not isolated incidents. For example, in 1934, Thelma Mitchell Rambo, the dean of women at Fisk University in Nashville, reported to the institution's president, Thomas Jones, that the national Negro secretary of the YWCA invited a group of Fisk women students to participate in an interracial seminar on religion that was being held on the campus of the University of

Kentucky in Lexington. Ten students were selected—they prepared for the event and worked with a religion professor on contemporary movements in religion. Dean Rambo said she had just received a letter from the National YWCA saying that the young students would not be allowed to come to the University of Kentucky but rather could go to the Black YWCA in the city. She said the letter stated the university's president had not permitted the Black women to be on campus. As an alternative, the Black national secretary of the YWCA stated she would find housing for the Fisk women in the homes of local Fisk alumnae. Dean Rambo noted that after a discussion with the students and their group's executive committee, they declined the invitation. Rambo said the students were disappointed, but it was the right decision.[45] President Jones (who was white) responded in a brief statement, "Under the circumstances outlined in your letter, I think you and the Executive Committee made the only decision possible. I do regret that it was not possible to go ahead with the original plan."[46]

From the beginning of the establishment of NACW, they monitored race issues. The membership, as noted, were all graduates of white institutions except for Howard and Fisk universities. So, the women knew firsthand the challenges of being on white campuses. In their 1926 meeting in New York City, Juliette Derricotte, national student secretary of the YWCA reported that she had visited twenty-five of the forty institutions on her list of white institutions where Black women attended. She gave her observations. She noted only five out of fifty-three Black women students at one white institution were not working their way through college. She noted that few Black women were awarded scholarships and were socially isolated. Derricotte outlined the major problems she viewed:

- Being barred from practice teaching
- Barred from using the swimming pool and classroom dancing
- Discrimination in grades
- Barred from participating in extracurricular activities
- Racist discussion of race and the race "problem" in courses such as anthropology
- Noted many groups doing interracial work and trying to improve race relations:
    American Federation of Youth
    American Youth Movement
    Student Volunteer Movement
    Federal Council of Churches of America
    Southern Interracial Committee
    Individual Church Boards
    YWCA and YMCA
    International College Students
    Cosmopolitan Clubs
    Fellowship of Reconciliation[47]

Considering the racism that many Black women experienced on these campuses, the group discussed if Black women who are financially impoverished should be discouraged from going to white institutions where "prejudice" existed. Also, they noted that many academically talented Black women dropped out of college due to financial reasons. But, due to location and personal preferences, as noted in the previous chapter, many Black women attended white institutions of higher education. Derricotte stated that many white colleges were attempting to limit the growing number of Black students who were attempting to gain admission. As it related to race and Black youth, she said there were many prejudiced white teachers who taught Blacks in the South, who she stated, were a "tremendous" problem as well. Hence, Black women students often had to confront racism in both predominantly white colleges and universities as well as HBCUs.

The final keynote speaker for the conference was Black scholar W. E. B. Du Bois. Noting Du Bois could speak about Blacks in white and Black institutions, he discussed the dilemma of Black students in both types of institutions. He said most Black colleges were poorly endowed, and their campuses were often physically unattractive with poor equipment and uneven teaching. He continued that Black colleges have to deal with the surrounding white communities and the politics of survival. He noted the positive aspects of students being in HBCUs and stated there was a positive *esprit de corps* where students could work together for a common cause (presumably race issues) and develop leadership skills and lasting friendships. In these institutions, Black students can avoid racism and have a happy college experience.

Du Bois noted that there were many advantages to attending white institutions. He said they had wealth, beauty, excellent equipment, and strong faculties. The notes said that Du Bois commented that students who attended white institutions were exposed to a superior culture. It's hard to believe this was stated considering Du Bois' lifelong scholarship on Black history and culture. In addition, his daughter, Yolanda, attended his alma mater, Fisk University. It is reported that Du Bois noted the value of a degree from a white institution, resulting in a passport to employment. Yet, despite these positive aspects for Black students in white institutions, Du Bois noted that Black students on these campuses are excluded from most aspects of campus life, even on liberal campuses. As a result, it was reported he said, these students develop a fighting attitude that they take out into the world after leaving these places. Finally, he noted these students are often educational misfits due to their training in these institutions. Du Bois emphasized he was not advocating which type of institutions Black youth should pursue, but he wanted to present his perspective on the pros and cons of both types. Black women's experiences in both types of systems were challenging, yet different. How the white women deans of students interacted with them is discussed in the book's next section.

White Deans of Women

In a history of the early deans of women entitled, *Deans of Women and the Feminist Movement: Emily Taylor's Activism*, Kelly C. Sartorium provides a history of the deans of women in white institutions primarily through a discussion of Emily Taylor, who served as dean of women at KU from 1956-74. Sartorium noted that Taylor was an active member of the National Association of Deans of Women and a feminist. Deans of women positions developed first throughout the Midwest and West, where larger numbers of women attended the public institutions opened to them beginning in the late 1800s. The first dean of women was Alice Freeman Palmer. Appointed at the newly founded University of Chicago in 1892, Palmer was one of the first women graduates of the University of Michigan (1876). After teaching school for a few years, she was appointed a history professor at Wellesley College in Massachusetts in 1879. Beginning in 1881 she served as interim and later permanent president until 1887. When she arrived at Chicago, she had distinguished herself as an example of the "new woman"—an educated, independent woman. Michigan awarded her an honorary doctorate in 1892. She represented the early wave of feminist deans who were also suffragettes. Palmer attracted other well-educated women to Chicago. Marion Talbot, a Boston University and MIT graduate in sanitation chemistry, was Palmer's assistant and later replaced Palmer when Talbot returned to Massachusetts. Palmer and Talbot were among the founders of the Association of the Collegiate Alumnae (ACA), the predecessor of the American Association of University Women (AAUW). Talbot organized the women deans and advisers in the Midwest in 1903 (the Universities of Wisconsin, Kansas, Michigan, Illinois, Iowa, Colorado, Ohio and Ohio State, Indiana, Northwestern; and small colleges as well: Lawrence (Wisconsin), Ripon (Wisconsin), Oberlin (Ohio), Beloit (Wisconsin)), and one college from the East Coast—Barnard.[48] The group expanded the following year to include the Universities of Nebraska, Missouri, Wyoming, Minnesota, North Dakota, California, and a few colleges from the East and the South. The women deans were largely scholars, and unlike Black women who obtained academic credentials and were frequently hired at HBCUs, the white women were overwhelmingly shut out of the professoriate due to sexism except in women's colleges. Being a dean of women sometimes provided them with faculty rank as an assistant or associate professor, which was the most a woman scholar could expect in a coeducational institution during this period.

The women deans in the heartland of the country were critical to understanding the field of women's student personnel. By 1915, 75 percent of all women in coeducational colleges were in the Midwest and West. As discussed in the previous chapter, Black women attended these institutions, and their numbers grew throughout the decades of the twentieth century. As these positions grew on coeducational campuses, deans of women tended to fall into two major categories: the strict disciplinarians who made women students abide by rules and regulations, or the deans who were the champions of women's personal autonomy and independence. These women were suffragettes and encouraged women students into careers. The author notes that Lucy Slowe and her former student mentee, Hilda Davis, fell into the latter category. Slowe preceded Taylor by a generation, but they all are viewed as the "feminist" deans of women of their eras. Sartorius observed that most white deans of women reproduced white cultural norms and sometimes exhibited racism and classism toward marginalized students. Indeed, the Black women students at most of these institutions experienced firsthand the lack of support of these deans. Sartorium noted that some women did recognize racism and sought to address it. Yet, neither the NADW nor the American Association for University Women—the organization of college women from accredited institutions that the NACW was based on—welcomed Black women into these groups until the 1960s.[49] Many women's deans upheld the exclusion of Black women from campus housing as was discussed in the previous chapter. Slowe worked to open the NADW to African American women deans after she was admitted as a member. As noted by the above letter, the national and regional and state conferences were frequently held in cities and hotels that barred Black participants. While Black women could join at the national level, regional chapters dictated the inclusion of Black women. It took twenty years for the NADW to change its segregationist practices. In 1937, Hilda Davis boycotted the national conference that was held in New Orleans where the hotel required Black participants to enter through the back doors and take the service elevators. In addition, Black members could not participate in meal events.[50]

Both the African American NACW and NAWDAC paralleled the white AAUW and NADW. However, the obvious issue of race required the Black organizations to address the issues of Black women and higher education. The issues discussed by the white deans reflected the different worlds that they lived in from Black women. The questions they asked about their roles were: "Why educate women? What could women graduates do with their education? Were they, like men, preparing for work in the public realm? If so, which employers would hire women?" During this early period, the women deans felt strongly that women students should major in the liberal arts like the male students, but also have courses that reflected the types of jobs that women could reasonably expect to obtain during this period—teaching and social work. When Lucy Sprague Mitchell was appointed as the first dean of women at the University of California at Berkeley in 1903, her biggest "obsession" was to find professions other than teaching for the women students. Mitchell was an honors Radcliffe College graduate in philosophy. Her appointment was due to the recommendation of Alice Freeman Palmer, with whom she lived in the household of the Palmer's, when she was a student at Radcliffe. Mitchell was appointed a lecturer in English as well as a dean of women. Like Palmer and Talbot, Mitchell was viewed as a progressive feminist according to her biography by Joyce Antler entitled, *Lucy Sprague Mitchell: The Making of a Modern Woman*.[51] This early group of primarily Midwestern and Western women deans concentrated on encouraging women students to pursue emerging new fields of employment rather than teaching, which was the primary occupation for women of all races.[52] However, as Sadie Tanner Alexander noted a decade later at the NACW conference, new fields were opening up for women, and Black women needed to be prepared. Even by 1909, the white deans of women reported that there were opportunities for women now in the dairy and poultry industries, journalism, philanthropy, library science, and business management. The women, all academics, studied women's wages, and by the 1930s produced a study for AAUW, the *Economic Status of University Women in the USA*. These early women deans were prominent in the advancement of women in the labor force. With the establishment of an employment bureau at Berkeley, Mitchell was one of the first deans of women to place women students in employment outside of teaching. Unlike the elite private colleges in the East, where the women students were not as focused upon employment after graduation, the women students in the major public land-grant institutions were provided significant guidance on employment. The women deans realized that marriage was an important goal of most women students; in the '40s and '50s, the students were provided pamphlets, such as "Your Job Future after the College," "Don't Try to Choose Between Marriage OR Career, but Get Ready for BOTH Home AND Job." While the traditional jobs for women were discussed in these publications, other positions such as medicine, pharmacy, the professoriate, law, and psychology were also placed on the list.[53] This was the same message Lucy Diggs Slowe expressed to the deans of Black women in the '20s.

As employment opportunities grew for white women, the Black women in these same institutions were still attempting to gain housing on these campuses and full participation in all aspects of campus life. The interracial interactions of Black women with white women were primarily through the YWCA. There were a handful of examples of instances of a white dean of women opposing segregation and the barring of Black women students on their campuses. For example, in the 1930s and 1940s, the dean of women of Berea College in Kentucky, Julia Allen was a former YWCA employee prior to coming to Berea. She sponsored interracial conferences at Berea and helped facilitate the integration of Black students back to Berea College in the 1950s. Likewise, at Oberlin, Dean Florence Fitch, also a former YWCA member, worked to facilitate interracial harmony on that campus. As noted in chapter two, both Berea and Oberlin were former abolitionist colleges, and these efforts reflected the histories of these institutions. The deans at Ohio University, Indiana University, and the University of Pittsburgh also worked to assist Black women students, particularly in student housing in the late 1940s, which was their major issue.[54] One dean lost her job because of her support of Black and Jewish women students who were both discriminated against. Ruth McCarn, a white civil rights activist, was appointed dean of women at Northwestern in 1937. Black women were not allowed to live on campus when she was appointed. She began advocating for Black women to live on campus after she arrived. McCarn was very conscious of the fact that Black women had to commute from Chicago or live in substandard housing in Evanston. She co-sponsored a conference on interracial affairs in 1938 with Howard University. McCarn also admitted the Black sorority, AKA in 1941 to the university's PanHellenic Council, the governing board of Greek organizations. This action brought significant opposition—particularly by white women Greek members. They were fearful that a Black woman could possibly emerge as president of the council. This bold move, in addition to McCarn's speeches that advocated integration and the equitable treatment of Jewish women, resulted in the president of the university, Franklyn Bliss Snyder, firing McCarn. Kelly C. Sartorius, historian of deans of women, pointed out the impact of McCarn's termination. Although President Robert Hutchins hired McCarn as the assistant dean at the University of Chicago, Sartorius observed:

> McCarn's very public dismissal by Northwestern sent a message to other deans of women that racial or non-Protestant civil right support could endanger the job of even an accomplished administrator like McCarn. . . . her dismissal nonetheless sent a chilling effect through the NADW. For those inclined to work on civil rights for non-majority populations, McCarn's departure from Northwestern and her hiring at the University of Chicago pointed out the importance of the attitude of the university president. A university's chief executive largely determined whether a dean of women could successfully and safely engage in controversial equity issues for non-white or non-Christian students.[55]

After this termination, with rare exceptions, few sympathetic white women deans spoke up for the equitable treatment of Black women students on their campuses or to avoid having conferences in locations where Black women could not stay or eat in the conference hotels. Their exclusion was simply viewed as the norm of the period.[56]

Since in most instances African American women could not live on campus, white deans of women woefully neglected them, with rare exceptions. As mentioned earlier, many Black students established chapters of Black Greek organizations for camaraderie, assistance in housing, and to have outstanding

African American women as role models. Ida Louise Jackson, who attended UC-Berkeley from 1918–22, was one of the earliest Black women to attend that university. She noted that she was instrumental in establishing the chapter of Alpha Kappa Alpha on that campus in 1921. Jackson noted there was an opportunity to also establish a chapter of Delta, but the university required a minimum of five women to establish a chapter. Jackson stated there were seven Black women at UC-Berkeley at the time. She said the majority decided they wanted to be AKAs. Remembering those days, in an oral history decades later, Jackson stated: "My reason [for wanting to establish an AKA chapter] was that some of the famous Black women then, Dean Lucy Slowe and Maudelle Brown Bousfield, *Dr.* Bousfield, and several of the outstanding women of the nation at the time in the field of education were members of Alpha Kappa Alpha. Dean Slowe was one of the original founders of AKA. So, the majority of us decided we wanted to join AKA."[57] Two of the seven women decided to establish a Delta chapter, but they did not have the requisite number. Jackson noted that AKA required that the dean of women sign and approve their application. When she went to see Dean of Women Lucy Stebbins for approval, Jackson said Stebbins had no idea there were Black women students who even attended the university. She recalled that the other two students who wanted to start the Delta chapter were not aware that the university required at least five members to start a chapter. Noting the lack of numbers to start a Delta chapter, Jackson recalled that Stebbins was uninterested and dismissive and said, "Why don't you girls all join one sorority? There are so few of you."[58] Jackson said that was proof in her mind that Stebbins was not concerned about the Black women. She said the Black women students had to convince Stebbins that AKA and Delta were very different and had different standards. They told her, "We were sold on Alpha Kappa Alpha." Jackson said the women were determined that there would be two and not one Black sorority on campus. In addition, she recalled: "We finally convinced her that we were going to stay in Alpha Kappa Alpha. And we had five [students]. Only two other Black women students were on the campus." Jackson noted, "She [Stebbins] didn't bother to do any research to find out how many [Black women were enrolled]. She just felt being Black, we all should [all] be one." Several years later, a chapter of Delta was also established once the Black women's enrollment had increased.[59]

Jackson's account of her experience of the invisibility of the Black women on campus shaped these women and others who had similar experiences gave them the determination to work on behalf of other Black women students in their professional lives. Having no status on campus resulted in Black women becoming extremely self-sufficient in determining how to navigate their way between the campus and the community. Jackson not only became an AKA one decade later, but she also became the national president of the sorority.

FIGURE 18. Kappa Chapter of Delta Sigma Theta sorority, University of California–Berkeley, 1921. Miriam Matthews Photograph Collections, University of California, Los Angeles Archives.

She completed her undergraduate degree from UC Berkeley in 1922 and her masters in 1924. In 1926, Jackson became the first African American to become a certified teacher in the state of California and the first Black person to teach in the City of Oakland.[60]

The Activities of the National Association of Women and Deans and Advisors of Colored Schools—the Challenges and the Quest for Refinement and Femininity

After Slowe founded the organization for deans of women in HBCUs (NAWDAC) in 1929, because of her training and visibility within the white National Association of Deans of Women, she was viewed as the leading authority of student personnel issues for Black women in the nation. As noted above, white deans of women consulted Slowe regarding issues related to Black women students in their institutions. However, Slowe's papers show she was constantly consulted for her advice on questions related to establishing and running offices that were established in HBCUs for oversight over the women students as these institutions grew. Women in these positions had little to no training or guidance, which is why Slowe's guidance and the organization were so important.

For example, in January of 1931, the new dean of women at Virginia State College in Petersburg, a state school, asked Slowe's advice on rules for students who live in their newly planned home economics practice house, something that some HBCUs had for their women students where they spent time living in such homes to show they could run a household. The dean, Ms. Whiting, asked, "With whom do they check out and in when they leave the campus?" "Who grants permissions for parties etc. in the city during this period?" "Are there set hours in the home for young men callers?" "How long a period are the students required to live in the home?" She also inquired whether there should be restrictions on women students on campus who didn't live in the practice house from visiting and if not, what their hours should be and whether she should have set conferences between the head of the practice house or should she meet only as problems arise.[61]

Slowe graciously responded that Howard didn't have a home economics practice house (certainly a concept she would have frowned upon since the last thing she would be interested in was preparing her students to be full-time homemakers). She responded that women who lived in the practice house should be treated like all other women students and bound by the same rules and regulations. She also said that the length of time women should spend in the house would depend on the course the student was taking to satisfy the requirements—in some instances, it's six weeks, and in others, it could be as much as twelve weeks. She also advised that the dean of women should meet weekly with the heads of the women's dormitories and not wait for a problem to come up. This was very much in keeping with Slowe's philosophy of keeping the women in her charge updated and in constant discussion about the nature of their work and the field of student personnel. Another state college dean of women from South Carolina also wrote Slowe the same year to say her biggest challenge was making her women students more "refined." She said the women students she worked with were "loud and harsh." Slowe had one of her assistants, Joanna Houston, send this Dean Slowe's statement and philosophy on this topic:

> With regard to a program for refining the manner of young women and giving them social finish. I should say that each problem and situation must be studied for itself; this is where the mind of the educator must work.
>
> As a general statement, I should say that the young women could be taught much by frequent participation in activities that call for the social graces and therefore make them conscious of their deficiencies. Teas and receptions to faculty members, administrators, and visitors, to whom women students always like to make a good showing, are valuable. We have used etiquette reading and discussion groups to great advantage; particularly effective were their demonstrations before the whole group. It must not be overlooked that idleness is conducive to disorder and general roughness of manner. The social

program for the dormitory should be designed to fill all the time which the director of the dormitory finds unused for business. Sundays and holidays need special attention. Leisure reading groups, hikes, excursions to places of interest, and some group participation in community uplift work will serve to educate young people as well as fill their vacant hours. The time is also important; people do not develop in one school year.[62]

The dean of women of Fisk University, Juanita Sadler, in 1933, expressed interest in the mentoring program that Slowe had at Howard. Fisk had always hired highly trained deans of women who held college degrees, had traveled widely, and came highly recommended by the leading authorities in student personnel.[63] Howard was its model. Slowe responded to an inquiry of Dean Sadler regarding the structure of this program. Slowe noted that becoming a mentor is the highest honor a senior woman can obtain at Howard. She explained that the sophomore and senior women select junior women in April. The selected mentors are assigned books to read over the summer pertaining to leadership, character, management, and what it means to be an educated person. She said the assignment of first-year women students to the senior mentors is done at the beginning of the year in a beautiful ceremony based on the Greek dialogue between Telemachus and his mentor in the Odyssey. The mentors are the ones who work with the new students throughout the year, and if there is a major problem, the mentors consult with Slowe and her office.[64] This program based on a Greek story reflected Slowe's background as an English professor, as well as her desire to ensure the women's students at Howard were exposed to what she perceived as important literature.

Mayme Foster who replaced Dean Sadler in 1937 also wrote Slowe. Foster's concern was a common theme with the deans of women at HBCUs. She said she wanted the Fisk women students to develop more social graces "to have them develop more concern about the small items of a social conduct on which the larger things are really based." She noted she wanted the women to develop a "higher level of womanhood," which was something that was constantly mentioned by Black women's groups—sororities, Black women's clubs, college deans, etc. Many other deans repeated Foster's comments regarding her perception of the college women at Fisk as well. Foster said that the women tended to be interested in participating in "ordinary activities of the lower level." She continued, the women were happy attending a "cheap local neighborhood nightclub" rather than attending a music recital or concert at a downtown music hall.[65] Indeed, Foster's characterization of the local nightclub as "cheap" reflected her bias and value system. The possibility that young women could be interested in both was not a consideration.

Fisk and Howard were always viewed as being the most progressive and liberal toward Black women students among the HBCUs. At both institutions, women students took part in self-governance and served on faculty-student disciplinary committees. At Fisk, women students could leave campus to go to approved restaurants and locations and could also ride in cars and take taxis, with permission. In 1938, the junior and senior female students collectively wrote a letter to the executive council (composed of the senior administrators) protesting the exclusion of a desired restaurant, the Club Del Morocco, from the approved list of places women students could go to off campus. Fisk rules stated that:

> Women at Fisk University are forbidden the attendance of any public places of amusement, which take on the character of nightclubs, or places of ill repute.[66]

The women noted that since this club was not on the list, Fisk administrators indicated to them that they would be liable to "severe punishment" by the executive council. The women lost this battle, with the university responding: "The Committee has reaffirmed its ruling promulgated several years ago in regard to the attendance of students upon public places in Nashville partaking of the character of a night club."[67] Fisk women students did have curfews and had to sign in and out when they left the dormitories. However, this was true of most colleges during this period. The time of the curfews varied by class status, with seniors in the 1940s being able to stay out until 10:45 p.m. Women students were able to attend the movies with a male date or with a group. However, they needed parental permission to attend football or other games on other campuses. Of the men, only freshmen male students were required to sign in and out after 7 p.m., and they had to be in the dormitory by 11:30 p.m. during the week and midnight on Saturday unless they had special permission. All male students were only required to notify the dean of men if they were going to be away overnight, but this did not require the approval of their parents.[68]

As early as 1930, in one of the annual meetings of the NAWDAC, this was a topic of concern. At the conference held at Fisk that year, Joanne Houston, who was the assistant to Dean Slowe at Howard gave a presentation on "Education for Leisure." She noted that Black women college students should be groomed for "leisure." She informed the group:

> The only way to make sure that the young woman in college is being prepared to take her place in a world where there is a great deal of leisure is to have a program of constructive leisure activities in the college.[69]

Houston stated the extra-curriculum aspect of this program was just as important as the academic courses the women were offered. She continued:

> It should aim at fostering a love of restful quiet and meditative solitude and a part should be directed at wholesome activities with contacts with people.[70]

Throughout the 1930s, both the NACW and the NAWDAC met annually with overlapping sessions. The former group was devoted to issues related to academic standards and issues related to Black women students and faculty regardless of the type of institution, and the latter organization was focused upon issues related to Black women students, faculty, and staff, and the qualifications and duties of the deans of women at HBCUs. The groups had some overlapping memberships, but they remained two separate organizations. Due to racial discrimination at hotels and cost, the meetings of both groups were held on Black college campuses. They met at colleges that had reached collegiate standing—Talladega, Tuskegee, Hampton, Howard, Wilberforce, Bennett, and Fisk.

As noted earlier, the NACW was interested in the academic aspect of Black women's higher education. Slowe pointed out in the 1930s conference that Black women educators had little to do with the curriculum of Black women students on these campuses. She said the NACW must be to Black women students what the white organization AAUW was to white women students. This meant providing oversight and guidance to what they are taught and the values stressed to them. She said that the role of their organizations was the development of the full women and not just maintaining petty rules concerning their behavior.[71]

The number of members and conference attendees grew over the years. In 1931, when the groups met at Talladega College in Alabama, there were twenty attendees from eleven colleges.[72] The group represented both private colleges and state land-grant institutions. Due to illness, Slowe had to miss this conference. The conference was presided over by Juliette Derricotte, the first African American dean of women at Fisk. She was a graduate of Talladega College ('18) and became very prominent in the area of women's education.[73] Although Slowe was not present, her concerns over how to make dormitories more like homes than places where women students are locked up and policed were discussed.

The body also had a robust discussion on whether women students should be allowed to smoke—a trend that was becoming more acceptable in society at large. The group was overwhelmingly against it. They outlined reasons for forbidding this trend: it was masculine and unladylike; detrimental to one's health; resulted in men not respecting women who smoke; resulted in men thinking women smokers are [sexually] "easy"; that tobacco is habit forming; and it's a fire hazard. The belief that smoking was masculine and unladylike reflected the extreme belief that Black women's reputations needed to be protected. Any act that detracted from being "respectable" and "feminine" should be avoided. The minutes of this session didn't note which women deans expressed these views. However, there were others who held an opposing view on this topic. Some noted that society was changing, and women who smoked were accepted. They noted that movies and popular culture portrayed women smoking. They also pointed out that some students already smoked prior to coming to college and that most dormitories were fireproof and did not pose any serious fire hazard. More likely than not, the women who held these views were not products of HBCUs or from the South. The reality is Black women were rarely viewed as the same as white women, and they were often harshly judged even by members of their own race who harbored conservative stereotypical notions about womanhood—so what was acceptable by white women in no way meant it would be accepted for Black women. The group ended with no resolution on the topic, noting that smoking is done in certain colleges but commenting that the issue hadn't presented itself in their institutions.[74]

Slowe missed this meeting due to illness, but in a survey she completed on this issue in 1924 for the Young Women's Christian Temperance Union, she indicated that there was not a problem with women students smoking at Howard. She said whether a young woman student smoked was a reflection of what type of mothers they had. The implication was a young woman's mother was the best determinant of their behavior. Hilda Davis, who was one of Slowe's first students and mentees at Howard, stated when asked about Slowe's views on smoking that women who smoked at Howard would be "sent home," meaning expelled. She said although Slowe believed in women's independence—she also had "high standards" for how she felt Black women should comport themselves.[75]

While this was an issue for the deans of women at other HBCUs including Howard, in 1935, Fisk female students won the right to smoke on campus, an extremely liberal privilege for women students at an HBCU. Nearly twenty years since Slowe expressed her view on women's smoking and almost ten years since it was discussed in the NAWDAC's conference, in administrative records of Fisk University, this privilege was discussed again in December of 1942, by the executive committee of the institution (including the deans of women and men, dean of the college, and other administrators and faculty) for clarification. They voted to allow women students to smoke in the student union.[76] A year later, the student council was asked by the executive committee to review the smoking rules and report their findings. The minutes stated that the rules should be clearly defined since there appeared to be ambiguity.[77] Smoking remained an issue at Fisk, and in November of 1945, the president noted that the executive committee of the college restated the rules and regulations of smoking on campus (since apparently the rules had remained ambiguous). The rules stated that indiscriminate smoking was not allowed on campus; smoking was only allowed in designated buildings and places and was not allowed in college halls including classrooms, on the Jubilee Hall campus (the women's area), or in front of the entrance of the chapel and the library; it stated that, while not encouraged, smoking would be "tolerated" in student rooms, faculty offices, and the lobby of the post office and bookstore, the Student Union and the International Student Center, and wash rooms and restrooms; further, with permission from the dean, smoking would be permitted in small informal graduate seminars.[78] These guidelines were for faculty, staff, and students without any regard to gender.

Credentials of Deans of Women at HBCUs

Both the NACW and the NAWDAC continued their work (both still headed by Lucy Slowe) on their advocacy for Black women in higher education—the latter organization focused specifically on issues of women students at HBCUs. During the Depression years of the mid-1930s, they continued their visits and research on the academic courses and standards of HBCUs. The members of NACW, as noted earlier, were all graduates of leading and prestigious colleges and universities. They attempted to impact the curricular offerings of HBCUs. At their annual conferences, they discussed the importance of offering a liberal arts curriculum and reiterated the importance of having a qualified vocational counselor for the growing number of women students.

At the 1935 conference of the women's deans and advisors, there was a survey of the credentials and number of women students that attended each institution. They also surveyed the number of women students who lived on campus and who lived off campus, and if the women's dean and advisor positions included faculty status. The situation varied greatly.

As reflected in the credentials of the above women, most had attended major institutions, had graduate degrees, and held faculty positions. These were the credentials that Slowe and the NACW believed necessary for a dean of women. However, many women deans in HBCUs at this period did not hold such impressive credentials. For example, the dean of women at the State A and M College in Orangeburg, South Carolina, did not list any college degree. She supervised 165 women in the dormitory and 65 day students. Johnson C. Smith, a private college in North Carolina, had a counselor of women instead of a dean. Mrs. H. L. McCrorey was a graduate of Atlanta University's normal department and had studied for six quarters at the University of Chicago, which was still a preparatory school for deans of women, and one summer at Harvard. She supervised eighty-eight women students with only twelve boarding on campus. McCrorey noted that the college did not have dormitories but would have one in the future. She did not have any teaching responsibilities.[79] The following year, a survey of thirty-eight Black schools that had deans of women or advisors attending the conference showed that twelve of the women had at least a bachelor's degree, nine had master's degrees, one had a normal school diploma, and six held no college degree at all (see chart 8). The institutions that employed deans without

CHART 8. Dean of Women's Credentials, 1935*

NAME	UNDERGRADUATE; GRADUATE DEGREE(S)	FACULTY STATUS	INSTITUTION	RESIDENTIAL VS. OFF-CAMPUS STUDENTS
Katherine N. Robinson	Wellesley; Boston University, MA English	Taught 12 hours/week	Cheyney State	70 vs. 37
Leah Lewis	Virginia Union; Columbia University, master's	Taught high school methods courses and student supervision 6 hours/week	Virginia Union	43 vs. 132
Tossie Whiting	University of Chicago; Teachers College, Columbia, master's	Taught 1 English class	Virginia State College	320 vs. 130
Ann Jackson	Univ. of Illinois; Columbia University (summer school)	Taught English 3 hours/week	Kentucky State College	114 vs. 196
Georgia Myrtle Teal	Cornell University; Columbia University	—	Wilberforce Univ.	235 vs. 122
Name withheld	—	—	State A&M College (SC)	100 vs. 65
Mrs. H. L. McCrorey†	Atlanta University Normal department; University of Chicago (6 quarters); Harvard (1 summer)	—	Johnson C. Smith (NC)	12 vs. 76

*Survey was taken at the 1935 women's deans and advisors conference.
†Position title was counselor of women instead of dean.

Dean of Women's Credentials, 1936*

MASTER'S DEGREE	BACHELOR'S DEGREE	NORMAL SCHOOL DIPLOMA	NO COLLEGE DEGREE
9	12	1	6†

*Survey of 38 Black schools that had deans of women and/or advisors at the 1936 conference of women's deans and advisors.

†Institutions that employed deans without any college degrees were the state agricultural and mechanical colleges in both North and South Carolina, St. Augustine, a private Episcopal college in North Carolina and Hampton Institute in Virginia and Downingtown Industrial School in Pennsylvania. (Source: National Association of Deans of Women and Advisors of Women in Colored Schools, Survey of Delegates to the 1936 Conference, Lucy Diggs Slowe Papers, Moorland-Spingarn Research Center, Howard University, Washington, DC [1936].)

any college degrees were the state agricultural and mechanical colleges in both North and South Carolina; St. Augustine, a private Episcopal college in North Carolina; Hampton Institute in Virginia; and Downingtown Industrial School in Pennsylvania.[80] Dormitories for women students were still being established on many campuses.

The gap in the training of the deans of women and advisors at HBCUs was often wide, as noted above. In every conference and other opportunities, Slowe emphasized the importance of a highly trained woman's dean, who is also an academic with faculty status. She had an opportunity to address a conference of men about the importance of the role of the dean of women in 1935 at a conference of National Association of Collegiate Deans and Registrars of Negro Schools. Slowe was the only woman on the three-day program.[81] Her presentation made an impact and the male organization requested to merge with the NACW. This proposal will also come later from the dean of men's organization as well. Slowe resisted merging the two all-women's organizations with those of men although she agreed they did need to hold joint meetings.

In the fall of 1937, Slowe became ill, resulting in her being away from Howard from mid-September throughout most of October. She never recovered and died at the age of fifty-four on October 21st. Her death was a devastating shock to the entire Black higher education community, particularly among Black women. Slowe had been the most vocal and significant spokesperson and visionary for Black women students in HBCUs. She wanted these institutions to prepare Black women for leadership and become "modern" women, being prepared for the current and future world, not one of the past. In addition, while so much of the curriculum of HBCUs prepared Black women in home economics and homemaking and teaching, Slowe fought strongly to not view these areas as the only calling for Black women students.

In the 1920s, she along with the NACW requested that courses be offered in HBCUs in new fields of employment for women such as library science, social work, pre-school training, and personnel work. In 1930, the NACW approached Howard University to offer courses in social work with no success. From 1931–35, Slowe was persistent in emphasizing that this was a new field of study and employment for women. Finally, in 1935, Howard began offering courses in social work. It was not until a decade later, in 1945, that they established an autonomous School of Social Work.[82] Slowe never lived to see the results of her advocacy for this field.

Slowe insisted that deans of women at HBCUs be highly educated and have faculty status. None of her writings, speeches, or comments reflected "god talk" or "race uplift" themes, which was the norm and found throughout the writings and speeches of many Black women educators and community leaders throughout the period in which she lived. While Slowe was indeed a woman of faith—none of her work mentioned God as the driving force of her work nor did she make religious references. As reported earlier in this chapter, early in Slowe's career she stated that she believed conservative religion was a handicap to Black women. The church had always been central to the Black community and African American women were staunch churchwomen. Previously cited historians Evelyn Higgenbottom and Bettye Collier Thomas have both produced important and powerful scholarship on the role of Black women in religious institutions. Slowe was relentless in her desire to free Black women students from the paternalism and infantilizing that she believed religion imposed on them. On this topic she wrote: "Frequently, Negro college women come from homes where conservatism in reference to women's place in the world of the most extreme sort exists." She said her aspirations for Black women students were not to be mere "helpmates" or "servants of the community"—but to live up to their potential. While she didn't advocate women ignoring their communities—instead, she believed they should develop leadership skills not just for women's organizations but for a larger society. In a keynote address she gave in 1934 at the NACW conference at Atlanta University, she said:

> The women students . . . must be prepared to shoulder the responsibility first of all for making a living because they are definitely committed in the modern world to developing their own individual talents and of being responsible for their own lives. Even if they marry, there is no guarantee that they will not be called upon to earn their own living. This fact, immediately brings us face to face with our whole economic order as it relates to the individual's employment, and no college is doing justice to its women students unless it prepares them to understand the economic world of which they must become a part. . . . The college cannot hope to send out into the communities women prepared to assume community responsibility and personal responsibility without seeing to it that they get ample opportunity for the practice of such responsibility in college.[83]

Sadly, all the issues Slowe fought and lectured against in her career—oppressive and demeaning rules and lack of leadership opportunities for women students and faculty, not only continued but also escalated. The decades of the '40s and '50s brought new voices on the topic of Black women's higher education.

CHAPTER 7

Deans of Women at HBCUs after Slowe
Tuskegee Institute and Bennett College

The changes that Slowe and the National Association of College Women (NACW) attempted to make on behalf of Black women students at HBCUs starting in the 1920s continued after her death. While the previous chapter highlighted the experiences of women students at Howard University during the Lucy Diggs Slowe years as dean, this chapter will discuss Tuskegee Institute and Bennett College and the efforts of these two institutions in developing programs for women's students in the 1930s–60s. Tuskegee will be discussed through the documents and activities of the deans of women and their efforts to provide agency to the women students from the late 1930s through the early 1960s. Bennett will be discussed from the efforts of the NACW and the National Association of Women's Deans and Advisors of Colored Schools (NAWDAC) who were members of the Bennett faculty to transform the curriculum of the college to make it relevant to the "modern" Black woman student. This chapter will also discuss the continuing role of the NAWDAC in building the deans of women's offices at HBCUs and the issues concerning the development of their women students, particularly in the era of the "modern woman."

The comparison of these two colleges will provide contrast to the discussion of Howard in the previous chapter. Howard was located in the nation's capital and perceived as being more liberal in attitude and prepared Black women students for a wide variety of fields. Ruth Brett commented, Howard was in the "vanguard" of Black women's student advancement (along with Fisk University). In contrast, Tuskegee was in rural Alabama and was a vocational/industrial college with stringent rules for its students, especially the women. Howard and Tuskegee were both established in the nineteenth century, Howard after the end of the Civil War in 1867 and Tuskegee, less than fifteen years later in 1887. Bennett became a women's college in 1926 with an African American male president, David D. Jones. His forward thinking for Black women's education with a stellar group of Black women faculty, who were committed to women's higher education and were members of the aforementioned NACW and NAW-DAC, resulted in Bennett focusing on a curriculum specifically to address the lives of Black women.

Tuskegee

When Ida L. Jackson went to Teachers College in New York to pursue a doctorate in education in the mid-1930s, Frederick Patterson, an Iowa State and Cornell University graduate in veterinary medicine and bacteriology, was appointed president of Tuskegee in 1935. Seeking to hire a well-educated dean of women in keeping with the recommendations of Slowe and the NACW, he contacted Jackson, who was highly recommended. Her initial goal had been to return to her hometown of Oakland and become a principal. However, while the school system allowed her to teach, they would not appoint her as a school administrator because of her race. As a result, Jackson took the position as dean of women and went to Tuskegee in 1937. Slowe, several months prior to her death, wrote Jackson an enthusiastic letter of congratulations and said: "Tuskegee should be congratulated in getting a person of your character, personality and training in such a strategic position ... [I] am sure that you will take advantage of every opportunity to assist our women in becoming the proper forces in our community life."[1] Slowe clearly thought the institution had turned a corner and was moving from the repressive, conservative treatment of women to a new day for the "modern" woman. Jackson immediately responded and said with Patterson as the new president, the institution was in transition. He had instituted student government (something that Slowe and NACW had emphasized that all colleges should establish), but that this change was in its infancy. Jackson responded immediately to disavow Slowe of her enthusiasm regarding her appointment. She reported her perception and challenges of being the dean of women at Tuskegee. She said the school hadn't changed (or advanced in its view of students/women) since the days of Booker T. Washington. She told Slowe her staff at Tuskegee was composed of three matrons, the former acting dean of women who was reassigned to be over housing, a secretary, and two clerks. Jackson noted that Slowe perhaps was already aware of these details. In closing she wrote, "This is essentially a men's school." She said she needed Slowe's sound advice.[2] After one year at Tuskegee, Jackson returned to California. Nearly fifty years later in an oral history recorded in 1985, Jackson reflected on that year at Tuskegee. She diplomatically stated that, while Tuskegee was a "great institution," nonetheless, working there was very challenging. She reiterated what she had written to Slowe in 1937 that Tuskegee was a college "geared for men." She ended her comments saying the institution had remained male centered "until comparatively recent years." She also noted the dean of men determined all of the social activities of the students.³

One of the biggest challenges of students as Slowe and her fellow colleagues like Jackson observed, especially the women on the campuses of HBCUs, were the stringent rules and regulations. The writer Langston Hughes was so disturbed by what he witnessed in his speaking tour in the 1930s of these campuses that he wrote an article of his experiences in *The Crisis* magazine in 1934. Hughes said that in the more than fifty Black colleges he visited, he felt like he was "going back to mid-Victorian England, or Massachusetts in the days of the witch burning Puritans."⁴ He noted draconian rules for both men and women students. He noted, 24-year-old grown men had to sneak to smoke a cigarette like they were little boys. On many campuses, card playing was viewed as a sin, although within the Black community, bridge and bid whist were two very popular and common card games. Hughes noted that many campuses banned dancing and noticed students were only allowed to march and not dance. Hughes questioned what century these colleges were in, considering it was the Jazz Age. As will be recounted in the testimonies of deans of women later, Hughes noted how campuses made extreme efforts to have men and women separated. He said campus officials acted as if it was "unnatural" for men and women to talk to one another.⁵

Hughes also criticized the stringent religious requirements and emphases on these campuses—mandatory chapel, weekly prayer meetings, Sunday services, "dull and stupid sermons, uninspired prayers, and monotonous hymns—neither intellectually worthy of adult minds nor emotionally existing in the manner of the old-time shouts."⁶

Jackson was replaced in 1938 by Jessie P. Guzman, another highly educated liberal arts college graduate. A southerner from Savannah, Georgia, Guzman earned her BA from Howard in 1919. She came to Tuskegee in 1923 as a researcher to work in the department of records and research with the noted Monroe Works, who produced the annual *Negro Yearbook*. With a master's degree from Columbia in 1929, Guzman took additional classes for a year from 1935–36 at the University of Chicago, and later, at American University in Washington, DC. Guzman worked at several HBCUs during this period. Although Guzman came to Tuskegee to be a researcher (and she later returned to this position), she was persuaded to serve as dean of women until someone who was trained in this field could replace her.

In 1944, Patterson found a highly trained dean of women for the institution. He appointed Jean Fairfax. Fairfax, from Cleveland, Ohio, and the daughter of college-educated parents, was a Phi Beta Kappa graduate of the University of Michigan ('41), and in 1944, she earned a master's in world religions from Union

Theological Seminary in New York City. She had experience working with the YWCA and the Student Christian Movement and been active in interracial organizations. In an interview with the author, Fairfax made the same observation as Jackson. She said Tuskegee was "male and militaristic." She said she felt the entire campus was "anti-student." She stated that she went to Tuskegee thinking she would develop great programs for the women students, but in essence, the administration wanted her to simply policewoman students' morals. She said students had to march to events down separate walkways. Fairfax noted that the experience was shocking to her. She recalled, at Michigan, Black students could not even live on campus. And, like the other Black women who had attended white institutions, they had enormous freedom in movement and personal lives because of the discrimination they encountered. Fairfax was stunned that Tuskegee expected her not to have male visitors in her apartment in the dormitory where she lived. From 1941 to 1946, during the World War II era, Tuskegee trained nearly one thousand Black pilots on the campus. The elite group of Black pilots became known as the "Tuskegee Airmen." Fairfax overlapped with these men on campus for two years. She stated there was a Tuskegee airman visiting her one evening, which caused a major uproar. Fairfax had an apartment in the women's dormitory. Some of the students, as a prank, pulled the fire alarm, which meant both Fairfax and her guest came out of her apartment. This incident became the talk of the campus. The dean who replaced Fairfax after this incident noted that Fairfax was a brilliant woman and dean and noted the male visitor "was fully dressed" and there was nothing "questionable" about what was happening in the apartment. She said after this happened, Fairfax "lost her pride" and left.[7] Fairfax had an outstanding career working in race relations in various organizations after leaving Tuskegee. She worked for the American Friends Service Committee as program director and traveled throughout Austria for several years. She also worked for the Southern Civil Rights Project for the American Friends and later worked for the NAACP Legal Defense Fund. Fairfax never worked again on the campus of an HBCU.[8] For women like Fairfax and her predecessor Ida Jackson, who had attended white undergraduate institutions, as noted earlier, they had complete freedom, albeit due to racist housing rules on the white campuses they attended. Living on the campus of most HBCUs required acceptance of the lack of personal autonomy, constant tracking of one's whereabouts, and oppressive rules, if you were a woman. For Black women who were from the South and products of HBCUs, none of these rules or expectations were upsetting or strange. This was the world they knew.

    Tuskegee was known as one of the most restrictive and difficult places to work in Black higher education. Under the principalship (and not presidency—so as not to offend southern whites with such a lofty title) of Booker T. Washington and later Robert Moton after Washington's death in 1915, the head of the school controlled all decisions. Even with Frederick Patterson becoming president in 1935, to appease the white community, the institution maintained strict discipline not only of its students, but as noted by the incident with Dean Fairfax, its faculty and staff as well. Both Jackson and Fairfax described the campus as being run like the military. The male students were organized in military regiments where they had to drill and perform guard duties. There was a commander of cadets. All students were required to have a Bible and attend daily chapel, and there was a system of merits and demerits.

While all students had to adhere to many rules, the next dean of women who replaced Jean Fairfax was Hattie Simmons Kelly who attended Tuskegee as a high school student. Kelly was a much older woman and was born in 1896 in North Carolina. She was sent to attend high school at Tuskegee in 1911 when Booker T. Washington was still alive and head of the school. Kelly graduated in 1915. She recalled that all of the female students had to wear uniforms and were required to make their own clothes and commencement dresses. The renowned industrial school required all of its students to work as well as study in evening classes and offered more than forty trades. All women students were also required to study domestic arts—regardless of their interest. Kelly said she took plain sewing, tailoring, dressmaking, millinery, cooking, and teaching. The students worked during the day and took classes in the evenings. Kelly stated she aspired to attend Fisk after Tuskegee but discovered she was not academically prepared to be admitted into Fisk. In an oral history conducted by the Radcliffe Black Women Oral History Project in the 1970s, Kelly also recalled how "strict" Tuskegee was. When she arrived at Tuskegee, the dean of women was named Mrs. Sue Helen Porter. Kelly said, Porter showed "no love toward you at all; everything was business." At Tuskegee, "your room was inspected, your trunks were inspected, your closets, your clothes; everything was inspected, and you were given demerits if anything wasn't just right. When you went to chapel, you marched out of chapel . . . if there was a button off your blouse, or if it was soiled—the white blouses on Sunday—you were pulled out of line." Female students had to enter the chapel through the bottom entrance which was a different entrance from the male students. She also noted, women students were confined to the campus.[9] Kelly stated, girls could only leave campus with an "admit" which was difficult to obtain. She said, "you couldn't go to town without a chaperone and they [Tuskegee administrators] were very, very strict."[10] In addition to the above, the institution read and censored student's mail. She recalled the dances were all military with the male students wearing military uniforms that were made in the tailoring department. The men were either captains or lieutenants. No dancing was allowed on campus until the 1930s with strict instruction regarding how close a couple could be to one another.

Because white philanthropy was critical to the survival of Tuskegee, it was important for the students to portray themselves as well-groomed, well-behaved and grateful students. Kelly recalled that students thought, "The whites that we knew were people who loved us, were people who were philanthropically inclined." She said when the white trustees were on campus, all the students had to dress in their uniforms (women students had to wear hats—that they made) and march in formation for the trustees. For students from the rural South, the opportunity to obtain an education was worth the stringent rules that were common to their upbringing. Kelly said the students were aware that lynching and other violence against Blacks happened outside their campus, which is why, in part, the overprotectiveness of the students was necessary.[11]

The restrictions at Tuskegee were legendary, and it was extremely difficult for those who were not born and educated in the South to endure the oppressive nature of the institution. Some Black men and women left as soon as the opportunity availed. For example, Horace Cayton, a sociologist who was born in Seattle, Washington, and graduated from the University of Washington and earned his doctorate from the University of Chicago, could not adjust to the strictness of the campus. He briefly taught at Tuskegee during the principalship of Robert Moton. Clayton found the conservative and accommodationist philosophy of the campus unbearable and asked to be relieved of his position. Moton responded, "I can understand your position . . . Most of the teachers from the North don't fit in. We have a peculiar situation down here, and I imagine you have to be born in it to really understand it. Our race needs all sorts of people; probably you could contribute more in the North. You have my permission to leave."[12] Similarly, two other male professors left for Howard the moment they had the opportunity. G. David Houston, who taught at Tuskegee briefly, wrote to a friend while there, "I must leave here as soon as possible." And E. Franklin Frazier, the sociologist who started his academic career teaching at Tuskegee, also left to teach at Howard, when he could make his exit. Frazier recalled that while at Tuskegee, he was admonished by his dean for walking around with too many books and feared white supporters and other whites in the area "would get the impression that Tuskegee was training the Negro's intellect rather than his heart and hands."[13]

The years after Kelly left Tuskegee in 1915, she taught in small rural towns in Alabama and Georgia in private schools. She returned to Tuskegee in 1923 to teach in the Children's School on campus, which was a primary school that served as a demonstration school for student teachers. After teaching for years in this school without any college degree, she pursued an undergraduate degree once the college department was established and earned her degree in 1934. Obtaining this degree resulted in her being appointed principal of the Children's School. By the 1930s, credentials became more important as the public schools in the South required teacher certification. In addition, Black colleges in the South were also growing from high schools to full collegiate status and required accreditation. Kelly noted how difficult it was for Blacks to obtain an education during that period in the rural South. She said although she finished high school in 1915, she wasn't able to obtain a bachelor's degree until 1934. By the 1940s, the Rosenwald Foundation and the General Education Board began awarding fellowships to African Americans to obtain graduate degrees to enhance the faculties of historically Black colleges. The pursuit of accreditation required faculty with graduate degrees. After Kelly's first husband died in 1944, the dean of education at Tuskegee, J. Max Bond, helped her to secure a fellowship to enter graduate school. Kelly, whose area was early childhood administration, was accepted into a doctoral program at New York University in educational administration where she could concentrate on rural education administration. She earned her master's but was summoned back to Tuskegee by President Patterson to assist him with an administrative crisis in the education department. After Kelly briefly served as acting dean of education, Patterson then asked her to become dean of women. After having two deans of women who were not products of the South or HBCUs, Patterson believed Kelly would be a better fit for the position. She was a daughter of Tuskegee and understood the culture of the institution. She said she resisted accepting the position because she was preparing to work in the field of rural school administration. She told President Patterson that she had no background in student personnel. He responded that since she had raised a daughter, she should be able to do the job. However, Kelly understood that being a dean of women required specialized training and it was not as simple as being the mother of a daughter.

Her devotion to Tuskegee and Patterson's plea resulted in her agreeing to accept the position.[14] Kelly recognized that being a dean of women now required specialized training. As was often the case, if an HBCU had a specific need, a faculty member would be sent to obtain training and credentials in a specific field. Such was the case with Kelly. She returned to NYU and transferred her doctoral program from rural school administration to personnel and guidance. Kelly didn't finish the program but completed enough courses, she believed, to administer a student personnel program. She noted that in the field of student affairs, few Black women deans were a part of the professional meetings and conferences in this field. Kelly said, "there were not more than three or four of us [Black women] but there were hundreds and hundreds of white women." She respected the expertise and efforts of the two Black women deans prior to her that President Patterson had hired—Ida Jackson and Jean Fairfax. Kelly said she wanted to build on the earlier efforts of these women to enhance campus life and leadership for the women students at Tuskegee. She said that white institutions had established a group called Associated Women's Students (AWS). Jackson had established an AWS group the year she spent at Tuskegee and when Kelly became the dean of women, she said she "capitalized" on this initiative.[15] The

AWS was originally an organization of white women students on coeducational campuses that was established in the early 1900s as a response to their rapidly growing population in higher education. Housing and personal guidance were important issues to address for these students. In 1939, there were eighty-four chapters of AWS that had been established on coeducational campuses. By the 1960s, there were more than three hundred chapters that existed on campuses. The chapters were overwhelmingly at large public campuses.[16] These groups encouraged women's self-government and leadership.

Dean Kelly at Tuskegee recalled that the women students at Tuskegee resented the monthly meetings that were required of the women's organization. It wasn't clear what the purposes of the meetings were because the women students didn't have any input or agency over their treatment and lives at Tuskegee. Kelly recalled the students complaining about mandatory chapel. They resented having to line up and march to chapel, having their clothes inspected, and having to sit separately from the male students in chapel. Kelly said that President Patterson was adamant that chapel would remain required. While the president had the final say in the matter, Kelly said a compromise rule was established (unclear by whom) that the women students could have three excused absences from chapel. This was not good enough for the women. Kelly noted that on one Sunday, the women students conspired to all be absent on the same Sunday. She said the students reasoned since they weren't absent for three services, they were not disobeying the rules. Yet, they were making a point to the administration. Actually, Kelly was sympathetic toward the women since as a student, she had experienced the same rules decades earlier. She didn't like the rules either. However, she said she was not a confrontational person, and she knew that the students wanted a fighter. Kelly was apparently unable to forcefully advocate for the women students. She admitted in her oral history that she never rocked any boats. She said she learned to follow the rules as a child, and she understood there was a hierarchy. Kelly noted: "Anywhere I go, I look to see who is in charge. I'm not a radical. I'm not a trailblazer, which is not a compliment, but I can't help it now. I follow the line that is set up."[17] Hence, unlike Slowe who was very vocal and outspoken on behalf of women students and herself, Kelley acquiesced to her superiors (who were male). She realized on the Tuskegee campus that she had no real clout. However, she did try to use influence with Patterson to have some concessions for the women students. President Patterson knew that Kelly was an obedient administrator who would not protest his orders and counted on her not to dissent from issues in which she disagreed. However, stringent rules were not just for students, as recounted earlier, a former dean was not expected to have male visitors in her apartment. Everyone, including faculty and staff, was expected to attend chapel on Sundays. Jesse Abbott went to Tuskegee in 1923 to join her husband Cleve Abbott, who had become a faculty member at Tuskegee in 1916. Cleve had been the only Black student at South Dakota State College and earned a degree in agriculture. R. R. Moton, the principal of Tuskegee, recruited him. Jesse Abbott was a native of Iowa and neither she nor her husband had attended an HBCU or lived in the South prior to coming to Tuskegee. In an oral history of her experiences and life at Tuskegee, she also noted that faculty were expected to attend chapel.[18]

Although Ida Jackson, the first dean of women hired by President Patterson, noted in her communication to Lucy Slowe in 1937 that Patterson was going to start a student government, it's unclear what that meant. While in other institutions that were developing student leadership, students served on or had their own disciplinary committees, at Tuskegee, students were barred from being members of the school's disciplinary committee. Kelly believed students should have been on this committee. With her counseling background, Kelly said she felt that students could offer valuable insight into the behavior of their fellow classmates. She recalled that male students were frequently disciplined for purchasing alcohol in neighboring counties since Tuskegee was in Macon County, which was a "dry" county. She said the male students were given three warnings and often put on probation or expelled for drinking alcohol. Kelly stated for women students, pregnancy resulted in an immediate expulsion. Kelly was sympathetic to the situations with the male and female students. She stated there was never any counseling—just discipline. She said before and after Macon County made alcohol available, she felt that students should have been allowed to determine whether they wanted to drink or not. Also, Kelly said she was "disturbed" when the discipline committee immediately sent a pregnant girl home. Kelly was very sympathetic toward the girls and said she would pray and speak with them and asked who she could call to help them.[19] Despite her support of such students, there was nothing she could do to change the attitudes toward pregnant women students.

Patterson brought in Ruth Brett to Tuskegee the same year that Kelly became dean of women. Brett became a major figure in student personnel and Black higher education. She worked in numerous HBCUs from the mid-1930s until her retirement in 1980. Her experiences and longevity in a diverse number of HBCUs results in her being an important source on these institutions regarding women as students, faculty, and administrators. During her long career, she was the first African American to be appointed to the Commission on Education for Women. She served on the National Board of the YWCA of America and the NAWDAC.[20]

Brett was a native of North Carolina and a 1935 graduate of Shaw University, a private Baptist Black college in Raleigh. She graduated at the top of the class at Shaw and benefited from the mentorship of William Stuart Nelson, who became the first Black president of Shaw in 1931. Nelson was a graduate of Howard

University and had a graduate degree in religion from Yale. Brett worked and lived in the home of President Nelson as a student helper and aide, and as a result, she had the opportunity to meet distinguished Black persons and many Black college presidents. After graduating from Shaw, Brett earned an MA at Hartford Seminary in religion, education, and psychology. Brett noted that Nelson was responsible for her first two professional jobs. In 1936, she became an assistant to the dean at the all-women's Spelman College in Atlanta, Georgia. When Nelson was appointed in 1936 as the first Black president of Dillard University, the private American Missionary Association college in New Orleans, he recruited Brett to become dean of women there in 1938. When Nelson left Dillard in 1940, Brett moved to the all-women Bennett College in Greensboro, North Carolina, as dean where she stayed for two years. She had attended summer schools each year since she earned her master's to earn her doctorate. She returned to Teachers College at Columbia University for a summer and a year in 1944 to complete her degree, which she achieved in 1945. With her doctorate completed, Brett benefited from her academic credentials and connections. President Frederick Patterson at Tuskegee was a member of the Bennett College Board of Trustees and appointed her acting personnel director at Tuskegee, to replace the male, J. Julius Flood, a Tuskegee alumnus who was on leave. When he returned the next year, Brett was appointed associate director of personnel. She had broad experience working and studying student affairs in HBCUs. Because Spelman and Bennett were both women's colleges, Brett noted the position working with the students was just titled dean since the entire student body was female.[21]

Brett was one of a few African American women with formal training in student personnel administration. This education reinforced the notion that student personnel was a field in which individuals who worked in student affairs needed solid credentials and training. Brett believed that women personnel administrators should have faculty status and not merely the title dean of women. Brett advocated for the title dean of students. She said that deans of women were viewed as housemothers, matrons, and women and expected to live on campus. Brett was mentored by Hilda Davis, who was dean of women at Shaw when she was a student. And Davis was one of Slowe's first mentees at Howard. Hence, Brett was very much in the Slowe tradition of believing that deans of women should not be expected to live in the dormitory. In an interview with the author, Brett noted that deans of men were not expected to live in the dormitory with male students. In fact, male dormitories often had women "matrons" who lived in their dorms. She noted that she did not live in the dormitory at Dillard, and when she accepted the position as associate director of student personnel at Tuskegee, one of the conditions of her accepting the position was her request that she would not be required to live in a dormitory.

Brett said she wanted to "have a life." Very conscious of the insular campus and Dean Fairfax's experience during her short period at Tuskegee, Brett did not want a similar situation. While Dean Kelly continued to serve as the dean of women at Tuskegee until she retired in 1962, Brett moved on four years later to take advantage of an opportunity to work in Germany at the University of Munich through the American Friends Service Committee to work with students who were refugees who had fled countries throughout Europe after the end of World War II. Brett overlapped with Dean of Women Fairfax for one year. As mentioned earlier, Fairfax also went to Europe through the auspices of the American Friends Service Committee to work. It is possible her experience resulted in Brett following suit. However, while Fairfax was very critical of her experiences at Tuskegee, Brett was not. She praised President Patterson and appreciated the opportunity to help develop courses and programs for both men and women students. Brett stated she had an opportunity to develop a student orientation course for freshmen, she worked with student leaders, and student government representatives, the campus life committee, student counselors, and helped with student placement in their senior year. She noted she accompanied students, men and women, to conferences and meetings outside of Tuskegee.[22]

When Brett was asked why her opinion on Tuskegee was so different from Fairfax, she noted Fairfax's educational background was very different from that of Tuskegee and said that Fairfax had a "very, very liberal attitude," and at Tuskegee, "there were just hard and fast regulations."[23] As pointed out earlier, Fairfax was not a product of the South or of an HBCU. Brett noted, unlike Fairfax, she didn't live in the dormitory nor did she work solely with the women students. She said, "I was working with the men and women." Brett pointed out that the campus changed significantly the year after Fairfax left. She also pointed out that student life changed dramatically after the war. The closed campus center that had been converted to a recreational center for the airmen was now opened for students for the first time, under supervision. Brett remembered:

> You see, it [Tuskegee] changed a good bit right after she [Fairfax] left. At least it was somewhere on the campus where they [students] could go and play ping pong, pool table games and things; like the army you know had provided, and there were more frequent dances. So, I think that you can say in all honesty that that group, that army group, liberalized Tuskegee's campus.[24]

When Brett was asked about Ida Jackson's and Jean Fairfax's view that Tuskegee was a "male" school, she agreed that during those years at Tuskegee, "men were definitely the persons who were recognized . . . women were there, [but they] just happened to be there."[25]

Indeed, the world Fairfax had experienced as a student at the University of Michigan at the end of the Depression and during World War II was vastly different from what Black women students at HBCUs experienced. In a discussion with Fairfax, as she reflected in her retirement on her life experiences in her early days as a student and later as a professional, she commented, the years she spent at Michigan were ones of "radical social and economic reform" and it included "many thoughtful Americans across class lines." Fairfax said although Michigan was a "big football/fraternity/sorority (black and white) campus," my buddies were the "socialists, communists, pacifists, Lincoln Brigade veterans, Michigan Daily types who were involved in endless debates about how we were going to be the generation to change the world!" She said after the war began in 1939, she participated in anti-war rallies. She said she participated in picketing of plants to support workers. She also helped organize the first women's interracial cooperative house at Michigan. She was involved in many other social, racial justice and peace activities. She attended Union Seminary in New York after Michigan and said she was committed to peace and economic justice. She said she had no idea what was happening at HBCUs during this period. Hence, when Fairfax came to Tuskegee with such views, as Brett noted, they were perceived as "very, very liberal." She was indeed a mismatch. Fairfax reiterated that most HBCUs "provided a very restrictive—even repressive or stifling—environment for nurturing social concerns and activism." Fairfax said there were protests and strikes on campus, but they were primarily about food or social restrictions (like chapel attendance). She repeated the fact that Tuskegee was very militaristic. She said she never met any conscientious objector while there [she had mentioned in our conversation that she knew many men at Michigan and Union Seminary who refused to register and had been jailed]. She stated students who did not conform to the views of Tuskegee were expelled. The desire to involve the women students (and she said *all* students) in interracial, social justice and the peace movement was not what she was expected to do. She said she was expected to be a policewoman and said, "I refused, and did not last long at Tuskegee."[26] The reality was Tuskegee was not Michigan or New York. It was in the rural South, where integration did not exist, and lynching was still a reality. Even on Tuskegee's campus, white visitors and trustees were segregated from Black students and faculty in seating, dining, and housing. Any attempt to have interracial groups would imply that African Americans were the peers and equal to whites. The students at Tuskegee were overwhelmingly poor and from rural areas where they were concentrating on obtaining skills to earn a living and be of use to their communities. Fairfax was indeed ahead of her time. However, by the 1960s, and the end of this study, there were indeed many interracial organizations, and Black women college students were prominent within these groups and racial justice movements.

After the departure of Fairfax and Brett, Dean Kelly remained dean of women at Tuskegee until her retirement in 1962.

It should be noted that all residential colleges, regardless of race, had rules for their women students. Describing the norm for white coeducational institutions, Kelly Sartorius stated:

> . . . by 1900, coeducational institutions placed deans of women in charge of what might be termed, "a college within a college." While women attended classes and libraries with male students, campuses divided them (the core institution) in separate housing, advising, and activities. Such sex segregation regulated women's conduct, controlled interactions between male and female students, prohibited premarital sex, and provided the supervision parents expected.[27]

Coeducation presented challenges of how students related to one another across the gender line.

Bennett College

The white Women's Home Mission Society and the board of education of the Methodist Episcopal Church founded Bennett in 1873 in Greensboro, North Carolina. For unexplained reasons, by 1926, there were four girls for every boy who attended the institution. Hence, at the recommendation of the founding organizations, Bennett transitioned from a coeducational college to a women's college in that year. David Dallas Jones was appointed the first president of the all-women's college. He was from Greensboro and held an undergraduate degree from Wesleyan University in Connecticut, a master's from Columbia University in New York, and honorary law degrees from Howard and Syracuse Universities. When he arrived, the institution had grown from a day school and a seminary to a college. At that time, 90 percent of Bennett alumnae were schoolteachers. With more than half the state of North Carolina being rural, there was a desperate need for trained teachers for Black youth in those areas.

The attractive aspect of Bennett for its students was that it was a women's college. Although Spelman was also a women's college, it was part of a consortium that included an all-male college and three coeducational colleges. While the Black coeducational land-grant North Carolina A&T was also in Greensboro, and the students at the two campuses enjoyed the activities and events at one another's campuses, Bennett was a stand-alone campus removed from others. The focus was 100 percent on the education and growth of the women of the institution. The small and intimate campus with overwhelmingly Black women faculty and a supportive Black president with an educated and active wife created a family environment.

When Bennett became a women's college, several members on the faculty and staff were Black women who were key members of the NACW and the

NAWDAC. Both organizations were steeped in the Lucy Diggs Slowe philosophy of education for leadership and independence for Black women. Among the women were Flemmie Kittrell who joined the faculty in 1928. She was a Hampton Institute graduate of 1924 and came to Bennett to teach in the high school. She earned a master's in home economics 1930 and a PhD in 1935 from Cornell University in home economics with a specialization in nutrition. These academic accomplishments made Kittrell the first African American woman to earn a doctorate in home economics and one of the first Black women to earn a PhD in general. During her twelve years at Bennett, after the high school closed and Kittrell earned advanced degrees, she served as dean of students and director of the home economics department. In 1937, Bennett established a department of home economics. Kittrell was also deeply interested in child development. Dr. Kittrell was president of the NAWDAC and Dr. Brett, who joined Bennett as dean of students in 1946, was vice president. Merze Tate earned a bachelor's degree from Western Normal College in Michigan in 1927 and a master's degree at Columbia University in 1930. She studied in Switzerland in 1931, was awarded a certificate in international studies, and became the first Black woman to earn a degree from Oxford University in 1935. In 1935, Tate was recruited to serve as dean of women at Barber-Scotia College in Concord, North Carolina. This was a small, all-women's junior college founded by Presbyterians (it became a four-year women's college in 1945, and coeducational in 1954, the year it became accredited). Because of Tate's extraordinary credentials, she was highly recruited after she returned to the States. She said she accepted a position at Bennett

FIGURE 19. Willa B. Player, President of Bennett College, 1955–66. Courtesy of the Bennett College Archives at the Thomas F. Holgate Library.

Deans of Women at HBCUs after Slowe

College after one year at Barber-Scotia. Tate said she enjoyed working at Barber-Scotia, but Bennett allowed her the opportunity to be a faculty member and also Bennett was in a city and the salary increase was substantial.

In 1936, she became chair of the division of social science where she taught history and political science. She established a weekly program in the chapel titled Contemporary Affairs, which attracted people from the college community and the town. Tate was a staunch feminist before the term became in vogue. She encouraged women's leadership and achievements and was very much in the mode of the women of the NACW. She remained on the faculty until 1941, when she taught at Morgan State College for one year, and in 1942, she completed her PhD at Harvard University in diplomatic history and international relations.[28] Ruth Brett, mentioned earlier, joined the administration as dean of students in 1940. She remembered President Jones as being "very forward thinking" on women's higher education and sought to make Bennett as good as any prestigious white women's college. Jones indeed was the most progressive and vocal male president on the education of Black women of his era.

Willa Beatrice Player was the most significant woman faculty member and administrator at Bennett. She was hired at the age of twenty-one by President Jones in 1930 to teach Latin and French in the college. A devout Methodist, she earned a BA from the Methodist Ohio Wesleyan College in 1929 in Latin and French and a master's from Oberlin College in 1930. She took a leave of absence during the Depression to travel abroad and study in France, and in 1935, she earned a certificat d'etudes from the University of Grenoble, France. She earned a PhD in student personnel from Teachers College, Columbia University in 1948. In her thirty-one years there, Player moved from the faculty to the administration. She was appointed director of religious activities; director of admissions; coordinator of instruction; acting dean, and in 1956, she replaced President Jones when he became ill and died.

Player devoted her entire career to Bennett, even declining an offer to become the first Black woman president of Spelman College.[29] Player was a Methodist, and the fact that the college was founded by the Methodist Church strengthened her commitment to the college, resulted in her remaining on the faculty, and subsequently, the administration as president. Both Kittrell and Tate ended up spending the bulk of their careers at Howard University. Although Howard University was the "capstone" of Black higher education, Kittrell and Tate recalled Bennett as the high point of their professional careers. In an oral history, Kittrell recalled that Bennett was her first professional position, and "it was the most satisfying job I've ever had . . . it was sad to leave Bennett; in fact, I wept."[30] Tate said she considered North Carolina her second home because of the fond memories, the lifelong friendships, and closeness of the faculty at

Bennett.[31] These distinguished women scholars were central to shaping the early years of Bennett's tone toward the students. While they moved on to the more prestigious Howard University, Bennett remained the institution they cherished in their professional careers. As we shall see, these early Black women faculty and administrators shaped the curriculum and set the model of modern Black womanhood for the Bennett Belles.

Reflecting on the contributions of the earliest Bennett faculty—all young Black women starting out in their careers, Susie Jones, the wife of President Jones, reflected on the importance of these women to the students and the college. She said, "There were people like Dr. Flemmie Kittrell, Dr. Merze Tate, and Dr. Willa Player, young women who constantly reminded the students what they could attain in their own lives." Mrs. Jones noted that while there were men who later also made contributions to the faculty, the Black women faculty were a "plus" because the women students were constantly stimulated, encouraged, and urged to move forward. They were exposed to young Black women as department chairs and administrators. Mrs. Jones also noted that Bennett was always criticized for constant faculty turnover. She said the college had limited funds for salaries, and President Jones believed it was better to have a young teaching faculty who would come and stay a few years and move on rather than have older faculty who had passed their peak. She said the young faculty gave the Bennett Belles a "sparkle" and enthusiasm.[32]

In spite of the highly educated Black women from elite institutions, President Jones invited Mary Mcleod Bethune, the prominent founder of the Daytona Educational and Industrial School for Negro Girls (1906), to be the baccalaureate speaker for the first commencement of the all-female class in 1930. He wrote: "We are graduating our first class from the college, and, of course, this will be quite an event with us; therefore, we are looking for someone who can bring a message of inspiration and hope to our girls and to our community."[33] In 1923, Bethune's school merged with the Cookman Institute of Jacksonville, Florida, under the sponsorship of the Methodist Episcopal Church. It later developed into a four-year coeducational institution. Although Bethune was considered the "female Booker T. Washington" and stressed domestic, moral, and industrial training ("head, heart, and hand"), she was held in the highest regard among Black women as well as the entire race. From her humble beginnings in Mayesville, South Carolina, to establishing a school for Black girls in Florida with just $1.50 was profoundly inspirational. Her story told young Black girls they could accomplish their dreams and goals, they simply needed to have them.[34]

Although, as discussed in our next section, home economics was a focus and part of the Bennett curriculum, it was not an all-consuming field of study the way it was in industrial and training schools.

Homemaking Institute

The Methodist Women's Home Mission Society recommended the establishment of a Home Making Institute when the college became all women. The religious women's group thought homemaking was important but not the only focus for the Bennett students and the Black women in the area. Despite the name, this Institute exposed the students and the public to a vast array of topics. This Institute was an annual event with various themes that ran for a week. The events were opened to the public and generated huge attendance. In 1927, the year of the first Institute—over three thousand people were in attendance. Each year it featured distinguished speakers from government, business, and white women's colleges and HBCUs throughout the country. Home making was discussed broadly—not simply how to be a good housekeeper; sessions covered the economics of being a good consumer, nutrition, and discussions on the various cuts of meats, etc. Home economic teachers and other educators attended and brought their students to take advantage of the information from this event. Unlike institutions such as Hampton and Tuskegee where domestic science was the primary focus for the women students, Bennett as a liberal arts college offered classes in household arts among other subjects. At its opening as a single-sex college, it offered classes in English, math, science, American history, and the Bible. Among the electives students could take were foreign languages, teacher training, biology, household arts, European history, and sociology. While the field of home economics was ultimately established as an area to major in, this department wasn't established until 1937. Kittrell was the architect of this department and later the division. She created a required course titled The Arts of Living. In a dissertation on Bennett College by Deirdre Bennett Flowers, the class was described as an orientation on living standards and aimed "to give a comprehensive idea and appreciation of life in an everyday setting." The course covered "personal hygiene, costume art, personality development, the use of time and money, and family and community life." The course was expanded to include helping students to deal with personal problems, etiquette, and social graces."[35] Dr. Brett emphasized the course was not an "aggressive" one for women to move into leadership in the manner in which Slowe had stressed for Howard women. Brett stated, "they [at that time] were still training you to be good women—acceptable women and that kind of thing and sort of fit into the convention."[36]

This course fitted into the type of training and exposure that the NACW advocated, to be carried out by the women who were deans on HBCU campuses. The committee of standards of NACW in their annual report in 1935 noted that the committee "studies the physical equipment of college, the training of the deans of women; housing and the position of women on the faculty. It gives equal consideration to the philosophy of education and of particular institutions, using as criteria opportunities for leadership [for women students], for display of [word unclear], for student government, for cultivating social amenities, for recreation, for more of the rounded development by lectures, concerts and discussion groups."[37] The forward to the organization's annual journal noted that while they were concerned with the education of Black people in general— their efforts were devoted "largely in the attempt to secure equal opportunities, particularly for women in Negro institutions." However, it noted the caveat that the organization "has always been aware of the problems of local groups of the race which must be the problems of all Negroes."[38]

The Depression of the 1930s and into World War II significantly changed higher education with an explosion of Black and white women attending college. The growth of public schools resulted in colleges terminating their high schools due to the growth of the nineteen state-funded land-grant colleges through the Second Morrill Act in 1890. These institutions were overwhelmingly attended by women since those colleges almost exclusively prepared their students for teaching. Bennett and other private HBCUs—especially, but not exclusively, those founded by white missionaries—were liberal arts colleges. The membership of NACW were products of liberal arts colleges, and they believed such a curriculum would make Black women more competitive and not pigeonholed. Yet, regardless of Black women's academic preparations, they overwhelmingly became teachers.

The need for teachers for Black students was dire in the South. A 1930 study by Fred McCuistion of the Julius Rosenwald Fund noted that 93 percent of Black southern schools were rural. The teachers were profoundly undereducated. Thirty-nine percent of all Black teachers in the South had less than a high school diploma and 58 percent had less than two years of education beyond high school. High schools in the rural South were still in their embryonic stage with 94 percent of Black students in elementary school and only 5 percent in high school. The study noted that the typical southern Black school teacher was a female of rural heritage, a high school graduate, with ten weeks of summer school.[39]

However, teaching positions for Blacks outside the South were difficult to come by because Blacks were barred from teaching at schools unless they were segregated. As a result, many educated Blacks from the North came south to teach. Whereas rural areas of the South attracted the least-prepared teachers, the opposite was true of urban areas. Major cities with Black high schools attracted Black educators with outstanding credentials from leading colleges and universities in the nation. Indeed, Blacks with graduate degrees and experiences studying abroad taught in cities like Washington, Baltimore, Atlanta, St. Louis, Kansas City, and Indianapolis. In his study of the *Negro College Graduate* in

1938, sociologist Charles S. Johnson pointed out, "teaching may be said to draw the poorest and the best types of college graduates. Both types find their way into the teaching field because there are so few jobs in other fields for them."[40] Susie Jones's father served as principal of the well-known Sumner High School in St. Louis, Missouri, during her youth. Both of her parents were graduates of the abolitionist Berea College, discussed in chapter two.[41]

The reality was rural schools sought out teachers who were skilled in industrial and domestic sciences. Also, white superintendents of schools viewed Blacks educated in elite liberal arts colleges as arrogant and proud. In 1918, when Julius Rosenwald visited Fisk University, he wrote Abraham Flexner, who was secretary of the General Education Board, "there seemed to be an air of superiority among them [Fisk students] rather than the spirit which has already impressed me at Tuskegee."[42]

Indeed, as mentioned with the adjustment of Blacks educated and born outside of the South teaching in colleges, this was the issue with those in the school systems as well. However, in this case, they were not sought out because there was a belief by southern whites that such people were not good "fits" for southern Black schools. In an early study that Du Bois and Dill published on Black teachers in the South, they noted these schools sought teachers with industrial and domestic science backgrounds. School systems were not interested in students trained in the liberal arts.

In 1937, the NACW held their annual convention at Bennett College. Dr. Kittrell was president of the Greensboro chapter of the organization. At the conference, Merze Tate gave a talk on "The Justification of the Women's College." Although Tate described herself as a "modern" woman who was clearly independent and extremely well-educated, world traveled, and successful, her comments as to the role of women's colleges to Black women were interesting in that they were both traditional and forward thinking. Tate's talk was void of the constant theme and charge that Black women need to help "uplift the race." She emphasized that Black women should seek self-actualization. Tate said that there are three reasons that women's colleges were important and unique: first, they are in a better position to develop women culturally and aesthetically; second, being separated from men at a critical period in the women's lives resulted in them developing a saner attitude toward sex and a higher moral character; third, and most important, women in single-sex colleges can approach the problems concerning life attitudes toward women. Although Tate, like most, if not all of the members of NWSA (and also NAWDAC—there were overlapping memberships), advocated and believed in Black women being professionals, she and they were painfully conservative in their beliefs regarding relationships with men and being in their company. There was an assumption that such closeness of the genders would result in "moral failings" on the part of the women and that they were all heterosexual. Also, Tate like all of the women of both groups stressed the need for Black women to develop culturally. She pointed out that obtaining intellectual knowledge was a given in college; however, she noted, "we expect all colleges to impart knowledge. I fear we have sometimes lost sight of the aesthetic contribution. Should not the women's colleges, especially those for our race, while not neglecting scholarship, lay greater emphasis upon the cultural?" Tate hastened to explain that while she believed that men and women are best educated separately at this period in their lives, she's not suggesting they should not have any contact. She said in a women's college the students don't have to worry about how they dress, their makeup, and their general behavior when men aren't around. However, she said she would advocate having coeducational activities, such as the visitation of men a few hours a week to see the women; a sensible number of term parties, teas, tennis matches and other sports meets, and picnics will suffice for interaction between male and female students. Tate stated that putting men and women together resulted in immoral acts (meaning sexual contact) being likely to occur. She said the college years are "when sex-consciousness is most acute."[43] She further stated, "we must face the fact that there is positive evidence of a disregard of the traditional moral code on every coeducational campus. The deans of women present will bear me out on this statement." Hence, deans of students on women's campus do not have the issues that deans of women on coeducational campuses have with heterosexual relationships. In another puzzling comment, Tate quoted Le Barron Russell Briggs, dean of Harvard faculty and president of Radcliffe College, saying "[women's colleges] do not exist for the competition of women with men, but for the ennobling of women as women." Tate continued that women's colleges aren't "endeavoring to turn out an army of masculine counterparts . . . nor is there a need to turn out an army of feminists." She noted the dilemma of the current college woman: they could be ultra-feminist and advocate women's rights forever or they can be ultra-feminine and serve men, produce the race, and keep house; or, she said they could do both. Tate told the women in the audience that current college women (assuming all students were heterosexual) had to contemplate whether to pursue a career, marriage, or both. Tate urged the members of NWSA to determine how to "salvage" the investment in time, money, and energy of these women in obtaining their college degrees. She said those who choose marriage have to determine how to make educated women's intellectual interests dominant and utilized. Tate, a lifelong single professional woman who had a highly successful career said, "It is probably true that the more highly educated a woman is the less content she is with woman's traditional activities in the home as a major and overwhelming portion of her own daily schedule." Tate noted that women who did not marry faced different challenges. She said this is the age of the modern women and women students have options, and it's the role of the members of the organization to assist college women in non-curricular issues and individual counseling. Tate ended her talk by saying college women should "enter to grow in wisdom; depart to serve better their country and their kind."[44] Tate clearly thought educated women should not waste their talents and intellect merely in the home but determine ways to satisfy both family and career. This topic became a consistent one especially as college enrollment of women soared. And, as will be discussed later, career and marriage was a significant topic for Black women college students.

HBCU College Women and Sports

Ensuring HBCU college women were poised, refined, and "feminine" continued to permeate discussions of the deans of women. The rise in women's sports after World War I became another challenge for the group. As discussed in chapter four, Black women on white college campuses participated in sports beginning in the teens. They also began majoring in the new field of physical education by the early 1920s. The Black women who were physical education majors as well as members of college sports teams from white institutions took their talents to work with girls in the Black community and Black colleges. Basketball was considered the most popular sport for college women during the 1920s through the 1940s. During this period, physical education classes for women initially stressed exercise and physical development. However, by the '30s, the field became more concerned with feminine refinement. Questions of femininity resulted in basketball being phased out and restricted only to intramural games. This view was expressed in white colleges and trickled down to Black colleges. Historian Patricia A. Graham in her study on women in higher education wrote: "The feminine ideal—as opposed to the feminist one—was stressed during the early and middle years of the twentieth century for college women."[45]

Institutions, such as Howard, Spelman, Fisk, Bennett, Tuskegee, and Hampton were very conscious of Black women's image of not being feminine and refined and ensured that their students and alums were readily recognizable by their grace and the way they publicly presented themselves. For example, Rosemary Reeves Allen, the head of physical education at Howard University in Washington, DC, from 1925 to 1967 stressed poise, beauty, and femininity in Howard women. Allen had an undergraduate and master's degree from the renowned Sergeant School of Physical Education at Boston University. She instilled within her students the notion of dignity, courtesy, and refinement. Her goal, she stated, was to make the women at Howard so distinctive that they could go anywhere in the world, and someone would say, "I can always tell a Howard woman when I see one because she walks in such beauty."[46] During the period that she was at Howard, up until the *1954 Brown v. Board* decision, which integrated public education, 80 percent of all Black women who taught physical education in high schools and colleges in the DC area were graduates of Howard. In addition to teaching at Howard, Allen taught physical education in the summers at Hampton Institute. She instilled within her students that beauty and health were synonymous, and that inner beauty would reflect outer beauty. The curriculum she established focused not only on sports, but anatomy, beauty, body aesthetics, charm, dance, and hygiene. Like other elite schools, Allen established annual events like the Beauty Bazaar, Christmas Program, Folk Fiesta, May Festival, Water Show, and Sports Day. Allen believed that light sports like archery, badminton, volleyball, and dance were acceptable sports for her students. While she didn't specifically name basketball, she commented in 1938, "The heavier sports have no place in a woman's life, they rob her of her feminine charms and often of her good health."[47]

In a report to the dean of the School of Liberal Arts, in 1939, Allen provided justification for why the women's physical education department should be its own department and not under the same administration as male students. She told him, "Women have problems that men do not understand—therefore, they get no sympathy," and the activities of the two departments are not the same. Allen said men should not teach any women's physical education courses, noting men "are not as well qualified to teach physical activities to girls or act as officials." She also appealed to the university to suspend intercollegiate and only allow intramural sports. Among the reasons she gave was intercollegiate competitions produce physical and emotional strain; it encourages rowdyism rather than cultural influences; attracts undo publicity to young women; distorts the students' value of athletics; curtails the freedom of a normal life, in which Allen argued that sports competitions bring about unwholesome experiences and becomes commercialized. She was able to convince the dean that competition was unhealthy and provided little cultural value for her physical education students.[48]

A similar view on decorum and how young women students presented themselves was made of Spelman students. Howard Zinn, a progressive faculty member who was terminated from the college in 1963 because of his activism in the civil rights movement said:

> "You can always tell a Spelman girl" alumni and friends of the college have boasted for years. The "Spelman girl" walked gracefully, talked properly, went to church every Sunday, poured tea elegantly and, in general, had all the attributes of the product of a fine finishing school. If intellect and talent and social consciousness happened to develop also, they were, to an alarming extent, byproducts.[49]

At one of the annual conferences of NAWDAC—there was a session titled, "Ideals in Physical Education for Women." A Miss Hoover, who was a physical

FIGURE 20. Thirteen members of the Bennett College basketball team in uniforms in front of Race Hall, 1930.

education instructor at Fisk, presented it. She repeated the prevailing view at that time that sports and physical education should be for health and enjoyment. She pointed out the "evils of strenuous competition." Unlike male sports on campuses where the teams competed for their various divisions, competition for recognition of women's teams was discouraged. Women should play light sports for the sake of enjoyment and not for winning pennants and trophies.[50]

By the 1940s, middle-class society and colleges determined that competitive sports were masculine endeavors. Women's basketball teams, in an attempt to distinguish their movements from the men's teams were given "girl's rules," which confined them to one part of the court, restricted them to a minimum number of dribbles, and required them to avoid physical contact with other players. To have women students avoid competition and tournaments and awards, games were overwhelmingly intramural so that a large number of women could participate and not a select few. As noted by the courses offered at Howard University, physical education courses began to require women students to stress good posture, class attendance, homework, and athletic activity. Varsity matches were replaced with "play days" and "sports days," in which the students combined games and various social activities.[51]

The Black press of the era also commented on the inappropriateness of women in sports:

> The girl who is too athletic is on the wrong track to becoming a wife. Men want feminine women, not creatures who are half like themselves and the other half resembling something else. It is only natural and logical because we loathe men who act effeminate and desire a man, all man. Men want women, all women. . . . being too athletic and consequently too mannish prevents her from being.[52]

This obvious sexist and homophobic statement reflected the thinking of the era. The one exception of a private school continuing basketball for Black college women was Bennett College. It had one of the top women's basketball teams in the nation in the 1930s. Despite the renown of this team, by the 1940s, the institution also succumbed to the belief that competitive basketball was inappropriate for women. Like Howard and other institutions, Bennett switched to intramural games and play day activities. In an insightful article on the basketball team at Bennett titled, "We Were Ladies, We Just Played Basketball Like Boys: African American Womanhood and Competitive Basketball at Bennett College, 1928–1942," this defensive title reflected the players' plea for the public to understand that although they played the game "like men"—they did not play by "girl" rules, and they also practiced by playing against the local Black high school boys' basketball team. One of the team's members said, "being a lady does not mean being prissy, it's just an inward culture . . . always being polite and not saying things to hurt people's feelings. You could be tough as I don't know what on that basketball court, but you still have those same principles." In the minds of these women, there was no contradiction in being a star basketball player and being a "lady." A former woman player who was then a coach wrote in support of women playing competitive basketball with "men's rules" versus the "girl's rules":

> Girls of today are red-blooded, virile young creatures, and are no longer content to conform to the masculine ideal of feminine inferiority and frailty. The clinging vine has given way to the freely moving, sensibly clad young Amazon of today. Such fineness of physique cannot be maintained or secured through the inadequacies of girls' rules in basketball.[53]

Despite this plea for Black women and girls to reject this notion of "femininity," this became a minority opinion. As Black women educated in white physical education programs went South to teach, they absorbed the view that competitive sports were not ladylike or feminine.

Basketball was a popular sport for Black college women in North Carolina beginning in the 1920s. Shaw University, Livingston College, Barber-Scotia,

North Carolina A&T, Bennett, and HBCUs in North Carolina, all had basketball programs. However, the quest to make Black college women "soft" and more "feminine" took place by the 1930s. For example, in 1937, North Carolina A&T University, the state's Black public institution, hired Ordie Roberts, a graduate of the University of Illinois. She established a physical education program for women students that included her interest in dance and tennis. In addition, modern and folk dance classes were introduced as "correctives" for students for posture and carriage. Roberts quickly advocated ending competitive women's sports—particularly basketball. She repeated the view that such activities were harmful to the physical health of the women. And she noted that all of the leading colleges in the country agreed and have eliminated such sports. As a result, the athletic committee voted to terminate intercollegiate competitive sports.[54] Within a few years, Bennett College, which had a winning and distinguished basketball team, also succumbed to pressure and discontinued its basketball team as well. In a front-page article in 1939 in the college newspaper, *The Bennett Banner*, it reported on twenty-five Bennett Belles who participated in a Sports Day at Hampton Institute. The article noted the sports and activities that the women participated in: hockey, volleyball, badminton, soccer, relays, and skits. It was clear the move toward non-competitive sports had been accomplished. There was no mention of basketball, and the article made clear the aim of sports for Black college women:

> It is hoped that such events will bring about a closer relationship between the schools; that the participants will feel a part of the group with regards to working toward the best of her ability for the good of the group; taking part for the self-satisfaction and not trying to be outstanding as such for prizes or praise.[55]

The comments of the article made clear competing for "prizes or praise" were not desirable attributes for Black college women. While Black male athletic teams were having Thanksgiving "classic" competitions for best teams, competition was perceived as a male prerogative.

When Bennett hosted the event in 1943, new sports had been added. The Belles participated in tennis, softball, badminton, archery, horseshoes, and relays. In addition, the women had a calisthenics exhibition. And, by 1945, fencing, handball, and juggling were also included.[56] By the 1950s, all of the women's colleges had replaced their teams with sports days, gymnastic exhibitions, May Days, and intramural games.[57]

As basketball was phased out in Black colleges for the women students, the sport of track and field was viewed as the worst for women students. From 1937 to 1948, the women's track and field team at Tuskegee Institute dominated the

Amateur Athletic Union. They won every year except in 1943 when they placed second to the Cleveland Olympic Club. While there were many outstanding women on the track team, Alice Coachman was considered the unrivaled star. She was an outstanding high jump and track star, winning twenty-six national championships, more than any other American women with the exception of her Polish-American rival, Stella Walsh. In 1938, Coachman won the Olympic gold medal in track, the first African American woman to do so. Nicknamed Tuskegee Flash, because of her speed, Coachman received little press coverage despite her record-breaking record as a sprinter and high jumper—because she was in a "man's sport." The *New York Times* only gave her one sentence of coverage when she won the gold medal. One observer of the press treatment of Coachman noted this comment when Coachman won the gold medal in the *Atlanta Constitution*:

> An all-round athlete, Alice is an outstanding forward on the basketball team in her college, but her instructors say confidentially that she's just a "fair" student in her home economics classes.

In other words, Coachman excels in male sports but isn't competent in the stereotypical women's area of home economics, a field in which Tuskegee was renowned. And, of course, no other classes were mentioned. The Black press coverage was different with headlines titled, "Tuskegee Star," "The Flying Miss Coachman," "Tuskegee's 21-year-old Speed Queen," "America's Number One Woman Track Athlete," "Alice Coachman Crowned National Sprint Queen." While the larger society viewed track as a masculine sport, the Black press attempted to portray Coachman in a feminine vein. In a 1941 feature article on the Tuskegee track team in the *Baltimore Afro-American*, the paper portrayed the women in a manner that reflected their femaleness—it said, "These young women, while mixing athletics with studies, enjoy all the pleasures and indicated desires to become a nurse . . . teachers, social workers."[58] Of Alice, they specifically emphasized her heterosexuality by saying Coachman was interested in being either a teacher or a social worker—but also the author noted, "being a good wife when she married will probably be the fulfillment of her secret ambitions."[59] While the NAWDAC, the deans of women at HBCUs, were concerned with how the decorum of the students continue to be developed, the NACW, the Black graduates of white liberal arts college, and Howard and Fisk Universities, were concerned with the academic standards and courses offered to Black women students. The next section will look at the impact of World War II and its aftermath with the mixed messages Black college women received. More Black women were attending college; their numbers surpassed that of Black men beginning in the 1940s and continue to do so today.

Activism and Intellect: Curriculum for Black Women Students

The growth of public high schools in the 1930s and '40s, resulted in an explosion of Black women attending state land-grant colleges. In 1928, there were 14,028 Black students who were admitted to college by high school certificates. Sixty-four percent of these students were women, and 73 percent of the students admitted by examination were women. The women matriculated primarily for two years to obtain credentials for teaching while the male students remained through the third and fourth year of college.[60] Eight thousand Black teachers were needed in 1928 to staff the growing public schools in the South. World War II resulted in men on coeducational college campuses being drafted for the military and resulted in most campuses becoming virtually all women. This section will discuss the efforts of the NACW and NAWDAC to transform the curriculum and prepare Black women for the new professions and opportunities opening to women during the war years and afterwards. In addition, with men away, opportunities for women in fields that were historically defined as male opened up to them. This resulted in college majors and positions unavailable to women in the past now opening up to white women. The members of NACW pushed to have Black women students exposed to such opportunities. The challenge, however, was the curricula at most HBCUs with rare exceptions, did not prepare women students for careers beyond teaching. Virtually all Black state institutions (and private ones as well) were preparing Black women for the desperate need for teachers in the South. This reality reinforced the social class divide. The NACW members focused on curriculum and standards and were products of white liberal arts colleges and universities or Fisk and Howard. This was not the curriculum offered to most Black women students. The group sought to change that by developing a curriculum specific to the needs of Black women. Bennett College was the test case for NACW. Although Spelman was older, had a larger faculty with better formal credentials, and ninety-four students in its college department compared to four students, when Bennett became an all-women's college in 1926, as noted previously, from the beginning, Bennett had Black leadership. The college's president and dean were Black men, and the ten faculty members were all Black women. Ten out of the twelve had attended HBCUs, and one held a master's degree. In contrast, by 1926, four white women had served as president of Spelman. That year it had eighteen faculty members, twelve of whom taught exclusively in the college department. All were white except for one Spelman graduate.[61]

One of the first professional positions Ruth Brett had was working in student affairs at Spelman as assistant to the dean in 1936 when Florence Read was president. Brett recalled that President Read was very kind to her but described

Read's administrative style as that of a dictator. She recalled Read as "paranoid" and having to be in charge of everything. Although there was a registrar and dean, she noted, Read ran everything. Brett stated the faculty and staff had little input into anything while she was there. Brett commented that in all of her professional experiences in most HBCUs, there was the "one person rule"—the president.[62] Hence, the Black women's organizations determined it was more desirable to work with Bennett since some of the key officers of NAWDAC had taught and served as department chairs and administrators at the college. In addition, there was a camaraderie and shared sense of purpose among the women, who themselves were Black women, and the Jones administration was very supportive of these endeavors.

In 1939, Bennett decided to completely revise the curriculum and adapt it specifically toward preparing Black women for their perceived role in society. Lucy Diggs Slowe's early years as dean advocated the importance of the curriculum for the "modern" woman and urged that fields like political science, sociology, and psychology to be offered. Bennett took this recommendation seriously. By 1940, Bennett had enrolled 354 students from 23 states and the District of Columbia. Its reputation had grown, attracting Black women from across the country. In North Carolina, the Black middle-class was populated primarily in the five largest cities: Raleigh, Durham, Greensboro, Charlotte, and Winston-Salem. It also attracted students from across the state. It was a small, beautiful campus with faculty and staff dedicated to the education of Black women. Dr. Brett stated that although she was dean of students, the entire faculty worked with the students, and she never felt she was the sole person responsible for the personal growth of the women. She said Bennett was a very welcoming and positive experience. Brett said that when a new faculty member came to the campus at the beginning of the school year, an old faculty member would invite them into their home. Throughout the year, the students and faculty worked closely together.[63] When she arrived, the administration and faculty were busy working on radically revising the curriculum to make it specifically relevant to Black women. Both Brett and Tate described the campus as a family.

With the input of the aforementioned women and faculty, in 1941, President Jones applied for a grant from the General Education Board (GEB) of the Rockefeller Foundation to conduct a three-year study of Black women college students to determine how Bennett should revise the curriculum to prepare its students for the changing world for women. He noted that such work had been done for white women but wrote, "no study has been attempted to establish the course that education take for women whose situations are similar to those of our students—namely, those women of a minority group from families of low economic status."[64] He also requested funding for the establishment for two practice houses for their new home economics department. The request was for a practice house for urban areas and another one for a rural area. Home economics majors would stay in one of the two homes for nine weeks as a part of their degree requirements. Each home would have four bedrooms and a kitchen. However, the rural practice home would have a community center and library, a laundry room and canning room, and space for gardening and chicken raising. The foundation funded the survey study for up to $7,500 over a one-year period but declined funding of the practice houses. It had received several requests for practice houses from other institutions, and the foundation decided to table decisions on such requests.[65]

Bennett worked in concert with the NACW to ensure empirical data on the status of Black women on HBCU campuses. One thousand questionnaires were sent to Black women college graduates. Four hundred questionnaires were sent to Bennett College alums who had graduated five or more years ago and six hundred to Black women graduates of other HBCUs. Dr. Brett was involved in collecting data for the project and visited an array of white women's colleges including Sarah Lawrence, Stephens, Bennington, Wellesley, Smith, Goucher, and Stephens. In addition, the study included visits to a couple of coeducational HBCUs—Tuskegee in Alabama and Fort Valley State in Georgia.

The study concluded based on the responses of the women that there was a need to provide courses that focused on the following areas:

Earning a Living
Communication
Consumer Education
Mental and Physical Health
Community Leadership and Citizenship
Home and Family Life
Recreation
Religion and Philosophy of Life

These were labeled "human living" topics. While Bennett prepared its students for careers, the respondents stated they felt they needed guidance and information on the various occupations they could pursue. In the area of consumer education, the women stated they needed more guidance in how to rent, buy, or build a house; how to buy life insurance; how to establish and build a savings account; how to invest wisely; how to understand interest rates; and the problems of purchasing on installment plans. The study noted the respondents requested more guidance in public speaking, how to write business letters, social responsibility, how to deal with racism in society, problems of courtship and marriage, information on sex education, and parenting information. The alums stated they would have benefited by doing their student teaching in the types of communities they would be working in. Interest in these areas clearly reflected these women students' plans on having agency over their lives and pursuing professional careers post-graduation.

In addition to the women's response from the survey, the college included the data from the visits to the women's colleges and the input from consultants who were scholars and college presidents of women's colleges. The Bennett faculty met monthly to discuss the findings and ponder how to implement this daunting task. The college was organized academically, in four divisions: the humanities, the social sciences, the sciences, and home economics. One of the outstanding aspects of Bennett College is the respect the institution had for its students. They encouraged leadership (since they had advocates for such by the NACW and NAWDAC faculty at Bennett). The study asked the alums and other Black women students for their opinions, which shaped the focus of the study. In addition, the college invited four students selected by their peers in their major to serve on each of the division committees and attend the regular faculty meetings. This was in direct contrast to the women's experience at Tuskegee where their opinions were not solicited on matters regarding changes on campus.

The committee concluded that there were too many requirements for graduation. The freshman class had seven required classes, sophomores had only one elective and seniors had three. The faculty and student representatives agreed to drop languages, chemistry, and survey of social sciences, general psychology, and a few other courses as requirements. They replaced these classes with new courses: consumer economics, which was required of all students; Negro history and the Negro in our culture. Courses in physical and mental health, religion and philosophy of life, community problems, and arts and crafts were also added. Courses that had previously been required for students in a given major were now opened to all students. These included: child psychology, nursery school education, family life, family management, household physics, the Negro in American literature, and community organizing.

In 1942 in the *Journal of Negro Education,* President Jones published an article titled, "The War and the Higher Education of Negro Women." This article discussed the impact of the war on opportunities for women during the war and afterward. He cited manpower studies and research from the American Council on Education of shortages in fields of employment such as management and administration, agriculture, and biology, medicine, engineering, and physical sciences, and areas of the social sciences, and arts and languages. Jones stated these studies indicated that women were not being prepared in those areas. He further commented, "If this is true of college women in general, then it is doubly true of Negro college women."[66] The article continued a discussion of the study that Bennett College along with the NACW conducted of Black women alumnae. He cited the study that Charles S. Johnson, the Black sociologist and first African American president of Fisk University, had made, *The Negro College*

Graduate. Johnson's study noted that only 11 percent of Black women college graduates fell within the categories of manufacturing and technical industries. He said there were two million women who were college graduates who could be trained for wartime positions and there were little more than a half million women in college (this included women of all races). Jones pointed out that he realized in the past Black women knew there were few employment opportunities for African American women in these fields. However, there was optimism that things were changing for women and African Americans.[67]

Jones noted that realistically most women would become mothers and many, homemakers. He used the well-quoted statement, "When you educate a man you educate an individual, but when you educate a woman, you educate a family."[68] He said during the war, homemaking and raising a family would be challenging and women needed to be prepared for how to handle these challenges. They would need to understand budgets and how to handle rationing. Women should be taught issues related to being a consumer during war and peace time. In addition, they should be exposed to courses related to psychology, nutrition, family life, etc. Finally, Black women needed to be cognizant of race relations and inter-group relations since there remained challenges in these areas.[69]

Because Bennett College was an all-women's college, it could focus 100 percent on women's concerns, curriculum, and activities. Coeducational HBCUs rarely had any special curricular focus for women students. Lucy Slowe always stated that coeducational colleges were a huge challenge to the growth and development of Black women students. Jones noted that Willa Player was on the subcommittee on women in college and defense, which included the dean of Barnard College, Virginia Gildersleeve; Dr. Lillian Gilbreth of Purdue; Dean Irma Voigt of Ohio University, Dean Margaret Jutin of Kansas State College; president of Wellesley College, Mildred McAfee; and president of Sweet Briar, Meta Glass. Jones always had his staff work closely with other major women's colleges and viewed Bennett students as preparing for the world as well as their communities.

With the momentum from the curricular reorganization based on the study conducted at Bennett and the grant from the GEB to implement the study, Flemmie Kittrell, who was a member of NACW and also the president of NAWDAC, approached Florence Read, the president of Spelman, regarding hosting a conference on the Current Problems and Programs in the Higher Education of Negro Women. Spelman College was named in honor of Laura Spelman Rockefeller, which resulted in Read having a direct connection with the officers at the GEB. Read would be an important ally for such a conference. The NACW had been working on issues on improving the curriculum for Black women at HBCUs since the 1920s. The proposed conference was the opportunity they had hoped for.[70]

In June of 1943, Kittrell met with Jackson Davis in the New York office to discuss the proposed conference. She indicated to him that President Read of Spelman had agreed to host the conference at Spelman the first week in September. In July, Kittrell sent him a copy of the proposed conference and again mentioned President Read's involvement.[71] The proposal submitted to GEB by Kittrell included a request for funding for a two-and-a-half-day conference with sixty invited participants. They would comprise the presidents of HBCUs, deans of women, deans of instruction, and instructors in education. The conference would discuss the issues that were surveyed by the Bennett and NACW study. The main topics were jobs, family (including consumer education), marriage, home, and courtship; health including mental, physical, and spiritual; and scholarship, leisure time, and human relations. Her notes also included discussing the topic of prostitution. It's unclear why this was a proposed topic.

Confident that the conference would be funded, Kittrell called the president of the predominantly male Association of Colleges and Secondary Schools for Negroes, Dean J. Hugo Jonson of Virginia State College, and told him that the GEB was sponsoring this conference and asked if his organization would have a joint meeting with the conference on Black women at the same time in Atlanta. Read rebutted this information and told the group that the proposal had not been funded and was still in the "inquiry" stage. Read mentioned that the American Council on Education had a subcommittee focused upon the Relation of Higher Education to the Federal Government and that the chair, Dean Margaret Morris of Pembroke College was concerned with women's colleges and wartime adjustments. She suggested using people from Sarah Lawrence and Stephens Colleges, white women's colleges, as consultants. Rufus Clement, president of Atlanta University, said he was not interested in a joint meeting and noted that a large group would create housing problems. The inability of Blacks to stay in hotels always presented issues of housing when there were conferences at Black colleges. He said the conference on women's issues should be separate. It's not clear if Clement was not interested in women's issues or did not want such a conference to meet at the same time as the organization of college presidents. Florence Read, who was a member of the ACSSN and president of Spelman, relayed this discussion to the GEB officials.

John D. Rockefeller, a major Spelman benefactor, also funded the General Education Board. Hence, Read held a close relationship with the GEB officials and functioned as their in-house informant.[72] The conference was not held in September and Kittrell approached the GEB about sponsoring the conference the following year. In October 1943, Kittrell asked Davis for funds for guest speakers, entertainment, and general costs. To impress upon him the urgency of the issue, she mentioned that the number of women on HBCU campuses had exploded. She noted that at Hampton, where she was the current dean, the new academic year resulted in 560 women enrolled and stated that the school had to turn away 500 others. She said they sent them to Virginia Union and St. Paul, two private HBCUs in the state. Kittrell also said that the Black land-grant college Virginia State had reached capacity and couldn't accommodate any more students. She said because of the dramatic increase in the number of women students, the deans of women at these institutions are experiencing new problems and others have intensified. She said these women felt a need to get together to confer and work on some constructive strategies for working with these students.[73] This explosion of Black women college students was a prelude to the social problems they would confront later as their opportunities for a higher education increased.

Jackson Davis wrote a memo to the file of Kittrell's visit and said he suggested a small study group of about twenty selected experts for a two-week gathering. Kittrell stated the conference's travel would be paid for by their institutions. She did indicate that she would go back to the planning committee to consider the study group versus a two-and-a-half-day conference. Davis also contacted Florence Read right away to let her know his suggestion to Kittrell to extend the time of meeting and reduce the number of participants. He wrote: "We [the GEB] raised the question with her [Kittrell] whether a smaller group more directly concerned with the higher education of Negro women meeting for a longer time as a work conference with some outside leaders and consultants might not be of more lasting benefit . . . Knowing of your interest, I would appreciate very much any ideas you may have about it." He said because of the difficulty of travel, the GEB was reluctant to encourage a large meeting. Of course, Read readily agreed and said, "A discussion by a smaller number of people, with the benefit of help from outside leaders and consultants, would be more profitable." She said she would wait for Dr. Kittrell to contact her since she was on the planning committee.[74] In a couple of weeks, Kittrell also responded that after conferring with her planning committee, they agreed to have a ten-day to two-week study group of fewer than twenty people to discuss the current higher education of Black women. This change of plans meant that very few of the deans of women at HBCUs could attend this event, although they were the ones who conceptualized the meeting. Of course, Kittrell had to agree with the GEB since they were the key funders.

Because of the greatly reduced number of people invited to this event (it was invitational only)—Kittrell had to confirm with the GEB that the gathering would not exceed twenty persons. The group would now be comprised of three members of the Commission on Higher Education; three members of the National Association of Deans of Women and Advisors of Negro Schools; and the rest of the participants selected by the presidents of HBCUs. The number did not include the speakers and consultants who would be brought in for their expertise.

The 1944 NAWDAC Conference

Six weeks prior to the Spelman conference funded by the GEB, the NAWDAC held their annual conference in April of 1944 in Durham, North Carolina, at North Carolina State College for Negroes. Since the Spelman conference had been delayed and reduced in number, the NAWDAC continued their discussion about the important issues of Black women students—especially during the war and afterward. Their theme was "Women's Students in Today's and Tomorrow's World." Flemmie Kittrell was president and Ruth Brett was the vice president of the organization, both former Bennett faculty and administrators. However, unlike the NACW, which was primarily concerned with academic standards and the curriculum for Black women students, as well as the employment status and advancement of Black women faculty and administrators, the NAWDAC as deans of women were more concerned with their social, personal, and spiritual life. At the Durham conference, the group discussed the social situation with Black women students during war times. Some of the topics covered were: How should colleges deal with GIs and women students? How should they deal with women students serving as hostesses at local USO clubs? How to prepare them for the many war-related jobs available to women. How are coeducational campuses coping with activities for women students since most campuses are virtually women's campuses?[75]

Jessie P. Guzman, the current dean of women at Tuskegee, told the group that because HBCUs were so diverse: small institutions, large institutions, private, denominational, or all-women's colleges, the social programs all varied. She said at Tuskegee, since the departure of so many male students due to the draft, as well as the training of cadets on campus, student programs were modified. In addition, the presence of the army flight school for the Tuskegee Airmen, as well as a local USO, required program modifications. She said the men who were army cadets participated in the same program as the regular male students. Dean Ruth Brett stated that at Bennett, they decided to sponsor some activity with the soldiers on Sunday nights. And, during the week, after the end of study hours, soldiers could visit students in a group in a designated place and engage in some activity. The representative from Lincoln University in Missouri, Miss LaRosa Hampton, said there was an urgent need for the institution to determine what kinds of activities to have for the women since there were no longer men around. She said the women had significant time on their hands, and she had to come up with new games for the women to learn that could be played with "limited space and with a minimum of hilarity and confusion."[76]

There was a discussion by the group as to whether it was wise to invite service men to their campuses for social activities. It was concluded that having service men on college campuses was a way for institutions to do their part for the war effort. However, the women said there had to be definite control over the men when they're on campus. These women deans had a preoccupation with, if not outright fear of, men and women being together.[77] In a meeting of the executive committee at Fisk University in 1942 on the question regarding military men and social events on campus, they decided that they would establish a special military register for the women's dorms. Soldiers were allowed to attend regular dances at Fisk only when their names were presented and were approved by the dean of women. The minutes of this meeting noted that while the institution would be hospitable and welcome servicemen, "our first interest is to the protection of our women students."[78] Again, the repeated belief that having men and women together unchaperoned and unwatched was dangerous.

The discussion of college women getting married was also discussed at length. Is marriage wise in wartime? The group brought in the director of Marriage and Family Council, Inc. from Chapel Hill to address this question. Mrs. Gladys H. Groves gave an address, "Family and Marital Status During War Times." She said there was no one answer, and it depended upon the circumstances and the couple, and no generalization could be made on the topic. Groves discussed three types of situations: the couple who married during the war; those who are in college and thinking about marriage; and those who are not yet facing this issue.

During and after WWII, there was an increase in the number of married women students. They overwhelmingly met their husbands in college; half got married before they graduated or in their senior year. This was the trend for white women students.[79] These data reflected white women college students; Black women outnumbered Black men on college campuses. Also, most HBCUs did not allow married women as students. There were no provisions on campuses for them. Groves counseled the deans of women that they should help their women students realize that marriage is a new way of life, and it does not settle all problems. She said for those women who are not engaged yet but are desirous of marriage, they should be made to understand there is a difference between the ideal of marriage and the reality of marriage. She said women should be helped to develop their own personalities and become their own person.[80] As pointed out multiple times, among officials at HBCUs there was a huge fear of women becoming pregnant. Writer Langston Hughes in his tour of Black colleges recorded his observations and said campus officials acted as if it was "unnatural" for men and women to talk to one another.[81] He recounted the story of a married woman student who came to Hampton Institute for a summer session and had to have permission from the dean of women to speak to her husband on the telephone. She said the phone bill mounted because there was a delay of the dean approving the call. The dean had to ensure that it was in fact the woman's husband and not some other man.[82] Dr. Thelma Bando recalled when she was on the faculty and assistant dean of women at Bishop College in the late '30s and early '40s, women students were not allowed to entertain male students in the dorm. Bando lived in a women's dorm. She said that men and women students had to sit outside on benches in public. She noted in her first year at Bishop, she made an error in allowing a young man to come into the lobby of the dormitory. She said he was an alum of the college and engaged to a woman who lived in the dorm. Bando said it was the beginning of the semester in September, and he was on his way to Nashville to attend Meharry Medical School. He dropped by on his way to say goodbye to his fiancé and spend the day with her. Bando, given the circumstances, assumed that having him sit in the dormitory's lobby would be acceptable. It wasn't. She said the wife of the president of the college called her and said to Bando that she heard there was a man in the dorm. Bando explained the situation and she said, "I certainly thought it was alright for him to sit in the living room." She was told, "That's against our regulations." I said, "Your regulations don't extend to alumni?" Bando said, "The young man wasn't a student but an alum." She said the rules were nonsensical.[83]

Mayme Foster, the dean of women at Fisk reported in January 1944 to the executive committee (president, vice presidents, and deans) that she learned that three women students married over the winter break. She said in two of the cases, the rules of the university regarding married students had been violated. Women students who planned to marry had to obtain parental consent, with their informing the institution of their approval. Foster noted only one of the three women had done so. Foster was the one woman on the executive committee; the men told her that they would empower her to enforce the present rule, or if she found extenuating circumstances, then she would use her own judgment in how she handled the issue.[84]

This topic was revisited nearly twenty years later when a professor in the education department at Bennett did a study and published an article titled, "The Married Student at Bennett College."[85] The author of the study, Professor Charles I. Brown, noted there were twenty-three married students at Bennett in the years of 1960–62. This group was interested in the college establishing a program and services for married students. The author of the study noted that while in the past, married women students were a rarity, since the end of World War II and the Korean Conflict, the influx of veterans on college campuses (due to the GI Bill) resulted in a dramatic increase in married women students. Professor Brown conducted a survey questionnaire that included structured and open-ended questions. He said his findings refuted the previous notion that married students were immature and suffered financial problems that would negatively impact their studies. He noted previous studies, including one by renowned anthropologist Margaret Mead, who stated such students lacked emotional and social maturity and were rushing to marriage and parenthood due to societal pressure. Indeed, marriage and babies skyrocketed after the end of World War II. However, Brown's research noted that the married women at Bennett ranged in age from twenty-three to forty-eight and had been married from five months to twenty-six years. He noted fifteen had no dependents and eight of the women did. However, none reflected financial problems. The conclusion of the study was emphatic: married women students are not an anomaly but a new trend in higher education. Brown ended the study by stating:

> There is one point that the authors felt should be made clear—that is that marriage is getting to be as much a part of college life in this country as are sororities, fraternities, and gay campus parties; and barring a world or national disaster, the number of collegiate married students is expected to increase. As to whether this situation bodes good or ill is a moot question. What this situation does mean, though, is that college married students are here to stay, as is indicated by the erection of facilities for married students at colleges all across the nation. This situation means that the married college students will not be contained to a voiceless and exceptional minority.[86]

The issue of student's physical and mental health was also discussed at the 1944 conference. Dr. Ruth Brett presided over this session. The group had invited Dr. Paul Cornely, the executive director of the National Student Health Association and faculty member of Howard Medical School. Cornely was renowned in the field of medicine and public health. He had both an MD ('31) and a PhD ('34) from the University of Michigan. He was the first Black person in the country to earn a PhD in public health. He explained the importance of having student health centers on campuses. He said African Americans died of diseases more rapidly than others and stated that it was important for Black colleges to take the health issue seriously. Howard was a university with a medical school and a hospital, so his recommendation for colleges was ideal, but not realistic for the population he was addressing. He spoke in the most ideal situations not understanding the profound financial limitations of HBCUs. He said colleges should have a full-time nurse and a full-time physician for every eight hundred students. And, if possible, the college should have a dentist and a psychiatrist. He recommended that colleges offer courses on good health and have forums on sex and marriage. These latter topics were those of interest to the women's deans.

Prior to the conference, Dean Kittrell published an essay in the *Quarterly Review of Higher Education Among Negroes* titled, "Current Problems and Programs in Higher Education." Kittrell was quite harsh in her assessment of Black women college students. She said while all college women have challenges, Black women students also have the burden of race, prejudice, and segregation. She noted the explosive number of Black women enrolled in college compared to men. She stated five times as many women were enrolled as men since the age of the military draft was lowered to eighteen. She stated this demographic shift in women's education would impact their attitudes toward family and the home, religious outlook, marriage, their participation in civic life and public welfare, their economic responsibility to society, and their point of view toward the war. Kittrell portrayed the average Black woman as uncouth. She gave the example:

> Let us cite briefly the role of the average Negro College woman graduate now working in Civil Service jobs in Washington. On her job she performs skills well—but is almost totally lacking in social attitudes which makes her liked by people . . . her health habits are poorer when she leaves college than when she entered and finds it difficult to live within her income and to manage her resources well, including her time.[87]

Kittrell continued that these women were not prepared to be good wives and mothers stating these women will have difficulties in their marriages because they won't be able to adjust to their new role. She continued, after such a woman marries:

> She is so tied down with home problems that she finds it impossible to participate in community activities for the common good of all. Her knowledge of voting is not adequate. These are some of the many problems we face with Negro College women graduates today.[88]

After this exhausting list of deficiencies that Kittrell attributed to the "average" Black woman college graduate, she did add a caveat that not all of these traits are found in all Black women college graduates—perhaps one or two, but "may I add here that our Negro Colleges are turning out some excellent women graduates who are able to take their place in the world with dignity and make their adequate contribution to the general welfare."[89] This view of Black women students and their "problems" as outlined by Kittrell was the preamble to the long-awaited conference several months later in June at Spelman College.

Black women students had to endure harsh rules and stereotypes. Dr. Thelma Bando who served as dean of women at multiple HBCUs recalled that the women were allowed to wear black, brown, gray, navy blue, white, and green. Students (and women faculty) couldn't wear prints or "loud" colors.[90]

Women Students in Today's and Tomorrow's World—Spelman College June 1944

The study group that was proposed at Spelman College by the Black women deans (NAWDAC) was finally realized (see chart 9). It was co-sponsored by the higher education commission of the Association of Colleges and Secondary Schools for Negroes and the General Education Board. It was only one week,

June 5–12, instead of the two weeks that the GEB had initially suggested. The opening keynote speaker on the topic "Issues and Challenges in the Higher Education of Negro Women" was Dr. Horace Mann Bond, president of Fort Valley State College in Georgia. He repeated the concerns of the moment that most colleges have become virtually all women because of the war. Institutions now recognize that the college curriculum has been woefully inadequate for women, and he said, "the war has sharply accented these general and special inadequacies." He discussed the need to revise the curriculum to develop a well-educated woman. Recognizing the difference in types of HBCUs, he said this revised curriculum could achieve this goal by 1) a liberal arts or general education; 2) vocational education; 3) a special type of education that is both liberal arts and vocational. He stressed the need for more social and cultural development for Black women students. This was something that the deans of women frequently discussed. He noted because the average Black college student is a product of social and cultural deficiencies, "Negro college students are in greater need of effective personnel service than the average American college students because of deficiencies in their experiences and opportunities."[91] Bond noted that Black students are doubly handicapped by restriction in job opportunities because of

CHART 9. Participants at the Conference on Current Problems and Programs in the Higher Education of Negro Women, June 5–12, 1944

NAME	TITLE	SCHOOL/ INSTITUTION	LOCATION
Mrs. Lucile M. Andrews	Superintendent of Hospital	Spelman College	Atlanta, GA
Mrs. Arnetta R. Ball	Freshman Personnel Advisor	Knoxville College	Knoxville, TN
Horace Mann Bond, (s)	President	Fort Valley State College	Fort Valley, GA
Anne M. Cooke, (c)	Coordinator of Communications Center	Hampton Institute	Hampton, VA
Mrs. Ann Cochran	Department of Education	Morris Brown College	Atlanta, GA
Mrs. Margaret N. Curry	Dean of Freshman	Spelman College	Atlanta, GA
Susie A. Elliot	Dean of Women	Howard University	Washington, DC
Jean Fairfax	Dean of Women	Kentucky State University	Frankfort, KY
Dutton Ferguson, (s)	Specialist	Office of Price Administration	Washington, DC
Margaret L. Fisher, (s)	Public Relations Secretary	Southern Regional Council	Atlanta, GA
Marth Jane Gibson	Professor of English	Talladega College	Talladega, AL

NAME	TITLE	SCHOOL/ INSTITUTION	LOCATION
Emma C. W. Gray	Dean of Women	Paine College	Augusta, GA
William Gray	President	Florida A&M College	Tallahassee, FL
Mrs. Grace Towns Hamilton	Executive Secretary	Atlanta Urban League	Atlanta, GA
Irene Harris	Executive Secretary	Phyllis Wheatley YWCA	Atlanta, GA
Mrs. Rebekah Jeffries	Dean of Women	Virginia Union University	Richmond, VA
Inez D. Jenkins	Dean of Women	Southern University	Scotlandville, LA
Ruth Jett	Administrative Secretary	Southern Negro Youth Congress	Birmingham, AL
Capt. Adele C. Kempker, USMC, (s)	Psychiatrist	Lawson General Hospital	Atlanta, GA
Flemmie P. Kittrell	Dean of Women	Hampton Institute	Hampton, VA
J. R. McCain	President	Agnes Scott College	Decatur, GA
T. E. McKinney	Dean	Johnson C. Smith University	Charlotte, NC
Mrs. Ernestine C. Milner, (c)	Director of Personnel	Guilford College	Guilford, NC
Alonzo G. Moron, (s)	Manager	University and John Hope Homes	Atlanta, GA
Florence M. Reed	President	Spelman College	Atlanta, GA
Ira De A. Reid	Chairman, Department of Sociology	Atlanta University	Atlanta, GA
Mrs. Estelle M. Riddle, (c)	Consultant	National Nursing Council for War Service	New York, NY
Alethea Washington	Professor of Education	Howard University	Washington, DC
Forrester B. Washington, (s)	Director	Atlanta University School of Social Work	Atlanta, GA
John P. Whittaker, (s)	Registrar	Atlanta University and Morehouse College	Atlanta, GA
Mrs. Cordella A. Winn	Acting Dean of Women	Florida A&M College	Tallahassee, FL
P. Q. Yancey, MD	Physician		Atlanta, GA
Idabelle Yelser	Chairman, Division of Education	Dillard University	New Orleans, LA
Louise Young, (c)	Professor of Rural Education	Scarritt College	Nashville, TN

(c) – Consultant (s) – Speaker

race but also because they are products of families where their parents are not educated and high schools that have poor or no guidance expertise. He said colleges need to do more for orientation, educational guidance and diagnostic and remedial measures. Bond outlined the same suggestions as the Bennett proposal: students should receive courses in psychology, sociology, history, economics, human geography, and personal development. And, these women should be prepared for citizenship and a strong family life.[92]

The conference participants discussed problems with the faculty at HBCUs. Having competent faculty was a critical issue. Most HBCUs were still building their faculties, and some were still striving toward accreditation. Not many HBCUs were represented due to the limited space. No one from Bennett was in attendance, perhaps because they were the ones who least needed to attend. There were five deans of women (not including Kittrell from Hampton); two deans of freshmen; faculty from Talladega, Dillard, Morris Brown, and Atlanta University; and there were members of government and nonprofit organizations; the only presidents who attended were President Bond who gave the opening address, President McCain of Agnes Scott, and of course, President Read of Spelman. There were no representatives from Tuskegee, although Jean Fairfax was in attendance. She was appointed dean of women the following year at Tuskegee, where she erroneously thought she could build programs for women students that were advocated at this conference. As noted earlier, her tenure was short-lived at Tuskegee.

The conference was highly publicized. The entire program and its findings were published in the *Quarterly Review of Higher Education Among Negroes*. And the *Spelman Messenger* carried an article on the conference with a photo of some of the attendees.[93] While there was a lot of excitement and hope on the part of the Black women in the NACW and the NAWDAC, by the following year, with the war being over, quickly the panic over Black women's higher education was basically over except in a few locations. The conference had little to no impact at all on Black women's higher education. Bennett College, who led the charge for this issue and had received a grant from the GEB to try to implement the new curriculum, continued their efforts in curriculum reform. After the conference at Spelman, President Jones approached the GEB for a second three-year grant to continue the implementation of the revamping of the Bennett curriculum. Since the GEB had provided the initial funding for this effort, as well as sponsored the recent conference on this topic, Jones felt confident that the foundation would continue their support. However, the notes in the files from the foundation reveal they were unenthusiastic about this endeavor and said Jones didn't make a strong case for why they should continue their financial support to Bennett. In the report submitted regarding the first three-year grant, it noted that the college was working on nine areas of change.

Intensive work had been done on three of the areas—communications, health, and earning a living. Jones said there were six other areas that needed to be addressed—consumer education, leadership and citizenship, recreation, family life, religion, and "general." The GEB fund had paid for the salary of the chair of the curriculum committee as well as the outside curriculum consultants. The travel of the administration to visit other campuses was also covered by the GEB grant. The GEB officers noted that only one-quarter to one-fifth of the faculty had visited other campuses, compared to administrators, like Ruth Brett. The foundation officer said they felt it was more important for the faculty to visit these institutions rather than staff members. Jones said that Bennett paid very low salaries to faculty, and they have very inexperienced faculty. Hence, he said it would benefit his faculty if they could visit institutions and observe the types of work done on these campuses. In the notes to the files, the officers note that they didn't feel Jones made a convincing argument. They said that there was constant faculty and staff turnover, so they thought the project "would never be completed as staff changes are more or less continuous."[94] The grant request was denied. It was unclear if the foundation officials did not view the curriculum restructuring to address Black women's specific needs as important. At any rate, it wasn't a topic they were interested in funding. As noted, the foundation had a relationship with Spelman and sponsored the event at that location. But this was not a Spelman project, but one initiated by Bennett College. The GEB was not financially or intellectually invested in Bennett or in a curriculum focused expressly on Black women students.

Undeterred, the Bennett College team continued to work on implementing their new curriculum. In 1946, their Homemaking Institute (which by this time was homemaking in name only), had the theme of "Opening Doors to Economic Security." Successful Black businesswomen were featured. In bold letters of *The Bennett Banner* highlighting the event, it proclaimed: "BUSINESS WOMAN HAILED AT BENNETT." The featured businesswoman was Mrs. Bertha Diggs, secretary of labor for the state of New York. In her address to the Bennett women and the audience, Diggs stated that hard work brings success. She indicated that in her position, she sets policy for the Labor Department for seven million working women. She was a native of Buffalo, New York, and said her background started out in public relations and counseling in adult education. She said she worked with various educational, political, and civic groups and also served as secretary of the Erie County Clerk's Office. She said as a result of these activities, she was able to make important contacts and be invited to key labor meetings. The message was to the women that you not only have to have credentials, but you also need contacts. Being visible and working in these various civic and political organizations gave her the contacts she needed to obtain her appointment. She told her female audience, while education was important, if there was a question of career versus family, then she felt the latter was more important. She was the mother of a twelve-year-old daughter. It wasn't clear how this advice impacted her own life since she was a working woman in a very high-profile position with a child.[95]

Other women profiled at the week-long conference were a florist from Darlington, South Carolina; a candy manufacturer from Birmingham, Alabama; a truck fleet operator from Scranton, Pennsylvania; and the treasurer of the *Pittsburgh Courier*, the renowned Black newspaper. There were several Black men also on the program: James Stamps, the branch manager of the Social Security Office in Chicago and George Streator, writer for the *New York Times*.[96]

This type of exposure of jobs in areas outside of the default position of teaching was viewed as a sign of progress for Black women students. And, while the need for teachers remained important, the goal was to provide Black women options and exposure to other opportunities that were available to them. The college continued to present to Bennett Belles a vast array of careers. A 1948 article in the college newspaper provided information on why home economics could lead to many different employment opportunities. It stated the image of home economics majors were "old-fashioned home girls" who were primarily interested in homemaking and marriage. The article said that while that was true to some extent, "there are employment opportunities in the field." It emphasized that home economics has not been saturated, and since it's a woman's field, there is no competition with men for positions. The article noted that women could do far more than teach with this degree. They could use the degree to become dietitians or home demonstration agents. Advanced positions included head dietitians in hospitals, industrial cafeterias, research specialists for the government, writers of subjects in women's magazines, and many other positions. These positions were all obtained from the Home Economics Association. These positions were available to white women who were products of programs that prepared them for the many opportunities. While Black women still overwhelmingly became teachers—a guaranteed position, Bennett provided examples of other professional options. The college showed the women not what they *should* become but what they *could* become.

The focus during this era was on heterosexual women. There were courses and forums on homemaking and having a good and happy marriage. At the Homemaking Institute of 1949, this theme was: "Today's Woman: Homemaker and Careerist." The theme didn't focus on either/or but indicated that women were expected to be both. An article in the student newspaper stated the planning committee noted the "problem" of young women was whether "it is important to have a happy home or a successful career . . . or whether the two can be combined."[97] This conference was dedicated to helping young women hear women discuss their lives and also participate in panel discussions on special topics.

The speakers were Dr. Adelaide Cromwell, from the sociology department of Smith College; Dr. Ruth Sloan, Chief of the Near East and African Branch of Public Affairs Overseas Program in Washington, DC; psychiatrist Dr. Marynia Z. Farnham of New York City; and Miss Bess Furman who wrote for the Washington, DC, office of the *New York Times*.[98] Dr. Farnham was the coauthor of a best-selling and controversial book in 1947 entitled, *Modern Woman: The Lost Sex*.[99] In response to the large number of women who worked outside of the home after the end of World War II, the extremely anti-feminist book argued that married working women experienced psychological disorders and threatened a happy married and family life. It is unclear how this speaker impacted the women students, but the issue of marriage and career became ones that were increasingly discussed in the following decade.

This theme as well as the speakers that were selected reflected the concern of women in HBCUs and other colleges regarding the increasing problems many Black women faced as their career opportunities and educational opportunities increased. Being a schoolteacher was not perceived as threatening to husbands and potential mates, which was an emphasis that was reinforced to Black women. However, pursuing fields that were not defined as "female" ones resulted in discussions within Black women college organizations and research regarding the social consequences of pursuing advanced degrees and careers not deemed within the "female sphere."[100]

As noted earlier, as a woman's college, Bennett had administrators who were aware of what the trends were with the education of white women, so they were able to devote their programs to accommodate women's needs in ways that were more difficult at coeducational HBCUs. Although white women college graduates were marrying younger, and in greater numbers after World War II, many of them did work although in significantly smaller percentages than Black women. In Linda Eisenmann's research of college women in the twenty years after World War II, she noted that by the mid-1950s, 40 percent of middle-class college women worked, more than women who were lower or higher class.[101] Kelly Sartorius's research notes in great detail how the deans of women in white institutions, especially coeducational ones, sought to prepare these women for varied employment options instead of teaching. Women's deans were also responsible for vocational counseling beginning at the turn of the century, a standard part of their positions.[102]

While Bennett Belles were well groomed and understood appropriate etiquette, the annual Homemaking Institutes exposed them to various options and examples of women leaders in their fields. Bennett also instilled within them the importance of being race-conscious activists. Both President Jones, and later, Willa Player, who succeeded Jones as president in 1956, supported student activism. Jones encouraged students not to patronize businesses that mistreated Black people. He also suggested that the students walk rather than ride in segregated transportation. And finally, the women were told to be of "service to our people."[103] Jones's advice to the Bennett Belles was the one Black people had heard since their days in the slave quarters. Not only were all Blacks expected to "help their race"—educated Blacks in particular were expected to help in this endeavor. In 1938, North Carolina theater owners agreed not to show films that portrayed Blacks as equals of whites and with Blacks being "out of character." This last comment meant showing Black actors not in servile stereotypical roles. As a result of this new decision of movie theater owners in North Carolina, the Bennett Belles organized a boycott of all movie theaters. They issued a statement in the local newspaper along with students from the neighboring state HBCU, North Carolina A&T:

> We hereby declare our intention to refuse to patronize these theatres until the resolution has been rescinded, or until the managers have changed their policy in re the resolution.[104]

President Jones's daughter, Frances, a junior at Bennett College, was at the forefront of the boycott. She organized an interracial group of students from across the state to join the boycott, including students from Duke University.[105]

Bennett's students and their community started multiple community service projects. In 1931 Dr. Kittrell established a laboratory school at Bennett. After the laboratory school was closed in 1938, the college opened a nursery school and an art school for children in the community. The college had the local students connect with Black women who were domestic servants and provided them classes in the "art of childcare." The art school provided classes to children in the community to enhance their appreciation of art and help them view it as a leisure pursuit.[106] During the 1930s, 74 percent of North Carolina's population lived in rural communities. Bennett's students were teachers in these communities, and some of them were from these small areas. They had speakers and did projects related to the tenant and sharecroppers' issues that were so prevalent throughout the rural South. Bennett Belles continued their activism and community service throughout the period of this book—in the '40s, the young women worked on projects related to World War II and focused on workshops and a summer institute related to enhancing home and family life and community leadership. Issues of health were extremely important to this group. In 1940, Bennett held a Child Health Institute, and they instituted a community health education program in the fall of 1944. Students voluntarily staffed the clinics during the summers that gave immunizations. The students read books and participated in storytelling for the children and participated in other forms of recreation. Like many other HBCUs, Bennett hosted conferences on civil rights and interracial relations. Black women students were very active in the YWCA, and chapters existed on private HBCU campuses. Some of the leading Black women in higher education worked for the YWCA throughout these decades of the '20s through the period of this book. Bennett Belles were selected to attend conferences related to racial harmony and cooperation, such as the Christian Citizenship Seminar of the Methodist Church.[107]

Black women students were prominent throughout the Black protest and civil rights movement. As early as the 1940s during World War II, Pauli Murray, who was in her second year of law school at Howard, formed a group of primarily women (since most of the male students had left for the military) to protest segregated lunch counters in drug stores and restaurants. She found a cafeteria near Howard that did not serve Black people and targeted it as a test case. Murray and her friends would sit at tables, at which they would be ignored. The group would picket outside the store with signs that said, "Our Boys, Our Bonds, Our Brothers are Fighting for YOU! Why Can't We Eat Here?" and other messages. Murray noted that the Howard administration was against the demonstration since they believed one should go to the court system to bring about change. Murray also noted the thought of Howard women being arrested was horrifying. She wrote:

> Many parents of Howard University students, particularly the parents of teenage girls, adhered to middle-class standards of respectability and would be horrified at the thought of their daughters tangling with the police, being arrested and thrown into jail. College administrators were conscious in those days of their role *in loco parentis,* were acutely sensitive to parental pressures and breaking the code of respectability enforced by parents . . .[108]

The protesters were successful in having the restaurant integrated. The loss of revenue was too much for the owner. Murray noted with pride the prominent role of the women students in planning and leadership and said, "Twelve of the nineteen demonstrators at the Little Palace on April 17th were women."[109]

The decade of the 1950s with the NAACP lawsuits challenging segregation in public education, and in graduate and professional schools' decades earlier, reached its peak with the landmark 1954 Supreme Court *Brown v. Board of Education* ending segregation of public education. Black women students and girls were prominent plaintiffs in all of these cases. Historian Marcia G. Synnott has written extensively on the major Black women pioneers of the desegregation of higher education in public institutions in the Midwest and South. While the activities of the women in these lawsuits are beyond the scope of this book, Synnott's work discusses the bravery and courage of six Black women who put their lives on the line for the cause of integration: Lucile Harris Bluford (University of Missouri), Ada Lois Sipuel Fisher (University of Oklahoma), Autherine Juanita Lucy and Vivian Juanita Malone (University of Alabama), Charlayne

Alberta Hunter (University of Georgia), and Henrie Dobbins Monteith (University of South Carolina). Three of these women sought entrance into all white professional schools—Bluford in journalism, Sipuel in law, and Lucy in library science. The other three students Malone, Hunter, and Monteith sought to enter as undergraduates.

Six of the Little Rock nine who integrated the famed Central High School in 1957 were young women. In other lawsuits as well, Black women and girls were present and often dominant.

By the 1960s, Black women college students were active in the civil rights protests throughout the country. Black women at Fisk, Bennett, Spelman, and other campuses were in the forefront of activism. Southern public colleges had to be conscious of fearing the wrath of the white politicians who funded these institutions. By the 1960s, student protests on HBCUs were in full force. However, many students at these institutions paid the price by expulsion. Spelman, although private and not subject to loss of funding like public HBCUs, had a conservative president, Albert Manley, who was not supportive of student activism in the civil rights movement. The book *Undaunted by the Fight: Spelman College and the Civil Rights Movement, 1957–1967* chronicled the struggles of the brave students who defied Manley and took part in sit-ins, the Freedom Rides, and the Student Nonviolent Coordinating Committee (SNCC). Black women at other institutions, such as Dianne Nash from Fisk who also co-founded the SNCC, were also active in the Freedom Rides. As the name suggests, SNCC was a student organization.[110] Black college students had a history of student protests against racism and discrimination as well as campus grievances.[111] Always conscious of Black women's image to society, the fashion magazine *Mademoiselle* highlighted the Bennett Belle sit-in protesters as "tough fighters on the picket line, young ladies at home."[112]

In keeping with the period of civil rights and social justice, the Homemaking Institute theme for 1960 was "Register and Vote, A Necessity for Good Citizenship." One of the activities for this theme was "Operation Doorknock," in which Bennett Belles went door-to-door in the Black Greensboro community to register the citizens to vote. This event resulted in the Belles registering 1,478 African Americans. NAACP attorney Thurgood Marshall (later a US Supreme Court justice) and Benjamin E. Mays, president of Morehouse College, were the keynote speakers for the Institute to kick off this event.[113]

In existence since 1927, the Homemaking Institute ended in 1965. As noted above the themes reflected timely issues of the day. The Institute always brought the most renowned speakers of the period of all races and genders. In addition to the ones already highlighted, they included First Lady Eleanor Roosevelt, anthropologist Margaret Mead, sociologist E. Franklin Frazier, and writer Langston Hughes.[114]

White deans of women discussed the same issues as the deans of women in HBCUs. Those in coeducational institutions had different concerns than those in women's colleges since the presence of GIs on campus wasn't an issue. The issue of men displacing women students after the war due to the Servicemen's Readjustment Act of 1944 that covered the tuition of returning service people was paramount. This significantly impacted white women in coeducational schools since male GIs flooded colleges. By the 1950s, the proportion of women in college had dropped from 50 percent before the war to 21 percent. Roger Geiger in his history of higher education after World War II stated, "women of the 1950s largely acquiesced in the domestic roles of housewives and mothers, to the consternation of latter-day feminists." He also noted that the era had the highest rate of marriage, the highest fertility rate, and the lowest divorce rate.[115]

This was not the case with Black colleges. As noted previously, high schools for Blacks in the South were rare except in cities until after World War II, so many Black veterans did not have the academic preparation to attend college. Those who did often were discouraged and counseled by white Veterans Administration personnel to pursue a trade, not a college degree. However, many did apply to HBCUs. In fact, these institutions could not accommodate the number of veterans who applied. According to one study, due to the limited facilities of HBCUs between 1946 and 1947, an estimated twenty thousand veterans had to be turned down.[116]

Howard University—which had undergraduate, graduate, and professional schools—witnessed an explosive increase in enrollment immediately after the war. The university's Annual Report of 1946–47 noted the enrollment went from 1,608 to 3,263 students in one year's time. It indicated that this is the first time since the Depression that the number of male students outnumbered the women students.[117]

During the war, enrollments continued to soar, led by Black women who already dominated the enrollments at HBCUs. For example, in the fall of 1944, Fisk had a record enrollment year of 600 students. Five hundred were women. It was noted that students came from all over the United States as well as several other countries. The report noted the university could have taken seventy-five additional students, but no dorm space could accommodate them. Fisk required all their students to live on campus unless they were from Nashville.[118] The following year, with male students on the GI Bill applying in great numbers, the executive committee discussed limiting the number of women students to 750 and prioritizing qualified veterans to return the college to a gender balance. However, returning veterans did not dominate the college enrollment. In 1947, Fisk had more than 1,000 students because of the influx of students on the GI Bill. However, the men represented just one-quarter of the students. Even with the GI Bill, women students still outnumbered male students. There were 468 male students with slightly more than 500 women students in 1947. As the men on the GI Bill graduated, the enrollment of the institution dropped. With the graduation of the GIs in 1951 and 1952, Fisk enrollment dropped 16 percent. Even with the Korean War from 1950–53, Fisk administrators noted that most Black GIs could attend one of the seventeen Black land-grant colleges, which were much cheaper (Fisk and Howard were the two most expensive HBCUs with tuition cost twice that of other Black institutions). Fisk administrators stated that the money saved in tuition at cheaper institutions could give veterans more money for housing.[119]

Until recently, the prevailing scholarship stated that after the war, women retreated from higher education and careers to focus upon being homemakers. The 1950s were viewed as a conservative era for women. Betty Friedan's 1963 best-selling feminist book, *The Feminine Mystique*, reinforced these views that have been challenged now by many scholars. Linda Eisenmann, in her book *Higher Education for Women in Postwar America, 1945–1965,* challenges this belief that women simply retreated to the home. Eisenmann's work demonstrates that women did not completely retreat from the workforce, and they continued in college and graduate school. Many were homemakers and mothers who devoted time to volunteer and to civic activities. However, she noted they were basically ignored as "incidental" students. Roger Geiger, in his assessment of this time period, noted that given the lower pay and interrupted employment of women (due to having children), the return on their investment would be 5 to 6 percent. He thought marriage was a better deal. He wrote, "Women doubled their total returns in the marriage-market, enhancing their income by another 5 percent." Geiger noted in purely financial terms it was more profitable for women to marry during or shortly after college by securing a high-earning spouse. He stated given the low pay of women wage earners and the disruption of having children, college attendance was not a good return on their investment except through marriage.[120] Of course, this belief was a common one since earning an "MRS" was viewed as a primary reason for women to attend college during this period. And for upwardly mobile women, attending college was a good investment to "snag" a high earning spouse. This attitude belittled women who were in college to better themselves, prepare for careers, may not have been heterosexual, or not focused on marriage. Despite the hype of the period, there is ample evidence that many college-educated women did desire a career.

Joanne Meyerowitz, in her essay "Beyond the Feminine Mystique: A Reassessment of Post-War Mass Culture, 1946–1958," examines popular monthly magazines read by both Black and white women during this period, including *Reader's Digest* and *Coronet*, *Harper's* and *Atlantic Monthly*, *Ladies' Home Journal* and *Women's Home Companion* and *Ebony* and *Jet* magazines. While the latter two publications were targeted to a Black readership, African American women read white women's magazines as well. These publications had a readership of twenty-two million and reached women of all races and backgrounds. Meyerowitz noted that these magazines advocated both domestic and non-domestic ideals. While there were frequent references to "femininity and domesticity," 60 percent of the magazines highlighted women with individual accomplishments. This was especially true of the Black publications since Black women graduates, as well as others, were prominently in the workplace. One-third of the magazines portrayed women who were unmarried or divorced or made no mention of a woman's marital status. Again, this was most pronounced with the Black publications. Only 15 percent of the articles in the magazines focused on women as wives and mothers.

While there were Black women who were homemakers, most Black women, whether they were college educated or not, worked. The events given by Bennett during the Homemaking Institutes provided their students as well as the women in the community with a vast array of career options. There were always discussions regarding career, community, and family.

Unlike white college women, whose enrollment numbers didn't surpass men until the mid-1980s, Black women have always outnumbered Black men in enrollment and graduation in the twentieth century except for the decade between the 1920s and '30s. However, Black women appeared to have a slow start: in the nineteenth century, as mentioned earlier, the demand for teachers was so great that they didn't need more than one or two years of normal school or college. There were only three Black women college graduates compared to twenty-five Black males with college degrees by the end of the Civil War. In 1890, thirty Black women had earned a baccalaureate degree, compared to over three hundred Black men and twenty-five hundred white women. In that year, white women constituted 35 percent of the undergraduate student population.[121] In her study of the women's movement of the nineteenth century, Eleanor Flexner reported that by 1890, white women had made such strides in medical fields since the Civil War that they were no longer a rarity in this area and numbered almost forty-five hundred.[122] However, by 1910, at Oberlin alone, more than four hundred Black women had attended. Sixty-one women had earned degrees from the ladies' department, the college's music conservatory, or the college.

As noted in earlier chapters, the demand for teachers was so great that Black women by the thousands flocked to the Black land-grant colleges that were established in the 1890s with the Second Morrill Act. In 1900, out of the 156 graduates of Black colleges, 22 were women. A survey in 1928 noted that Black women comprised 64 percent of the enrollment of the seventeen Black land-grant colleges. Hence, Black women were attending educational institutions in large numbers; they simply didn't graduate in the early decades.

The following chapter will discuss the role of foundation support in advancing the education of Black women over a twenty-year period that overlaps with the Depression and World War II.

PART FOUR

CHAPTER 8

The Beginning of the Black Female Professoriate

As noted in the previous chapters, Black women had attended a vast array of colleges since the mid-nineteenth century. Beginning in the early 1920s, they began earning doctoral degrees in various fields. In 1921, three African American women earned PhD degrees: Eve Dykes from Radcliffe College in philology (the study of literature and linguistics); Sadie Tanner Mossell in economics from the University of Pennsylvania; and Georgiana Simpson from the University of Chicago in Germanic languages.[1] All three women were products of Washington, DC's Black elite and white undergraduate institutions or Howard.

Dykes's father and three uncles were all graduates of Howard University. Dykes graduated from Howard in 1914. She taught for one year, and with financial support from one of her uncles, attended Radcliffe College to pursue her master's in philology. Since Howard wasn't accredited until 1921, Dykes had to obtain a second baccalaureate degree from Radcliffe, which she earned in 1917 (magna cum laude); she then earned her master's in 1918 and the doctorate in 1921. She wrote a six-hundred-page thesis on the "Pope and His Influence in America from 1715–1850." In addition to the financial support of her uncle, Dykes received a scholarship from Radcliffe College for five semesters. Upon graduation, she returned to Washington to teach at the prestigious Dunbar High School.

Sadie Tanner Mossell Alexander also came from a long line of educated family members. Her aunt, Hallie Tanner Johnson, was a physician and founder of the Nursing School at Tuskegee Institute. Her father, Aaron Mossell, was a graduate of Lincoln University in Pennsylvania and the first Black person to earn a law degree from the University Pennsylvania (1888). Her uncle Louis Baxter Moore was the first African American to earn a doctorate from the University of Pennsylvania (1896) and was the dean of Teacher's College at Howard University. Because Mossell's aunt and uncle lived in DC, she moved from her home in Philadelphia to attend the renowned M Street High School (which was renamed Dunbar High School). After graduating from high school, her mother had her return home to Philadelphia to attend the University of Pennsylvania—the family school. She graduated from Penn in 1918 and received a graduate fellowship from the Graduate School of the University of Pennsylvania and earned a doctorate in economics in 1921. Unable to find employment in white companies, Mossell worked for one year at a Black insurance company in North Carolina before returning to Philadelphia to marry. The employment situation remained the same, so she returned to the University of Pennsylvania to earn a law degree and enter into practice with her then husband Raymond Pace Alexander. She graduated from Penn's law school in 1927 and became the first Black woman to pass the Pennsylvania State Bar.

Georgiana Simpson was much older than Dykes and Alexander. Simpson was a product of the Washington, DC, public schools and normal schools in the 1870s. She earned all three of her degrees from the University of Chicago in Germanic languages. She subsequently went to Germany to study languages and literature. She taught at the M Street School (later Dunbar) until 1931, when she joined the faculty at Howard.

The fourth Black woman to obtain a doctorate was also a product of Washington, DC's educated elite—Otelia Cromwell. Cromwell's father was the prominent newspaper man, John Cromwell, editor of *The People's Advocate*. She was the first Black woman to graduate from Smith college ('00), where she earned a degree in classics. She earned a master's in literature from Columbia University in 1910 and a PhD in Elizabethan literature from Yale University in 1926, becoming the first Black woman to earn a doctorate from Yale. Her brother John Cromwell Jr. graduated from Dartmouth in 1906 with a degree in mathematics and became the first Black certified public accountant in the country.

With the exception of Sadie Tanner Alexander, all of these women became teachers, and later, professors. Even with these distinguished Ivy League degrees, the job market relegated these women and their Black male counterparts to work in the segregated world of Black education. They were not considered for teaching appointments at white women's colleges. And, given these women's strong classical education, they were not highly sought after in many Black colleges that emphasized industrial education or the land-grant colleges that were the last to achieve accreditation. Of course, the students who had the great privilege of having such highly trained teachers in high schools reaped the benefits of their knowledge and world travels. The leading Black high schools, as well as many private liberal arts Black colleges benefited from them.

A doctoral degree was not necessary to obtain a tenure-track position in US colleges and universities until the end of the middle of the twentieth century. However, for those institutions seeking to move from secondary to collegiate status, advanced degrees were increasingly required for the accreditation. African Americans lagged behind whites in obtaining graduate degrees, especially African American women.[2] By 1928, when the Southern Association of Colleges and Secondary Schools began to rate and accredit African American colleges and postsecondary schools, graduate education became an important credential for accreditation. Between 1928 and 1948, two foundations, the General Education Board (GEB) and the Julius Rosenwald Fund (JRF), began awarding fellowships to African Americans for advanced training. The officials at these two foundations recognized that HBCUs were beginning to appoint Black presidents (all of the Black land-grant colleges had Black presidents) and that these campuses would want to have Black faculties. In addition, the public schools for Blacks in the South in the late '30s began requiring teachers to have degrees and certifications. The GEB was instrumental in aiding in this regard.

The grants given to African American women for undergraduate training by the GEB from 1923 to 1929 were specifically to study home economics, library science, and general education at Hampton Institute with the requirement that the grant recipient would return and work in the South. Female students from Hampton, Howard, Fisk, and Tuskegee were targeted to receive funds.[3] These funds were to prepare for the need of teachers (women) to teach home economics in schools in the South and the field of library science, which required a college degree by 1930.

While the GEB-funded fellowships for advanced graduate studies came later, their initial funding was for the above-mentioned areas. This funding was a godsend to the Black women overwhelmingly from rural areas, who had not obtained undergraduate degrees or who had attended unaccredited institutions that didn't have the faculty at the time to prepare them for the certification that they needed. Over and over, the women fellowship recipients expressed their gratitude. For example, Mabel Myers Stinnett, a 36-year-old divorced mother from rural Tennessee, had a high school diploma from Tennessee State College and was a home demonstration agent. She received a fellowship in 1929 to attend Hampton Institute, where she earned a bachelor's degree in home economics. Her fellowship report noted that until the state required a degree to teach home economics, "most anyone who had a fair idea of home economics could teach." She said:

> The fellowship made it possible to concentrate and thus do better work, because of the time could be spend in study instead of doing work to help pay bills at the school . . . [the fellowship] caused me to study and plan those things that should be taught to help that class of girls who will never finish high school, who will drop out of school in the seventh, eighth, or ninth grade, who will someday be homemakers and mothers. It gave me an opportunity to improve myself.

> I wanted to earn my BS but did not have money to attend school. It also caused me to form a determination to study more and do research work in home economics. I am trying to put away a little money for that purpose despite the depression and salary cuts and I hope to go away to study in the summer.[4]

By 1936, Stinnett was employed as a home economics teacher in Nashville.

Similarly, Grace Mae Sullivan from Kentucky was the head of the department of home economics with a bachelor's degree from Hampton Institute. She was awarded a fellowship in 1932 to obtain a master's in home economics and childcare at Iowa State University. In her fellowship report, she wrote in 1936:

> The scholarship gave me a whole year of undisturbed study, heretofore I was forced to work and go to school. Graduate work is very expensive, and most Negroes are not financially able to spend a whole year in school without some aid. I consider this the best year's study I have had.[5]

Again, the stress of the relief of the financial burden it would take to obtain a degree was mentioned over and over. Eunice Powell, from rural Mississippi who obtained a high school diploma from Alcorn College in 1919 was a teacher of home economics in the school after she graduated. In 1930, with a GEB fellowship, she went to Hampton Institute to obtain a bachelor's degree. She told the foundation:

> It was possible for me to receive a BS in one year. Without this aid, Three summers' work would have been required, involving extra expenses for railroad fare. It was possible for me to study without financial worry.[6]

Powell returned to her old position after obtaining her bachelor's from Hampton.

Many of the recipients of both fellowships mentioned financially supporting parents and siblings. For example, Josie Wilhelmina Roberts earned a BA in music from Talladega College in Alabama in 1929. When she obtained a fellowship from the Rosenwald foundation, she was a public-school teacher of music and taught music to the sixth grade at the elementary school at Bethune—Cookman College. She received funds to study at the Oberlin Conservatory of Music. In her report to the GEB, she said, her father died before she completed college:

> leaving my mother to struggle with five children. I immediately upon finishing my AB began helping my younger brothers in their education, never dreaming that I should have the opportunity for music at the Conservatory. After many years of experience in institutions in the music department, I finally had a part of my ambition accomplished through the graciousness of the Rosenwald Fund. I shall never forget Mr. Rosenwald and the "great spirit" that still carries on for humanity. God bless his memory, his family

and the fund. Although I was not granted further study, I am so proud of the hundreds who are benefiting as I did, through its administration and hope it may go on forever. I remain, very gratefully yours.[7]

Another candidate stated in her job application to the National Urban League that her undergraduate education was average to limited. She said:

> I attended a small southern college where the atmosphere was too Conservative to allow for much stimulus to original creative thinking—Too much rote work. I never felt that I was giving full expression to my mental capabilities while there.

Despite these limitations, she said she was grateful she had attended an HBCU:

> It offered more individual contact with instructors than a larger one.
> It was coeducational and gave me opportunity for a gradual development of wholesome contact with the opposite sex.
> I was glad I attended a wholly Negro college first because I developed along with the best in my own race without the danger of a feeling of racial inferiority.
> I worked to help myself through college and have supported myself entirely since graduation. At different times, I have helped relatives over difficult periods.[8]

Her reflections on her poor educational preparation mirrored that of many other women.

As will be discussed, despite the fact that Black women college students outnumbered Black men beginning in the 1940s, they were enrolled overwhelmingly in teacher training colleges. In contrast, Black male students were not. This dramatically impacted Black women's college graduates' opportunities to qualify for graduate schools.

With these two sources of foundation support, many talented African American men and women were able to pursue and complete graduate school during this twenty-year period. Harry Green noted in his study of African American holders of doctorates by 1945, four-fifths of these recipients earned them after 1930. However, of the 381 Black American holders of doctorates and professional degrees by that time, only forty-five were women. This was not due to a lack of interest but to the lack of qualifications of many women applicants. An analysis of the top five undergraduate institutions that produced fellowship recipients showed that two were all-male: Lincoln University in Pennsylvania and Morehouse College in Atlanta. The other three—Fisk University, Howard University, and Virginia Union—were coeducational non-public institutions with strong liberal arts and professional schools. None of the teacher training schools or Black land-grant colleges, where most Black women were enrolled, was even in the top twenty undergraduate programs whose graduates received fellowships. However, in reviewing the applications of several hundred Black women applicants to both the GEB and the JRF fellowship programs, it is particularly revealing that more than half of them had attended summer sessions at their own expense at Harvard, Columbia (Teachers College), University of Pennsylvania, Cornell, Michigan, Ohio State, Iowa, Minnesota, Wisconsin, Kansas, and the University of Chicago.[9] These women made personal sacrifices to improve their academic backgrounds.

In order to address the need for faculty with advanced degrees, the Rosenwald Foundation created a program to finance the graduate studies for students from Morehouse, Spelman, Atlanta University, Howard University, Fisk University and Meharry Medical College in Nashville, and Dillard University in New Orleans. While the GEB initially ensured that Black schools in the South maintained home economics and industrial education, the Rosenwald Foundation focused primarily on funding students from liberal arts and white institutions, although they did fund persons who didn't attend such institutions. The GEB did fund fellows for doctoral studies as well. The Rosenwald Foundation restricted its awards to African Americans between the ages of twenty-four and thirty-five to attend graduate and professional schools (although they did make exceptions to this criterion in compelling circumstances). Rosenwald did not require its recipients to work at a Black institution in the South (although at the time for most Black academics, there were no other options).[10] The foundation also funded writers, visual artists, and dancers.

While Black academics had these two sources of funding, it was clear, given a choice, most preferred the Rosenwald Fellowship. That foundation sought to provide funding to talented Black academics of promise to raise the level of HBCUs to that of white colleges. The GEB, heavily tied to the notion of Black subservience and industrial and domestic education, sought to fund a different type of fellow, although many prominent academics received both GEB funding and Rosenwald funds. A Rosenwald Fellowship was viewed as more prestigious. Kenneth Manning, in his biography of Ernest Just, the eminent Black zoologist who served on the faculty of Howard University and whose professional survival depended on the largesse of the Rosenwald and the GEB noted, "Blacks looked to the Rosenwald first, the General Education Board second" for funding.[11]

Building up the credentials of the faculty of HBCUs coincided with the NAACP's quest to dismantle segregated higher education institutions. Throughout the 1930s, the NAACP challenged the "separate but equal" decision of the Supreme Court's 1896 *Plessy v. Ferguson* case. States that continued to segregate Black students in public higher education began offering tuition stipends for such students to study out of state if there wasn't a major or program available to them in their state. This was initially the case for both graduate, professional, and undergraduate education. For example, Alice Carlotte Johnson, a 1934 graduate of Virginia Union University, applied to the white University of Virginia in Charlottesville to pursue a masters in French. They denied her application because of her race. The NAACP took up her case, and as a result of publicity about her rejection in the Black press, to avoid litigation from the NAACP challenging their "separate but equal" ruling, the Commonwealth of Virginia gave Johnson a scholarship to attend Columbia University, where she earned a master's in English and comparative literature.[12] As state by state used this tactic to avoid integrating their colleges, this became a great vehicle for Black students in the South to attend superior and prestigious institutions outside the South. For example, Phyllis Wallace, from Baltimore, took advantage of this opportunity. She became the first Black woman to earn a doctorate in economics (Yale '48.) At the time of her high school graduation, Maryland had two Black state colleges—Coppin State and Morgan State. She noted she looked at both catalogs and determined which fields weren't offered at either institution. She chose economics and received a stipend to attend New York University. She excelled in the field, graduated in 1944, and anticipated returning to Baltimore to be a teacher like most Black women college graduates. However, her advisor encouraged her to continue her studies in economics and recommended her to Yale. At Yale, she went into the field of international economics, earning a master's in 1944 and a PhD in 1948. She was the recipient of the General Education Graduate Fellowship and a Rosenwald Fellowship for her support at Yale.[13] These race-based stipends made all the difference in the lives and careers of the Blacks who took advantage of them.

In 1938, the Supreme Court ruling in favor of the NAACP lawsuit *Gaines v. University of Missouri Law School* resulted in an increased number of African Americans applying to graduate and professional schools. One GEB Fellow of the 1930s, Rose Butler Brown, who was the first Black woman to earn a doctorate from the Harvard School of Education (1937), recalled that after the *Gaines* decision, "Negroes [poured] into Northern universities to seek advanced degrees. Despite the Great Depression, money was now available to qualified Negro teachers as never before . . . they flocked to Teachers College, Columbia University."[14]

Indeed, so many African American went to Teachers College, Columbia University in the 1930s and 1940s that it was not uncommon for a third of the student body to be Black.[15] According to a 1938 GEB report, Columbia University had graduated 121 graduate students (men and women) compared to eighty-one from the University of Chicago and sixty-six from Howard University.[16]

Dorothy Height, who became a national civil rights leader and head of the National Council of Negro Women, recalled during the Depression of the 1930s, she was a full-tuition scholarship student at New York University. She said that since there were no jobs to earn money, she tutored some of the Black women who came from the rural South to attend Teachers College. She stated that many in the Harlem community looked down on the women from the South as they struggled academically. Height noticed that as the NAACP fought to have the salaries of Black teachers in the South equalized to that of white teachers in the South, she noted many Black teachers were in jeopardy of losing their jobs because of their lack of required credentials. Thus, "every college credit counted." Harlemites could be quite disdainful of these teachers from the rural South. Height said these people would comment, "She's at Columbia U to take two points in penmanship" and similarly disparaging types of comments. Height commented that one of the women she tutored had an extremely poor educational background and had been taught to memorize instead of analyzing materials.[17]

There was a vast difference in the applications of African American women who attended the elite and selective Seven Sisters colleges and other northern white colleges who were funded by the GEB program. Their applications, as well as those from Spelman, Fisk, and Howard universities, were assured awards. Recommendations from Florence Read, the president of Spelman College from 1927 to 1944, for faculty and students who applied for GEB fellowships were readily awarded with rare exception. In statistics from 1947 to 1955 supplied by Spelman College to the GEB, 111 Spelman alumnae had attended graduate and professional school in that nine-year period with GEB awards.[18]

Although the Black women who were products of the above elite institutions were very competitive and were able to obtain their doctorates, students from land-grant and small unaccredited schools were not. Such was the case of Naomi Mill Garett in 1944. The Rosenwald Foundation awarded her a fellowship at age thirty-nine to work on a doctorate in French at Columbia University. The foundation waived the thirty-five-year-old criterion because of Garrett's outstanding application and references. She earned an AB from Benedict College in South Carolina in 1927 and attended summer school at Howard University during the 1930s. She earned a master's degree from Atlanta University in 1937. When her fellowship ended in 1945, in her report to the foundation, she stated that Columbia accepted very little of her previous college work. Dismayed, while she had hoped to work toward a doctorate, she wrote:

> Nearly all of the graduate work that I did at Atlanta (where I received my master's degree) and at Howard University had to be considered undergraduate hours to give me the number of acceptable credits required for admissions. Thus, I shall have to spend two years in residence here.[19]

Although Columbia accepted few of Garrett's previous college credits, her professors praised her academic ability. And as heart-wrenching as her letter was, the foundation did not award her additional funds to allow her to complete her doctorate.[20]

Given that Black students were awarded these fellowships to enhance Black colleges (hence, not competing for jobs in white institutions), Black women often received enormous encouragement and support from white male professors in their graduate programs, even in male-dominated fields. For example, Beatrice Yvonne Black, a 1939 Phi Beta Kappa graduate of Smith College, obtained a master's and completed work toward a doctorate in mathematics from Brown University. When the Rosenwald Foundation contacted the dean at Brown to inquire about Black's status as a student and whether the foundation should continue support of her degree, the response was enthusiastic. The dean noted the dearth of Black mathematicians in the country and said a Black woman should be more marketable than a "white woman or even a white man." Clearly that was news to any Black person seeking employment on the same basis as a white person. However, another white male professor echoed the dean and noted Black's ability and noted her employability. He wrote:

> I am aware of the need for better preparation of the Professor of mathematics in Negro colleges. Miss Black will find a position more easily than would a white woman taking a Ph.D. in Mathematics, and she ought to be very useful.[21]

Authorities at Yale University were equally as enthusiastic regarding Evelyn Boyd who was also completing a doctorate in mathematics. Like Black, Boyd was also a Phi Beta Kappa graduate of Smith College (1945) and a member of the mathematics honor society Sigma Xi. The director of the Graduate Mathematics Program at Yale reported to the Rosenwald Foundation in 1947 that Boyd was "highly gifted" and that the number of Black mathematicians in his estimation would never be large, and Boyd had a bright future and "serves a definite need in the [Black] community."[22]

Another gifted applicant, Leila Smith Green, applied to pursue a PhD in organic chemistry at Radcliffe College to work with prominent Harvard professors in 1938. Green was a Howard University graduate who had an impressive academic record and had amassed scholarships from Howard to support her undergraduate education and graduate studies at Howard. When Rosenwald officials asked Will W. Alexander, a white Methodist minister in Atlanta and the former executive director of the Commission on Interracial Cooperation from 1919–30, his opinion of Green's application, he responded that he had had a personal interview with her and found her "mature and well-balanced"—more than her youth would have indicated. However, he commented: "The only question that remains is how much weight to attach to the testimony of her professors at Howard as to her preparation and ability for the work in chemistry which she proposes to undertake."[23] It turned out that Green was awarded the fellowship, and she received rave reviews from her Harvard professors—she was the superior student that her Howard professors had indicated. After her first year, a Dr. Bartlett from the chemistry department at Harvard wrote in his report of Green: "Miss Green has shown herself to be a remarkably good student—in fact her mid-year grade was the highest in the class." He said her work and ideas were original and urged the Rosenwald Fund to continue their support of her for the next year. A Dr. Ross noted, "She [Green] has proved herself to be both capable and independent. Her research is quite good," and he noted all of her professors have very high respect for her and recommended her continued financial support. Finally, the chair of the organic chemistry department, Dr. Louis Fieser, wrote: "Miss Green is a student of outstanding ability and has been doing work of the highest grade . . . She seems to me to be highly deserving of continued support from the Rosenwald Fund."[24] The fact that Alexander would question the highly supportive references by Green's Howard professors is galling. He was a minister and not a chemist. It was unclear if his skepticism of the positive reference for Green was because she was a Black woman.

In confidential comments the foundation's selection committee also voiced skepticism of awarding two other outstanding Black women scientists fellowships. Viola Goins (later Palmer) applied in the field of public health and bacteriology. She attended Oberlin from 1929–31 and began graduate studies at Yale, but she had to transfer to Michigan due to finances. She noted Michigan was less expensive. She had studied at the University of Paris and had an outstanding record. The third candidate was Charlotte Smith, a 1937 graduate of Mt. Holyoke who earned a master's at Howard in 1938 in anatomy and endocrinology. The minutes of the all-male selection committee noted they had originally viewed these three women as "definite gambles." However, they discovered that the women were actually "brilliant." As with Green, the notes stated, "Henry Moe, usually the most conservative member of the Committee, after interviewing these candidates and talking with their professors, strongly urged their appointments." The skepticism of these women's abilities, in spite of their attending outstanding institutions, obtaining top grades and stellar references, reflected the difficulties many women experienced in their academic and professional careers.

Unlike many white women who received advanced degrees and were later unemployed or underemployed due to gender and nepotism rules, most educated Black women did have employment opportunities available to them albeit in Black educational institutions. Black colleges readily employed them. Black women served on the faculty of the all-male Morehouse College in Atlanta, as well as at leading coeducational institutions, such as Howard and Fisk Universities. While many white firms that she applied to rejected Sadie Tanner Alexander after she earned a doctorate in economics in 1921, she received numerous offers to teach in

HBCUs. In an oral history, Alexander noted she was offered teaching positions at Fisk, Howard, and Atlanta University.[25] Anna Julia Cooper was an 1884 Oberlin College graduate earning a PhD in romance languages from the Sorbonne at the age of sixty-five without foundation support. When she responded to a survey of Black college graduates in the 1930s, for the question: "length of time between graduation and first employment," she replied, "not a moment."[26]

Foundation records through the applications and final reports of the Black women fellowship recipients provide a glimpse into their backgrounds and work in HBCUs. The application and report of Shirley Graham (later Du Bois) is a classic example. In her 1938 application, Graham noted that she was the daughter of a Methodist minister and that she grew up in a home "fiercely devoted to 'service' and 'race pride.'" She attended Howard School of Music from 1926–27, and in 1928, she moved to Paris to study musical composition and orchestration at the Sorbonne, becoming fluent in French. Graham returned to the States the next year and taught for two years in the department of music at Morgan State College in Baltimore. In 1931, she applied to Oberlin College as an advanced student and earned a bachelor's degree in music in 1934, and a master's in music history and criticism in 1935. Like so many of the middle-class Black women, she studied and traveled virtually every summer. She had studied multiple summers at Columbia University and one summer at Vassar College during the 1920s and '30s. In addition, Graham studied piano, organ, voice, harmony, and orchestration privately. After graduating from Oberlin, she was appointed head of the fine arts department at Black land-grant Tennessee Agricultural and Industrial State College in Nashville. In her Rosenwald application, she noted she planned to attend Yale School of Drama. Graham said she had an extensive background in art and music, as well as Greek, architecture, sculpting, painting, and an array of other courses. She said when she went to Tennessee to teach, her classrooms had no equipment or materials for the teaching of art. She said, however, this didn't discourage her. She reflected:

> I had my own "Art Through the Ages," hundreds of prints which I had used at Oberlin, prints, and photographs and memories of Paris. Carefully, I prepared my lectures. What brought me up short was the realization, slowly borne on me, that pupils had no idea what I was talking about. Most of them had come from the rural districts of the Mississippi Valley. Even those who had come from towns or cities had never been inside an art gallery or concert hall. And, yet, they wanted to know. I saw hunger for beauty. I laid aside my prints and even my book and lecture notes. We went outdoors and began to study. From the hills and trees and bushes we learned color by comparing the green of the campus to the blue of the sky, and we saw that sky at sunrise as well as at noon and sunset. Finally, we began copying these things on paper. Out of soap, we carved objects and animals with which they were familiar. I

know all this was kindergarten technique, but they did begin to get the feel for the line and form and color. When, by special permission, I was able to take them into an art gallery, they were able to see. And I myself, recognized new fields opening up before me. I taught the girls line and color in their clothing—how to match and contrast the color of their skin; I showed both boys and girls how green grass and bright flowers transform bare, muddy yards and how cream-colored paint would lighten drab, dark rooms. At Oberlin, I had learned to correlate the arts one to another—on this campus, I learned to correlate art with life and everyday living.[27]

Graham's moving essay to the Foundation clearly demonstrated the challenges of teaching in institutions with no resources and students who have had no exposure to cultural institutions, such as art galleries or museums. As she indicated, Graham grew up in a family where "service" to the race was stressed. She quickly learned to turn the lecture of the Eurocentric content into one that the students could relate to. She started with the basics that the class could comprehend until they could move into the students' understanding the class materials. Graham stayed in this position only one year. In 1936, she was appointed during the Depression to be the director of the Federal Theater Project in Chicago, part of Franklin D. Roosevelt's Works Progress Administration. Graham was awarded the fellowship and attended Yale Drama School from 1938–41.

Academic Couples

The fellowship opportunities resulted in numerous academic couples obtaining fellowships. While most state institutions established rules regarding spouses working at the same institution, many couples often did and found ways to get around these laws. Both foundations provided stipends for dependent family members. However, only in rare instances did a wife relocate with her husband (and not vice versa—since there was no expectation that a husband would be dependent upon his wife). Black marriages were different from the average white family, where it was expected that the wife would accompany the husband and that he would be the primary breadwinner—this was not the case with Black couples. This became clear when the GEB inadvertently included a family stipend to a Howard Medical School faculty member's stipend who had received a fellowship for further studies in his specialization. The fellowship recipient's wife was also a professional and remained in Washington to continue in her job. When the foundation discovered its error, one of the officers wrote to the dean of Howard's medical school. He noted the error and stated that foundation would not ask for the money to be returned since it was the foundation's error; however, he added, "It is my personal opinion that a fellow's independent wife should be encouraged to accompany him even if that means a reduction in their double income—I think the fellow is happier, and often his wife profits quite as much from the new environment as he does." He ended by telling the dean that the foundation hoped that he would "keep this in mind" when recommending future fellows.[28]

Young academic couples managed to enhance their careers and maintain their marriages in a variety of ways. In 1937 and 1939, the Rosenwald Fund awarded graduate fellowships to Bonita and Preston Valien, respectively, to pursue their doctorates in sociology at the University of Wisconsin. In 1940, Kenneth and Mamie Phipps Clark shared a joint fellowship awarded to them toward their doctoral studies in child psychology at Columbia University. The fellowship was renewed twice. Other couples also applied and received separate fellowships. Viola Goins, while a 1938 Rosenwald Fellow working on her doctorate in bacteriology at the University of Michigan, married another Michigan doctoral student in sociology, Edward N. Palmer, a Rosenwald Fellow of 1939.[29] Another Michigan couple who were both Rosenwald Fellows were Cornelius Lacy Golightly, a philosophy major and 1941 Fellow. His wife was Catherine Cater Golightly, a literature major and 1943 Fellow. Cornelius earned his doctorate in 1941 and continued his studies in religion at Harvard. Catherine was employed at Fisk University during this period but applied for a second fellowship to complete her doctorate, while Cornelius was employed on the faculty at Howard University.[30] Commuting marriages were common among this group.

Unlike the conservative GEB, the Rosenwald Fund supported African American couples and demonstrated no apparent bias toward them. In fact, their annual report of 1943 highlighted the Golightlys as an example of a "talented couple."[31] Another "talented couple" were Hugh and Mabel Smythe, who married in 1939 and were both Rosenwald Fellows in different years, fields, and institutions.[32] Mabel Smythe held fellowships from 1940–42 for work toward her doctorate in economics at the University of Wisconsin. She earned this degree in 1942. Hugh held Rosenwald Fellowships during the years 1939–45 and worked on his doctorate in anthropology at Northwestern University. His studies were interrupted by World War II, which put his fellowship on hold. He earned his doctorate in 1945. After earning her doctorate, Mable Smythe was appointed assistant professor of economics at Lincoln University in Missouri, and by 1944, was associate professor and acting chair of the department of economics. By this time, Hugh Smythe had been honorably discharged from the army and was teaching at Atlanta University and Morris Brown College. The Smythes' commuting marriage finally ended in 1945, when they both obtained positions at Tennessee State University. Although the Drs. Smythe lived in different cities for a number of years, they coauthored numerous articles and a book.[33]

Margaret and Charles Lawrence also received Rosenwald Fellowships. Margaret Morgan, a Cornell University graduate, married Charles Lawrence during her second year of medical school at Columbia University in 1938. After their wedding, they spent the summer together, then began a commuting marriage when Margaret returned to medical school and Charles attended graduate school at Atlanta University. In 1939, Charles was awarded a Rosenwald Fellowship to work on a doctorate in sociology at Columbia University. As a result, he was able to join his wife there. They returned to a commuting relationship in 1941 when Charles had a position in Atlanta as a member of the staff of the South Field Council of the Student YMCA. By this time, Margaret had earned her medical degree and was completing her residency at Harlem Hospital. The next year in 1942, she and Charles were both able to obtain another Rosenwald Fellowship. After his fellowship expired, his Rosenwald file noted he was able to have a part-time job in New York while he completed his doctorate. After he completed his degree, he and Margaret moved to Nashville, where they secured faculty positions. He joined the faculty of Fisk University, and she attended Meharry Medical School. As with other Black academic couples who sacrificed living separately temporarily to accomplish their academic aspirations, in her biography written by her daughter Sara Lawrence Lightfoot, Margaret describes the daily letters that she and her husband wrote to each other while they were separated, and how they cheered each other's ambition and accomplishments. Her daughter Sara noted that: "Marriage and professional life had been comfortable companions because she and Charles cared so deeply about both pursuits, and because her husband felt enhanced, not diminished by her ambition."[34]

While some African American academic couples met as students, others met on the job. Virginia Lacy and Edward Allen Jones are one such example. She was a GEB Fellow in library science at the University of Illinois in 1937–38. Because of Lacy's training and degrees in library science, she was recruited to Atlanta University (AU) as head of cataloging at the Arnett Library in 1939. When the School of Library Science opened at AU in 1941, Lacy became a founding member of the school. The same year, she married Edward Allen Jones, a professor of foreign languages at neighboring Morehouse College. However, like the Lawrences, he left shortly after their wedding to complete his doctorate at Cornell University. Two years later, Virginia left for two years to complete her doctorate at the University of Chicago. Thus, it wasn't until 1945 that the couple was reunited in Atlanta. Virginia, who was the second African American in the country to earn a PhD in library science, was appointed dean of the School of Library Science. Edward became chair of foreign languages at Morehouse College. They remained at the Atlanta University/Morehouse campuses for their entire professional careers.[35]

When Lacy Jones recalled these events for the Radcliffe Oral History Project in the late 1970s, the interviewer was incredulous, and apparently did not realize that this personal history was not unique to this couple. When asked questions regarding their loneliness for each other, Jones informed the interviewer that she and her husband had professional goals and recognized that these fellowships would enable them to earn terminal degrees without debt and result in professional advancement in academe.[36]

Indeed, these fellowships were a godsend and, if awarded, one had to take advantage of these opportunities to obtain advanced degrees at prominent institutions. As noted from the many fellowship recipients' final reports, these awards allowed these students to pursue their degrees full-time and not forfeit their salaries. In the past, students had to attend for repeated summers to pursue these degrees.

Winona Lee also met her husband on a Black college campus. Lee, a recent master's graduate from the University of Iowa in theatre and drama, was hired in 1951 as a faculty member of Kentucky State College (KSC, later University). Within nine months of starting her position, she married Joseph Grant Fletcher, the acting chair of the English department and head basketball coach at KSC. In 1962, Winona left for a year and a half to pursue a doctorate at Indiana University. She left her nine-year-old daughter with her husband Joseph and a niece, a Kentucky State student. During this period, she drove the three-hour trip from Bloomington, Indiana, to Frankfort, Kentucky, on the weekends. When she returned to her classes at KSC, she drove back and forth between the two cities to complete the remaining requirements for the doctorate. On this schedule, Winona earned her doctorate in 1968. In the years between 1964–68, she noted that she took her daughter with her on research trips around the country as she worked on her dissertation. She said this exposure to scholarly research resulted in her daughter earning a doctorate years later.[37]

Joseph Fletcher was a GEB fellowship recipient in the 1930s but never completed his doctorate at Columbia due to family responsibilities. He was eighteen years Winona's senior and encouraged her to pursue her doctorate because he knew the degree would enhance her career. In 1971, Winona was invited to join the faculty at Indiana University as a two-year visiting professor. While there, she helped to develop the African American Studies Program at IU. After Joseph retired from Kentucky State in 1978 and the institution began to lose its identity as a historically Black college, Winona Fletcher said her husband encouraged her to accept Indiana University's invitation to join the faculty. She accepted and became a full-time, tenured professor and served as associate dean of the College of Arts and Sciences from 1981–84.[38]

Reflecting on the twenty-seven years she spent on the faculty at Kentucky State College, Fletcher noted that all Black colleges hired married couples and said these institutions could not have existed without them. Fletcher also noted, as did another married Black woman faculty member, by hiring two persons, the college got a better financial deal. She remembered that the college campus was like a family, and despite the fact that faculty members had extremely high teaching loads and low pay, the sense of community and commitment to the students made the experience exciting and rewarding.[39]

Dr. Mildred Barksdale, who was discussed in chapter three, also met her husband Dr. Richard Barksdale in the 1950s when they were teaching at North Carolina Central University. They married in 1960 and joined the faculty at Atlanta University. Mildred was hired to establish and head the special education department and Richard was hired to chair the English department. Like Dr. Fletcher, Dr. Mildred Barksdale noted that Black faculty couples were the norm on most Black college campuses. She said these institutions needed the expertise of the Black women scholars, who were frequently as well educated as the male faculty. She recalled that at least a third of the faculty at Jackson College when she was an undergraduate in the 1930s were faculty/staff couples (later Jackson State College).[40]

At least three Black college presidents met their wives in graduate school or while working at the same institutions. Sadie Gray (later Mays) met Benjamin Elijah Mays in the mid-1920s when they both taught at South Carolina State College. They married in 1926. She earned a bachelor's degree (a second bachelor's because she was a graduate of the unaccredited Paine College) from the University of Chicago in 1924, and Benjamin E. Mays earned a master's from the University of Chicago in 1925 in religious studies. Sadie received a Rosenwald Fellowship in 1930 and earned a master's in social work from the University of Chicago in 1931. Benjamin Mays earned a PhD from Chicago in 1935. He was the first dean of Howard University's School of Religion by then. Sadie taught at the Howard School of Social Work. By 1940, Dr. Mays was appointed president of Morehouse College in Atlanta, where he served in that position for twenty-seven years. After becoming the wife of a college president, Sadie's life changed. She noted in the Rosenwald Foundation follow-up survey of former fellows that she was primarily a homemaker and taught part-time in Atlanta University's School of Social Work. However, she noted that she felt her work when they lived in Washington, DC, "was significant." Now, she said, "most of my work now is volunteering with students, the Urban League, the YWCA, Girl Scouts, and children's home and church."[41] A college president's wife was not expected to earn a salary, even when she worked and made significant contributions on these campuses.

Susie Williams Jones met David Dallas Jones, who became president of Bennett College, when they also were both students at the University of Chicago. Susie, a graduate of the University of Cincinnati, was taking additional undergraduate summer courses to enhance her credentials. David Jones was pursuing a graduate degree. After they married, as discussed in previous chapters, he was appointed president of Bennett College in 1926. As noted in chapter seven, Susie was very active on the Bennett campus and served as registrar without pay.

Likewise, Ethel McGhee was a 1919 graduate of Spelman College. She earned a diploma from the New York School of Social Work in 1925 and was later employed by Spelman as an advisor and teacher of sociology. In 1930, McGhee was awarded a Rosenwald Fellowship to student personnel development at Teachers College, Columbia University. She returned to Spelman in the position of dean of women. In 1932, she married John W. Davis, president of West Virginia State College. In her follow-up survey to the Rosenwald Fund in 1944, she said she was a "housewife with an eleven-year-old daughter; but was on the Board of Trustees at Spelman and a representative on the Kanawha Council of Girls Scouts. I am most grateful for my fellowship. On a college campus, I use the information I gained in my studies."[42] So, all of these educated wives of college presidents utilized their knowledge to benefit the students on the campus and beyond.

While many Black women married to Black male academics were employed, many were not allowed to work on the same campus due to nepotism laws, especially at state institutions. For example, numerous women who were fellowship recipients noted this issue. Edmonia Louise Walden, who received a Rosenwald Fellowship to attend the University of Chicago in 1930 and earned a master of arts in home economics in clothing and textiles, was on the faculty of West Virginia State College. However, in 1936, she wrote: "I married a gentleman working on the same faculty. A rule was passed that no two people in the same family could draw state checks. So, I was dropped along with several others in 1933. However, I was asked to return to work as a part-time worker in the institution." She noted she worked from 1:30–3:30 each day.[43] She didn't say in what capacity.

Hilda Lawson was a Rosenwald Fellow from 1937–40 and earned a doctorate in English from the University of Illinois in 1939, at the age of twenty-four. After obtaining this degree, she was hired by Lincoln University in Missouri, a state college, to teach graduate students for their MA program. In 1941, she married a colleague on the faculty, Dr. Sidney Reedy. This brought her teaching appointment to an end at the institution. She reported to the Rosenwald Fund in 1944 that she was no longer employed "because Lincoln's Board of Curators opposed the employment of wives of faculty members. Silly, isn't it?"[44]

Finally, Ruth Brett, discussed earlier, left Fisk University as dean of women in 1953 to marry historian Benjamin Quarles. They were hired (again an academic couple) to join the faculty and staff of Morgan State College in Baltimore. Dr.

Quarles was hired to head the history department and Dr. Brett was hired to be the director of the counseling center. Since Morgan was in a state that didn't allow wives to work at the same institution as their husband, Dr. Brett said she was advised by the institution's president, Dr. Martin Jenkins, not to change her name. Hence, she was always Dr. Ruth Brett instead of Dr. Ruth Quarles. She and Dr. Quarles stayed at Morgan State until their retirements (Dr. Quarles in 1974 and Dr. Brett in 1980). Dr. Brett noted that another woman faculty member at Morgan who married a faculty member was advised the same strategy. In one other instance, the academic wife was already married and had her husband's last name, so this strategy couldn't work for her.

Black Women Faculty at Fisk

Archival records provide insight into the hiring of women faculty and administrators during the presidencies of Thomas E. Jones and Charles S. Johnson at Fisk University. Jones was the fifth and last white president of Fisk University, and he served in this position from 1926–46. Charles S. Johnson became the first African American president of Fisk in 1946. In 1928, Jones hired Johnson to become the chair of the sociology department at Fisk. As the number of Black women earning graduate degrees increased beginning in the 1920s, they began to join the faculty at Fisk in the Jones years and continued to add to their numbers during the Charles S. Johnson years. In addition, the growth of Black women in student affairs had a prominent place at Fisk, with some of the early African American women trained as deans of women being employed at the institution.

Thomas Elsa Jones, a Quaker and graduate of Earlham College and Hartford Theological Seminary was appointed president of Fisk University in 1926 and served until 1946. Coming from a career of Quaker mission in Tokyo and on the faculty of Ohio State University, he had no experience in race relations or as a higher education administrator.[45] (He succeeded President Fayette Avery McKenzie who served from 1915–25. McKenzie resigned after student and alumni protests of his paternalistic and dictatorial style.[46]) Charles Johnson was president of Fisk from 1946 until his sudden death in 1956.

Like Howard, Fisk attracted a strong research-oriented faculty, and both institutions competed for many of the same top Black scholars. In 1927, Jones contacted Sadie Tanner Alexander, mentioned earlier, who held a PhD and a JD degree, about a faculty position at Fisk. He said the university was in the process of establishing a department of business and commerce and he wanted her to be a professor in this department, saying she was "eminently qualified to help us develop here a strong school for the education of young Negro businessmen."[47] He also noted that Fisk was planning to establish a law school, and her husband, Raymond Pace Alexander would be a candidate for a faculty position there.[48] As mentioned earlier, academic couples were a huge plus to HBCUs, and they were welcomed except in the instances of the states that didn't allow wives to work at the same institutions as their husbands. Alexander responded by declining the offer stating she had just completed law school and "as soon as I am admitted to the Philadelphia Bar, I expect to enter my husband's office and devote my entire time to the practice of law."[49]

In 1930, Fisk appointed nine research professors; none were women. However, four of the nine were African American (Charles S. Johnson, E. Franklin Frazier, Elmer S. Imes, and St. Elmo Brady). Ambrose Caliver, who was on the faculty since 1917, was promoted by Jones from assistant dean to dean of faculty during the summer of 1927, becoming the first African American dean of the university. He left to complete his PhD at Columbia in 1929. Alrutheus Ambush Taylor, another African American, was appointed dean. Taylor remained in this position until his death in 1955.[50] Caliver and Taylor's appointments were a part of Jones's push to address Black alumni and students, who demanded a greater Black presence on the faculty and administration. A few Black women emerged on the faculty—Lillian Cashin, a Fisk alumna with graduate degrees from the University of Chicago and Columbia University. Cashin graduated from Fisk in 1908 and later earned a master of arts from the University of Chicago. In 1915, she returned to Fisk to teach in the university's high school. When it closed in 1927, she joined the faculty of the university in the English department in 1928 and ultimately became chair of the department. Cashin's fields were English, comparative literature, and drama. Although she was not a playwright, she helped establish the Fisk University StageCrafters, the student theater group. Cashin also organized annual playwriting contests on campus. She joined with other renowned Black faculty in theater and drama to establish the Negro International Dramatic Association as well as regional theater tournaments among Black colleges and universities.[51]

Jane Ellen McAllister was also appointed to the faculty in 1928 as professor of education. McAllister was extremely precocious and graduated from Talladega College, another AMA sister college of Fisk in Alabama, when she was 19 years old in 1919. She entered the University of Michigan in 1920 for graduate work and earned a master's degree in 1921. She subsequently taught at Southern University between 1919–27 with periods off for graduate studies and a two-year teaching assignment at Virginia State University as principal of their training school. She returned to Louisiana and worked in teacher training and schools established by the Rosenwald Foundation, General Education Board, the Slater Fund, and the Phelps-Stokes funds throughout the state. In 1926, McAllister entered a doctoral program at Teachers College at Columbia University and graduated in 1928, becoming the first Black person to earn a doctorate from Teachers College. Building on her work in Louisiana, McAllister's dissertation was entitled, "The Training of Negro Teachers in Louisiana."[52]

Jones was reluctant to hire McAllister despite her stellar education and experience. Fisk was starting a graduate program in education that would offer a master's degree. When Jones was approached about hiring McAllister by Mabel Carney, a professor at Teachers College, Jones contacted Leo Favrot, of the General Education Board with whom McAllister had worked. Jones told Favrot that "of course, I have been looking for a man, but Miss McAllister's records seems so satisfactory that I would like to have your reaction to her for this post."[53] Favrot responded favorably stating:

> Miss Jane Ellen McAllister is unquestionably a young woman of outstanding promise in the educational field. She has an unusually bright mind and with it a pleasing personality. I have known her for several years and consider her remarkably successful as a teacher. Her experience has been, so far as I know, largely in the training of elementary teachers. While in Louisiana, she rendered an extremely important service in the field of extension work among Negro teachers in service. She was respected and honored by the white parish superintendents for her knowledge of this field and her ability to direct the work of teachers.[54]

Despite the above positive assessment of McAllister, Favrot continued that while she was wonderful with elementary school teachers, he could not attest to her skills as an administrator and how well she could work with teachers at the secondary level and other departments of education that would be developed at Fisk. He noted that Professor Mabel Carney at Teachers College was extremely enthusiastic about McAllister. Jones said he wanted someone with a national reputation. Favrot told him to speak with professors McAllister had studied with when he was in New York. Favrot ended by saying he believed McAllister was better suited for a place like Hampton, where she could direct teacher training and work with elementary students in rural areas. But he qualified the statement to Jones ending, "However, as I have already said, my opportunity to judge her ability for the particular position which, I understand, you wish to fill, has been limited, and I should not be willing to trust myself entirely."[55]

Indeed, Jones contacted every person McAllister had worked with and also her Columbia professors.[56] Her advisor and mentor, Mabel Carney was the head of the rural education program at Teachers College and urged Jones to consider McAllister. He expressed concern over her youthfulness (McAllister was twenty-seven). Carney noted that despite McAllister's age, she was not only the first African American woman to earn a doctorate from Teachers College in education but also the first Black woman in the world to do so. She also pointed out:

> In personal appearance Miss McAllister is one of the most attractive girls I have known of either the colored or white race. She is so light in color that she

is frequently regarded as full white and is in every respect a young woman of unusual charm and personality. We all expect her to be one of the outstanding leaders in Negro Education in a few years, and it is for this reason that I thought you might be interested in her availability at the present time.[57]

The reference to Black women's complexions happened repeatedly when whites were trying to convince other whites why they should admit or hire a Black person (implying she's not really *that* Black). McAllister was hired. Although Fisk was not her only option for employment, she decided on Fisk over Spelman College in Atlanta. In her letter of acceptance, McAllister told Jones, although she had not visited Fisk's campus, her acceptance was based on the growth and development of the department and later School of Education. However, knowing the enormous administrative burdens most Black colleges placed on faculty, McAllister insisted that Jones agree on certain issues:

> Since considering the service which Fisk proposes to render in the future, I have been able to make my decision without visiting the college. I consider it a privilege to have a share in this work. Therefore, I accept the position, which you have offered me as in education with the understanding that I shall have classes in psychology and education, and no clerical work or work as registrar unless that work appeals to me more than teaching . . . I am sorry that I was not able to give you my answer sooner, and I hope that the delay has not inconvenienced you seriously . . . I anticipate with keenest pleasure my work with you in Fisk.[58]

When McAllister arrived at Fisk, she was the only faculty member in the education department with a doctorate. She was appointed as a full professor. McAllister immediately began working with students and attempted to build a relationship between Fisk and the Nashville School board. In 1929, she was appointed head of the department, the first African American woman head of a department at Fisk. She wrote a proposal during that year on establishing a cooperative training program between Fisk and Nashville Public schools since Fisk no longer had lab schools for their students to work in. McAllister, in mid-year, realized that Jones's promotion of her to head of the department was verbal and not in writing. She pressed him on this matter. Jones hedged. In April of 1930, McAllister wrote Jones a one-and-a-half-page typewritten letter. She went directly to the point:

> I hope not to be forced to believe that throughout the year you have forgotten intentionally that in a conference in May 1925, you assured me that I was head of the department of education. In reply to my question, "I shall be head of the department?" You said, "Yes, and in addition, I should like to have you carry on the educational work of the Dean's office.["][59]

McAllister also pointed out some slights that she wanted to inform Jones about—she noted that Jones had also told her that she was a member of the graduate committee, yet she had never been invited to any of the meetings with the other department chairs. She said the dean's office also had no clue that she was supposed to be department head of education. McAllister diplomatically stated that she had been so busy working that she hadn't had a chance to bring this up. She ended with several demands (requests):

> I feel I owe it to myself to ask you: 1) to include my name on those committees on which all heads of departments are supposed to serve by virtue of their administrative duties, and 2) To make any other adjustments, which will show the position on which, you agreed that I was to hold when I accepted work for this year. The position, which we agreed upon, was that of head (and not acting head) of see the justification and necessity of this request . . . Very truly yours[60]

Jones sheepishly responded within two days:

> I hereby officially recognize you are Head of the Department of Education and have been since the beginning of the school year on or about September 14, 1929. Your engagement was for the school year 1929–1930 . . . I regret that lack of records has caused you any embarrassment.[61]

However, Jones had made a grievous error in verbally appointing McAllister head of the department. In a letter to Leo Favrot, Jones anticipated the return of Ambrose Caliver from Columbia with the completion of his PhD in the fall of 1930. He said that with the establishment of the master's program in education, Caliver would become the head of the department. While Jones was extremely complimentary of McAllister's efforts, nonetheless, he didn't see her in the top position. He wrote:

> Miss Jane McAllister (*although she was Dr. McAllister*) has already made a big place for herself at Fisk and I think is going to demonstrate not only here, but throughout the South, that her work has a real value in the field of postsecondary education. Professor Snell, who was in Yale University last year on a Fellowship from the General Education Board, is a white man from Alabama, who did his bachelor's and master's work in Psychology and Education at Peabody College. His year at Yale has grounded his training into excellent shape and he is giving splendid courses in this field. Miss Belle Parmenter, who has been with us for years, is also a good teacher . . . With these four in the Department of Education, I believe we are not only able to give majors in Education and Psychology but actually to do work leading to the Master of Arts Degree.[62]

McAllister was a woman who spoke up for herself. At the end of the academic year of 1929–30, McAlister contacted Jones regarding her status for the following year and her salary since she was considering her options. He increased her salary by $300, perhaps as an appeasement, from $2,200 to $2,500. When she received her contract on May 15, 1930, for the following year, McAllister refused to sign it without assurance of her administrative status. Jones told her he was waiting to hear from Dean Caliver but she would be retained as a full professor with the increase in salary. After McAllister returned to her family home in Vicksburg, Mississippi, for the summer, she accepted a position at Miner Teachers College in Washington, DC, where she was appointed professor and head of the education department effective September 1930. Miner had just transitioned from being a normal school to a four-year teacher's college.

Ironically, at the last minute, Ambrose Caliver did not return to Fisk. President Herbert Hoover appointed Caliver in 1930 to the new position of Senior Specialist in the Education of Negroes in the US Office of Education. He remained in the post when Franklin Delano Roosevelt was elected President two years later and joined FDR's "Black Cabinet." He never returned to Fisk.

McAllister's decision not to return to Fisk was a huge loss. She was a distinguished educator. And, although Jones readily acknowledged her talents, he was not willing to elevate her to the position she deserved. Furthermore, McAllister was the first Black woman full professor with a PhD at Fisk. She was an important role model and symbol for the African American students on campus and for the people in the Nashville and Tennessee area in her desire to assist in their children's education. However, unlike Black women scholars who were a part of an academic couple that an institution could underpay as the spouse, and avoid a commuting marriage, McAllister was an independent single woman.

Fisk was a small college (despite the university label). It was not until 1944 that it enrolled its largest number of students, 683; hence, the small faculty. While African American women did slowly join the teaching force at Fisk—the initial appointments of academic Black women were through the dean of women's department. For example, Sadie Daniels, hired in 1935, was employed as director of physical education for women. This was a position suggested by Juliette Derricotte when she became dean in 1928. Women faculty were at lower ranks than male faculty and were paid less (which was the case on all campuses). In 1935–36, there were forty faculty members of whom seven were women. One was African American (Lillian Cashin), the others were deans of women, and the director of physical education for women.

Cashin's salary was $2,800, when she was hired by Jones in 1928, and the salary remained the same until she died in 1945. Sadie Daniels, who was employed in 1935, was appointed at $1,800. In 1940, she wrote a letter of complaint to Jones that she had not received a raise since that time. She stated:

> I really do not know when I have been so discouraged and disappointed . . . this is my third time I have asked you for a raise but have not yet received any

consideration. You told me each time I asked that my work was satisfactory, and I fitted into the University life nicely.

The first time I asked you for a raise, you told me I was the best physical education teacher you had since you had been at Fisk. Last year when I asked for a raise in salary and status, you said you were considering me already because I deserved it having served my probationary period satisfactorily.[63]

Other women also expressed concern over salary offers for positions at Fisk. An African American woman biologist, offered a position in the department of biology in 1944, rejected the position due to a low salary of $1,500. The applicant had an undergraduate degree from Howard, a master's in science from Ohio State University, and graduate work at Columbia and the University of Chicago beyond the master's degree. She thanked Jones for the job offer but stated she had been interested in years of teaching at Fisk:

> I do feel however, that my preparation and experience in the field of biology warrants a better salary than you have offered. Throughout my professional career, my salary was never so low. If therefore an amicable adjustment can be made in the matter, I would be willing to consider a nine-month contract and be very happy to serve you.[64]

Jones responded that although the salary was low, he believed it was basically a foot in the door for the candidate and said he could only offer her the rank of instructor (which was common for women faculty). He concluded by stating he was sure she would find the work at Fisk "interesting."[65] In her final communications, the candidate, Madeline Clarke Foreman, told Jones, coming to Fisk would require major personal and professional adjustments. Since faculty lived on campus, she noted she would have to store her furniture and rent her home to come to Fisk. Plus, more importantly, she would like to be paid what she was worth. Jones wasn't willing to budge, and the candidate turned down the offer.[66]

In 1944, other women rejected Jones's offer. One white woman candidate from the University of Wisconsin wrote him a short rejection with no attempt to renegotiate saying: "Though the position offered at your school sounds very interesting, I find myself unable to accept it. My responsibilities are such that I can agree to no less than $1300 as a salary."[67]

Although African American women were obtaining PhDs in greater numbers by the 1940s, none were employed at Fisk until after Jones retired in 1946, with the exception of McAllister who left after her first year.[68] Jones still relied on faculty who were willing to sacrifice livelihood for the privilege of teaching at Fisk. In the past, the faculty had been comprised of many white members of the American Missionary Association. Faculty members were required to live on campus. For many highly educated Black women, particularly those with PhDs, Howard readily employed them and so did other DC institutions, such as Miner Teachers College, where Jane McAllister became a department head and full professor in the late 1920s. Likewise, Otelia Cromwell, who was the first Black woman to graduate from Smith College in 1900 and earned a PhD in Elizabethan literature from Yale in 1926, also spent her entire professional career teaching at Miner Teachers' College. Many other early Black women worked for the National YWCA and in other positions, such as Saddler, who went to work in Washington, DC, with Bethune. Fisk was often able to attract its alums back, particularly the women in the dean of women's position. However, as the years progressed, professional growth and salaries were an important aspect of attracting faculty of both genders.

As the Second World War came to an end, Jones resigned his position of twenty years to become the president of his alma mater, Earlham College in Indiana.[69] While he expressed great concern in helping many Black women students throughout his presidency, Jones was less sensitive to the employment of women scholars. He underpaid them and wrote that he preferred male faculty for positions over women. Women were hired at lower ranks. And, while Lillian Cashin served on the faculty from 1928–45, he never raised her salary during this period. Fisk certainly benefited from Jones's leadership in obtaining accreditation and the growth of the student body.

Joseph Richardson, a historian of Fisk University, noted that Fisk was not only an intellectual hub with highly productive scholars in economic and social research but also the center of writing, arts, theater, and music during the Jones presidency. By the 1930s, distinguished artists and writers were on the faculty—including Black male writers—James Weldon Johnson, Arne Bontemps, and Robert Earl Hayden. Artist Aaron Douglas joined the faculty in 1937. And as mentioned earlier, Cashin's works with the theater added greatly to the robust environment of the campus. There were annual music and theater festivals.[70]

The Fisk trustees accepted Jones's resignation, and as they sought to appoint a new president, their meeting minutes stated that they thought it might be time to employ an African American president. As noted earlier, Howard University had employed an African American president since 1926; Atlanta University appointed John Hope in 1929 as its first Black president and Hope had served as president of Morehouse College in 1906. This was the direction of private Black higher education. The Fisk trustees' minutes noted:

> It was also felt that the best available man, regardless of race, should be selected, but in the event that two men of practically equal abilities should be found; perhaps the time is past due for selecting a Negro president.[71]

The committee also emphasized that Fisk should always have an interracial faculty and continue to focus upon the world community.

The Charles S. Johnson Years—1946–56

Charles S. Johnson was appointed the first African American president in 1946. Johnson was a University of Chicago–trained sociologist and an expert in race relations. He was a researcher at both the Chicago Urban League and the National Urban League in New York City prior to being recruited to the faculty at Fisk in 1928. With funding from the Laura Spelman Memorial Fund, Johnson established the renowned Department of Social Research Relations Institute at Fisk. With significant foundation support, this department produced first class research on issues of race.

In 1942, Johnson became director of the Race Relations Institute at Fisk established by the AMA. The Race Relations Institute was also funded through the Julius Rosenwald Foundation, where Johnson was co-director of their Race Relations department. The Rosenwald Foundation, established by Julius Rosenwald, the president of Sears, Roebuck and Company, in 1917, was a non-profit organization established to aid "the well-being of mankind." The foundation built schools in the rural South for Blacks from 1928–48. As noted earlier, it funded graduate and professional fellowships for 999 African Americans. Johnson's affiliation with the foundation world included the Phelps-Stokes Fund, the Carnegie Corporation, the General Education Board (which also funded graduate fellowships to African Americans during this period), the American Council on Race Relations, and the Bureau for Intercultural Education. Thus, the appointment of Johnson was a major event for Fisk, especially African American women scholars.

As Director of the Race Relations Institute, Johnson attempted to hire Marion Cuthbert to Fisk as his associate director. Cuthbert was in one of the small groups of highly trained women in the field of race relations and women affairs. Born in Minnesota and educated at the University of Minnesota and Boston University for her undergraduate degrees, she subsequently earned her master's in psychology and a doctorate in higher education from Teachers College, Columbia University. She wrote a pioneering dissertation on the higher education of Black women entitled, "Education and Marginality" in 1942 (which will be discussed in the following chapter), the year she earned her doctorate. Like Slowe, Derricotte, and a handful of other Black women scholars in the field of higher education and race relations, Cuthbert discussed the unique challenges Black women faced in higher education and society. She served as a dean of women at Talladega College in Alabama in 1927, and by 1932, she was employed in the office of the National YWCA that worked in the area of developing "Negro" leadership, staff development, and interracial relations. She traveled globally in this position, conducting workshops on interracial relations. She was a liaison to the National Conference of Social Work, the

National Urban League, affiliated with the United Council of Church Women, and the NAACP, where she served as vice president of the board of directors. Hence, Cuthbert's presence at the Race Relations Institute would have been a major hire. Johnson offered her a salary of $3,200—far more than Jones would have thought to offer her. But, the Race Relations Institute maintained its own budget, and Johnson knew that Cuthbert was in great demand. She thanked Johnson for the offer and indicated that she was being considered for several other positions in New York, so she would get back to him. Johnson quickly responded:

> I do not doubt that there are many offers of challenging posts in New York and its environs. What I want to impress on you most firmly now is that you should give serious consideration to a slightly different but most challenging job of helping to build a new and exciting program in the field of race relations which so much needs your personal and professional resourcefulness. We all hope very much that you are going to give a reasonably prompt response to this matter.[72]

Within a few days, Cuthbert sent a telegram to Johnson declining the offer. She had decided to accept a faculty position at Brooklyn College, one of the City Colleges of New York. This was a significant appointment because the City Colleges of New York were beginning to hire top African American faculty in these institutions. She was appointed to the department of personnel services, where she counseled women students and taught in the department of sociology and anthropology, in which after two years, she taught full-time becoming the college's first Black tenured faculty member.[73]

In a lengthy follow-up letter Cuthbert told Johnson:

> I know my telegram was disappointing to you and in several ways my decision is disappointing to myself. But as I reviewed the matter, I saw that the reasons for declining the post outweighed those for accepting.[74]

Cuthbert said she knew the Fisk position would require a lot of travel and that at this point, she preferred to stay put and do some writing. She said she wanted to spend time writing and doing research—tasks she noted "that cannot be done under circumstances of so much moving about. As your Associate, I would have a good deal of travel in connection with the race relations program, I am sure."[75]

Cuthbert ended by graciously telling Johnson:

> I think I could do your work and I know I should enjoy being associated with you. I am particularly sorry that my decision deprives me of this latter satisfaction. I was greatly pleased that you thought of me for this important work and appreciated your offering me the position. My best wishes for finding the good person to go forward with you in your great work.[76]

By remaining in New York City, Cuthbert was not only able to serve on the faculty of Brooklyn College, but she also continued to work with the National YWCA as well.

Johnson was in close contact with many Black women scholars, and they consulted him regarding positions elsewhere as well as requesting references for fellowships. Johnson was constantly asked by Black and white institutions for referrals for faculty and administrative positions. Mary Huff Diggs, an African American woman who had recently earned a PhD in social work from Bryn Mawr, consulted Johnson in 1946 regarding several job offers she had received. One was to become the superintendent of a state training school for girls in the state of Maryland, which came with a competitive salary, a chauffeur, and living stipend. The other position was at a state HBCU in the South to establish a program in social work. Diggs said she wasn't against going South, but she wanted to go where she thought she would be most needed, and her skills utilized to the fullest. She said money wasn't the primary issue as well. Johnson said he would discourage the job at the HBCU unless the president could assure her financial support for the program and tie-ins to the department of public welfare and other colleges. He said if Fisk had a School of Social Work, then he would hire her himself. He also stated that several northern colleges who said they were willing to hire a Black faculty member had approached him, and he wanted to nominate her for such positions if she would agree. He told her that he would "do some more scouting around" for a good post for Diggs and to expect to hear from him again soon. Within months, Diggs had been offered a full-time position at Hunter College in New York—one of the City Universities of New York—becoming the institution's first full-time Black faculty member. Johnson's glowing reference on her behalf and Diggs's stellar qualifications sealed the deal.

In a letter to Johnson in December of 1946 congratulating him on being appointed president of Fisk, Diggs related her experience of her first semester at Hunter. She said she thoroughly enjoyed her job and noted there were a few stares at first by faculty and students, but her reception had been positive. She said the Black women students were beside themselves with pride and joy. She noted the only issue that concerned her was one that almost every Black faculty has experienced in a white institution where there are few if any other Black faculty. She noted that every problem related to a Black student was referred to her. She wrote, "I've had to use diplomacy in refusing to allow all problems of Negro students from no matter what departments to be loaded on me."[77]

She also stated that she had prepared herself to help the race, and sometimes when she was reflective, she wished her setting could be duplicated in a Black school. Johnson assured her, "In my opinion, you are serving the Negro race immeasurably where you are. You are helping to build this confidence indirectly, but more surely than by any reports you could make on the capabilities of the race."[78]

Hence, as Johnson entered his presidency of Fisk, his commitment to race relations meant he believed that Black people should be in all types of institutions, and that meant predominately white ones as well. That belief was not universal.

The year Johnson became president of Fisk, he published an article on the faculty, and he requested a detailed report from Dr. Charles Thompson, dean of education at Howard University, on the shortage of faculty members for HBCUs. Johnson pointed out in the early years of missionary-funded schools and colleges, salaries were more like stipends than actual salaries. Johnson outlined the dilemma of faculty in many HBCUs—excessive teaching load, absence of rank or salary schedule, lack of tenure or retirement, and no insurance. He indicated in many colleges, salaries are negotiated between the candidate and the president. He noted, because of the above, there were high turnover rates among the faculties at HBCUs. Johnson noted good salaries tended to correlate with good faculties. Johnson called for a raising of standards, for faculty with advanced degrees and evidence of scholarship, along with higher salaries.[79]

Thompson's memo to Johnson outlined the challenges facing current HBCUs. Fisk and Howard used to be the most competitive and desirable places to work for well-trained scholars. As a result of the end of World War II and the GI Bill, there was a great demand for college faculty. He estimated that somewhere from 750 to 1,000 faculty and staff of HBCUs were needed due to their growth. He also estimated that there was a 15 to 20 percent increase in staff needed to handle the enrollment surge. Thompson's memo noted that many men who taught before the war were returning and entering other professions. He stated that many first-rate Black scholars were leaving to work for the government or other non-academic agencies. In addition, because of the improvement of salaries in public schools, many academics were moving into that area. Finally, he said, there was a movement by some white colleges to hire Black faculty. And he said the competitive salary scales at white colleges had reduced the number of white faculty who used to come to teach in HBCUs. In a report to the board of trustees, Johnson told them that the minimum salary for a full professor at Fisk in 1947 was $3,500, which put them in the lowest two-thirds of salaries in a study of minimum salaries of full professors across the country.[80]

Johnson worked diligently to attract top faculty and provided leaves for current faculty members to complete degrees and for research and study. Johnson's early presidency coincided with a loss of students due to the reduced numbers of veterans attending college and also to the loss of male students to the military draft. In a January 1951 board of trustees meeting, they discussed the loss of one hundred male students and predicted that the draft would impact 60 percent of the male students at Fisk. They proposed offering working students in the City of Nashville to take afternoon, evening, and Saturday classes to offset the decline in residential students. The board also proposed a reduction in the teaching staff due to the drop in enrollment. Johnson said the difficulty in a reduction of faculty was that he had recruited some of the best faculty for the university in the past years. These new faculty members represented the best in a long history at Fisk. He was advised to eliminate eight faculty positions. Ideally, given the anticipated reduction in enrollment for the following year of 1951–52, they calculated that at least eighteen faculty members should be cut but the board agreed to the mandatory eight.[81] The board minutes of October 1951 indicated that 30 percent of the faculty had been given salary increases.[82]

Despite budgetary constraints, Johnson was able to hire numerous Black women faculty members. President Johnson hired Madeline Clarke Foreman, the biologist with whom President Jones refused to negotiate a reasonable salary and rank in 1944, as an associate professor in 1949.[83] He brought other women faculty on as instructors. Johnson was able to employ Coragreene Johnson, a PhD in English from the University of Michigan who had recently graduated in 1942 but had taught at Spelman, Atlanta University, Bennett, and Tillotson. She was hired at the associate professor rank. The second Black woman PhD Johnson recruited was Evelyn Boyd, the second Black woman to earn a doctorate in pure mathematics. Boyd was a Phi Beta Kappa graduate of Smith College with a master's and PhD from Yale University. She was hired as an associate professor. Boyd had taught part-time at NYU and had worked for three summers as a mathematician at the US Bureau of Standards in Washington, DC. She only stayed at Fisk for a couple of years and returned to work for the federal government again and later in industry with IBM.[84]

Johnson suffered from migraine headaches. His schedule required nonstop meetings, travel, and correspondence. Despite the stresses of being a college president, Johnson worked around the clock and throughout the summers on various boards and projects. In his report to the board of trustees in 1949, in addition to his report of his activities of the university, he listed nearly a full page of other activities he was involved in—including both national and international meetings and organizations. He served on the Fulbright Board for foreign scholarship; the United States National Commission for UNESCO; the International Commission on Conservation of World Resources. He was an official US delegate to the United Nations. And he served in the following boards and organizations: the Commission on Higher Education; the Jersey Roundtable for Industry and Education; the American Council on Race Relations; the Southern Regional Council; the Board of Home Missions of the Congregational Church (AMA Department of Race Relations); the Whitney-Payne foundation;

American Social Hygiene Association; National Tuberculosis Association; and the Board of the Nashville Community Chest. Little wonder that in October of 1956, he dropped dead of a heart attack on the train platform on his way to a Fisk board meeting at the age of sixty-three. His sudden death was a blow to Fisk and the Black higher education community. His emphasis in the years as president on scholarship and high standards and stellar faculty was a part of a greater legacy. During his presidency, the university became the first HBCU to have a Phi Beta Kappa chapter. It also established a chapter of the Association of University Women. Johnson championed the advancement of the race through scholarship and diplomacy—he worked to uplift the race through encouraging both men and women. His papers are full of correspondence of former male and female students and colleagues. Dr. Gladys Inez Ford, who was on the faculty at Fisk for forty-one years and worked with both Jones and Johnson, said that Charles S. Johnson was the best president she ever worked with. She recalled him as fair and having high ideals and treating women with respect. She stated he was not paternalistic but a person who viewed women as intellectual equals.[85]

Very few Black women served on the faculty at Fisk during the Jones years of 1926–46. President Johnson sought to expand the number of women during the nine years of his presidency in tenured and high ranks. However, the women he attempted to hire often had more geographically appealing and more financially remunerative options. The faculty of Fisk was always small—rarely more than forty-five to fifty people (full-time). Despite the small number of Black women faculty, Fisk was known as being a pioneer in the dean of women's programs for their women's students. Juliette Derricotte began and set the standards for efforts in other HBCUs.

The Quest for Gender Equity at Howard

Howard University's history of Black women faculty was vastly different from Fisk's. Howard had a long history of hiring Black women faculty, like many other HBCUs. However, they were underpaid and relegated to lower ranks. From the oral histories and papers of these women scholars, the only administrative positions a Black woman academic could aspire to, with rare exceptions, were dean of women, or head of the department of home economics or women's physical education.

While the names of prominent Black male scholars, such as Alain Locke, Sterling Brown, John Hope Franklin, Benjamin Mays, Howard Thurman, Ernest Just, E. Franklin Frazier, Rayford Logan, Ralph Bunche, Frank Snowden, and Charles Hamilton Houston, who taught at Howard are well known, little is known of the equally impressive list of Black women who joined the faculty immediately after Mordecai Johnson became president in 1926.[86]

Like their male colleagues, they were often the first Black woman to graduate from a given program and university, and like their male colleagues they were nationally and internationally prominent. Among these women faculty were Dorothy Boulding Ferebee, Merze Tate, Flemmie Kittrell, Dorothy Porter, Inabel Lindsay, and Patricia Roberts Harris, who will be discussed in greater detail later.[87] Unlike many of the distinguished Black male faculty who left for other posts in national organizations, government, and administrative positions in other HBCUs, Black women faculty remained at Howard their entire professional career. Their options to move to other more prestigious positions were virtually non-existent due to their race and gender. Institutional and personal papers in the Moorland-Spingarn Research Center at Howard provide four decades of history of women faculty and administrators at the university. In addition, oral histories of many of these women are also found in the Radcliffe College Black Women Oral History Project.[88]

As noted earlier, all three of the first Black women PhDs were offered faculty positions at Howard. Two of the women accepted. Eva Dykes who earned her doctorate in English philology from Radcliffe and Georgiana Simpson who earned a doctorate in Germanic languages from the University of Chicago accepted. Sadie Tanner Alexander who earned a doctorate in economics did not become an academic and declined the offer.[89] Many other Black women "firsts" joined the faculty. Dorothy Ferebee graduated from Tufts Medical School in 1924 and joined the Howard Medical School faculty in 1930. She remained at Howard until her retirement in 1968. She served as director of the Howard Medical Center from 1949–68. In addition to her professional duties at Howard, Ferebee was very much in the race "uplift" tradition. She was the national president of the National Council of Negro Women, an umbrella organization for Black women's clubs, and national president of Alpha Kappa Alpha (AKA), the oldest Black women's sorority that was founded at Howard in 1908. She was also the medical director of a health program sponsored by AKA in Mississippi.[90]

Dorothy Porter Wesley was a 1928 alumna of Howard and was the first Black woman to earn a master's in library science from Columbia University (1932). She was appointed to the staff at Howard in 1932 to establish the special collection and worked in the Moorland-Spingarn Collection. She remained at Howard until her retirement in 1975. Inabel Lindsay was a 1920 alumna of Howard University. She earned a master's in social work from the University of Chicago in 1937 and returned to Howard to join the faculty in that same year. By 1945, Lindsay became the first dean of the School of Social Work at Howard, a position she held until her retirement in 1968. Flemmie Kittrell, mentioned in previous chapters, was the first Black woman to earn a PhD in the field of nutrition (Cornell 1938). In 1944, she joined the faculty of Howard University to establish and become dean of the first School of Home Economics. Like

Ferebee, Kittrell's work took her beyond the campus and into rural towns and developing countries of the world to work on issues of nutrition. She served as dean until her retirement in 1972. Merze Tate was the first Black woman to earn a degree from Oxford University (bachelor's in literature in 1935) and the first Black woman to earn a PhD from Harvard (government and international relations in 1941). Tate joined the faculty at Howard University in 1942.

While many women faculty and administrators predated the presidency of Mordecai Johnson, all of the women discussed in this chapter overlapped with the tenure of Johnson. While Johnson is well known for developing Howard into the "capstone" of Black higher education, he is also well known for his many controversies, disagreements, and disputes with Howard faculty, staff, and alumni. While Johnson was without question misogynistic and sexist, he had many confrontations with male administrators and faculty as well. It was clear that the issue with him was power and control.[91]

For example, one of the best-known women who served as both administrator and faculty member was Lucy Diggs Slowe, highlighted in chapter six. Slowe was a Howard graduate of 1908. Slowe became dean of women at Howard in 1922 and predated Johnson's appointment. Their first major confrontation came a few months after Johnson's arrival. In January of 1927, Slowe received a complaint from a Howard parent that a male professor had used "improper and vulgar" language in a class of female students. Slowe discussed this incident with the professor, who then sent Slowe a letter attacking her motives and her morals. When Slowe approached President Johnson about the matter, he supported the offending male professor. Only after Slowe threatened to resign did Johnson refer the matter to the board of trustees. The accused professor was subsequently placed on leave of absence with half-salary. Although Slowe could not confirm this, she suspected that Johnson never presented the facts of the situation to the board.

With her insistence in upholding the dignity and respect of the Black women students, her challenge of Johnson's decision resulted, according to one of her friends, "in a persecution of Dean Slowe [that] was continuous and heartless."[92] Slowe fought with Johnson on many issues related to the women students at Howard. He repeatedly denied Slowe raises and attempted to strip her authority. The final straw was when Slowe became ill unexpectedly in 1937; Johnson sent a message to her that if she didn't return to work immediately, he would replace her. After receiving this message, she died. While Slowe's illness was the obvious cause of her death, the callousness and insensitivity of Johnson's message to her was never forgotten or forgiven by Slowe's friends and family.[93] This event was widely referred to as the "Death-Bed Ultimatum."[94]

Another Howard alumna who served on the faculty for decades was Inabel Burns Lindsay. Lindsay graduated from Howard in 1920 with honors and was awarded an Urban League Fellowship to attend the New York School of Social Work. After a year of study in New York, she returned home to St. Joseph, Missouri, to care for her ill mother, and taught public school for one year. She married by 1937 and had earned a master's degree in social work from the University of Chicago School of Social Service Administration. She was then invited to join the faculty at Howard to assist in establishing a School of Social Work. She was appointed director of the Program of Social Services. In 1944 the Howard University trustees voted to establish an autonomous School of Social Work. In 1945, Lindsay was appointed the first dean of the School. By 1952, she had earned a doctorate in social work from the School of Social Work at the University of Pittsburgh.[95]

Lindsay, in several oral histories, was very candid concerning the status of women at Howard during the Johnson presidency and of her experiences on the campus. Despite the many women faculty members at Howard and the appearance of egalitarianism, Lindsay stated that women were usually paid less and were subjected to gender bias. She stated she became dean of the School of Social Work (SSW) by default. She explained that Johnson wanted to appoint a qualified man for dean ("chauvinistically they wanted a male dean"). However, Johnson could not find a man to take the job because men could command higher salaries in the government and other private agencies and places like the National Urban League. During the search for a dean, the Association of Schools of Social Work evaluated the school of social work for accreditation. Howard officials were alerted that the school could not become accredited with her as acting dean. With this news, Lindsay said, "the university administration very promptly changed my title to dean. I became the dean by happenstance."[96] She served in the position until her retirement in 1967. Under her leadership, the SSW grew in size and reputation. Lindsay's goal was not to make the Howard School of Social Work the best Black school of social work but a distinguished school of social work for all. The school attracted both Black and white students.

Despite the renowned status of the Howard SSW, Lindsay noted that President Johnson was extremely paternalistic toward her and women faculty in general. She recalled that Johnson never referred to her as Dr., Dean, Professor, or even Mrs. Lindsay, but rather, called her "daughter." She said she did not think he did this out of malice but rather this "reflected the culture of which he was accustomed."[97] Johnson, an ordained Baptist minister, felt, according to Lindsay, that women should be subordinate. She was the only woman on the dean's council for years and was not expected to make any contributions or suggestions at these meetings. Lindsay found sexism a much greater barrier to her professional career than race:

> I was in a predominately Negro institution, so that race was secondary. Sex, however, was not. There were women on the faculty, of course, many of them,

very fine, outstanding ones who were recognized and accorded to a degree the same academic opportunities of promotion and tenure, although there again, I think the bias of sex operated for all women. They didn't get promoted as readily, nor to as high a rank as a man. But, when it came to administration—outside of Home Economics, Nursing or Physical Education, which, of course, had a woman head of the physical education department, women didn't move into the central administration of the University.

Historian Rayford Logan was Lindsay's supervisor as interim dean of the Graduate School in 1943 when the School of Social Work was a division and attempting to earn accreditation. His diary entries are full of very favorable comments from Lindsay and they clearly had a collaborative and cordial relationship. One diary entry noted that in the course of the division being upgraded to a school, the new federal child welfare program offered Lindsay a position as consultant. Her salary would have been $3,200, and $3,600 with overtime, while her salary at Howard was just $2,500. Lindsay ended up remaining at Howard to ensure the success of the new school.[98] Her devotion to developing strong social workers was more important than moving to a federal job as many of her male colleagues did. Lindsay recalled, "The salary was low. There wasn't anybody [men] who was interested in sacrificing to that extent." As noted above, when it was clear that the school of social work could not become accredited without a permanent dean, it appears that Lindsay put building the school of social work above a larger salary.

Despite Johnson's documented sexism toward many women faculty and administrators at Howard, he was not universally disliked. Dr. Ferebee stated that while many male physicians at the Howard Medical School resented her position at the university, she found an ally in Mordecai Johnson. She noted:

> I think that sexism [at Howard] was a very common practice, and still is . . . I think that, even though I experienced discrimination and a great deal of jealousy on the part of many of the men physicians and the men directors, I had a stanch ally at Howard University in the person of Dr. Mordecai Johnson, the president. He was absolutely superb in seeing that both men and women whose qualifications were recognizable received the kind of recognition to which they were entitled. So that for a long time, my service as medical director of Howard University Health Service largely was due to Dr. Mordecai Johnson's approval of me, and the fact that the physicians who were opposing me were a subterranean faction, were never able to reach me because of the citations and recognition given me by the university president.[99]

The views of Johnson by many of the women were varied. Like many of the men who had experienced difficulties with Johnson, there were other members of the faculty and administration who admired what Johnson did for the institution. Nevertheless, the prevailing wisdom during his administration

FIGURE 21. Merze Tate, Professor of Howard University, 1942–77. Courtesy of Western Michigan University Archives and Regional History Collections.

was that women were not treated as equal members of the faculty. Merze Tate is another stark example of inequality.

Merze Tate, who joined the faculty in 1942 as a replacement faculty during World War II, experienced enormous sexism at Howard. She was appointed in 1945 as a tenured full professor—one of the earliest women to be a tenured full professor. In a phone interview with the author, Tate expressed her outrage at the manner in which she was treated at Howard, noting that she was underpaid despite her impressive credentials, which included having degrees from Oxford and Harvard and studying in Geneva, the University of Berlin, and Paris.[100] Rayford Logan, who served as chair of the history department at Howard while Tate was in the department, refutes Tate's charges of sexism. Tate was convinced that she was treated differently because of her gender. She confronted Logan in a faculty meeting in 1954 about summer school appointments telling Logan pointedly that she felt he showed favoritism to male faculty members. She said she and another woman faculty member, Marie Wood, had been assigned only one course each instead of two like the men. Logan wrote long diary entries concerning the matter and noted: "I tried, in vain, to point out that there was no discrimination against her because of her sex. I said that such an idea was 'silly.' She still insisted that he had been unfair to her, had violated their agreement [to sign summer school appointments on a rotating basis] and he had done so because she was a woman."[101] Logan also pointed out that classes were assigned based on need. Tate stated that her graduate level course on American Diplomatic History had not been assigned. He stated, "I pointed out that she knew as well as the rest of us that the Department had decided as a matter of policy not to offer any graduate courses in the Summer School since the Summer School insisted upon a minimum number of students."[102]

Despite Logan's arguments put forth in his diary, and he apparently told Tate, she always believed her gender was the reason. However, from primary sources, it is clear that Logan supported Tate from the moment she was hired. In fact, there was originally a decision to be made whether to hire Tate, who was African American, or Caroline Ware, who was white. In correspondence to Dean Charles Thompson[103] regarding considering Tate and Ware for the interim position in the history department, Logan stated, the decision would not be easy. Both were equally qualified. Both had attended Oxford and had doctorates from Harvard. Ware studied at Oxford for a year before attending graduate school at Radcliffe, while Tate earned a degree from Oxford.[104] However, Logan noted, "Tate is colored, but a personality problem. Ware is white, lives in Vienna, Virginia, but a more mature scholar and probably less of a personality problem. I lean towards Tate." In the end, he recommended and hired Tate for the position.[105]

The fact that Tate, who was the first Black woman to earn a doctorate in international relations from Harvard, had to beg for a position at Howard is a story of blatant sexism. Any Black man with her stellar credentials would have been hired in a heartbeat. Tate and Ware initially sought a position in the government department at Howard, which was small due to the absence of male faculty during the war. When the chair of the department, Eric Williams, learned that his options were both women candidates, he wrote to one of his Howard male colleagues, "I'm suppose, apparently, to make a choice between Caroline Ware and Merze Tate. What have I done to deserve that?"[106] He hired neither woman. This is when Logan rescued them to the department of history. Their contracts starting in 1943 were year to year. Tate was kept on for another year through 1944. With the war over by 1945, Tate sought a permanent position on the faculty. Learning of a position opening in geography and geopolitics, she submitted a two-and-a-half-page letter of application noting she had taken every geography course offered to supplement her study of history, economics, sociology, and government. Tate was ultimately hired as a tenured member of the history department and became one of the earliest tenured women on the faculty.[107] She remained on the Howard faculty until her retirement in 1977.

Ware also ended up on the faculty. She interviewed several times at Howard. After teaching temporarily in history, at the end of the war, she became director of research for the School of Social Work. She was passed over for positions in government and history and was rescued by the School of Social Work, which was noted to have had a woman dean, Inabel Lindsay. Ware remained in this position at Howard until she retired in 1961.

In a 1993 oral history, Dorothy Porter Wesley, who was also a graduate of Howard and a member of the library staff for more than forty years (1932–75), commented on her life at Howard. Like Slowe, Lindsay, and Tate, Wesley recalled her experience at Howard as being discriminatory as a woman:

> At Howard at one time, it was a completely male situation, and they didn't think even the dean of the School of Social Work [Inabel Burns Lindsay] amounted to anything. The dean of students—the woman dean—had to go to the dean of men to get a roll of toilet paper sometimes.[108]

The interviewer inquired if she was referring to the problems of Lucy Diggs Slowe at Howard and Wesley responded no; it was the dean who replaced Slowe. However, Wesley recalled that "Slowe was powerful, she was very strong. She fought Mordecai and everybody."[109]

Wesley stated again that women were significantly underpaid. She recalled during the Johnson presidency, women's salaries were not equal to men's in the same rank. She stated, "My salary was always low. I never made any money. I resigned a couple of times, but they made me go back [laughter]."[110] Salary issues were not always gender specific, however. Rayford Logan also threatened to resign when he discovered that three of his male colleagues and friends had been promoted to what was the equivalent of a distinguished professor level. Unlike Porter, and the other women who did not receive increased compensation when they protested, Logan did prevail and received an increase from $5,000 to $6,000.

Although many of the women found it difficult to work under the conditions of Mordecai Johnson, they remained at Howard for a lifetime. Howard remained the most prestigious institution for Black academics, and especially for Black women academics, who were not able to move into presidencies or deanships or to the faculties of a handful of white colleges that began to hire token Black male faculty in the 1960s. For example, many of the men moved on. Eminent male faculty like Ralph Bunche, John Hope Franklin, Ernest Just, Percy Julian, Howard Thurman, Benjamin Mays, and Abram Harris Jr. left for white institutions when the opportunity presented itself, with the exception of Mays, who became president of Morehouse College. Very few Black women scholars were offered such options, and even those who were graduates of the Seven Sisters colleges, were never invited to join those faculties. Once a Black woman scholar was appointed to the faculty of Howard, she had no other options that exceeded what Howard offered.

Despite the fact that Howard was the "capstone" of Black higher education and a comprehensive university with stellar professional schools, it was a very difficult place to work. John Hope Franklin noted in his autobiography, *Mirror to America*, his feelings about Howard. After working there for some years, Franklin stated in a meeting with Logan and others that while he had worked in other Black colleges that were run on the "plantation system," meaning the presidents considered themselves masters and the faculty slaves, he said, at none of those schools had the presidents treated the faculty with as little respect as President Johnson had.[111]

Because Howard was the preeminent institution of Black higher education, and it boasted an enviable faculty of Black men and women of the highest educational backgrounds and enormous accomplishments, they were confined in their professional mobility, and hence, most had to endure the treatment of Johnson.

Women Faculty Club

The women faculty at Howard established the Women's Faculty Club in 1940 due to their growing numbers and their interest in affairs impacting women at Howard. The Women's Faculty Club consisted of not only women faculty but included professional library staff, the dean of women, the educational directors of the women's dormitories, the dietitian, the household manager, women physicians, and the nurses in charge of women students. They not only belonged to women's organizations on campus, they also overlapped in many national organizations.

The women faculty at Howard seemed to have a close sisterhood and camaraderie, especially visible in the Women Faculty Club. Senior women faculty chaired the group. While the majority of women faculty at Howard were African American, there were white women, such as Caroline Ware, and women of other races and nationalities. They were welcomed into the organization and were listed in reports and announcements. The extent that they participated isn't known. The few programs and minutes that exist reveal that the leadership was Black women faculty. However, the 1950 annual program of the organization was in appreciation of Indian women "who have served and who are serving their country."[112] Both Merze Tate and Flemmie Kittrell had spent time in India. Tate had just returned from a year's Fulbright fellowship in India (1950–51). The organization's goals were not only for fellowship among the professional women employees of Howard but also concern for the women students. The newsletters of the organization noted with pride the women's professional accomplishments, their degree attainments, publications, fellowships and awards, sabbatical leaves, promotions, and new hires.

The women met monthly in the evenings at one of the member's homes. They also had luncheon meetings. This group of women—many of whom taught and worked at Howard together for decades—were also members of other organizations. Hence, their relationships were not just professional. These women cared about women's rights and gender equity. According to a 1949 program that summed up the year, Dr. Ruth Ella Moore, who was the president of the group that year, noted that more than half of all employees at Howard University were women; the director of the Health Service was a woman (Dr. Ferebee); key women worked in the budget office in payroll and bookkeeping; there were women students in all ten schools including engineering and architecture; and women were on the faculty of all schools except engineering and architecture.

This group kept data on women's advancement, or lack thereof, at the university. Merze Tate and Dorothy Ferebee were active members of the DC chapter of the American Association of University Women, a non-profit organization founded in 1881 by a group of white women college graduates to advance the issues of college women. As discussed, the organization was restricted to women who were graduates of accredited colleges. Howard was one of a handful of Black colleges that met this criterion. When the Howard women faculty attempted to establish a chapter on campus in the early 1950s, they discovered they were ineligible for membership due to lack of information on the women faculty. The Women's Faculty Club (WFC) immediately established committees to assess the status of women faculty at Howard.[113]

One of the major reasons for their ineligibility was because of salary discrimination. Tate chaired a committee on the status of women at Howard during the 1960s and found that, "we had a salary scale for professors, associates, assistants, but the women were always at the lower level of the scale, seldom in the middle, and never at the top."[114] The committee also revealed that male faculty were always given preference in opportunities to earn additional salary by teaching through summer school appointments. On this issue, Tate stated, "women were out."[115]

The senior women faculty used their status to speak on behalf of *all* women at Howard. Since they were scholars, they compiled data to appeal to the administration. The first report released in the academic year of 1953–54 noted that in the School of Liberal Arts, there were seventy-three full-time male faculty and thirty-one full-time female faculty members (tenured/tenure track). Twenty-six of the men were full professors and only four women were full professors (Tate in history, Anne M. Cooke (Reid) in drama, Flemmie Kittrell in home economics, Charlotte Watkins, English). There were twenty-two male associate professors and eight female associates; seven male assistant professors and three women assistant professors, eighteen male instructors and fourteen female instructors, and female assistants (laboratories).[116] There were twenty-seven departments— fourteen with female faculty and thirteen without. Physical education for men was an exclusively male department, and physical education for women and home economics were women-only departments. Both of these latter departments had women department heads. These three gender-specific departments were not factored into their report but noted as exceptions.

Only one department that had male and female faculty had a woman department head that was a full professor—drama. A woman, who was an associate professor, headed the botany department. The female full professor department head was the lowest paid head for someone with a full professor rank, and her salary was $1,252 below the maximum for her position in the academic year 1953–54. The woman professor who served as chair of botany was an associate professor and also earned a lower salary than her male counterparts who served as department heads at the associate professor rank. Her salary was $751 below the maximum for that category. In addition to the data on the dearth of women department chairs and the fact that they consistently earned less than their male counterparts, the report demonstrated that women throughout the liberal arts departments were at the bottom of the pay scale despite their years of service.[117]

Tate, a full professor since she accepted a full-time position in 1945 and one of the most outspoken women on the faculty, monitored assiduously the salaries of the men in her department. Her academic credentials were unmatched by anyone at Howard. She was highly published by major academic presses, a consultant to the State Department, and had an international academic reputation, and she accomplished this all as a Black woman. She mentioned this repeatedly to the senior administration, and in an extensive follow-up letter to a face-to-face meeting with the Dean of the College of Liberal Arts J. St. Clair Price in 1951 about her salary inequities. Blunt and to the point, she wrote:

> As a sequel to our recent conversation regarding my status in the history department, I deem it judicious to express my sentiments in a formal letter so there will be a written record and no misunderstanding, delay or circumvention.
>
> Stated briefly, my position is that I shall not quietly accept a status and a salary in the department inferior to that of any other member, except the chairman. This stand, I feel, is justified by simple comparative facts. If remuneration is based upon academic preparation, honors, degrees, experience, publications, travel, prestige, and the publicity and glory a professor brings to Howard University and not upon personal, fraternal, and differences-in-sex considerations, then I stand second to none of the regular members, and in some instances surpass the head of the department.
>
> Not one of the members has had the academic preparation in first class American and English Universities that I have had. Not one has been elected to membership in the two most outstanding honor societies: Phi Beta Kappa and Pi Gamma Mu (National Social Science Honor Society). Moreover, I hold two more degrees than any other member: The Oxford B. Litt. and an honorary D. Litt from Western Michigan College. In addition, I have studied in Geneva and Berlin.
>
> My teaching and administrative experience is second only to that of the chairman and in versatility surpasses his. No other member has been requested to teach in so many different fields or have been assigned such a variety of subjects, including European, English, American, Diplomatic, and

> Military History, International Politics, Political Science, Geography and Geopolitics. Other members of the department teach only in one field. Since coming to Howard University, I have taught twenty-five different assignments. Whenever new subjects have been introduced or courses left when a teacher is on leave or becomes ill, I have been requested to teach them.[118]

Tate had been asked to save the Army program by teaching in that program where she had seventy men in one class. She pointed out when a course was available that had only eight to twelve students, that course was given to another professor. She noted her extensive publication record—books published by Harvard and Oxford presses, and two other unpublished manuscripts, ready for press—and her extensive global travel and work with the State Department. She stated, "no other member [of the history department] has studied or taught abroad as many years; no other member holds a degree from a foreign university; no other member has represented Howard University and the United States with credit in more far-flung places or on a UNESCO seminar at Lake Success; no other member has been invited to lecture for a second year in a foreign land or to represent the United States in the Foreign Service."[119]

Finally, Tate told him that it's expected that women faculty be "silent and saintly" and to accept "a supinely and inferior status and salary and still carry the heaviest burden."[120] She told them as a single woman, her salary was even more important than married men with working wives.[121] She asked for a response in writing. She received one from the dean of the university who basically said that salary increases were based on the recommendation of the dean of her school. He told her to contact her dean. It was clearly a case of passing the buck.[122] Tate was convinced that Black women *were* expected to simply be missionaries and work without mention of salary. The Black women faculty, well known and accomplished academics, were not bible-quoting women who made religious references as many other women did in other institutions.[123] For example, Merze Tate interviewed Eve Dykes in 1977 for the Black Women Oral History Project. Dykes, as mentioned earlier, was one of three Black women to earn a PhD in 1921. She taught at Howard from 1929–44 in the English department. A devout Seven Day Adventist, Dykes left Howard to teach at the unaccredited Black Seventh Day Adventist college in Alabama, Oakwood College. Dykes was the only faculty member with a PhD on the faculty when she arrived at Oakwood in 1944. Due to her religious convictions, she wanted to assist the college in obtaining accreditation—which it did in 1958. In the Radcliffe Oral History interview, Tate brought Dykes up to date on the status of women at Howard and their efforts for gender equity. Tate asked Dykes: "Do you think your sex has had anything to do with your status in places? Do you think if you'd been a man, with a Harvard degree, you might have had a higher salary at Howard University?" Dykes responded that she didn't have any idea about salaries, when she was at Howard, but she knew women earned less in all schools and departments. Tate told her about the study of salary and promotion discrimination of women at Howard the women faculty conducted. Dykes responded: "I have tried to be satisfied, because my main interest isn't money. I've tried to be pleased, I mean, but as far as being rebellious or bitter because of the discrimination that is made between men and women." She said while at Oakwood, someone told her that a group of male faculty members had received promotions and raises. She asked the college president about this, and he told her that she didn't get a raise because she was a woman. Dykes responded that she had to pay the same price for a loaf of bread as male professors. So, Dykes clearly was one of the "saintly" women who said money wasn't an issue. Considering that Dykes was the most educated faculty member on the campus and left the top Black university to serve on the faculty of an unaccredited religious college and was underpaid reflected her exploitation because of her gender and religious devotion.[124]

As Dorothy Porter Wesley noted in her oral history, women faculty and professionals earned the lowest salaries. Even though the Black women faculty represented the most educated women in academe and were often pioneers in their fields and the first to earn degrees in their fields, they were shockingly in ranks lower than men who were not their academic equals. The WFC had the deans of their respective schools send them annually the names, ranks, and salaries of the men and women faculty. By 1961, the ranks of women to full professors had barely moved. Only one additional woman had been promoted to full professor—Dr. Virginia Woods Callahan, Professor of Classics. Callahan, who was white, was hired in 1945 as an associate professor, the same year that Tate was hired. She earned a PhD in classics from the University of Chicago in 1941. She was highly published but was not promoted to full professor until 1960—fifteen years later.[125]

Although the ranks of women faculty in the School of Liberal Arts remained low, they were significantly better than women in the professional schools. Nearly half of the faculty of the School of Liberal Arts were female—eighty-seven women. This meant that a large part of Howard's teaching staff was women in very low ranks. The School of Dentistry reported in 1961 that there were seven women on the faculty—three associate professors, two assistant professors, and two instructors. One of the women was head of the department of oral hygiene.[126] While there were women faculty in the medical school, their ranks were low. Ruth Ella Moore, who taught at Howard from 1940 until she retired in 1973, chaired the department from 1947–58; yet, Moore was never promoted beyond the rank of associate professor. Likewise, Dr. Dorothy Boulding Ferebee began her career at Howard's Medical School in 1927, first as a clinician in obstetrics. Two years later, she taught courses in nurse's training and for second-year medical students and became the physician to the women students. In 1949, she became the director of the health center of the university and held that position until her retirement in 1968. Yet, after decades in the medical school, she retired at the rank of assistant professor of preventive medicine.[127]

These women were not only extraordinary individuals in their respective fields, but many of them were the founding deans of their schools. They were leaders in their professions, held impressive and prestigious fellowships, and taught and influenced the lives of thousands of students over the course of their careers. They also lectured and taught globally on Fulbright fellowships and by invitations to universities throughout the world. They were leaders in national organizations within the Black community as well within their professions. Merze Tate, like most of her female colleagues, was active in women's organizations as well as those related to civil rights groups like the American Association of University Women (AAUW), the National Association of Colored People (NAACP), National Council of Negro Women, National Association of College Women, and the major African American sororities.[128] The influence of these women and their activities was vast and wide reaching. Their influence and impact at Howard and to the larger society have been overlooked. While many of the well-known Black male faculty left for better positions amid dissatisfaction with Mordecai Johnson as president, the women faculty did not have that option. They created a community of support for one another and worked to make life for women at Howard better.

Current scholars are beginning to look at the contributions of women scholars at Howard. In a recent book on the Howard School of International Relations, author Robert Vitalis discusses the birth of the field of international relations. He noted Merze Tate's importance to the field, as well as her horrible treatment at Howard. Vitalis stated that Tate was "the most accomplished international scholar at Howard." He also commented, "The real tragedy is her marginalization at Howard, the discrimination she endured as one of the few women teaching in the social sciences (and one of the only women in the United States teaching international relations in the 1940s, 1950s, and 1960s), and her disappearance from virtually all retrospective accounts of African American intellectual life and internationalism."[129]

There was a true sisterhood of women faculty at Howard from the 1930s through the 1960s and early 1970s. By the late '60s and early '70s, the old guard, pioneer women faculty began to retire. Compared to women who taught in other HBCUs, the Howard women were a very academically privileged group who lived in the national capital and never had to live in dormitories as so many of the early Black women faculty did on small growing Black colleges. Howard women faculty had the opportunity to work with a highly distinguished group of women who held national and international prominence. Like many Black women college faculty members at HBCUs, they changed the lives of students and improved the world. They were able to not only teach undergraduates but graduate and professional students as well. Their contributions were enormous. At the funeral of Dr. Dorothy Ferebee in 1980, Patricia Robert Harris, longtime colleague of Ferebee at Howard and fellow member of the FFC, noted in her eulogy the impact that gender had on Ferebee's career at Howard:

> Broad as her leadership was, how sad to think that the double handicap of race and sex shackled the talents and energies of this woman. I have often wondered what she could have done and where she might have led others had her leadership been accepted by our entire society earlier. Howard University, which has nurtured and maintained so many educated Black men and women, gave her a base from which to work (and even at Howard University, where race was not a factor, the virus of sexism limited her activity, a fact of which she was acutely aware).[130]

These women faculty served for more than fifty years in the service of Howard University. As much as they accomplished and contributed to the university and their professions, as Patricia Robert Harris noted, had they not been constrained by gender, the institution and society would have gained so much more.

Unlike the Howard Black women, the women in other HBCUs had to contend with the lack of contracts, poor living conditions, lack of ranks, and pensions, etc. For example, Louise Thompson Patterson was one of the earliest Black women graduates of the University of California-Berkeley. She earned a bachelor's degree in economics in 1923. Because teaching positions were not available for Black women in Northern California, she was able to pass as a Mexican and work as a secretary. Patterson learned of a teaching position at a Black school in Arkansas in 1925: Pine Bluff Agricultural, Mechanical, and Normal School. This was one of the seventeen Black land-grant institutions. Patterson wrote an inquiry about the position and she immediately received a telegram from the principal of the school offering her the position with the lofty title of head of the Department of Commerce. Patterson had never been south, but she was eager to make a contribution to the education of Black students. The institution was of junior college rank. She said when she arrived, the campus looked like fifty acres of cow pasture and only 21 of the 411 students were of college level.[131] Her dormitory was mice infested, and she said the school was decades away from being a "college." Despite the poor preparation of her students, she put her all into making the best of the situation. She noted the classes were frequently disrupted because white planters required the students to pick cotton in the fields. Their classes had to revolve around the planting season. One of the male teachers at the school owned a Model T Ford, and Patterson said, out of boredom the two of them would ride around the countryside. She said they always made it back in time for the mandatory 10 p.m. curfew of her dormitory. As was the situation discussed regarding Jean Fairfax at Tuskegee earlier, Patterson, not a Southerner and not familiar with the norms of Black colleges and the area, was not aware that her personal and social life would be monitored. The independent and outspoken Patterson would not let her life be controlled by the school. The principal of the school, Robert Malone, a Tuskegee graduate, instructed the matron of the dorm to inform Patterson that her behavior of riding around in a car alone with a man in the evening and night was "inappropriate." Patterson ignored the warning. Patterson was also reprimanded for not attending church on Sundays. She told the principal, "I didn't sign a contract to go to church."[132] To avoid the issue of living in the dormitory, Thompson sent for her mother, and she was able to rent an apartment in a house across from the campus. She decided to leave the school at the end of the year; however, she stayed through the summer to teach a group of teachers who taught in the rural schools. Patterson said none of these teachers had more than a fourth-grade education. She devoted eight weeks to teaching these women. She wrote Hampton Institute for a position because she heard it was the most well-endowed HBCU and was hired to teach in the department of business administration.[133]

Patterson's excitement about Hampton Institute faded after she arrived. The college was indeed beautiful and on the scenic Chesapeake Bay in Virginia; however, it didn't meet the expectations she had of the school. Unlike her experience in Arkansas, at Hampton the principal, most of the administration, and department heads were white. The school stressed the "Hampton Idea," which focused completely on industrial and moral training for the students. She said it was rumored that the teachers in the trade school were members of the Klan. She said the students were treated like servants and segregated from whites on campus—the workers, faculty, administrators, etc. She was appalled at the rules and regulations for the students, especially the women students—they couldn't wear stockings, use cosmetics, or curl their hair. The lengths of their skirts were measured, but this was the norm in most HBCUs, and as was discussed earlier, Hampton Institute was the model for Tuskegee. For someone like Patterson, who like the other Black women who went to white undergraduate institutions and were not allowed to live on campus, these restrictions were shocking, she said, for the students at Hampton who were older—one thirty-six-year-old woman student was put on probation because she went shopping in town without a chaperone. Black and white teachers were not to associate with one another. Unsatisfied, Patterson left Hampton, moved to New York, and secured a graduate fellowship from the National Urban League to study social work. She never worked at another HBCU.[134]

Thelma Bando (Howard '32) and Helen G. Edmond (Morgan State '33), were both hired to teach and work at the Virginia Theological Seminary and College in Lynchburg in 1934. Edmonds was hired as a professor of History and dean of women and Bando as professor of English and assistant dean of women. The institution was a poor church school, and Bando said the school depended upon funding from church donations. She said their salary was $100 a month, plus room and board. However, for the first three months, they never were paid but received promissory notes. She said the parents of the students were extremely appreciative of their dedication and work and often brought them fruit from their farms. She and Edmonds lived on campus in a dorm. She recalled that, although she didn't get paid, the experience was positive. She said the school was like a family. The students worked as well. She recalled they did her laundry, and if you did not want to go to the dining room, they would bring the faculty members food to their room on a tray. Bando said her father had to wire her money for train fare to come home to Philadelphia during the Christmas holidays since she hadn't earned any money. Neither she nor Edmonds returned the next year.[135] Bando became assistant dean of women at Bishop College in Texas, and Edmonds went to graduate school at The Ohio State University and earned a master's in history and the following decade earned a doctorate from the same institution in 1946 with assistance from the General Education Board Fellowship.

As noted earlier, President Charles S. Johnson wrote an essay in 1946 titled, "Faculty" that addressed the abysmal salaries and conditions of faculty members at an HBCU. He said the pay was basically a stipend rather than a salary. He noted most schools didn't have a salary scale, tenure, retirement, insurance, etc., and all compensation was negotiated with the president.[136] This issue was reflected in a diary entry Rayford Logan, chair of the history department at Howard, wrote in July 1955. He wrote that a former young Black woman colleague, who had previously taught at Howard for nine years, Marie Wood, called him to say that she received a phone call from the president of Livingstone College in North Carolina, an institution founded by the African Methodist Episcopal Zion Church. The president accused her of "lacking character" and "being unethical" because he learned she had accepted a position at Alabama A&M instead of Livingstone. Logan advised her to tell the Livingstone president that "negotiation is not a commitment." The Livingstone position would pay $4,800 a year with no rank specified. The position at Alabama A&M offered a salary of $6,000 and the rank of full professor, but Wood discovered that that position was a disappointment as well. Wood contacted Logan when she arrived in September to say the housing was poor (she had to live in the dormitory) and the food was "abominable." She had a commuting marriage, and later in the semester her husband was hospitalized in the veterans hospital in DC. One of her former colleagues in the Howard history department told Logan he informed Wood that if she quit in the middle of the year, she would probably never have another job at any [Black] land-grant college.[137] It's unclear what Wood did, but it is unlikely that she returned to the institution.

Most Black women faculty faced challenges, whether they were at the capstone at Howard that was viewed by most as the pinnacle of Black higher education, or talented married Black women faculty who were a part of an academic couple who ended up spending their careers in one location because it kept the couple in the same location, or the many single Black women faculty who went to various institutions that made them the best offer, and there were also married academic women who had commuting marriages. HBCUs were not monolithic—the land-grant colleges always had Black presidents. Many of the private colleges, especially those founded by American Missionary Association initially, had white presidents and faculty as well as some of the area places like Howard University, the all-male Lincoln University, and others. Most who left records noted the low salaries but said their reward came from the success of their students, and most remained at these institutions throughout the period studied in this book.

Because salary rates were often higher than for teaching at an HBCU, many highly educated persons taught in prominent high schools, like Dunbar High School in Washington, DC; Crispus Attucks in Indianapolis (actually Merze Tate taught there prior to teaching at Howard); and Sumner High School in St. Louis, Missouri. Adding to the complicatedness of securing a position, Black graduates from white and liberal arts colleges, such as Fisk and Howard, often were met with disdain from some Black schools. Inabel Lindsay stated she accepted a teaching position in Kansas City, Missouri, at a grade school in 1922. She immediately experienced hostility from her principal. He told her that he wanted no part of a college graduate. He was a product of a normal school and that was what he preferred as a teacher. Lindsay said she had requested to teach in the high school where the principal was a Howard graduate. However, she said the board of education assigned her to the grade school to a principal who did not know her. Lindsay assumed the board of education did not want to show any favoritism by assigning her to work with a Howard alum. Lindsay said she and another college graduate were appointed to this school. She recalled in their first faculty meeting that the principal told the other teachers, "We've got two college graduates assigned to us this year. I don't know what they're coming here for. They ought to go down to the high school." By the second semester, Lindsay transferred to the high school.[138]

Mary E. Branch and Tillotson's College

Teaching at HBCUs did often require a missionary zeal and attitude. For example, Mary Elizabeth Branch, a Black woman educator and college president who is little known within Black and women's higher education, falls within the self-sacrificing category. Born in 1881, Branch attended high school and normal school at the Virginia Normal and Industrial Institute, a preparatory and high school. She immediately began teaching in rural Blackstone, Virginia. Her biographical information does not provide exact days of her employment. Teachers were constantly in demand as Black schools expanded, so Branch was recruited to teach at her former normal school the next year, which she accepted. She attended Columbia University for a bachelor's and master's in English in 1925. With these advanced credentials, Branch was recruited to serve as dean at the all-girl Black Vashon High School in St. Louis. This opportunity came with a substantial increase in salary and a retirement pension, which was unheard of in southern Black colleges or public schools. After several years in this position, in 1930, she was contacted by the American Missionary Association to head the women's Tillotson's College in Austin, Texas. The previously coeducational school, whose first class was in 1884, was, like all Black "colleges," a preparatory school and later a high school. The institution had unstable leadership; there had been ten presidents in the forty-six years of the school's existence. In a survey of Black colleges conducted by the United States Department of Education, the college was recommended to be closed. Branch declined the offer to head the school twice. The school maintained a high school of fifty students and had only sixty-five young women in the college department. Just as Eve Dykes, one of the first three Black women to earn PhD, resigned her position at Howard that came with faculty rank and a pension, to go to an unaccredited religious institution in Alabama, Branch, likewise, changed her mind and resigned her position with pension in St. Louis that paid twice as much as the "presidency" of Tillotson, which had no pension. Branch stated she prayed over this decision and said she accepted the position because "my people and I are forever in debt to the early missionaries who came South to teach them after the Civil War. This is a real chance to help pay that debt."[139]

Accepting the position without seeing the condition of the campus (which was horrendous), dilapidated buildings, very few books in the library, and ruined furniture. However, as expected, a Black woman could perform the "holy impossible."[140] Branch wrote hundreds of letters appealing for books, new and used, to individuals and used bookstores. She sought to increase the school's enrollment, which was at a junior college level and unaccredited. Only one faculty member held a master's degree. Branch immediately began speaking at Black churches in an attempt to increase enrollment. She raised funds to offer scholarships to the top two Black girls in every high school in Texas. And, like Hampton and Tuskegee, Branch, in an attempt to raise the level of academically prepared students, admitted students who would work on campus to cover 90 percent of their cost. In 1931, Branch had the high school discontinued and upgraded the college to a four-year institution. By 1933, she had recruited new faculty—all of whom had master's degrees. This brought the rating of the school to that of Class B by the Association of Colleges and Secondary Schools of the Southern States. There was not a roster of the new faculty available for review, but considering it was a woman's college and Branch instituted a four-year home economics program to attract students, it's highly probable that the faculty were dedicated Black women who wanted to contribute to the education of these young women. Branch responded to alums who requested that the college return to its previous coeducational status. This was done in 1935. The college established a football team the next year and the college reputation and enrollment grew. New buildings emerged—a home economics practice house and a men's dormitory by 1937; in 1939, the college's enrollment was 400, including 140 men. By 1943, Branch succeeded in having the college fully accredited with a Class A rating by the Southern Association of College and Secondary Schools. Branch fulfilled her mission and commitment to Black youth to work for a quality education for them. She became ill and died in July of 1944.

It's unclear why Branch has been so overlooked in African American educational and women's history. She saved an institution that had been recommended for closure.[141] She is omitted in two important Black biographical sources—Rayford Logan's and Michael Winston's *Dictionary of American Negro Biography* and the prominent biographical encyclopedia *Black Women in America* by Darlene Clark Hine.

CHAPTER 9

Education and Marginality
The Conclusion

This chapter will discuss the challenges and consequences Black women college graduates experienced within the Black community as a result of their college education. It will also discuss a series of important studies on Black women college graduates that started in the late 1930s and continued through the 1950s. This chapter concludes by highlighting expanded opportunities for Black higher education after the civil rights legislation.

From the antebellum period until the 1960s, Blacks were encouraged to pursue an education to benefit the race. This was to compensate for the education denied to them and to reap the freedom education would bring them. As noted earlier, education was important for the entire race—gender notwithstanding. However, over the century, many Black men changed their attitudes toward gender equity and roles. While Blacks needed the efforts and contribution of everyone, as Black women's educational attainment exceeded that of Black men after the 1930s, a backlash emerged in many aspects of the community. Black men graduated from colleges beginning in the 1820s due to their ability to attend all-male colleges. Thus, they had an educational advantage over Black women for decades. In addition, they had access to strong liberal arts colleges and professional schools. As noted in previous chapters, while some Black women in the nineteenth century attended white institutions in the North and New England, the greatest number throughout this book attended Black state land-grant colleges that prepared teachers. Even the private Black colleges produced a large number of teachers. At the end of the nineteenth century, Black male graduates outnumbered Black women graduates four to one.

In addition to having an educational advantage, Black men also had a political advantage. The Fifteenth Amendment ratified in 1870 provided all men the right to vote. During this brief period of Reconstruction, twenty-two Black men served in the nation's Congress, scores of others served in local and state elected offices, and with the establishment of Black land-grant colleges, all the presidents of these institutions were Black men. Hence, a leadership class of

Black American men emerged. At the same time, a small cadre of feminist, race-conscious, articulate, primarily Oberlin-educated Black women also emerged as active leaders and speakers within the Black community, locally and nationally. While interested in the Black community as a whole, they also voiced concerns about the status of Black women. Unlike articles prior to the Civil War that were published in Black publications that praised the accomplishments of Black women and urged them to join with Black men in pursuing an education, during Reconstruction, the tone changed. Articles in Black publications stated a woman's sphere was in the home and education for women should be primarily for moral education and for the preparation of marriage and motherhood. Titles, such as "Shall Our Girls Be Educated?" "The Homemaker," and "Women's Exalted Station" appeared throughout the 1880s and 1890s in the *AME Review*, the widely read publication of the African American Episcopal Church. These articles glorified homemaking and encouraged Black women to seek an education that would "prepare their sons for manhood." These articles shaped the views of many Black people going into the twentieth century.[1]

Anna Julia Cooper, Oberlin graduate of 1884 and a professor at Wilberforce University in Ohio, hit the emerging sexism head on with a publication titled, *A Voice for the South*. In 1892, the publication noted the paucity of Black women who had obtained a higher education and blamed the lack of encouragement from Black men as a primary reason. She wrote: "I fear the majority of colored men do not yet think it worthwhile that women aspire to higher education . . . Let money be raised and scholarships be founded in our colleges and universities for self-supporting worthy women." She noted that women should not fear that being classically trained would lessen their opportunity for marriage, which was the prevailing theory of the period. Responding to this view, she said education makes women's standards go up:

> The question is not now with the woman, "how shall I so cramp, stunt, simplify and nullify myself as to make me eligible to the honor of being swallowed up into some little man?" . . . but the problem, I trow, now rests with the man as to how he can so develop his God-given powers as to reach the ideal of a generation of women who demand the noblest, the grandest and the best achievements of which he is capable; and this surely is the only fair and natural adjustment of the chance.[2]

Cooper was widowed after two years of marriage and never remarried.

Black women were the poorest of the race and worked either in agricultural or domestic work. The establishment of the nineteen Black land-grant colleges that prepared teachers was life altering for the thousands of Black women who attended. Although only half of these institutions offered college-level courses, their preparatory and high school departments prepared teachers. Because the demand for teachers was so great with the establishment of elementary schools, women flooded these institutions.

As the number of college-educated Blacks grew in the nation, a record of their progress was first reported by sociologist W. E. B. Du Bois in his two studies, *The College-Bred Negro* (1900 and 1910). The number of Blacks in college after 1920 grew in large numbers.[3]

Studies on Black college students only noted the graduates—not the hundreds who never completed the degree. By 1910, more than four hundred Black women had attended Oberlin.[4]

In the landmark study, *The Negro College Graduate* (1938), sociologist Charles S. Johnson stated the number of Black graduates grew dramatically. From 1920 and 1933, the number of Black college graduates from northern colleges increased 181 percent (from 156 to 459), and for Black colleges, the increase was 400 percent (from 497 to 2,486). His study interviewed and surveyed 5,512 Black college and professional school graduates from across the country. The graduates ranged from those finishing in 1890 to 1936. Johnson wanted to determine the factors that motivated the graduates to attend college, their philosophy of race, and their adjustment to life after college. Two thousand of those surveyed were women. He noted that women graduates were significantly younger than the men, reflecting their recent opportunity to attend college. He noted that 55.7 percent of the women in the study were under thirty years of age compared to 27.9 percent of the men. Johnson stated three-quarters of all the Black women graduates were under forty years of age. He noted that the older graduates of both genders were motivated to "help the race" and by "race leadership" as primary reasons for attending college. Johnson encouraged Marion V. Cuthbert to continue the study of Black college graduates and focus specifically on the women for her dissertation at Teachers College at Columbia University.[5]

Cuthbert was born in St. Paul, Minnesota, and attended the University of Minnesota, and later transferred and graduated in 1920 from Boston University with a degree in liberal arts. As was the case of most college-educated Black women in the North, she had to go South to teach in a segregated school. After graduating from BU, she served as teacher, and later, principal in the Burrell Normal School in rural Florence, Alabama. She left that position in 1927 to become dean of women at Talladega College in Alabama. Like so many Black teachers, Cuthbert attended summer school at Teacher's College in 1928 and 1929. In 1930, she received a fellowship from the National Council of Religion in Higher Education and was able to complete a full year in residence at Teacher's College and earned a master's degree in psychology in 1931. After graduation, she remained in New York and joined the staff of the National YWCA. Her dissertation, "Education and Marginality: A Study of the Negro Woman College Graduate" (1942), continued and expanded the study of Charles Johnson.

Cuthbert surveyed 172 Black women college graduates from forty communities throughout the country. Ninety-nine had attended HBCUs, sixty-two had attended northern colleges and universities, seven had attended institutions in the West, and four studied in New England. Forty-five of the women also held master's degrees. The women surveyed had all graduated between five and ten years of the study. Hence, they were all graduates in the 1930s. Cuthbert also surveyed fifty-eight non-college graduates as a control group. The purpose of Cuthbert's study was "to discover and describe the situation arising from the marginal life which results from the college education of Negro women." She stated the study was sociological and that psychologists could explore this topic from their perspective in further studies. The study concluded that many college-educated Black women were marginal and often lived in between two worlds, which impacted their social relationship with others and caused friction in marriage.

Since Cuthbert's education and work setting was in white settings outside of the South, it impacted her questions and assumptions. Because of the nature of her interracial work with the National YWCA, she valued such relationships. Her questionnaire had multiple questions on the women's relationships with white people. Some examples of questions: "Describe any interracial work in which you're engaged"; "How many white friends do you have?"; "What white people do you know best?"; "What are some of the things you can do with Negro friends that you can't do with white friends?" There were multiple questions along these lines. Considering that most of these women were living in the Jim Crow South, where even the YWCA segregated them in its branches, the questions did not take this into consideration. There were some interracial efforts through church groups, but overwhelmingly, Black women devoted their community and civic activities within their race. One respondent wrote regarding one of the questions about white friends, "Since I live in the South, there is no need to answer this question [what do you do with your white friends]." She said the one thing she knew she couldn't do with a white person was be their houseguest.[6]

However, a little over a third of the respondents (36.7 percent) had white friends. Cuthbert noted that making white friends began "with friendships formed during college days; in student-movement contacts of a variety of types; in relationships with faculty; and in a number of activities concomitant with the college experience." Cuthbert also noted that Black women had white friends as a result of professional contacts and activities. Again, 80 percent of Black women were teachers in segregated schools at that time. And, while the prevailing view was that education lessened a Black woman's opportunity for marriage, 80 percent of the women in the study were married.

Cuthbert's study was important and coincided with the aforementioned conference on Black women in higher education that convened at Spelman in 1944 and also the annual conferences of the Black Women Deans and the National Association of College Women, who stressed research and the collection of data on Black women in higher education. The Black college women of the 1930s and early '40s were studied multiple times. In 1943, a master's thesis was conducted at the University of Michigan entitled, "Student Problems Encountered Daily by Deans of Women at Sixteen Colleges for Negroes," by Georgia C. Brown. This study surveyed the "problems" that deans of women at sixteen HBCUs faced during a four-week period during the 1942–43 academic year. Each dean was provided a form to be filled out weekly detailing the issues (labeled "problems") that they encountered to provide the reader with an understanding of the many tasks of deans of women. The institutions surveyed included private ones—Howard, Fisk, Dillard, Talladega, Bennett, Shaw, Knoxville, Virginia Union; the two industrial colleges—Hampton and Tuskegee; and multiple state and land-grant colleges—Florida A&M, Prairie View, North Carolina State, Morgan State, Southern, and Cheyney Teachers College. Brown discussed the history of the dean of women position and how with the continued increase in the number of Black women in colleges, especially those attending coeducational colleges, has led to continued issues. One of these issues, which these colleges perceived as a problem, was: "Can proper relationships between young men and women students be maintained when they were thrown together so continuously and so casually as they would be both inside and outside of class? Can proper social standards be set up and enforced?" She discussed (as was discussed at Bennett) whether Black women students should have a different curriculum from men. Brown concluded there were eight main areas that the deans of women were most involved with, although only two issues—social and disciplinary—required the most attention with women students. Brown said the social issues were primarily "boy-girl" relationships. A dean expressed concern over young women spending too much time with a male student, or a first-year student spending time with a student who was a senior, or young women being concerned that they did not have a boyfriend. Disciplinary issues seemed routine college issues: young women being late for dormitory curfew, leaving campus without permission, smoking, drinking, using profanity, cheating on exams, and too many extracurricular activities.[7]

Two additional dissertations on Black college women were produced in 1948 and 1949. Willa Player, previously mentioned and a long-term faculty member of Bennett College, later became its president. She produced a new curriculum for the college in response to a survey from the early 1940s. This survey, funded by the General Education Board, was discussed at length in chapter seven. The college utilized her research to produce a curriculum that responded to the comments of Black women graduates and current students. The new curriculum included courses that provided the students with information on careers, civic and community engagement, health and consumer education, and family and home life. These themes were integrated with the academic curriculum. Another dissertation written by a Black woman scholar, Ina Bolton, "The Problems of Negro College Women," was completed in 1949 for a doctorate in education from the University of Southern California. Bolton's higher education started at the Black land-grant Prairie View State College in Texas and shifted to the predominantly white Washburn College in Topeka, Kansas, in 1930. In 1933, she earned a master's degree from the University of Kansas and began a career in student affairs. After earning her master's, she served for six years as dean of women at the Alabama Agricultural and Mechanical College for Negroes, a land-grant college. She left the college in Alabama to become professor of philosophy and dean of women at Lincoln University in Missouri, another land-grant college.[8]

Bolton was a prominent leader and figure among the deans of women and was the fourth National President of NAWDAC. Bolton's dissertation surveyed 278 women and interviewed fifty women at six coeducational land-grant colleges with A ratings. She studied women who graduated between 1935 and 1945. As noted earlier, during this period, Black college women were young. The average age of the women in the study was 28.3 years old, ranging from twenty-four to forty-seven.[9] The colleges were in Alabama, Arkansas, Kentucky, Oklahoma, Missouri, and Texas. Bolton, a minister's wife, held views of traditional and conservative women. She explored four areas of the impact of college on women: curricular, economic, social, and psychological. She assumed that all Black women students were heterosexual and destined for marriage and family. She asked, "How many schools give any real assistance in the all-important problem of securing the right husband, or a husband, and the fundamental problems of marriage in all its relationships? And, the problem of rearing children, providing them with a sound cultural background?" Bolton believed that women should have a different curriculum from men and not be "subjected to the rigors of a curriculum which were designed for the masculine activities of life, and which had little to do with preparing women for professional, vocational, domestic and social activities appropriate to their sex."[10] Bolton objected to the belief of many educators that women should have a "man's" education and be like men. Her questions to the women in the study reflected her belief that certain fields and professions were beyond the reach of Black women. She asked the women if they thought they received training for vocations that were not open to them because of their race, training, or location (she did not ask because of their gender). Like Cuthbert's study, Bolton asked about their preparation and involvement in civic and community affairs: "Did they vote, were they active in organizations like the Parent Teachers Association? Were they prepared to have leadership roles in these groups?" Forty-seven percent of the women were married and the rest were divorced or widowed. The women were overwhelmingly teachers (59 percent), and 16 percent were housewives. Education and home economics were the top two majors of the women in the study (59 percent). This reflected the curricula of all land-grant colleges. Some of the respondents in the study indicated that college had lessened their interest in marriage, and a quarter of the women said they wished they were men. This was a question Bolton had asked under the psychological problems section of the study. Bolton did not elaborate on or probe this finding or note why the question was asked. Three-quarters of the married women in the study said they did not plan to give up their jobs after marriage, and a third of the married women who did not work outside the home said they regretted having to give up their career for marriage. Bolton's conclusions and recommendations were that these institutions were failing the women students for not preparing them for their lives after college. She noted the colleges failed to provide vocational and guidance counseling and gave no access to psychological services. She recommended that these colleges offer mandatory classes for women on marriage, childcare, personality development, and consumer education. Since marriage at that time was a union between a man and a woman, it was curious that Bolton's suggestion for a class on marriage would be just for women. Should not this have been a class for all students? The notion that only women needed to understand their roles in marriage and how to maintain a happy and healthy home seemed outdated.

Bolton's views were conservative and disappointing. Throughout the existence of the women of the National Association of College Women, who were the graduates of white colleges and Howard and Fisk, they were concerned with developing the young women students' leadership. The women who were members of the NAWDAC, the dean's group, represented a different mindset. These were women who were primarily Southern born and products of HBCUs. Bolton's study noted that many women stated they lacked freedom in their choice of majors, minors, or electives. Women students should be free to take any courses and major in anything they were interested in. But their responses indicated that they did not have this freedom. Others dictated their lives. One got the sense that there was a lack of advisement at their institutions. These women were stuck in a no-choice situation with no room for negotiating their course selections. In her dissertation, Bolton doesn't cite or acknowledge the important work on Black college women by Charles S. Johnson or Marion Cuthbert. Johnson attempted to survey every living Black college graduate. Their work should have been a point of comparison from her research.

The studies specifically on women were during and after the war years when the number of Black women in college continued to grow. In addition, while most college-educated Black women, especially in the South where there were segregated schools, were teachers, other employment avenues were expanding for Black women. Inabeth Lindsay recalled that her mother was very disappointed that she did not become a teacher. Born in St. Joseph, Missouri, Lindsay said all of her friends went to college in Iowa, Nebraska, and Kansas, which were accessible. She said that because Black students couldn't live in the dormitories, her mother sent her to Howard instead, so she could live on campus and "be protected" by adults. Lindsay said she was barely sixteen (she finished high school at age fifteen) when she went to Howard. While a student, one of her male professors told her about a new field of social work that was emerging and that there were scholarships available through the National Urban League to attend the New York School of Social Work (which is now Columbia School of Social Work). She said when she explained what social workers did, her mother assumed she would be working in the slums with derelicts and criminals. Lindsay recalled:

> In the little Mid-western town where I was born and reared, there was very little else for a Black girl to look forward to other than teaching or working in someone's kitchen. So it was just assumed that I would become a teacher like my brother and sister.[11]

In her oral history, Lindsay reflected she was deeply appreciative that her Howard professor, Dr. Williams, informed her about the field of social work. She said that she had no idea there were other professional outlets other than teaching. Lindsay stated, had she known there were other professional options, she may have chosen another career path. She said, "Had I known that women could be lawyers, could be doctors, could be other professionals. I might have chosen differently." She said she liked the law and thought she would have been a great lawyer. However, she said, "I never in my life heard of a woman lawyer as a youngster." She said she never met a Black woman librarian.[12]

Lindsay's comments reflected the reality of most Black young women of her era. Teaching was viewed as the only route to not becoming a domestic servant or working in farm labor. The annual Bennett College Homemaking Institute throughout the late '20s through the '40s provided its students and people in the area with an expanded array of careers.

Throughout the 1940s, and into the 1950s, there were more educational opportunities opening up for Black women. Many had benefited from the fellowships previously discussed. Also, the National Scholarship and Fund for Negro Students were matching and placing Black high school youth in white colleges. Black publications, such as *Ebony, Jet,* and *Negro Digest* highlighted the many successes of Black women and men. Cuthbert's study highlighted topics on Black women found in *The Crisis* magazine (NAACP), *Opportunity: A Journal of Negro Life* (National Urban League); and the *Journal of Negro Education* (Howard University)—all Black intellectual publications. A study of Black popular magazines from 1946–58, the period when the emphasis on marriage and domesticity to women was thought to be at its peak, found that this was not the case in Black publications. More than 60 percent of the articles highlighted women's individual accomplishments. A third of the articles did not mention women's marital status. For example, in an August 1947 article in *Ebony* showcasing Black women attorneys, there was no mention of their marital status. The article, "Lady Lawyers: Seventy on Battle for Sex and Race Equality in Courts," noted that there are nearly eight thousand women attorneys, but only seventy were Black and their road has been paved with anti-feminist prejudice and braving the cold shoulder of men. However, the article noted the first Black woman to become an attorney was Charlotte Ray, who graduated from Howard Law School in 1872. The article had four pages of photos and biographical information on the women, noting that while twelve Black men were judges, there was just one woman at that point, Jane Bolin.[13] The magazine profiled Black women in various positions, including the only Black mechanic for American Airlines. The article noted that this woman was a mother of two and while she was a "good cook," she was a better mechanic.[14] The article clearly indicated that her career in a male field did not diminish perceived notions about traditional female roles.

Other articles chronicled the professional success of individual Black women and testified to their progress, talents, skills, and intellect. A 1959 article showcased Bernadine Carrickett Washington, a buyer for a major women's fashion market in Chicago. She was described as a pioneer in the field and was one of the best-known buyers in her field. She traveled to Seventh Avenue in New York six times a year to purchase more than one thousand dresses and suits for stores in Chicago. While there was no mention of her marital status, the article described Washington as a "trim, energetic fashion expert known as being business- and lady-like."[15] Finally, in December 1959, *Ebony* featured an extensive cover story on "Negro Girls on Capitol Hill: Once Rare, Their Numbers Are Increasing." The article noted that Christine Davis started as a member of the congressional secretarial pool twelve years earlier; she was not allowed to use the House of Representatives cafeteria. She had to appeal to the Speaker of the House to end this discrimination. As the first Black secretary to work on Capitol Hill, she is one of the top-ranking and highest-paid "girl Fridays."[16] The article featured five full pages of various Black women in their offices with the representatives they worked for. It highlighted Black women who started as interns, and one woman was a research assistant working on her doctorate. One woman stated she was hired as a full-time staff member for a summer while a student at Howard and continued as a part-time staff member while in college. The article stated there were currently 32 Black women in 19 of the 536 lawmakers' offices; while this was a start, the author wrote that many more Black staff should be hired.[17] The article noted the women in these positions worked closely on a daily basis with the leading politicians of the nation. This resulted in them being very helpful to Black leaders in the country.[18]

The leading white anti-feminist Dr. Marynia Farnham, who was mentioned earlier as a speaker at one of the annual Homemaking Institute conferences at Bennett College, said that "stories about famous career women" were the "propaganda of the feminists" and that such stories undermined the "prestige of motherhood."[19] Such views resulted in discussions in the popular and the Black intellectual press on the consequences of the perceived gender imbalances in educational attainment. The discussion concluded that these women will not be desirable marriage partners. When Black women deans began to discuss how to make Black women students better prepared to be wives and mothers, the emphases shifted to learning social graces and discontinuing competitive sports that were perceived as too "masculine." In the 1940s, a debate over this issue was discussed in the newly founded *Negro Digest*. Established in 1942, it was patterned after the *Reader's Digest*. Within a year, the publication had a national readership with a circulation of more than fifty thousand a month. In 1947, a series of articles discussed the issue of educated Black women and marriage. The novelist Ann Petry wrote a humorous article titled, "What's Wrong with Negro Men?" Petry was from Old Saybrook, Connecticut, and had a degree in pharmacy from the University of Connecticut. After marrying, she moved to Harlem and became a successful writer. Petry's piece noted that many Black men professed to have progressive political views, but when it came to women, they were in the "dark ages." She pointed out that given Black people's political and economic reality, for a Black man to have a wife who lived up to the idealized expectation of doing "pure womanly chores" was unrealistic. She said the overbearing and demanding expectations of many Black men demonstrated that sexism bonded men and transcended race and socioeconomic status. She concluded, "In this respect, he [the black man] is as medieval as his white brother."[20] Pauli Murray, who has been discussed throughout this book, wrote a piece a few months later, "Why Negro Girls Stay Single." She argued that it was racism and sexism that had created the conflict between Black men and women. Economic necessity had propelled Black women to seek college educations. She denounced what she called outmoded notions of gender roles. Racism kept Black men from obtaining jobs and earning livable wages.[21] Both Murray and Petry rejected the notion that Black women must hone their domestic skills after working all day.

Black women's marriage eligibility became a major topic of concern during this period. Jeanne Noble was a 1946 graduate of Howard University and earned a master's degree from Teachers College, Columbia in 1948. She taught in her hometown in Albany, Georgia, at Albany State College until 1950, when she was hired as dean of women at Langston University in Oklahoma. She left that position to pursue her doctorate at Teachers College. She continued the study of Black women college graduates. Noble was a psychologist, and like Cuthbert, surveyed Black women college graduates from both Black and white institutions. She queried 412 women from six major cities. Seventy-one percent graduated from Black colleges and 29 percent graduated from white institutions. As with the other studies, Black women graduates were young. Sixty percent were under the age of forty. Unlike the other three studies, by the time of Noble's study, 62.5 percent of all Black college graduates were women and just 35.6 percent were men.[22]

Noble asked the women what they felt they got out of college and if it met their expectations and if there were disappointments. As was noted by Petry and Murray (and many others), eighty-nine of the women in Noble study said they were in college "to prepare for a vocation." This was their *primary* reason for attending college. They were not seeking a husband, as with the overwhelming number of women in most Black colleges except the private ones like Howard and Fisk that had more gender balance. In spite of this, 75 percent of the women were married or had been married. However, 50 percent of the women said their husbands earned less money and were employed in lower-socioeconomic-status jobs. This was often the case in the past, and the stigma did not exist as much as it did by the 1950s. For example, in an autobiography of Mamie Fields, who was a 96-year-old South Carolinian raised in the "race uplift" tradition, recalled that her mother was better educated than her father. She said this was a common phenomenon:

> Dad could read, write, and count well, but Mother was better educated than he. The difference didn't matter in those days the way it might now. Dad respected Mother's education, but that didn't mean he felt he was less because he didn't have the same. He was proud of his wife.[23]

Black women were continuously put on the defensive. They were sexually exploited throughout slavery and given the reputation after Emancipation of being immoral. Ironically and unfortunately, as Black colleges were established, these institutions established harsh rules that reinforced the notion that Black women were wild, untamed, and needed constant surveillance. Noble's work also made that point: "Her [the Black woman's] education in many instances appears to have been based on a philosophy which implied that she was weak and immoral and at best she should be made fit to rear her children and keep house for her husband."[24]

The women in Noble's study said they were defensive about their educational accomplishments and said that even though they had the desire, they would not seek degrees beyond the baccalaureate because of the impact it will have on men. It was not the case that these women were male-centered; they were sensitive to the fact that Black men, unlike white men, had been emasculated throughout their lives. While it was supposed to be a "man's world," Black men frequently saw Black women support the family partially, and sometimes, solely. Unlike in white society, often the mother was the central figure in Black families. In the Johnson 1938 study, the Black graduates of both genders stated their mother was the one who motivated them to obtain a college degree.

All of the women interviewed for Noble's study spent years in HBCUs—Thelma Bando, Hilda Davis, Ruth Brett, and Jean Noble all said that marrying was an obsession with most of the Black college women and most would drop out of college if they had the opportunity to marry. This was why Slowe, as mentioned earlier, would not allow Howard women to date men who were in servant positions at the university. Bando said women were not very discriminating in their choice of husbands or felt this was their only opportunity to meet someone. Hilda Davis noted, "Any woman who looked [at] something different from marriage was thought to be queer." She continued, "All through the years, marriage has been the goal for most women, and so they would give up the chance to earn degrees; and then especially with the Black men who were achieving, they wouldn't want women who were their equals."[25] This societal pressure stifled any woman who may not have been heterosexual or one who truly wanted to continue and pursue graduate or professional studies.

The women in Noble's study spoke of the pain they felt because they had obtained more education than Black men. One wrote:

> I would like to comment on the fact that there are so many Negro women college graduates. If it hadn't been for the economic necessity, I don't feel that they would have done it. Sometimes I feel that Negro women feel guilty about the education they do have. Of course, I feel that all women have this feeling, but it is more prevalent among the Negro group. They are more conscious of the fact that accomplishments may prevent them from getting married. I have actually had them ask me how they can put on brakes, to keep from being A students and presidents of clubs, and so forth.[26]

As Ann Petry pointed out, the belief by many Black men that educated, working Black women demeaned the status of Black men transcended socioeconomic backgrounds. Many professional Black women with educated, professional husbands battled the same sexist views. For example, Inabeth Lindsay, mentioned earlier, said she didn't work the first year she was married because her husband felt she should be at home.

> I didn't work because my husband had some old-fashioned ideas about women working. . . . But I got bored to death.[27]

Lindsay said she had been raised to work and everyone in her family had to earn their keep. Further, she said she felt guilty about receiving the scholarship from the National Urban League to become a social worker, yet she wasn't working. She stated:

> I did feel very guilty over that. But, after I'd been married eleven months, I was quite bored, and guilty about not doing anything, because I said my mother worked too hard and spent too much money on my education for me not to be doing something with the education that was made possible.[28]

After her year's agreement with her husband not to work, she was hired by Charles S. Johnson at Fisk University to work on a research project for him in Springfield, Illinois, which she accepted. It was to work on a specific project. She said once she was known as a social worker, before she was hired for the faculty at Howard, she had an endless number of social service agencies contacting her about employment. She said a Black social worker was rare at that time.[29]

Lindsay was able to convince her husband that she wanted to work and their marriage survived. This wasn't the case with Dr. Dorothy B. Ferebee, the director of the Health Center at Howard. She began teaching on the faculty of the Medical School in 1927. In 1930, she married Claude Ferebee, a dentist who was on the faculty of the Howard University School of Dentistry. After the first year of their marriage, Claude Ferebee had a personal dispute with the dean of the School of Dentistry and was fired. Because he was fired, Claude expected Dorothy to leave her position at the School of Medicine in solidarity as his wife. In her oral history, she said the marriage had problems from the start because he was jealous that she had a thriving medical practice in addition to her faculty position at Howard. She also had a national reputation as Supreme Basileus (President) of the national Alpha Kappa Alpha, the nation's first and oldest Black sorority (1939–41). Dorothy Ferebee was also the medical director of a very successful health project called the Mississippi Health Project (started by AKA President Ida L. Jackson), where she and other health volunteers would go to rural Mississippi Delta to provide health care, inoculations, etc. to poor Blacks in the summer. This was a program through AKA that continued for seven years. She and her husband had a set of twins the second year of their marriage. Before knowing she was having twins, Dorothy said she hoped the child would be a boy to please her husband. She said:

> He was becoming more and more resentful of everything I was doing as a woman, because what I attempted seemed to turn to gold, and his efforts turned to mud . . . The fact that I became busier and had perhaps a larger group of patients, that didn't sit too well with him . . .[30]

Dorothy said Claude became more and more unhappy, and he asked her to give up her medical practice since he had started a dental practice. She said, "he insisted that I give up my work. Of course, I wasn't going to do that."[31] She said

Education and Marginality   295

he resented her prominence with the Mississippi Health Project. He moved to New York to set up a practice where his father was also a dentist. Dorothy commuted back and forth to New York, but in the end, the marriage couldn't work, and he asked for a divorce and Dorothy said she responded, "It is my pleasure to give you your freedom. Thus, in a very calm fashion, we were divorced."[32] Professional jealousy and male ego destroyed their marriage. Dorothy said that her husband was an outstanding dentist, and he was able to establish a thriving practice. However, it was simply a fact that she had far more patients than him. She pointed out, "I am a doctor, and he is a dentist," and this distinction disturbed him.

As Ann Petry's article noted, many Black men who professed to be progressives were actually profoundly regressive when it came to the gender issue. For example, Rayford Logan's biographer, Kenneth Janken noted:

> As a radical in politics, Logan consistently stood for women's rights. He believed not only in women's civil equality but also that the improvement of their material conditions and their inclusion in the political process were fundamental to the success of African decolonization and independence.[33]

However, these beliefs did not transfer into his personal life and marriage. Janken said:

> In his [Logan's] personal life, he held fast to traditional gender roles, and he nearly completely dominated Ruth [his wife] . . . He restricted her intellectual and cultural growth in ways he defined. For example, when she wanted to pursue a professional singing career, Logan told her the penalty for such a choice would be the end of their marriage; he would not stand for his wife to have a career, and that settled the matter.[34]

Logan's wife, Ruth, had been a voice major and was the director of the college choir at Virginia State when they met. She also taught music at Virginia Union. This career ended with her marriage to Logan.

Black men of all socioeconomic status embraced the notion that highly educated women jeopardized their marriage opportunities. When the wealthy Mary Church Terrell graduated from Oberlin in 1884, her father threatened to disinherit her when she decided to take a teaching position at Wilberforce College. She stated:

> It was held by most people that women were unfitted [sic] to do their work in the home if they studied Latin, Greek, and higher mathematics . . . I was ridiculed and told that no man would want to marry a woman who studied higher mathematics.[35]

But, like most of these women, Mary Church did get married. She married Robert Terell in 1891, a graduate of Groton Prep School, Harvard College, and

Howard University Law School. He became a judge and a strong supporter of Mary Church Terrell's national prominence as the national president of the Black women's club movement and a charter member of the National Association for the Advancement of Colored People (NAACP).[36]

Dr. May Edward Chinn, the only woman doctor in Harlem for fifty years, also recalled her father being embarrassed by her educational pursuits; he not only discouraged her but provided no financial support to her. Chinn's mother was a live-in domestic at the estate in Irvington, New Jersey, for the New York jeweler, Charles Tiffany. Chinn benefited from growing up as a child in the Tiffany family, and she had the opportunity to learn classical music, French, and German. For high school, her mother saved her wages and sent Chinn to the Bordentown School, a coeducational boarding school for talented Black youth. The school taught industrial courses but also had a classical curriculum that included Latin. After Tiffany died and the estate was sold, she and her mother moved back to New York City where she completed high school at a public school there. She earned a BS from Teachers College. Excelling in science, she became the first Black woman to graduate from the Columbia Bellevue Hospital Medical School, now New York University Medical School. After medical school, she became the first woman to intern at Harlem Hospital. Her father did odd jobs when he couldn't find employment. While Chinn's mother supplied the steady income to the family and encouraged her education, Chinn's father believed a woman's role was in the home. Chinn recollected:

> My father objected to me going to college, number one . . . his idea of a girl was that you got married and had children. He was of a different generation. A girl that went to college became a queer woman. And, he didn't want to be the father of a queer girl.[37]

Her reference to her father's fear that she would be a "queer" was the first time someone mentioned the belief that certain types of education made women prone to becoming homosexuals. Chinn not only was rejected by her father, but she also received little recognition from the Black community for years; she was resented by Black male doctors and segregated by white hospitals. She said Black male doctors fell into three categories: "1) those who acted as if I wasn't there; 2) those who took the attitude 'what does she think that she can do that I can't do?'; and 3) the group that called themselves support[ive] by sending me their night calls after midnight."[38] Chinn noted Black male doctors referred their poor patients who couldn't pay them to her. Nevertheless, she continued to serve the poverty-stricken and largely unemployed population in Harlem.

Throughout the 1950s and 1960s, Black women and girls put their lives on the line as plaintiffs, activists, and community leaders, and worked for meager wages as teachers. In a study of Black women who attended one of the eleven HBCUs in Texas between 1930 and 1954, historian Merline Pitre noted, Black women students at all these campuses were steered into the gender-specific field of teaching. She continued:

> Regardless of the institution these women attended from the 1930s through 1950s, the education they received tended to be more practical than classical . . . it is an understatement to say that the majority of black females who graduated from college became teachers. Teaching provided them with professional work, a skilled vocation, and a lucrative salary, albeit lower than white women and black men.[39]

In Johnson's study of the Negro college graduate, he noted that the salary of a white woman teacher who attended a land-grant college was $1,655 in 1936 and the salary of a Black woman graduate of a Black land-grant college was $973. He calculated that a white women land-grant graduate who taught elementary school earned 81 percent more than a Black woman graduate of a Black land-grant college. If the white woman graduated from a university, then her salary was 86 percent higher. If the white woman taught high school and was a land-grant graduate, then she earned 77 percent more than her Black counterpart, and if she was a university graduate and taught high school, then she earned 108 percent more than a Black woman teacher.[40] Cuthbert commented in her dissertation that in spite of all of the upset over Black women college attainments, they were in the "poorest paid" jobs with the largest number of Black women.[41]

By the 1960s, the civil rights movement was in full force with tremendous participation of Black women. Major demonstrations were started and led by Black women. The one by the women at Howard University spearheaded by Pauli Murray in the 1940s is but one example. The important women who volunteered to be plaintiffs in major higher education lawsuits have already been mentioned. In 1964, a civil rights Bill passed guaranteeing Blacks equal rights in education, public accommodations, voting, employment, public facilities, and federally assisted programs. As with Emancipation a century earlier, Black people eagerly anticipated putting their newly acquired rights to the test. Black women, in particular, had much to look forward to since they remained at the lowest rung of the economic ladder.

In 1965, a controversial report by Daniel Patrick Moynihan was published where he characterized the Black family as pathological due to its "matriarchal" structure. In 1965, only 25 percent of Black families were headed by women. The next year *Ebony* magazine did a special issue on *The Black Woman*. Shockingly, the editors of *Ebony* agreed and were uncritical of Moynihan's assessment of the Black family. John Johnson, the publisher, wrote a tribute to Black women—he noted what they had endured through slavery and how the "Negro woman became the dominate family figure in a slave culture that was designed to eliminate all vestiges of family life for the Negro."[42] He stated that Black women were varied in their history and their status—and that there are Black women who are still "mammy" to wealthy white women's homes, while having a son graduating magna cum laude from an Ivy League college. He noted the Black woman is a prostitute, an ambassador, a cab driver, a civil rights worker, a teacher, preacher, doctor, poet, cook, housewife, fashion designer, and novelist. It was to these women that the issue was dedicated.

The editorial page also acknowledged the long history of Black women's contribution to the race from Sojourner Truth, Harriet Tubman, and all the Black women who were the teachers of our youth for decades. It noted that Black women:

> said, 'yes' when asked to tear up her roots in the South to migrate to better jobs for Negro men in the North. She can glory in the fact that as the matriarch in the family, she kept the children in line and urged them to better themselves at all costs, pinched out the money from a barely living income to make the down payment on a home and cooked and cleaned in the white man's house to put food into her children's mouth when the male in the family found it impossible to get a job.[43]

Now with the new civil rights legislations and legal segregation outlawed, in a section of the editorial entitled, *The Past Is Behind Us,* it said all the above is in the past and it is now time for Black women to put the slave past behind her and become the "wise counsel and guidance to her husband and children and yet remain a wife and mother instead of an iron-handed family boss." This profoundly insulting comment was followed by the instruction of "The Goal Today," which was "the immediate goal of the Negro woman should be to establish a strong family unit, where the father is the dominate person, and the children are brought up to respect not only their parents but the rights of others."[44] The article instructed Black women to focus on homemaking and volunteer community work. In addition, she should emulate the Jewish wife and mother who "pushed her husband to success, educated her male children first and engineered good marriages for her daughters. A born psychologist, she often guided her husband to success without ever diminishing him."[45] What these men described was their desire for Black women to be like their perception of the idealized white women. Noting that Black women are now moving into white collar jobs and into offices as secretaries and stenographers, "while the pay is often tempting, the family unit is more important than money."[46]

Finally, the editorial ended up saying "the future is bright" with new opportunities. Now Black men can have improved training and better job opportunities, allowing the Black woman to spend more time at home with her family. Again, she was told to stress educating their sons, so that Black girls can look forward to having them as future husbands. Indeed, Black men had been kept back, as had Black women. Scholars who have analyzed the attitudes of Black men on this topic note they embraced the middle-class "ideal American husband" as described in the above view of working women and the impact on the psyche of men. Anthropologist St. Clair Drake wrote a response in the *Negro Digest* to the Murray and Petry articles about Black men and sexism, titled "Why Men Leave." He agreed that if Black men could not live up to the standard of being a successful husband by being the breadwinner; he often deserted the family. Drake put the blame on the wife stating, Black women's steady employment "weakened" Black men's position in the family.[47] Dayo F. Gore said Drake and other Black male intellectuals of this period (the 1950s and '60s) in their discussion of the destruction of Black manhood, "rarely addressed the issue of Black women's exploitation or sexism in Black communities. Thus, their proposed solutions often reinforced dominant gendered norms and male supremacy."[48]

The special issue on Black Women also had an article by the religious scholar, C. Eric Lincoln who continued the thesis that Black women need to step back and let Black men be the head of the race. He wrote:

> The patriarchal family—a family with a man at the head is a cherished American institution . . . The American *ideal* is to have a father at the head of the household . . . To be middle class means to conform to a cluster of values, attitudes and behavior patterns which are already set by the prevailing society.[49]

According to Lincoln, Blacks should accept unquestionably the "values, attitudes and behavior patterns" of the prevailing society. Obviously, no Black woman would balk at her husband making the wages he deserved and obtaining the positions he deserved. However, the danger of the *Ebony* editorial and the Lincoln article was that they were discouraging married Black women from obtaining an education or seeking employment. He continued:

> A husband who is making enough to support his family will often feel his manhood has been challenged if his wife insists upon working and particularly if she throws in his face the fact that the additional creature comforts of the home came from her paycheck. If the woman should, by any chance, make more money than her husband, the marriage could be in real trouble.[50]

As stated before, all of these comments have the assumption that all women desire to be married. Many did not. *Ebony* published an article in 1958 on the topic "Why Don't They Marry?" This article explored the reasons both men and women stayed single. All of the people highlighted were successful professionals.

It was the usual argument that being a professional woman worked against them being married. In the Letters to the Editor the following month, a woman advised career women "don't sacrifice marriage for a career," another wrote, "I like my life just as it is."[51] Cuthbert's and Bolton's dissertations reflected that many women held this view. Furthermore, there was an assumption that all women were heterosexual. They were not. Also, most Black women *were* married, albeit many to men who earned less money than they did. In a society that celebrated and expected men to be the primary, if not sole, economic provider of the family, this issue was one that impacted Black men's self-esteem and sense of masculinity. American society constantly demeaned and reduced Black men to boys. Thus, having a wife who was more educated and earning more money was a reminder that he was less a man than those men who were white.

The irony of this editorial is the fact that it instructs Black women on motherhood and how to be a good mom when Black women had raised generations of white kids and took care of white households. This was the Black women's specialty since enslavement. And, ironically, that same issue had an extensive article on Black women civil rights activists in the South. Phyl Garland, a Black woman journalist, wrote an extensive article titled, "Builders of a New South: Negro Heroines of Dixie Play Major Role in Challenging Racist Traditions." The author paid tribute to the courageous Black women who put their lives on the line and suffered brutality and being arrested protesting on behalf of civil rights. Photos and interviews with women such as Fannie Lou Hamer, Ella Baker, Daisy Bates, Rosa Parks, Gloria Richardson, Annie Devine, Ruby Robinson, and Marion Wright [Edelman] demonstrated Black college women working in the Delta of Mississippi along with Black women sharecroppers for the freedom of Black people.[52] It was hard to believe that an article so powerful about what Black women were willing to sacrifice for the race could be in the same issue with an editorial admonishing Black women for their contributions to the race.

Articles about dual career couples negated the editorial of the special issue. Two examples are in 1965: there was a feature article titled, "Woman Fills Man-Size Union Job" about Lillian Roberts, who was based in Chicago and was the vice president of the international labor group, the Federation of State, County and Municipal Employee (AFL-CIO). The article stated, "attractive Lillian Roberts, a 36-year-old Chicagoan, is proving her sex is no handicap in performing her job." It noted she was the first Black woman union vice president for the United States or Canada. There was a bitter union strike happening in New York against the New York Department of Public Welfare, and Mrs. Roberts led one of the most difficult strikes in the union's history. She did so well that the New York union offered her a promotion with a much higher salary. Roberts accepted the position on a temporary basis and moved to New York, returning home to Chicago two weekends a month. The married Roberts and her husband, who was a printer, had two foster sons. Her mother took care of the sons while the father was at work. Roberts's mother said she planted the seeds of social protest in her children, and she approved of her daughter's move to New York. The five-page article had photos of the Roberts family together walking with their sons, holding their hands, and playing games; portraying Roberts studying labor history at the University of Chicago; and kissing her husband goodbye from O'Hare Airport. The caption noted the couple were deciding if the entire family would move to New York. In addition to Lillian's promotion and substantial raise, the union guaranteed her husband a position as a printer.[53]

Two months later, another article featured on a dual career couple who were both chemists. The article was titled, "Scientific Couple Find Success in Albuquerque." Kenneth and Katheryn Lawson were recently married. She graduated from Dillard University in the natural sciences and earned a master's degree from Tuskegee Institute in organic chemistry. Like many Black women academics, she taught at an array of HBCUs seeking better salaries and teaching conditions. Katheryn taught at North Carolina A&T, Grambling College, Bishop College, Talladega College, Savannah State, and Central State (Ohio). She was a chemistry instructor when she met her husband, Kenneth. He had earned a bachelor's in biology at Central State and was working on a master's degree when they married.[54] In 1954, Katheryn was recruited by the University of New Mexico to work on a doctorate in radiochemistry. Kenneth said that the offer for Katheryn was too good to pass up, and they moved to Albuquerque. She started on her doctoral program, and Kenneth continued his master's at the university as well but also took a job as a chemist-bacteriologist laboratory technician for the city's sewage division. Within two years, Kenneth was promoted to superintendent of Albuquerque's sewage division. In 1957, Katheryn had earned her doctorate in radiochemistry and was hired as the head of the biochemistry research department of the veterans hospital. The next year, she was offered a job at the prestigious Sandia National Laboratories in their Crystal Physics Research Division. Like the article on the Robertses, this article featured the Lawsons in multiple settings. They had two sons while Katheryn was a doctoral student. Both Lawsons were shown in their work settings, and multiple settings with their sons: one with the dad and his son, and another with Katheryn with a son in the kitchen while she's cooking, and a couple of others with the entire family—out in their backyard, and in their den with their sons and two dogs. The Lawsons said "togetherness" was their key to happiness. They said they strongly believed that there is "strength in unity."[55]

In both articles, it showed the family moved because of the wife's job opportunities and the husband agreed that it was the right move. In both instances, they decided based on what was best for the family. These were modern families. This was no different from the decisions the academic couples made when both received fellowships. The article noted that the salaries of both the Lawson's were very lucrative, both making five figures.

Not only did the families come out ahead, these two examples demonstrated what the outcome could be when a couple works as a team and not one person subordinating the other. The *Ebony* editorial team was completely out of step with modern times. Phyl Garland, the Black women associate editor of *Ebony*, was no doubt responsible for these forward-thinking examples of Black couples. Many articles did not mention the marital status of women at all. The magazine constantly profiled Black women in a positive manner.

However, the editorial of the special issue did not represent the views of all Black men. While many men did believe that women should subordinate themselves to men, others did not, like the two examples above.

The previously cited dissertations on Black women college graduates indicated their desire to continue to work when married, if possible. Inabeth Lindsay commented that her sister had to quit her job as a teacher once she got married because some school districts required that women teachers be single. There was a history of married women being discriminated against in the workplace. Nepotism laws were also instituted so a married couple could not work at the same institution. Lindsay stated she had always planned to work, and the year she stayed home after getting married was extremely boring. She said all the women did was have "bridge parties, and teas, club meetings and people were very limited in their concerns about social problems and what was going on in the community. I just thought it was a waste of my time."[56]

The belief that marriage trumped everything in a woman's life was evident in 1951, when in the yearbook of the Howard Dental School a comment was printed about the five women in the graduating class:

> Let us remember the ladies—diligently pursuing the title of DDS which sooner or later will take a secondary position to the title of MRS.[57]

From the antebellum era until the mid-60s, the end of this book, Black women were urged to obtain an education for the elevation of the race. Black parents relocated to communities that ensured their children had an education before Emancipation. The Black women, who were educated in the seminaries in the North at Oberlin prior to the Civil War, overwhelmingly went South to teach their people.[58] Black women in the North and New England had a seventy-five-year educational advantage over their Black sisters in the South. As noted repeatedly, public high schools didn't exist throughout the South for Black people until after World War II, except in cities. James Anderson noted that 90 percent of Black students attended private schools run by Black churches, colleges, and missionaries.[59]

While Black women in the South were trained to be teachers, the Black women who attended colleges outside the South and the two elite Black colleges of Fisk and Howard had more professional options. For example, the first Black woman to graduate from Wellesley College in 1887 became a physician in 1893, graduating from the Women's Medical School of New York. Charlotte Ray graduated from the Howard University Law School in 1872 and became the first Black woman law school graduate, the first woman admitted to the District of Columbia Bar, and the first woman to be admitted to practice before the DC Supreme Court. Several decades after Emancipation, these two Black women went into what was considered male careers. However, both women believed these professions were important for the race and took advantage of their opportunities.

Constance Baker Motley, who attended Fisk University for one year in 1942, noted her female classmates' wealth and the careers they pursued. She said several of the girl's fathers were doctors. The women came to Fisk because it was the college (like Howard) for upper-middle-class Blacks. Motely noted that many of these students were the second and third generation in their families to attend college. She recalled that at least five women in her class became doctors and one an attorney.[60]

The women of the NACW established this organization to work for Black women college students, primarily in HBCUs, to help them have high standards and develop leadership on their campuses. HBCUs were very conservative, and the independence and freedom that the NACW women received in their undergraduate institutions were at odds with what was expected on the residential campuses at HBCUs. Despite the years of efforts to impact the treatment and advancement of Black women, in the end, the organization appeared to have little impact. Opinions of the group were like the Blind Man and the Elephant story. In a conversation with Ruth Brett about the impact of NACW, she stated that the group's membership had great intentions, but the life experiences of the members were so removed from the realities of the women students in the South at most HBCUs that they were ineffective. She said they were idealogues who were overwhelmingly born, educated, and worked outside the South. They held degrees from elite colleges and graduate and professional degrees from prestigious institutions, were world-traveled, attended international conferences, and their children went to elite private schools. These out-of-touch views were reflected in some of the questions the Cuthbert's study asked the Black women college graduates. Hilda Davis, who was a Howard alum and a member of the group, stated when asked if she thought NACW had any significant impact on the education of the women students at HBCUs, she responded, "Oh yes, very much." She said the organization elevated the importance of the role of deans of women on these campuses. Jeanne Noble, also a Howard alumna, commented that being a dean of women was the highest administrative position a Black woman could aspire to at an HBCU (although Howard had a couple of women's deans in female-dominated fields, i.e., home economics and social work). Finally, Jean Fairfax commented that she never perceived the position of dean of women as a key administrative one. She said they were basically campus police officers hired to enforce social rules and keep women students out of the bushes with male students.[61]

To be fair, the members of the NACW were sincere and dedicated to helping to enhance and raise the academic standards of HBCUs and ensure that Black women students were exposed to a larger world than their overwhelmingly rural backgrounds. Hilda Davis noted that the women of NACW in Washington, DC, had a tutoring program for years to help prepare Black students to attend top colleges.

The dissertations that were done in the '40s and '50s on Black women college students and graduates also had little impact. They were rarely, if ever, mentioned in discussions of Black higher education in articles or conferences. Many Black women prior to the 1950s who came from white undergraduate colleges and universities to work at HBCUs left and never returned. However, these women worked on behalf of the race outside of HBCUs. Among them were Jean Fairfax who worked for the American Friends Service Committee, and the last twenty years of her professional career, worked for the NAACP Legal Defense Fund, combating patterns of discrimination in higher education. Ida Jackson returned to California as the first Black teacher in Oakland. Louise Thompson Patterson became an activist in the Communist Party. Marion Cuthbert worked for the National YWCA, and later, became the first Black faculty member at Brooklyn College.[62] Reviewing the early records of the women who were members of the sororities Alpha Kappa Alpha and Delta Sigma Theta demonstrates the type of lives and level of academic achievements these women had accomplished. By 1921, the women were doctors, dentists, lawyers, pharmacists, social workers, and in graduate school. Many of these women traveled the world and noted their trips to Europe. In an AKA report from 1927, one member reported she traveled abroad in Europe for ten weeks noting the countries she visited but stated she spent most of her time in France. The sorority members valued foreign travel and established a scholarship in 1926 for their members to study abroad. The award was given every other year. The first recipient was Ethel Harris Gubbs, director of math for the public schools in Washington, DC, who used the award to study mathematics at the University of Berlin. In subsequent years, other women went abroad, including Merze Tate who won the award in 1931 to attend Oxford University.

These were the women who organized to advise and shape Black women students. The social class distinctions were vast. While the organization of the deans of women in HBCUs that was started in 1929 by Lucy Diggs Slowe had a specific focus on women's leadership, independence, and autonomy, that was not the case at most HBCUs with rare exceptions. This book has discussed the rules and challenges those women students faced on many campuses. After World War II when more categories of work developed, it finally appeared that women would have more options. And by the mid-'60s, with the new civil rights laws, there was room for much optimism. In spite of the editorial for the special issue of *Ebony* magazine, there was no turning back for Black women. For Katheryn Lawson, who had taught at more than five HBCUs, having the opportunity to pursue her doctorate at the University of New Mexico changed her life. She received funding directly from the university, unlike the lucky few who received the previously discussed fellowships from the '20s–'40s. She and her husband now had options that transcended teaching at HBCUs. They were able to earn their graduate degrees and move into lucrative, high paying jobs as a couple. Black women read these articles of successful Black women and were inspired by the expanding opportunities for them.

Recent scholars have created a body of scholarship that has updated the Black male–centric history of the Black struggle in the nation. It was a collective effort and Black women and girls have paid a high price for the continuous commitment they made on behalf of the race. Marcia Synnott, as noted earlier, has written about the significant role of Black women as plaintiffs in key higher education cases. She wrote: "Black women have participated almost equally with black men in both the public sphere of civil rights activism and in higher education."[63] Likewise, Gary Ford Jr.'s book highlights the important, but often overlooked role of Constance Baker Motley. She was the only woman lawyer with the NAACP legal defense fund, argued fifty-seven cases in the Supreme Court, and played a key role in the desegregation of higher education institutions (University of Mississippi and the University of Georgia) as well as public-school cases. Ford wrote:

> To comprehend the anatomy of the marginalization of Constance Baker Motley in the historical narratives of the civil rights movement, one must first understand the larger history of the movement and the lack of credit given to many black women who led struggles to abolish slavery, enact anti-lynching laws, abolish poll taxes and white primaries, and gain women's suffrage, fair housing, and temperance. Long before the civil rights movement of the 1950s and 1960s, Sojourner Truth, Harriet Tubman, Anna Julia Cooper, Ida B. Wells-Barnett, Mary Church Terrell, Mary McLeod Bethune, and Dorothy I. Height were some of the black women who worked to eliminate racial discrimination and other racial inequalities. They served as role models both for black female actors who fought to eliminate Jim Crow during the civil rights movement and for contemporary black female actors.[64]

Race uplift was a collective effort. V. P. Franklin's recent study, *The Young Crusaders: The Untold Story of the Children and Teenagers Who Galvanized the Civil Rights Movement* indicated how many were children and teenagers. The first paragraph of this study states:

> It may surprise many readers to learn that the largest civil rights demonstration in United States history was not the August 1963 March on Washington,

but the system-wide school boycott in New York City on February 3, 1964, when over 360,000 elementary and secondary school students went on strike and thousands attended "freedom schools" opened throughout the city.[65]

The book cover portrays a group of Black girls protesting.

Black women started their quest for education with the abolitionist colleges and continued in a wide variety of colleges over the past century and a half. They experienced issues of racial discrimination in most of the white institutions. But some Black women noted encouragement and support by white faculty. Both Charlotte Hanley and Phyllis Wallace had supportive white male advisors. Both were economics majors in the 1940s; Hanley attended Barnard College and Wallace attended New York University. Hanley was originally a math major, and she was advised to switch to economics because it offered more lucrative employment options. Her advisor secured her a job to work as a researcher with the National Bureau for Economic Research. Several years later, she became the first Black person hired at the Federal Reserve Bank of Chicago as an economist. Wallace assumed she would return home to Baltimore after graduation to be a teacher since that was the norm for Black women. At NYU, she was an outstanding student and graduated Phi Beta Kappa. Noting her academic talent, her advisor encouraged her to continue to graduate school in economics and recommended Yale. She earned a master's and a PhD at Yale. At Yale, Wallace was denied the opportunity to be a teaching assistant because of her race and gender. She received funding from the Rosenwald Foundation. Like Hanley, Wallace also worked at the National Bureau for Economic Research and became an expert in international economics. Likewise, Inabeth Lindsay said when she was at Howard, one of her male professors encouraged her to consider social work and told her about a fellowship sponsored by the National Urban League to attend the now Columbia School of Social Work. So, there were no across the board racial and gender experiences among students.

As this study ends, the writings and arguments of W. E. B. Du Bois, a staunch supporter of Black women's rights, are instructive. He challenged the misogynist views of his brethren. He constantly wrote essays celebrating Black women's successes and condemning the racism and sexism they experience by white women as well as Black men. When white women denied Black women access to their colleges, he said that white women were far more racist than the men and characterized them as "unyielding in their racism."[66] As editor of the NAACP *The Crisis* magazine from 1910–34, he constantly highlighted the educational accomplishments of Black women by putting them on the cover of the magazine. From 1910–20, Du Bois discussed support for women's suffrage. With the erosion of Black men's rights and the push for suffrage by Black women leaders and activists, many Black men were alarmed and embraced conservative views of womanhood. The discussions reflected in *The Crisis* reflected the same sentiments of the special issue's editorial of *Ebony* in 1966.

In an address in 1912, at the white National Women's Suffrage Association, Du Bois condemned "Anglo-Saxon manhood," which conservative Black men had embraced. He also denounced the racism of white women who discriminated against Black women. On this topic, a 1914 editorial stated:

> The southern white women who form one of the most repressed and enslaved groups of modern civilized women will undoubtedly, at first, help willingly and zealously to disfranchise Negroes, cripple their schools and publicly insult them.[67]

Du Bois made it clear that racism and sexism were dual issues that Black women continued to face. In response to a special issue of *The Crisis* on women's suffrage, conservative Howard professor Kelly Miller protested the notion of women's suffrage.

Miller stated the readers should not be "misled" and assume Du Bois and the Black women who presented the case for women's suffrage represent most Black people. He said:

> Sex is the one fixed and unalterable separatrix of mankind. Women's sphere of activity falls mainly within while man's field of action lies largely without the domestic circle... Woman is physically weaker than man and is incapable of competing with him in the stern and strenuous activities of public and practical life... Suffrage is not a natural right, like life and liberty.[68]

Du Bois responded that Miller's views were "ancient" and informed him that "women were successful in practically every pursuit in which men are engaged." Du Bois made the logical argument years earlier that, "votes for women means votes for Black women," which obviously the entire race would benefit from. This should have been the reasoning of the people who wrote the *Ebony* editorial—which eluded them: that when more Black women are educated and hold well-paying employment, then there are more benefits to their families and the race.

Finally, in Du Bois's essay titled, "The Damnation of Women," he condemned the country for its treatment of Black women, but he gave his greatest criticism of Black men. The essay began by discussing women from his youth and his comment that "they existed for men and not for themselves." Du Bois described the oppression of women and said, the "future woman must have a life of work and economic independence. She must have knowledge. She must have the right to motherhood at her own direction." He chronicled the suffering and debasement of Black women during slavery and mentioned the things he was willing to forgive the white South for, but he said there was one thing he could never forgive:

> neither in this world nor the world to come: its wanton and continued and persistent insulting of the black womanhood which it sought to prostitute to its lust.[69]

He reminded the reader that "after the [Civil] war, the sacrifice of Negro women for freedom and uplift is one of the finest chapters in their history." He notes the many contributions they had made—but in a direct comment to Black men, he informed them that Black women had done far more than they had for the race:

> As I look about me today in this veiled world of mine, despite the noisier and more spectacular advance of my brothers, I instinctively feel and know that it is the five million women of my race who really count. Black women (and women whose grandmothers were black) are furnishing all our teachers: they are the main pillars of those social settlements, which are called churches; and they have with small doubt raised three-fourth of our church property.[70]

The experiences and impact of Black women and their higher education over the century and a half discussed have been impressive, but not without hardships and often condemnation. While the editorial in *Ebony* magazine advised Black women to step aside and allow Black men to take charge, the educational attainments of Black women have continued to exceed those of Black men. The late 1960s opened more opportunities for Black students with special admissions programs by private organizations and white institutions. Black women have taken advantage of these opportunities and exceed Black men in open admissions, non-selective, as well as highly selective, institutions. Currently, compared to Black men, Black women earn 64.1 percent of bachelor's degrees, 71.5 percent of master's degrees, and 65.9 percent of doctoral, medical, and dental degrees. African American women lead in enrollment at the most prestigious and highly selective institutions. As far back as 2006, a study noted this trend, and in a survey of twenty-six highly selective institutions (including the Ivy League, Stanford, Duke, Emory, the University of Chicago, Georgetown, etc.), Black women represented from 50.5–71 percent of the Black student population in all but three institutions—California Institute of Technology, Massachusetts Institute of Technology, and Notre Dame. Black women students exceed Black men students at top public institutions as well (UC–Berkeley, UCLA, Michigan, UNC–Chapel Hill). Their attendance at these institutions results in their acceptance into leading graduate and professional schools. Black women outnumber Black men in HBCUs as well (62%) and Spelman, the all-women's college, has the highest graduation rate of any HBCU (78%).[71]

Although Black women have surpassed Black men in all aspects of higher education, as noted from this study, for decades Black men were in the lead in terms of degrees and educational attainment. And, the 1966 *Ebony* editorial asked Black parents to educate sons at the expense of their daughters; Black men exceeded Black women in doctoral and professional degrees until that period. The ages of Black women with graduate and professional degrees are younger than Black men because it's only been in the past four decades (post 1960s) that they were able to reap the benefits of the civil rights movement. In 2014, there were 109,000 living African American men of all ages who had doctorates compared to 98,000 African American women. However, African American women under the age of forty have more doctorates than Black men—41,000 versus 18,000.

As noted, the mid and late 1960s opened greater higher educational opportunities for African Americans. Black women, especially those who were graduates of HBCUs, who were overwhelmingly schoolteachers and in other traditionally gender-based helping professions before, now had other options. When the report of Black women dominating the most elite institutions in the nation was released, as with the *Ebony* editorial of 1966 on the danger of Black women's educational attainments, there was an alarmist discussion of this data. An editorial in the *Journal of Blacks in Higher Education* commented:

> The fact that black women significantly outnumber black men at these institutions will have a spillover effect in graduate school, in professional positions, and in leadership posts in our society. The fact that far more black women than black men will achieve the credential of a diploma from these top schools means that far more women than black men will be admitted to the nation's best graduate and professional schools. In turn, far more black women than black men will go on to become lawyers, doctors and corporate leaders.[72]

There was no celebration but alarm at the educational attainment of Black women—especially since they tended to dominate in the most elite institutions in the country. The comments that these women would surpass Black men in leadership and prominent professional positions were not lost on the reader. The sentiment projected was that this is a serious problem. Throughout the quest for an education and a desire to "help the race," Black women were constantly reminded of the social consequences of achievements that were deemed too high for a woman. In one issue of the *Journal of Higher Education*—on the front page it posted:

STATS OF THE WEEK   Percentage of Black women married in 1970—54%
                    Percentage of Black women married in 2005—35%

Indeed, the educational gap between Black men and women does present issues in a patriarchal society for Black men and women. However, Black women have options for partnership—in terms of sexual orientation as well as interracial options. Despite this alarm, as the author told Jean Fairfax this study would end in the '60s, she commented that she was in the South in the '60s the weekend the Student Nonviolent Coordinating Committee was born. She observed that Black women college students were prominent in the leadership; moreover, she said, Black women were key in all aspects of racial justice activities, "in state legislatures and agencies, as leaders in black coalitions that were organized to assume justice for blacks in public higher education." Educated Black women were prominent as civil rights advocates, lawyers, and community women. Black women never stopped using their talents for the race and their community. Scholars have written about these women and their contributions. While the struggle to combat Jim Crow was prominent in the Black community activism, as Pauli Murray noted, Jane Crow remains the challenge for African American women.

As we reflect on over a century of Black women's quest, purposes, and experiences in higher education covered in this study, we must circle back to the importance of Lucy Diggs Slowe and the women faculty at Howard University. Slowe challenged and took on the paternalism and sexism of HBCUs. Through her brilliance, she established an organization that was dedicated to advancing the education and leadership of Black women students. A quote by Lucy Diggs Slowe reflected her core philosophy for Black women: that they "develop their talents to their highest extent." In addition to her work in emphasizing to the presidents of HBCUs that the deans and counselors of women should be trained in the field of student personnel but also have academic credentials with faculty status, she also prepared a group of women students at Howard to serve in these positions. She established a class at Howard to develop student leaders.[73] The senior Black women faculty at Howard with Merze Tate and others at the helm were unrelenting in their efforts to expose the gross inequities women faculty experienced in salary and rank. This was the case in all HBCUs; however, the fact that the Howard women had tenured positions and were some of the most distinguished Black women academics in the country, allowed them to express their grievances to the male administration. In addition, the Howard women's faculty was a sisterhood that resulted in their speaking not only for themselves but for others. These women were prominent and heads of national women's organizations, such as the National Council of Negro Women and the major sororities Alpha Kappa Alpha and Delta Sigma Theta, so their influences spanned far beyond Howard University. These were the voices of Black women faculty and students. And, as Merze Tate stated, Black women historically were expected to "saintly approach and accept silently and supinely an inferior status and salary and still carry the heaviest burdens." As this study has shown, by the mid-1960s, this view has been challenged.

Notes

Abbreviations

AKA—Alpha Kappa Alpha
AWS—Associated Women Students
GEB—General Education Board
HBCU—Historically Black College and University
NAACP—National Association for the Advancement of Colored People
NACW—National Association of College Women
NAWD—National Association of Deans of Women
NAWDACS—National Association of Women's Deans and Advisors of Women in Colored Schools
YWCA—Young Women's Christian Association

Introduction

1. *The Weekly Advocate* (January 7, 1837).
2. Woodson, *The Education of the Negro Prior to 1861*.
3. David Walker, *Appeal to the Coloured Citizens of the World, but in Particular, and Very Expressly, to Those of the United States of America, written in Boston, State of Massachusetts, September 28, 1829* (Boston: David Walker, 1830).
4. Ibid.
5. Baumgartner, *In Pursuit of Knowledge*.
6. Johnson, *The Negro College Graduate*.
7. See Greene, *Holders of Doctorates among American Negroes*.
8. Cuthbert, *Education and Marginality*, 99–100; Bolton, "The Problems of Negro College Women Graduates," 1–227; Noble, *The Negro Woman's College Education*.
9. Pauli Murray, *Song in a Weary Throat* (New York: Harper and Row, 1987).
10. Cooper, *Beyond Respectability*; Giddings and Morrow, *In Search of Sisterhood*; Hine, *Black Women in White*; Shaw, *What a Woman Ought to Be and to Do*; Evans,

Black Women in the Ivory Tower, 1850–1954; Collier-Thomas, *Jesus, Jobs, and Justice*; Neverdon-Morton, *Afro-American Women of the South and the Advancement of the Race, 1895–1925*.

11. Boyd, Fuentos, White, ed. *Scarlet and Black, Volume 2*; Walton, *Women at Indiana University*.

12. For more on this topic, see Perkins, "The Impact of the Cult of True Womanhood on the Education of Black Women," 17–28.

13. See Painter, *Sojourner Truth*, and Washington, *Sojourner Truth's America*.

14. *Plessy v. Ferguson, 163 U.S. 537* (1896).

15. Franklin, *From Slavery to Freedom*.

16. See for example Gaines, *Uplifting the Race*; Linda M. Perkins, "The National Association of College Women, 65–75; Higginbotham, *Righteous Discontent*; Ford, *Constance Baker Motley*.

17. See Hendricks, *Fannie Barrier Williams*; Ransby, *Eslanda*; Giddings, *Ida*; May and Cooper, *Visionary Black Feminist*; Rosenberg, *Jane Crow*; Cooper, *Beyond Respectability*.

18. Du Bois, "The Talented Tenth."

19. Higginbotham, *Righteous Discontent*.

20. For more on this topic see Perkins, "Merze Tate and the Gender Equity at Howard University," 516–51.

21. See Perkins, "Lucy Diggs Slowe," 89–104; Perkins, "The National Association of College Women," 65–75.

22. Perkins, "Merze Tate and the Gender Equity at Howard University," 516–51; Perkins, "The History of Black Women Graduate Students, 1921–1948," 53–67; Perkins, "For the Good of the Race," 80–103.

23. Solomon, *In the Company of Educated Women*.

24. Geiger, *American Higher Education since World War II*.

25. Jenkins, "Enrollment in Institutions of Higher Education of Negroes, 1953–54," 139–51.

26. Herbolt, "Never a Level Playing Field," 104–8.

27. Cuthbert, *Education and Marginality*.

28. Noble, *The Negro Woman's College Education*.

29. See Welter, "The Cult of True Womanhood," 151–74; Linda Perkins, "The Impact of the 'Cult of True Womanhood' on the Education of Black Women," 17–28.

30. Perkins, "Women's Education in the United States," 254–56.

31. Franklin, *Black Self-Determination*.

32. Bell, *Degrees of Equality*.

33. Anderson, *The Education of Blacks in the South*.

34. *The Negro Family: The Call for National Action* (Washington, DC: Office of Policy, Planning, and Research by the Department of Labor, 1965); "The Negro Woman: A Special Issue," *Ebony*, 21, no. 10 (August 1966): 112.

Chapter 1. Education for "Race Uplift"

1. Litwack, *North of Slavery*, 64.

2. See Campbell, *The Slave Catchers*; Franklin and Schweninger, *Runaway Slaves*.

3. "The Kidnapping Case: Narrative of the Seizure and Recovery of Solomon Northrup," *New York Times* (January 20, 1853); Solomon Northup, *Twelve Years a Slave*.
4. Quoted in Jordan, *White over Black*, 554.
5. Foote, *Black and White Manhattan*. Woodson, *The Education of the Negro Prior to 1861*, 27.
6. Wright, *The Negro in Pennsylvania*, 53.
7. Moss, *Schooling Citizens*, 1–3.
8. May, *Some Recollections of Our Antislavery Conflict,* 40.
9. Higginbotham, *Rightest Discontent*.
10. May, *Some Recollections,* 40.
11. Ibid.
12. Ibid.
13. May, *Some Recollections*, 72.
14. Moss, *Schooling Citizens*, 18.
15. Franklin, "In Pursuit of Freedom," 114.
16. Welter, "The Cult of True Womanhood," 151–74.
17. See Palmieri, *In Adamless Eden*; Nash, *Women's Education in the United States*; Chambers-Schiller, *Lee Virginia Liberty;* Perkins, "The Impact of the Cult of True Womanhood on the Education of Black Women"; Perkins, "Women's Education in the United States, 1780–1840, by Margaret Nash."
18. *The Rights of All* (New York, September 18, 1829): np.
19. Butcher, "The Evolution of Negro Women's Schools in the United States," 24.
20. Ibid.
21. *Freedom's Journal* (New York, March 23, 1827); *The Colored American* (New York, December 8, 1838).
22. *The Liberator* (Boston, December 3, 1831).
23. Ibid.
24. *Genius of Universal Emancipation* (March 1832): 1862–1863.
25. Quoted in *The Liberator* (November 17, 1832).
26. *The Liberator* (April 27, 1833).
27. Quoted in *Freedom's Journal* (August 10, 1827).
28. Perkins, "Black Women and Racial 'Uplift' Prior to Emancipation," 317–34.
29. Sherwood, *The Oblates' Hundred and One Years,* 5, 29, 34.
30. *Special report of the Commissioner of Education on the Improvement of Public Schools in the District of Columbia, 1871* (Washington, DC, 1871): 205–6.
31. Perkins, *Fanny Jackson Coppin and the Institute for Colored Youth*.
32. Moss, *Schooling Citizens* (online resource).
33. Quoted in Butcher, "The Evolution of Negro Women's Schools in the United States," 20.
34. Ibid.
35. Quoted in Wormley, "Myrtilla Miner," 451; Foner and Pacheco, *Three Who Dared,* 119.
36. Null, "Myrtilla Miner's 'School for Colored Girls,'" 254–68.
37. Quoted in biographical sketch, "Myrtilla Miner," in James, James, and Boyer, eds. in *Notable American Women*, 548.

38. Quoted in Sterling, *We Are Your Sisters,* 189–90, 193.
39. Quoted in Sterling, *We Are Your Sisters,* 190.
40. Ibid.
41. Quoted in Sterling, *We Are Your Sisters*, 201.
42. Ibid.
43. Ibid., 191, 203.
44. James, James, and Boyer, Biography Sketch in *Notable American Women,* 548.

Chapter 2. Abolitionist Colleges

1. American Baptist Free Mission Society, "American Baptist Free Mission Society Report on the New York Central College, McGrawville, NY," 1850.
2. New York Central College List of Students, compiled by Catherine M. Hanchett; *New York Central College—A Beacon on the Hill* (documentary film).
3. Institute for Colored Youth, the Officers and Students and the Annual Report.
4. Hanchett, "The Later Careers of Some African American Students from New York Central College."
5. Ibid.
6. For details on Mary Edmonia Lewis, see Buick, *Child of the Fire.*
7. For details on the Edmonsons and their attempt to escape slavery, see Ricks, *Escape on the Pearl.*
8. Quoted in Pacheco, *The Pearl,* 129–30.
9. Quoted in Mary Kay Ricks, "A Passage to Freedom: During Washington's era of rampant slave trading, two sisters embarked upon a remarkable journey and became a cause celebre for the Abolitionist Movement" in *Washington Post Magazine*, February 17, 2002, p. 20; Pacheco, *The Pearl,* 139.
10. Pacheco, 134–35.
11. Ibid., 135.
12. Ibid., 137.
13. Letter quoted in Fletcher, *A History of Oberlin College*, 1:170.
14. Ibid., 1:171.
15. Ibid., 1:210, 2:507.
16. Fletcher, *A History of Oberlin*, 1:249–50.
17. Baumann, *Constructing Black Education at Oberlin College,* 29.
18. There is a debate about which college was the first HBCU. Ashmun Institute in Oxford, Pennsylvania, was chartered in 1854 by a white Presbyterian minister, John Miller Dickey, for the education of Black ministers to evangelize in Africa and to provide religious leadership to Blacks in the United States. The institution's name was changed to Lincoln University in 1866. It remained all male until 1953. See Bond, *Education for Freedom.* The Institute for Colored Youth was founded by Quakers initially for the education of delinquent boys on a farm school outside of Philadelphia—the school was unsuccessful, and it closed in 1846. The Black community of Philadelphia requested that the Quaker founders move the school to Philadelphia and by 1849, the school opened in the Black community. In 1852, the Black community asked if the Quaker managers would include girls in the school and they agreed. The school became a renowned college

preparatory school and employed throughout the 19th century the most educated Black men and women of the era. Fanny Jackson Coppin, an Oberlin graduate, was a teacher and later principal from 1865–1902. The institution closed in that year and was moved to Cheyney, Pennsylvania to become a "Tuskegee" at Cheyney. While the institution had Quaker origins, it was a totally different institution in mission and focus. The strong classical curriculum was erased to mirror the industrial emphasis of Tuskegee Institute. The Quaker Board of Managers sold the school to the state of Pennsylvania in 1922 when it became a state normal school. For details on the history of the Institute for Colored Youth and its move from Philadelphia to Cheyney, Pennsylvania, see Perkins, *Fanny Jackson Coppin and the Institute for Colored Youth*, 307–30. Wilberforce College in Xenia, Ohio, was established in 1856 by the White Methodist Church for the primary and secondary education of the children of southern slaveholders (not unlike the mulatto students who attended interracial Oberlin College in Ohio). After the beginning of the Civil War, the students ceased attending. In 1863, the college was purchased by the African American Episcopal Church, a Black denomination. This coed institution offered both preparatory and collegiate liberal arts curriculum. See McGinnis, *A History and Interpretation of Wilberforce University*.

19. Henle and Merrill, "Antebellum Black Coeds at Oberlin College," 10.

20. Key Events in Black Higher Education in the *Journal of Black Higher Education Chronology of Major Landmarks in the Progress of African Americans in Higher Education*.

21. Conor Grant, "Revisiting Middlebury's Racial History" in *The Middlebury Campus*, March 19, 2014.

22. Lawson and Merrill, "The Antebellum Talented Thousandth," 143–44.

23. Fletcher, *A History of Oberlin*, 2: 50–78.

24. Ibid., 2: 524.

25. Quoted in Lawson and Merrill, *The Three Sarahs*.

26. *Bulletin of Oberlin College*, New Series 345, November 1834: 4

27. 1 Corinthians 14:34 "Let your women keep silence in the churches: for it is not permitted unto them to speak; but *they are commanded* to be under obedience, as also saith the law. 35 And if they will learn anything, let them ask their husbands at home: for it is a shame for women to speak in the church" (King James Version *Bible*).

28. Coppin, *Reminiscences of School Life and Hints on Teaching*, 17.

29. Coppin, *Reminiscences*, 17.

30. Flexner, *Century of Struggle*, 37.

31. *Catalogue of Oberlin College, 1860–1861*, 40.

32. Coppin, *Reminiscences*, 17.

33. Coppin, *Reminiscences*, 25.

34. Coppin, *Reminiscences*, 13, 17.

35. Coming and Hosford, "The Story of LLS: the First Women's Club in America," 10–13; Programs of the LLS, LSLSA Minutes, Executive, 1859–1874; *Oberlin Archives*, Oberlin College Library, Oberlin, Ohio.

36. See Painter, *Sojourner Truth*; Margaret Washington, *Sojourner Truth's America*.

37. Fletcher, *The History of Oberlin College*, 2: 845, 881.

38. Coppin, *Reminiscences*, 18.

39. *Lorain County News*, February 4, 1863.

40. *Lorain County News,* February 10, 1864.
41. Fletcher, *A History of Oberlin,* 2:720.
42. Coppin, *Reminiscences,* 19.
43. Fletcher, "Against the Consensus," 206.
44. Fletcher, "Against the Consensus," 216.
45. Coppin, *Reminiscences,* 19.
46. *Oberlinana,* Oberlin College, 1883.
47. *National Anti-Slavery Standard,* July 9, 1864.

48. Ibid. Jackson's words basically repeated what was often heard at Oberlin: "the *mind* and the *heart,* not *color,* makes the man and the woman too. We hold that neither men or women are much better or much the worse for their *skin.* Our great business here is to educate the mind and the heart, and should deem ourselves to have small cause to be proud of our success if we should fail to eradicate, in no long time, the notion that nature had made any such difference for either to associate with the other as beings of common origin and a common nature. We believe in treating men according to their intrinsic merits—not according to distinctions over which they can have no control. If you are a young gentleman of color, you may expect to be treated here according to your real merit; and if white, you need not expect to fare better than this." Professor Henry Cowles quoted in Robert Fletcher's *A History of Oberlin,* 2: 526.

49. Quoted in Sterling, *We Are Your Sisters.*

50. Norris was one of the few members of the Class of 1865 who did not respond by appearance or by letter of regret to the 25th class reunion. (See *Reunion of the Class of 1865,* Oberlin College, Program, 11). Henle and Merrill, "Antebellum Black Coeds at Oberlin College," 9.

51. Quoted in the *Oberlin Evangelist* (September 1, 1862), 149.
52. Quoted in Quarles, *Black Abolitionist,* 113–14; Fletcher, "Against the Consensus," 224.
53. Coppin, *Reminiscences,* 15.
54. Fletcher, "Against the Consensus," 224.

55. In 1946, Fisk University appointed its first Black president, Charles S. Johnson. See Richardson, *A History of Fisk University.*

56. Woodson, *The Education of the Negro Prior to 1861,* 276.
57. Du Bois, *The College-Bred Negro.*

58. Wilson, "The Witness to Impartial Love: John G. Fee and the Founding of Berea College," in *Berea College: An Illustrated History,* 9–31.

59. Ibid.
60. Rogers, *Birth of Berea College,* 18.
61. Quoted in Wilson, *Berea College: An Illustrated History,* 12.
62. Nelson, "Experiment in Interracial Education at Berea College," 13–27.
63. Ibid., 21.

64. Sara G. Stanley and Edmonia Highgate, Norfolk, to William Woodbury, July 21, 1864; Sallie Doffing, Norfolk, to William Woodbury, August 29, 1864; Clara Duncan, Norfolk, to William Woodbury, August 29, 1864; Sara G. Stanley, Norfolk, to George Whipple, October 6, 1864, *American Missionary Association Papers,* Amistad Research Center, New Orleans, Louisiana. For more details regarding Black women teachers with the AMA see, Linda M. Perkins, "The Black Female American Missionary Association

Teacher in the South, 1861–1870" in Crow and Wadelington, eds., *Black Americans in North Carolina and the South* (1984), 122–36.

65. Rogers, *Birth of a Berea College,* 107.
66. Quoted in Rogers, *Birth of a Berea College,* 111.
67. Quoted in Rogers, 161.
68. Ibid., 119.
69. Quoted in Wilson, *Berea College,* 18.
70. Ibid., 27.
71. Marion B. Lucas, "Berea College in the 1870s and the 1880s: Student Life at a Racially Integrated Kentucky College" in *The Register of the Kentucky Historical Society,* 98, no. 1 (Winter 2000), 2.
72. Richard Sears, *Roster of Black Students at Berea College.*
73. Lucas, 7.
74. Lucas, 9.
75. Lucas, 22.

Chapter 3. College-Bred Black Women at Predominantly White Institutions in the Post–Civil War Era

1. Sidhu, "The Andersons of Shoreham."
2. Perkins, "The National Association of College Women," 65–75.
3. See *Annual Reports of the Normal College of the City of New York,* 1874–1882. Hunter College Archives.
4. *Registrar Record Book,* Hunter College Archives.
5. Ibid.
6. Solomon, *In the Company of Educated Women,* 142.
7. Grunfeld, "Purpose and Ambiguity," 216.
8. *16th Annual Report, 1886,* 40, Hunter College Archives.
9. Ibid., 219.
10. Murray, *Song in a Weary Throat,* 66.
11. Ibid., 67.
12. Ibid., 69.
13. Ibid., 69. Pauli Murray was an outlier when compared to the other educated Black women of her generation. She was a strong advocate for her race, but she was also a strong feminist and was one of the founding members of the National Organization for Women. She was active in cases for the socialist Workers Defense League. She was not a club woman or member of a sorority. Unlike the women discussed in this volume who focused on decorum and appearances, Murray dealt with gender and sexual identity issues and always wore pants, rarely skirts or dresses, and often passed and disguised herself as a boy and/or a man. She and a woman friend dressed in boy scout suits and hitchhiked on a freight train in the 1920s. Murray wore her hair short and was very small without noticeable female breasts and portrayed herself as male. And, she used men's bathrooms. For more on Murray's gender identity issues see the chapter "I Would Gladly Change My Sex" in Rosenberg, *Jane Crow,* 115–40.
14. Du Bois, *The College Bred Negro,* 34.

15. Ibid.

16. Ibid., 35.

17. Carey and Walker, "Profiles in Courage," 106–31.

18. Anderson, *The Education of Blacks in the South*, 189.

19. Cromwell, *The Other Brahmins,* 139.

20. Gatewood, *Aristocrats of Color,* 247.

21. *The Splendid Record of Wellesley's Negro Alumnae* (Records of the Dean of the College: Wellesley College Archives, 1963).

22. Harriett A. Rice, "On the Mountain Top," *Wellesley Magazine* (June 1943), 298.

23. Biographical Records of Harriett A. Rice Folder, Alumnae Association Records, Wellesley College Archives (Wellesley, MA, n.d.); McLeod, *Daughter of the Empire State.*

24. McLeod, *Daughter of the Empire State,* 1.

25. Rudd, Jean, with Lionel Bolin, "Transcript of Interview with the Honorable Jane M. Bolin," *Jane Bolin Papers*, Schomburg Center for Research on Black Culture, New York Public Library Archives.

26. Jane Bolin Offutt, "Wellesley in My Life," 92.

27. Ibid., 92.

28. Ibid.

29. Ibid.

30. Du Bois, *The College-Bred Negro,* 264.

31. Henry Parsons Dowse, *Radcliffe College* (Boston: H. B. Humphrey, 1913).

32. Alberta Scott Biographical Data Sheet, Radcliffe College Collection of Biographical Data on African American Students, Schlesinger Library, Radcliffe College, Cambridge, MA., pg. 1, "Alberta V. Scott," *Boston Globe*, June 23, 1898 (1875–1902); "Alberta V. Scott," *Bost Guardian*, September 2, 1902.

33. "Interview of Margaret McCane by Her Daughter on January 1, 1981," Margaret McCane Papers, Box 1, Folder 4, Schlesinger Library, Radcliffe College, Cambridge, MA.

34. Ibid.

35. Mary Gibson Huntley, "Radcliffe in My Life," Mary Gibson Huntley Papers, Box 4, Folder 45 (Personal Papers), Schlesinger Library, Radcliffe College, Cambridge, MA.

36. Charlotte Leverett Smith Brown Biographical Data Folder, Radcliffe College Collection of Biographical Data on African American Students, Radcliffe College Archives, Schlesinger Library, Cambridge, MA, p. 29, n.d.; Huntley, *"Radcliffe in My Life,"* Mary Gibson Huntley Papers, Box 4, Folder 45 (Personal Papers ed), Schlesinger Library, Radcliffe College, Cambridge, MA.

37. Margaret P. McCane to Ellen Henle, January 9, 1982, Margaret P. McCane Papers, Folder 5, Schlesinger Library, Radcliffe College, Cambridge, MA.

38. John F. Moors, Boston, Massachusetts to Ada L. Comstock, President of Radcliffe College, Ada Louise Comstock Records of the President, Radcliffe College, 1923–1943, Folder 10, (June 9, 1925). Ada Louise Comstock Record of the Office of the President, *Radcliffe College*, 1923–1943, Folder 10.

39. Ibid.

40. Ibid.

41. Ibid.

42. Ibid.

43. Ellen McKenzie Lawson, "Early Black Students at Radcliffe: The First Twenty-Five Years (1898–1933)" in author's possession, n.d.

44. "Discussion in Re: Carrie Lee," Partial Transcript of NAACP Board Meeting, n.d., Smith College Archives, Smith College, Northampton, MA.

45. W. E. B. Du Bois, "A College Girl," *The Crisis* 8 (1913), 293.

46. Moorfield Storey, Boston, Massachusetts, to Reverend Marion LeRoy Burton, Smith College, October 14, 1913, Carrie Lee Folder, Individuals 1917, Box 1789, Smith College Archives, Smith College, Northampton, MA.

47. Biographical Sheet, Faculty Records, Bo–Br, Box 42, Ruth Bowles Folder, Smith College Archives, Smith College, Northampton, MA.

48. Mary White Ovington, Brooklyn, New York, to Joel Spingarn, October 23, 1913, Carrie Lee Folder, Individuals 1917, Box 1789, Smith College Archives, Smith College, Northampton, MA.

49. White, *A Man Called White,* 336.

50. Ibid., 337.

51. Roster of Black Undergraduates Who Attended Smith College, 1900–1974, Black Students Folder, Admissions Office Records, Smith College Archives, Smith College, Northampton, MA.

52. Jefferson Church, Springfield, Massachusetts, to Mary Lyon, November 17, 1845, Mary Lyon Collection, Series A, Sub-Series 2, Mount Holyoke Archives, South Hadley, MA.

53. In 1949, a journalist from the Black *Ebony* magazine inquired regarding when the first Black women attended the college and how many were currently enrolled. The person who responded noted that Mt. Holyoke started keeping records of students by race in 1883 and hence there may have been Black students prior to that time. She noted the college at that time had twenty-four Black alumnae and five Black women were currently enrolled from the Bronx, New York; Washington, DC; Atlanta, Georgia; Brooklyn, New York; and Roselle, New Jersey. Doris Deskin, assistant director of the New Bureau, Mount Holyoke College, August 1, 1949, to Elisa C. Hawkins, Chicago, Illinois, Afro-American Students/Alumnae File, Folder 1, Mt. Holyoke College Archives.

54. "Course records for History 265," paper by Martha Ralston Perkins, Archives and Special Collection, Mount Holyoke College, South Hadley, MA.

55. Alumnae Biographical File for Hortense Parker, Class of 1883, Archives and Special Collections, Mount Holyoke College, South Hadley, MA.

56. Helen Calder, "Dear Mamma, November 14, 1894," Helen Calder Papers, Archives and Special Collections, Mount Holyoke College, South Hadley, MA.

57. Florence Purington, Dean, Mount Holyoke College, October 11, 1913, to Ada Comstock, Carrie Lee Folder, Individuals 1917, Box 1789, Smith College Archives, Smith College, Northampton, MA.

58. *Black Women Oral History Project,* "Interview with Frances H. Williams," October 31, 1977; "Interview with Frances Williams," October 9, 1991; "Frances Williams, Class of 1919, Alumnae File," Archives and Special Collections, Mount Holyoke College, South Hadley, MA; "Frances Williams," *Transcript-Telegram* (Massachusetts), February 2, 1983, 26.

59. "Alumnae files of Alice Stubb, 1926 et al.," Archives and Special Collections, Mount Holyoke College, South Hadley, MA.

60. Guy-Sheftall and Stewart, *Spelman,* 47.

61. "Black and White Americans," Course Records for History 265, Fall 1973, Folder 1, History Department, Background Materials, Archives and Special Collections, Mount Holyoke College, South Hadley, MA.

62. Ibid.

63. Quoted in Dean Karen Tidmarsh, Bryn Mawr College, "History of the Status of Minority Groups in the Bryn Mawr Student Body," p. 1, Collection 9JG, Bryn Mawr College Archives, Bryn Mawr College, Bryn Mawr, PA.

64. Horowitz, *The Power and Passion of M. Carey Thomas.*

65. Du Bois, *The College-Bred Negro,* 36.

66. M. Carey Thomas, Bryn Mawr College, to Georgiana R. Simpson, Washington, DC. May 2, 1906. M. Carey Thomas Papers, letter book 34, p. 320; Bryn Mawr College Archives, Bryn Mawr College, Bryn Mawr, PA.

67. M. Carey Thomas address to 1916 College Opening; reprinted in *The College News,* Bryn Mawr, October 11, 1916: 1.

68. Miss Grace Hutchins to Marion Edward Park, January 3, 1926, in Marion Edward Park Letters, Office Files, 1922–42, Racial Discrimination Folder, Box 24, Bryn Mawr Archives, Bryn Mawr College, Bryn Mawr, PA.

69. Marion Edwards Park to Grace Hutchins, January 8, 1926, in Park Letters.

70. Horowitz, *The Power and Passion of M. Carey Thomas,* 444.

71. M.Carey Thomas, Bryn Mawr to Virginia Gildersleeves, Barnard College, New York City, December 12, 1930, Gildersleeves Papers, Barnard College Archives, Barnard College, New York, New York; Virginia Gildersleeves, Barnard College to M. Carey Thomas, December 15, 1930, Gildersleeves Papers.

72. Marion Edward Park, Bryn Mawr, PA, to Mrs. Paul H. Douglas, Northampton, MA, April 27, 1927, Marion Edwards Park Papers (1922–42), Box 29.

73. Durr, *Outside the Magic Circle,* 56.

74. Durr, *Outside the Magic Circle.*

75. Johnson, *Southern Women at the Seven Sister Colleges.*

76. Ibid., 84.

77. Ibid., 90.

78. Minutes of Five College Conference, Mount Holyoke College, October 30–31, 1936, in *Records of the President's Office,* 1DB, 1899–1966 Folder, Conference of Five Colleges: Minutes, 1916–40, Wellesley College Archives, Wellesley College. Wellesley, MA, 1.

79. "Number of Students in the Entering Class," Admissions Committee Minute Folder, Box 1, McBride Papers, Bryn Mawr College, Bryn Mawr, PA.

80. Dean Jane Louis Mesick, Simmons College, Boston, MA, October 6, 1936, to President Marion Edwards Park, Bryn Mawr College; Marion Edwards Park Office Files, Racial Discrimination file, Box 24.

81. President Marion Edward Park, Bryn Mawr College to J. L. Mesick, October 7, 1936, Park Office Files.

82. Minutes of Five College Conference (October 30–31, 1936), 1–2.

83. Minutes of the Five College Conference (October 30–31, 1936), 2.
84. Minutes of the Five College Conference (October 30–31, 1936), 2.
85. Minutes of the Five College Conference (October 29–30, 1937), 3.
86. Newspaper clipping, 1897, in Anita Florence Hemmings Folder, Vassar College Archives, Vassar College, Poughkeepsie, NY.
87. Quoted in 1897 newspaper clipping, "Negress at Vassar" in Anita Florence Hemmings Folder.
88. Various newspaper clippings of the Hemmings affair, in Anita Florence Hemmings Folder, 1897. Vassar College Archives.
89. W. E. B. Du Bois to Dr. Henry MacCracken, May 15, 1930, in *Presidential Papers* (May 1930), Vassar College Archives, Vassar College, Poughkeepsie, NY.
90. W. E. B. Du Bois, "Postscript," *The Crisis;* No Author, "474 Students Enrolling in 1953, Win $197,000," *Opportunity News,* 1953 (August 1932), 266.
91. Christmas, "A Historical Overview," 4–5.
92. The Daisy Chain was a prestigious Vassar commencement activity dating back to 1884. Vassar students were selected in their sophomore year based on leadership and willingness to assist seniors with commencement activities. Those chosen carried chains made of daisies.
93. Beatrix McCleary, "Negro Student at Vassar," *Vassar Alumnae Magazine* (1946), 16.
94. "Du Bois Suggests that Vassar have 100 Negro Students." *Vassar Miscellany News* (April 4, 1942), 1.
95. Christmas, "A Historical Overview," 3.
96. Hurston, *Dust Tracks on the Road,* 169.
97. Hurston, *Dust Tracks on the Road,* 170.
98. Quoted in *Different Voices: The Experiences of Women of Color at Barnard* (New York: HEOP Office of Barnard College, 1996), 12.
99. Interview with Jean Blackwell Hutson with Linda M. Perkins, June 5, 1997. New York City.
100. Virginia Gildersleeves, Barnard College, to the Reverend James H. Robinson, n.d. reprinted in the *Barnard Bulletin* (March 1, 1943), 1.
101. Editorial, "Where Do We Go from Here?" in *Barnard Bulletin* (March 1, 1943), 2.
102. Height, *Open Wide the Freedom Gates,* 31.
103. Ibid., 32.
104. Statement written by Charlotte Hanley Scott to Carolina Niecy in Barnard College Archives, African American Student Folder, Barnard College, New York.
105. Telephone interview with Charlotte Hanley Scott with Linda M. Perkins, June 9, 1997.
106. Francis L. Monroe King to Regina Elstone, November 26, 1973, in the History Department.
107. Andree L. Abecassis, "Black at Barnard: A Survey of Policy and Events," *Barnard Alumnae Journal* (Spring 1969), 4.
108. Janet Novas, "Black Women in Science from Mount Holyoke: A Biographical Sketch of Two Mount Holyoke Alumnae: Dr. Barbara Pierce '43 and Dr. Jean E. Armstrong '48" paper written for History 381, Mount Holyoke College, History Department

Records, Series D, Course Records, Papers for History 381 (Spring 1988) Mount Holyoke College Archives, Mount Holyoke College, South Hadley, MA.

109. Transcribed alumna interview with Felice Schwartz, Smith College Archives.

110. National Scholarship Service and Fund for Negro Students—Opportunity News, "More Success Stories among Year's Top Award Winners" (New York, NY, 1951).

111. NSSFNS—Opportunity News, "More Success Stories among Year's Top Awards Winners" (New York, NY: NSSFNS 1952).

112. Jordan and Gordon-Reed, *Vernon Can Read!*.

113. NSSFNS—Opportunity News, "474 Students Enrolling in 1953 Win $197,000" (New York, NY: NSSFNS 1953).

114. "Personal Interview, Felice Schwartz," Sophia Smith Collection, Smith College Special Collection, Smith College, Northampton, MA (1971).

Chapter 4. Major Public Universities and Black Women in the Heartland

1. Bordin, *Women at Michigan.*

2. Ibid.

3. Dykes Jr., De Witt S., "Ida Gray Nelson Rollins (1867–1953)" in *Notable Black American Women,* Smith, ed., 496–97.

4. Bordin, *Women at Michigan,* 38.

5. Dykes Jr., De Witt S., "Ida Gray Nelson Rollins (1867–1953)" in *Notable Black American Women,* Smith, ed., 496–97.

6. Bordin, *Women at Michigan.*

7. Attaway and Barritt, *Women's Voices,* 1.

8. Ibid., 25.

9. Ibid.

10. Ibid., 26.

11. Ibid., 28.

12. Ibid., 29.

13. For more information on Blacks educated in the North who went South to teach see Linda M. Perkins, "The Black Female American Missionary Association Teacher in the South, 1861–1870," in *Black Americans in North Carolina and the South,* Crow and Hatley, eds., 122–36.

14. Painter, *Exodusters.*

15. Breaux, "We Must Fight Race Prejudice Even More Vigorously in the North."

16. Larry M. Peace, "Colored Students and Graduates of the University of Kansas" in Du Bois, *The College-Bred Negro,* 36.

17. Breaux, "We Must Fight Race Prejudice," 87.

18. *The Crisis* annually reported the institutions and accomplishments of Black students in both HBCUs and predominantly white colleges; among the latter were Cornell University, Columbia University, University of Minnesota, Oberlin College, Des Moines College, University of Kansas, University of Illinois, University of Chicago, University

of Cincinnati, Kansas State, Western Reserve. See *The Crisis* issues: July 1913, 6(3), 116; July 1914, 8(3), 133–35; July 1915, 10(3), 141.

19. Ibid., 40.

20. Peace, "Colored Students and Graduates of the University of Kansas," 39.

21. Lawrence, Kansas, *Topeka Plaindealer* (May 30, 1913), quoted in Breaux, "We Must Fight Race Prejudice," 250.

22. Parker, *Alpha Kappa Alpha through the Years 1908–1988*, 118.

23. "Delta Chapter, Alpha Kappa Alpha, University of Kansas" in the *Ivy Leaf*, (December 1921), 1(1), 20.

24. Breaux, "We Must Fight Race Prejudice," 3.

25. Breaux, "We Must Fight Race Prejudice," 244.

26. Ibid., 234–35.

27. Giddings, *In Search of Sisterhood*.

28. See the personal statements that Black women college students and graduates sent to Du Bois that are published in his *The College Bred Negro* (1900), 54–55.

29. See Wolters, "The New Negro on Campus."

30. Even liberal Oberlin by the end of the nineteenth century had become more conservative and discriminatory towards Black students and barred them from memberships. See Bigglestone, "Oberlin College and the Negro Student, 1865–1940," 198–219; Waite, *Permission to Remain Among Us*.

31. McCusker, "The Forgotten Years of America's Civil Rights Movement," 22–23.

32. Ibid.

33. Ibid., 31.

34. Ibid., 36.

35. Sartorius, *Deans of Women and the Feminist Movement*, 125–26.

36. Hill and Hill, ed., *Invisible Hawkeyes*, 24–25.

37. The NAACP segregation cases of Donald Murray against the University of Maryland's Law School in 1935 and the Supreme Court Lloyd Gaines against the University of Missouri Law School in 1938 moved to dismantle segregated professional schools. Murray v. Pearson, 169 Md. 478, 182A.590(1936) and Missouri ex rel. Gaines v. Canada, 305 US 377 (1938).

38. On this topic, see Verbrugge, *Active Bodies*.

39. Breaux, "We Must Fight Race Prejudice Even More Vigorously in the North."

40. *Ivy Leaf*, (May 1924), 3(1), 19; (1925), 4(1), 18; (September 1930) 8(3), 6.

41. *Ivy Leaf*, (December 1930) l (8), no. 4, 11.

42. Ibid.

43. Inez Patterson, *Temple University Hall of Fame,* http://owlsports.com/hof.aspx?hof=249.

44. Ibid.

45. Jenkins, "The Negro Student at the University of Iowa."

46. Ibid., 19.

47. *Ivy Leaf Magazine*, May 1924, 3(1); *Ivy Leaf Magazine*, 1925, 4(1); *Ivy Leaf Magazine*, September 1930, 8(3); *Ivy Leaf Magazine*, December 1930, 8(4).

Chapter 5. Black Women and Historically Black Colleges

1. For information on Black women who moved south to teach see: Linda M. Perkins, "The Black Female American Missionary Association Teacher in the South, 1861–1870," in *Black Americans in North Carolina and the South*, eds. Crow and Hatley, 122–36.

2. Mack, *Representing the Race*, 4.

3. Hylton, *Virginia Union University*, 37.

4. Ibid., 47.

5. Butcher, "The Evolution of Negro Women's Schools in the United States."

6. Ibid.

7. O'Brien, "Lois Irwin, Barber College and Christian Altruism in Alabama, 1926–1927," 322–38.

8. Jenkins, "The Black Land-Grant College in their Formative Years," 63–72.

9. McCluskey, *A Forgotten Sisterhood*.

10. Ibid.

11. Ibid., 83.

12. Ibid.

13. Talbert, *The Sons of Allen*, 267.

14. Bond, *Education for Freedom*.

15. Jones, *A Candle in the Dark*.

16. Anderson, *The Education of Blacks in the South, 1860–1935*.

17. Jenkins, "The Black Land-Grant College in their Formative Years," 69.

18. Wolters, *The New Negro on Campus*, 10.

19. Dill and Du Bois, *The College Bred Negro American*.

20. Perkins, *Fanny Jackson Coppin and the Institute for Colored Youth, 1865–1902*.

21. Logan, *Howard University*.

22. Frankie V. Adams Oral History in the *Black Women Oral History Project*, Schlesinger Library, Radcliffe College (April 20 and 28, 1977), 2–3.

23. Linda M. Perkins, Dr. Gladys Forde Interview, October 23, 2010, Houston, Texas.

24. Ibid.

25. Ibid.

26. Linda M. Perkins, Dr. Mildred Barksdale Interview, March 5, 1994, Urbana, Illinois.

27. Anderson, *The Education of Blacks in the South, 1860–1935*.

28. Black Women Oral History Project, Interview with Frances Mary Albrier: Women in Politics Oral History Project (1977–78).

29. Ibid.

30. Linda M. Perkins, Interview with Dr. Thelma Bando, November 4, 1986. Baltimore, Maryland.

31. Logan, *Howard University*, 36–38.

32. Ibid., 98–99.

33. Ibid., 104.

34. Ibid.

35. Ibid.

36. Ibid., 170.

Chapter 6. The Emergence of the Deans of Women at HBCUs

1. The Board of Trustees promoted Slowe to full professor the following year in 1923. However, she didn't receive an increase of her $3500 salary. Miller and Pruitt-Logan, *Faithful to the Task at Hand*, 116.

2. Raymond Wolters, *The New Negro on Campus,* 17.

3. Ibid., 71–72.

4. Ibid., 115.

5. Quoted in *The New Negro on Campus*, 72.

6. Miller and Pruitt-Logan, *Faithful to the Task at Hand*, 87–93.

7. Solomon, *In the Company of Educated Women.*

8. Sartorius, *Deans of Women and the Feminist Movement,* 24.

9. Lucy Diggs Slowe to Juanita Saddler, Howard University, November 16, 1933, *Lucy Diggs Slowe Papers*, Moorland Spingarn Research Library, Howard University, Washington, DC.

10. Sartorius, "A Coeducational Pathway to Political and Economic Citizenship," 161–83.

11. Perkins, Interview with Thelma Bando.

12. Ibid.

13. Ibid.

14. Slowe, "The Dormitory—A Cultural Influence," 11–14.

15. Linda M. Perkins, Interview with Thelma Bando, November 4, 1986. Baltimore, Maryland.

16. Ibid.; Linda Perkins, Interview with Hilda Davis, Newark, Delaware, June 15, 1987. This belief was also the expectation of nineteenth century white women as well. See Barbara Welter's "The Cult of True Womanhood."

17. Antler, *Lucy Sprague Mitchell.*

18. Wolters, "The New Negro."

19. Interview with Thelma Bando.

20. For example, see Joyce Antler's biography of Lucy Sprague Mitchell, one of the earliest deans of women. Antler, *Lucy Sprague Mitchell.*

21. Quoted in Miller and Pruitt-Logan, *Faithful to the Task at Hand,* 134.

22. Quoted in *Faithful to the Task at Hand*, 123–24.

23. *Faithful to the Task at Hand*, 142.

24. Higginbotham, *Righteous Discontent,* chapter seven.

25. Ibid. and Collier-Thomas, *Jesus, Jobs, and Justice.*

26. Linda Perkins, Interview with Hilda Davis, Newark, Delaware, June 15, 1987.

27. Proceedings of the Conference called by the College Alumnae Club of Washington, DC (1923), unpublished document in Lucy Diggs Slowe Papers, Moorland Spingarn Collection, Howard University.

28. Ibid.

29. Ibid.

30. Ibid.

31. Ibid.

32. Ibid.

33. Report of the Committee on Standards, *Journal of the National Association of College Women* (1924), 43–48.

34. Proceedings of the Conference called by the College Alumnae Club of Washington, DC (1923).

35. Lucy Diggs Slowe, "The Education of Negro Women and Girls" speech given at Teachers College, Columbia University, March 11, 1931, reprinted in the Memorial Education of the *Journal of National Association of College Women by the College Alumnae Club of Washington,* p. 14.

36. Ibid.

37. Perkins, ed., "The Black Female Professorate at Howard University, 1926–1988."

38. Slowe, "Higher Education of Negro Woman."

39. Frazier, E. Franklin. "A note on Negro education," *Opportunity* (1924) 2, 75–77.

40. Lucy Diggs Slowe, "The Education of Negro Women and Girls" speech given at Teachers College, Columbia University, March 11, 1931, reprinted in the Memorial Education of the *Journal of National Association of College Women by the College Alumnae Club of Washington,* p. 14.

41. Minutes of the Executive Committee Meeting of the Fifth Annual Convention of the National Association of College Women, April 13 and 14, 1928, Atlantic City, New Jersey, in Lucy Diggs Slowe Papers.

42. Annie Bailey Cook, Harrisburg, Virginia, to Beulah Clark Van Wagenen, Hampton Institute, Hampton, Virginia, November 15, 1936, in Lucy Diggs Slowe Papers.

43. Quoted in Miller and Pruitt, *Faithful to the Task at Hand,* 97.

44. Ibid., 99.

45. Thelma Mitchell Rambo, Dean of Women, Fisk University, Nashville, Tennessee, Letter to President Thomas E. Jones, Fisk University, November 6, 1934.

46. President Thomas Jones, Letter to Mrs. Thelma Mitchell Rambo, Dean of Women, Fisk University, November 8, 1936.

47. Derricotte, "Schools I Have Seen."

48. Sartorius, *Deans of Women and the Feminist Movement,* 25.

49. Ibid., 4–5.

50. Ibid., 124.

51. Antler, *Lucy Sprague Mitchell.*

52. Sartorius, *Deans of Women and the Feminist Movement,* 26.

53. Ibid., 39.

54. Ibid., 122–23.

55. Ibid., 125.

56. This conclusion was based on the discussion of Black women deans of women who recalled exclusion from various conferences because of locations.

57. "Oral History of Ida Louise Jackson: Overcoming Barriers in Education," interviewed 1984–85 (Oral History, University of California Black Alumni Series, The Bancroft Library, University of California–Berkeley), 19.

58. Ibid.

59. Ibid.

60. "Oral History of Ida Louise Jackson: Overcoming Barriers in Education," interviewed 1984–85 (Oral History, University of California Black Alumni Series, The Bancroft Library, University of California–Berkeley).

61. Lucy Diggs Slowe, "Attachment in Lucy Diggs Slowe, Letter to Miss Tossie P. F. Whiting, Dean of Women," January 27, 1931, Virginia State College.

62. Attachment in Lucy Diggs Slowe, Letter to Miss Tossie P. F. Whiting, Dean of Women, Virginia State College, January 27, 1931. Lucy Diggs Slowe Papers.

63. Fisk along with all of the other HBCUs founded by the American Missionary Association hired highly educated women trained in student personnel. Many of these women worked at multiple campuses—Talladega, Fisk, Dillard.

64. Dean Lucy Diggs Slowe, Miss Juanita J. Saddler, Dean of Women, Fisk University, Nashville, Tennessee, November 16, 1933. Lucy Diggs Slowe Papers.

65. Mayme U. Foster, Dean of Women, Fisk University, Nashville, Tennessee, to Dean Lucy D. Slowe, Howard University, Washington, DC, February 17, 1937, Slowe Papers, Moorland-Spingarn Research Center, Howard University, Washington, DC.

66. The Women of the Junior and Senior Classes residing in Jubilee, Letter to Fisk University Executive Committee, March 19, 1938.

67. Mayme U. Foster and A. A. Taylor, 1938, Thomas Jessie Jones Papers, Fisk University Archives, Nashville, TN.

68. Ibid., 47.

69. NAWDAC, *Minutes of the Conference of the National Association of Women's Deans and Advisors of Colored Women,* Lucy Diggs Slowe Papers, Moorland-Spingarn Research Center, Howard University (1930).

70. Ibid.

71. NAWDAC, *Minutes of the Conference of the National Association of Women's Deans and Advisors of Colored Women,* Lucy Diggs Slowe Papers, Moorland-Spingarn Research Center, Howard University (1930).

72. Colleges that had representatives were Talladega, Bishop, Morgan, Fisk, Tennessee State, Knoxville, St. Augustine, Tuskegee, Virginia Union, and Virginia Institute.

73. Juliette Derricotte was born in Athens, Georgia, in 1897 and received a public speaking scholarship to attend Talladega College in Alabama. She graduated in 1918 and attended the YWCA Training school in New York City. After she completed the summer course, she was hired that fall to work in the YWCA's headquarters as the Secretary of the National Student Council where she visited college campuses throughout the country, planning conference events and helping young women develop leadership skills. In 1924, she became a member of the World Student Christian Fellowship where she traveled globally as a delegate from American campuses. She earned a master's in religion in 1927, and in 1929, she resigned her position at the National YWCA to become the Dean of Women at Fisk University in Nashville. A rising star in women's higher education, global affairs, and interracial issues, she was tragically killed several months after this conference at Talladega in a car accident on her way to her parents' home in Georgia on a school break. Because of segregated hospitals, she was denied admittance to the local hospital near the accident. She had to be driven 35 miles to a Black hospital in Tennessee where she died. A Fisk student who also was riding with her died as well.

74. NAWDAC, *Report of Conference Proceedings*, Lucy Diggs Slowe Papers, Moorland-Spingarn Research Center, Howard University (1930), 6.

75. Interview with Linda Perkins, Davis, Hilda, Newark, Delaware, June 15, 1987.

76. Minutes of the Executive Committee (December 14, 1942), Board of Trustees Minutes, President Thomas Jones Papers, Fisk University Archives, Fisk University, Nashville, TN.

77. Minutes of the Executive Committee (October 18, 1943), President Thomas Jones Papers, Fisk University Archives, Fisk University, Nashville, TN.

78. President Thomas Jones, Letter to the Fisk Faculty and Staff (November 21, 1945).

79. National Association of Deans of Women and Advisors of Women in Colored Schools, Survey of Delegates to the 1936 Conference. Lucy Diggs Slowe Papers, Moorland-Spingarn Research Center, Howard University, Washington, DC, 1936.

80. Ibid.

81. National Association of Collegiate Deans and Registrars, Program of the 1935 Conference at Howard University, Lucy Diggs Slowe Papers, Moorland-Spingarn Research Center, Howard University, Washington, DC.

82. Carter, "The Educational Activities of the National Association of College Women, 1923–1960."

83. Lucy Diggs Slowe, "'The College Woman and the Community,' Opening Speech at the National Association of College Women at Atlanta University, April 1934," *Journal of National Association of College Women*, Memorial Edition (1939); Sartorius, *Deans of Women and the Feminist Movement*, 20–21.

Chapter 7. Deans of Women at HBCUs after Slowe

1. Lucy Diggs Slowe to Ida Jackson, July 27, 1937, Washington, DC, Lucy Diggs Slowe Papers.

2. Ida Jackson to Lucy Slowe, July 31, 1937, Tuskegee Institute, Lucy Diggs Slowe Papers.

3. University of California Black Alumni Series, "Oral History of Ida Louise Jackson: Overcoming Barriers in Education," interviewed 1984–85 (Oral History, University of California Black Alumni Series, The Bancroft Library, University of California–Berkeley), 54.

4. Hughes, "Cowards from the Colleges," 226 28.

5. Ibid.

6. Ibid.

7. Linda M. Perkins, Interview with Jean Fairfax, Phoenix, Arizona (October 1987); A. Lillian Thompson, Interview with Hattie Simmons Kelly (April 1, 1977a.), 74.

8. Katharine Q. Seelye, Jean Fairfax, "Unsung but Undeterred in Integrating Schools, Dies at 98," *New York Times* (March 1, 2019). https://www.nytimes.com/2019/03/01/obituaries/jean-fairfax-dead.html.

9. A. Lillian Thompson, Interview with Hattie Simmons Kelly (April 1, 1977a).

10. Ibid., 35.

11. Ibid., 49

12. Quoted in Cayton, *Long Old Road*, 98–199.

13. Hall, *Black Separatism in the United States*, 59.

14. Thompson, "Interview with Hattie Simmons Kelly," in *Black Women Oral History Project* (Radcliffe College, 1977a), i–138.

15. A. Lillian Thompson, "Interview with Hattie Simmons Kelly (April 1, 1977)," 74–75.

16. Sartorius, *Deans of Women and the Feminist Movement*.

17. Thompson, "Interview with Hattie Simmons Kelly," in *Black Women Oral History Project* (Radcliffe College, 1977a), i–138.

18. A. Lillian Thompson, "Oral History of Jesse Abbott" (Oral History, *Black Women's Oral History Project*, Schlesinger Library, Radcliffe College, Cambridge, MA, 1977b), 28.

19. Thompson, "Interview with Hattie Simmons Kelly," in *Black Women Oral History Project* (Radcliffe College, 1977a), i–138.

20. Larry Crowe, *Oral History of Dr. Ruth Brett Quarles, History Makers* (November 11, 2003). https://www.thehistorymakers.org/biography/ruth-brett-quarles-39/.

21. Ibid.

22. Linda M. Perkins, Interview with Dr. Ruth Brett, Baltimore, Maryland, June 1987.

23. Ibid.

24. Ibid.

25. Ibid.

26. Fairfax, Jean, "Jean Fairfax, Phoenix, Arizona to Linda M. Perkins, UCLA," September 21, 1987.

27. Sartorius, "A Coeducational Pathway to Political and Economic Citizenship," 161–83.

28. Joseph Harris, "Professor Merze Tate (1905–): A Profile," in *Profiles*, The Graduate School of Arts and Sciences, Howard University, Washington, DC, 1981.

29. July stated President Jones told him about the offer to Player and "wasn't happy about it." July, Robert W., "Confidential Memo to the Files," December 8, 1952, GEB Box 41, folder 373, Rockefeller Archives Center. July noted that Jones informed him that Player turned down the job at Spelman to remain at Bennett, "this is, of course, a great relief to DDJ."

30. "Oral Interview Flemmie P. Kittrell," *Black Women Oral History Project*, Radcliffe College, Cambridge, MA, 1977.

31. "Oral History of Merze V. Tate," *Black Women Oral History Project*, Radcliffe College, Cambridge, MA, 1978. Both Tate and Kittrell spent the bulk of their careers at Howard University—Tate from 1942–77 and Kittrell from 1944–72.

32. *Black Women Oral History Project*, Susie Jones, July 11, 1977, 16–17.

33. Jones, David D., "David D. Jones to Mrs. Mary McLeod Bethune, Bethune-Cookman College, Daytona Beach, Florida," February 27, 1930, Mary McLeod Bethune Papers, Amistad Archives.

34. Bethune, Mary McLeod, "Mary McLeod Bethune, President to President David D. Jones, Bennett College for Women, Greensboro, North Carolina," March 14, 1930, Mary McLeod Bethune Papers, Amistad Archives.

35. Flowers, "Education in Action."

36. Perkins, Interview with Dr. Ruth Brett, Baltimore, Maryland, June 1987.

37. Howard, Juanita, "Standards Committee Report," Southern Regional Conference of the National Association of College Women (Virginia State College, St. Petersburg, VA, October 13, 1935).

38. National Association of College Women, "Forward," *Journal of the National Association of College Women,* 1935.

39. McCuistion, "The South's Negro Teaching Force," 21.

40. Johnson, *The Negro College Graduate,* 227; Many highly trained Blacks, including those with PhDs, taught high school. For example, Edward Bouchet, the first black to earned a PhD in the nation (in physics from Yale, 1876) taught high school for his entire professional career at the Institute for Colored Youth in Philadelphia. Likewise, Charles Turner, who earned a PhD in biology from the University of Chicago in 1907 also taught high school in St. Louis until his death in 1923. Anna Julia Cooper who earned a PhD in French from the University of Paris in 1925, also taught high school in Washington, DC, her entire career. Many others like Merze Tate, who had studied abroad every summer, taught high school.

41. *Black Women Oral History Project,* Susie Jones, 16, 34.

42. Harlan, *Separate and Unequal,* 104.

43. Tate, "Justification for the Women's College."

44. Ibid.

45. Graham, "Expansion and Exclusion."

46. Quoted in Grundy, "From Amazons to Glamazons," 126.

47. Ibid.

48. Allen, Maryrose R., "Maryrose Reeves Allen to Dean Charles H. Thompson, College of Liberal Arts, Howard University," October 14, 1939.

49. Quoted in Lefever, *Undaunted by the Fight,* 15.

50. Ibid.

51. Ibid.

52. Quoted in Ivora (Ike) King, "Feminine Yet Athletic" in *Baltimore Afro-American,* September 19, 1931, 13.

53. Rita Liberti, "We Were Ladies, We Just Played Basketball Like Boys: African American Womanhood and Competitive Basketball at Bennett College, 1928–1942," *Journal of Sports History* 26 (1999): 567–584; Letter quoted in *Baltimore Afro-American,* April 5, 1930, 14.

54. Quoted in Grundy, "From Amazons to Glamazons,"130.

55. "Bennett Join in Fall Sports Day," *The Bennett Banner,* vol 10, no. 2, December 1939.

56. "Queen Carol Carter Reigns Over May Day," *The Bennett Banner,* vol. 14, no. 8 (May, 1945), 1; "Bennett Hostess, Collegiate Sports Day," *The Bennett Banner,* vol 12, no. 6 (May 1943), 1; "Bennett Hostess, Collegiate Sports Day," *The Bennett Banner,* vol. 12, no. 6 (May 1943), 1. "Queen Carol Carter Reigns Over May Day," *The Bennett Banner,* vol. 14, no. 8 (May, 1945), 1; "Bennett Hostess, Collegiate Sports Day," vol. 12, no. 6 (May 1943), 1.

57. Grundy, 131.

58. Lansbury, "Baltimore Afro-American," 1940, Quoted in Jennifer H. Lansbury, "'The Tuskegee Flash' and 'The Slender Harlem Stroker': Black Women Athletes on the Margin," *Journal of Sports History.*

59. Ibid.

60. Noble, *The Negro Woman's College Education,* 89.

61. Lockwood, "Bennett College for Women, 1926–1966."

62. Perkins, Interview with Dr. Ruth Brett, Baltimore, Maryland, June 1987.

63. Ibid.

64. President David D. Jones, Bennett College, to Dr. Jackson Davis, General Education Board Papers, Rockefeller Archive Center (May 3, 1941).

65. Dr. Jackson Davis to Dr. David D. Jones, Bennett College, General Education Board Papers, Rockefeller Archive Center (June 4, 1941).

66. Jones, "The War and the Higher Education of Negro Women," 329–37.

67. Ibid.

68. Ibid., 336.

69. Ibid.

70. Letter from Flemmie Kittrell to Jackson Davis, General Education Board Papers, Rockefeller Archive Center (July 3, 1943).

71. Ibid.

72. Memo to File: "Re: Conference on Education of College Women in War Time," Jackson Davis's file of the General Education Board Papers, Rockefeller Archive Center (July 29, 1943).

73. Memo to the file: "Flemmie P. Kittrell, Hampton Institute" in Jackson Davis's file of General Education Board Papers, Rockefeller Archive Center (October 4, 1943).

74. "Letter from Flemmie Kittrell to Jackson Davis, July 3, 1943," General Education Board Papers, Rockefeller Archive Center, n.d.

75. National Association of Deans of Women and Advisers to Girls in Negro Schools, "Findings of a Conference on Current Problems and Programs in the Higher Education of Negro Women," *Quarterly Review of Higher Education Among Negroes,* vol. 12, no. 4 (October 1944).

76. Ibid.

77. Ibid.

78. "Minutes from Executive Committee Meeting, September 28, 1942," Jones Papers, Fisk University.

79. Geiger. *American Higher Education since World War II,* 46.

80. Langston Hughes, "Cowards from the Colleges," 226–28.

81. Ibid.

82. Ibid.

83. Linda M. Perkins, Interview with Thelma Bando, 1986, Baltimore, Maryland.

84. Minutes of the Executive Committee Meeting, January 22, 1945, Jones Papers, Fisk University Archive; *Fisk Student Handbook* (1946), 30.

85. Brown, "The Married Student at Bennett College," 183–87.

86. Ibid.

87. Kittrell, "Current Problems and Programs in the Higher Education of Negro Women," 13–15.

88. Ibid.

89. Ibid.

90. Perkins, Interview with Thelma Bando.

91. National Association of Deans of Women and Advisers to Girls in Negro Schools, *Findings of a Conference on Current Problems and Programs in the Higher Education of Negro Women*, 208.

92. Ibid.

93. Kittrell, "Current Problems and Programs in the Higher Education of Negro Women," 13–15; National Association of Deans of Women and Advisers to Girls in Negro Schools, *Findings of a Conference on Current Problems and Programs in the Higher Education of Negro Women*; Spelman College, "Conference on Negro Women's Problems in Higher Education," 10–11, 24; National Association of Deans of Women and Advisers to Girls in Negro Schools, *Findings of a Conference on Current Problems and Programs in the Higher Education of Negro Women*; Spelman College, "Conference On Negro Women's Problems in Higher Education," 10–11, 24.

94. Memo to file: A Second Grant of $7500 for work on curriculum construction and reorganization (June 30, 1944), General Education Board, Rockefeller Archives Center, Sleepy Hollow, New York.

95. Pinkard, "Bertha Diggs, Labor Secretary, Attributes Success to Hard Work," 1, 4.

96. Ibid.

97. Banner, "Homemaking Institute '49 Features Career and Home," 1.

98. Ibid.

99. Farnham, a psychiatrist affiliated with the New York State Psychiatric Institute and Hospital, argued that "contemporary women in very large numbers are psychologically disordered and that their disorder is having terrible social and personal effects involving men in all departments of their lives as well as women." This book became a national bestseller and contributed to both the return to domesticity in the post–World War II decades and the psychoanalytic antifeminist movement.

100. Noble, *The Negro Woman's College Education*.

101. Eisenmann, *Higher Education for Women in Postwar America, 1945–1965*.

102. Sartorius, "Counseling US Women for Economic Citizenship," 831–42.

103. Flowers, "Education in Action."

104. "Theatres are boycotted by Students," *The Winston Salem Post*, 8, 37 cited in Flowers, "Education in Action," 176.

105. Flowers, "Education in Action," 183.

106. Ibid.

107. Ibid., 213.

108. Pauli Murray, *Song in a Weary Throat*, 203–4.

109. Ibid., 208.

110. For more information on the role of Black college students in the Civil Rights Movement see: Carson, Clayborne, *In Struggle: SNCC and the Black Awakening of the 1960s* (Harvard University Press, 1995) and Monteith, Sharon, *SNCC's Stories: The African*

American Freedom Movement in the Civil Rights South (University of Georgia Press, 2020) and Gasman, Marybeth, "Instilling an Ethic of Leadership at Fisk University in the 1950s," *Journal of College and Character* 2, no. 2 (2001).

111. See Wolters, *The New Negro on Campus*.
112. Guitar, "Bennett's Proper Pickets."
113. Lockwood, "Bennett College for Women, 1926–1966."
114. Ibid.
115. Geiger, "Higher Education in the 1950s," 45.
116. Herbolt, "Never a Level Playing Field," 104–8.
117. Howard University, "Annual Report, 1946–47," 1947.
118. (No author) "Fisk Has Record Enrollment of 600."
119. Memorandum for Faculty on the State of the University, Office of the President, Charles S. Johnson Papers, Fisk University Archives, Box 42, Folder 7 (1952).
120. Geiger, "Higher Education in the 1950s."
121. Cooper, *A Voice from the South*, 174; Graham, "Expansion and Exclusion," 766.
122. Flexnor, *Century of Struggle*, 182.

Chapter 8. The Beginning of the Black Female Professoriate

1. Linda M. Perkins, "The History of Black Women Graduate Students, 1921–1948." The undergraduate degrees of these women were Howard, University of Pennsylvania, and the University of Chicago, respectfully. Dykes, like most graduates of Black colleges, had to get a second baccalaureate degree from Radcliffe since her degree from Howard wasn't deemed the equivalent of a Harvard/Radcliffe degree. Both race and gender hindered African Americans from gaining access to graduate school.

2. The first Black man to earn a PhD was Edward Bouchet in physics from Yale University in 1876, also his undergraduate institution. Unable to obtain a college professorship because of his race, Bouchet taught physics and chemistry at the Institute for Colored Youth in Philadelphia for twenty-six years but resigned in 1903 because of Booker T. Washington's impact on changing the school's curriculum. The first white woman earned a doctorate in 1877. By 1900, their number had grown to 204, but Black male holders of doctorates had increased to only twenty. Eells, "Earned Doctorates for Women in the Nineteenth Century," 648; Greene, *Holders of Doctorates among Negroes*.

3. Ibid.

4. Mabel Myers Stinnett, "Fellowship Report Cards," 1936, Fellowship Follow-up Cards, General Education Board Papers, Rockefeller Archives, Sleepy Hollow, New York.

5. Grace Mae Sullivan, "Fellowship Follow-up Report," 1936, General Education Board Papers, Rockefeller Archives, Sleepy Hollow, New York.

6. Eunice D. Powell, "Fellowship Follow-up Card," 1933, General Education Board Papers, Rockefeller Archives, Sleepy Hollow, New York.

7. Josie Wilhelmina Roberts, "Fellowship Follow-up Card," 1935, General Education Board Papers, Rockefeller Archives, Sleepy Hollow, New York.

8. Ibid.

9. Perkins, "The History of Black Women Graduate Students."

10. Ibid.

11. Manning, *Black Apollo of Science.*

12. Strayhorn, "Alice Carlotta Jackson," 19.

13. MIT, "Phyllis A. Wallace."

14. Browne and English, *Love My Children,* 17–18.

15. Crocco and Waite, "Education and Marginality," 69–91.

16. *General Education Board Annual Report* (Sleepy Hollow, NY: Rockefeller Archives Center, 1938).

17. Height, *Open Wide the Freedom Gates,* 33.

18. "Roster of Spelman College Graduates Who Have Attended Graduate and Professional Schools," 1955, in General Education Board Papers, Folder 283, Box 38, Rockefeller Archives, Sleepy Hollow, New York.

19. Naomi Mill Garrett, "Final Report of Fellowship," Fellowship Files, Julius Rosenwald Papers, Nashville, Tennessee (1945). Garrett's career had a happy ending. Without additional funding from the Rosenwald Foundation, Garett took a job as a bookkeeper and a second job to pay her tuition. She completed her course work in 1947 and accepted a job on the faculty at West Virginia State College (now University). In spite of her enormous teaching load at West Virginia State, Garrett continued to work on her dissertation. She received a fellowship from the Ford Foundation in 1951 and graduated in 1954. She was awarded a Fulbright to Paris in 1958–59. Prior to coming to Columbia, she taught two years in Haiti. She ultimately became the head of the Foreign Languages Department. She traveled extensively and attended cultural festivals in Africa, Europe, the Caribbean and Latin America. In 1972, she joined the faculty of Denison University, a white liberal arts college in Ohio as university professor. She was the first African American woman to teach at Denison and also the first woman to teach in their Black Studies Department. She remained until her retirement in 1979. Denison University Archives (Vertical Files, Naomi Mill Garrett) and correspondence from her great nephew, David E. Nicholson, Washington, DC, November 1, 2021, including a Garrett CV, her biography in Who's Who of American Women (197–973).

20. Ibid.

21. Richardson, R. B. D., Dean, Brown University to George M. Reynolds, Fisk University, March 21, 1941, Beatrice Yvonne Black Fellowship File, Rosenwald Fund, Julius Rosenwald Papers, Fisk University Archives, Nashville, TN.

22. E. Hille, *Director of Graduate Studies in Mathematics* (Nashville, TN: Julius Rosenwald Papers, 1947).

23. Will W. Alexander, Administrator at the United States Department of Agriculture to Raymond Paty, Director of Fellowships, Julius Rosenwald Fund, Chicago, Illinois, March 22, 1936.

24. Dr. P. D. Bartlett and Dr. William F. Ross, Letter of Reference for Leila S. Green, 1939 and 1940.

25. "Sadie Tanner Mossell Alexander," *Black Women Oral History Project*, Radcliffe College Archives, Radcliffe College, Cambridge, MA, 1977.

26. "Anna Julia Cooper Papers," Negro College Graduate Questionnaire, Moorland-Spingarn Collection, Howard University Archives, Washington, DC, 1971b.

27. Shirley Graham, "Personal Statement in Shirley Graham File," 1938, Julius Rosenwald Foundation, Fisk University Special Collection, Nashville, TN.

28. Robert A. Lambert to Dr. Numa P. B. Adams, Dean of Howard University Medical School, July 19, 1939.

29. "All Fellowship Records are found in the Julius Rosenwald Foundation Papers," Julius Rosenwald Foundation Papers, Fisk University Special Collection, Nashville, TN.

30. "Exhibit A," 1943, Folder 6, Box 386, Julius Rosenwald Foundation Papers, Fisk University Special Collection, Nashville, TN.

31. Ibid.

32. "Hugh H. Smythe Fellowship Folder, Mable Smythe Fellowship Folder, Folders 7 and 8, Box 448, Julius Rosenwald Foundation Papers, Fisk University Special Collection, Nashville, TN.

33. Ibid.

34. Lawrence-Lightfoot, *Balm in Gilead,* 152, 238.

35. "Interview of Virgina Lacy Jones," October 10, 1978, Oral History, *Black Women Oral History Project*, Schlesinger Library, Radcliffe College, Cambridge, MA.

36. Ibid.

37. Kathy Perkins, Interview with Dr. Winona Lee Fletcher, July 26, 1994, Chicago, Illinois.

38. Ibid.

39. Ibid.

40. Linda M. Perkins, Interview with Dr. Mildred Barksdale, 1994, University of Illinois.

41. Sadie M. Mays, "Followup Questionnaire," 1944, Julius Rosenwald Papers, Fisk Special Collection.

42. (Mrs. David) Ethel McGhee, "Follow-Up Card," 1944, General Education Board, Rockefeller Archives Center.

43. Edmonia Louise Walden Grider, "Follow-Up Report," 1936, General Education Board, Rockefeller Archives Center.

44. Hilda Lawson Reedy, "Follow-Up Card," 1944, Julius Rosenwald Foundation, Fisk University Special Collection, Nashville, TN.

45. Richardson, *A History of Fisk University, 1865–1946,* 102–3.

46. Ibid.

47. Thomas E. Jones, President of Fisk University, Letter to Dr. Sadie Mossell Alexander, June 22, 1927, Folder 15, File 1, Jones Papers, 1926–46.

48. Ibid.

49. Sadie Mossell Alexander to President Thomas Jones, July 14, 1927, Folder 15, File 1, Jones Papers.

50. Richardson, *A History of Fisk University, 1865–1946,* 113.

51. Miller, "Holding Center Stage," 152.

52. Williams-Burns, "Jane Ellen McAllister," 342–57.

53. Thomas E. Jones, President of Fisk University, Letter to Leo M. Favrot, March 1928, General Education Board.

54. Leo M. Favrot, Field Agent, Letter to Dr. Thomas E. Jones, President, Fisk University, March 28, 1928.

55. Ibid.

56. See Jones's correspondence on McAllister in his Papers at Fisk University, Jane Ellen McAllister Folder, Fisk Archives.

57. Mabel, Carney, Teachers College, Columbia University, Letter to Dr. Thomas Elsa Jones, President, Fisk University.

58. Jane Ellen McAllister, Letter to Dr. Thomas Elsa Jones, City Club of New York.

59. Jane Ellen McAllister, Letter to President Thomas E. Jones, May 6, 1930; Jane Ellen McAllister, Letter to President Thomas E. Jones, Fisk University, April 11, 1930.

60. McAllister, Letter to Jones, April 14, 1930.

61. Thomas E. Jones, President of Fisk University, Letter to Dr. Jane Ellen McAllister, April 17, 1930.

62. Thomas E. Jones, President of Fisk University, Letter to Mr. Leo Favrot, Baton Rouge, Louisiana, January 24, 1930.

63. Sadie E. Daniels, Letter to President T. E. Jones, Fisk University, April 18, 1940.

64. Madeline Clarke Foreman, Letter to Thomas E. Jones, President, Fisk University, July 1, 1944.

65. Thomas E. Jones, Letter to Mrs. Madeline Clarke Forman, July 7th, 1944; Richardson, *A History of Fisk University, 1865–1946*.

66. Madeline Clarke Foreman, Washington, DC, Letter to President Thomas E. Jones, Fisk University, July 22, 1944.

67. Evelyn S. Bourden, note to President Thomas E. Jones, Fisk University, August 5, 1944.

68. Greene, *Holders of Doctorates among American Negroes*. According to Greene there were forty-five Black women PhDs by 1946.

69. Richardson, *A History of Fisk University, 1865–1946*.

70. Richardson, *A History of Fisk University, 1865–1946*.

71. Trustee Committee on President, Report of Trustee Committee Meeting, April 10, 1946, Fisk University, Thomas E. Jones, Fisk University Archives, Nashville, TN.

72. Charles S. Johnson, Letter to Miss Marion Cuthbert, New York, NY, June 14, 1944.

73. Jessie Carney Smith, ed., *Notable Black American Women* (Detroit, MI: Gale Research Inc, 1992).

74. Marion Vera Cuthbert, Letter to Dr. Charles S. Johnson, Fisk University, June 26, 1944.

75. Ibid.

76. Marion Vera Cuthbert, Letter to Dr. Charles S. Johnson, Fisk University, Nashville, Tennessee, June 16, 1944.

77. Mary Huff Diggs, Letter to Dr. Charles S. Johnson, President, Fisk University, December 30, 1946.

78. Charles S. Johnson, Letter to Dr. Mary Huff Diggs, Hunter College, January 3, 1947.

79. Johnson, "The Faculty," 471–83.

80. Charles H. Thompson, Memorandum to Dr. Charles S. Johnson, Re: Recruiting Teachers and Faculty Salaries, October 1st, 1947.

81. Board of Trustees of Fisk University, Minutes of the Executive Committee of the Board of Trustees of Fisk University Held at 133 East 40th Street, New York, NY, January 23, 1951, Folder 9, Box 14, Charles S. Johnson Papers, Fisk University Archives, Nashville, TN.

82. Fisk Board of Trustees, Minutes of the Meeting of October 16, 1951, Folder 9, Box 14, Charles S. Johnson Papers, Fisk University Archives, Nashville, TN.

83. Charles S. Johnson, Report of the President to the Board of Trustees of Fisk University, October 25, 1949, Folder 13, Box 14, Charles S. Johnson Papers, Fisk University Archives, Nashville, TN.

84. Kathy Perkins, Interview with Dr. Winona Lee Fletcher, Chicago, Illinois (July 26, 1994).

85. Linda M. Perkins, Dr. Gladys Forde Interview (Houston, Texas: October 2010).

86. Holloway, *Confronting the Veil*; Williams, *In Search of the Talented Tenth*; Logan, *Howard University*.

87. These are just the most prominent of the women faculty and among the earliest to serve.

88. Evelyn Boyd, *Biographies of Women Mathematicians*, https://mathwomen.agnesscott.org/women/granvill.

89. Eva Dykes, interview by Merze Tate, November 30 and December 1, 1977, *Black Women Oral History Project*. OH-31, T-32/Eva Dykes, SL. Interview with Sadie Tanner Mossel Alexander. Alexander Family Papers. (Philadelphia: University of Pennsylvania Archives, 1977).

90. Dorothy Ferebee, interview by Merze Tate, December 28 and 31, 1979, *Black Women Oral History Project*. OH-31, T-32/Dorothy Ferebee, SL.

91. For lengthy discussions of Johnson's battles with various Howard faculty and administrators, see Logan, *Howard University*.

92. Note attached to the letter from Clarence Harvey Mills to Lucy Diggs Slowe, January 11, 1927, Slowe Papers, Howard University: Moorland-Spingarn Research Center (hereafter, MSRC). For a more detailed discussion of Slowe's negative experiences with Modecai Johnson see Logan, *Howard University*, p. 292; Perkins, "Lucy Diggs Slowe," 89–104; and Scott, "To Keep My Self-Respect," 70–76.

93. Perkins, "Lucy Diggs Slowe." Also see "The Trials of a President," *Time Magazine*, (March 1938), 13.

94. See memorandum to the Howard Board of Trustees by members of the Executive Committee of the General Alumni Association in which they outline President Johnson's "hate, ill will, and malice" towards Slowe and noted while she was critically ill, Johnson sent Slowe a message that "she should turn to her duties immediately or a successor would be in her place within twenty-four hours"; because of this, the memorandum stated that the family of Slowe requested that Johnson not appear or take part in any aspect of her funeral service. Quoted in Miller and Pruitt-Logan, *Faithful to the Task at Hand*, 233–34.

95. Inabel Burns Lindsay, interview by Marcia McAdoo Greenlee, May 20 and June 7, 1977, *Black Women Oral History Project*, OH-31, T-32/Inabel Burns Lindsay, SL.

96. Ibid., 24.

97. Ibid., 24.

98. Rayford Logan Diary, entry of March 4, 1943, Folder 2, Box 4, Library of Congress, Washington, DC.

99. Dorothy Ferebee, interview by Merze Tate. December 28 and 31, 1979, *Black Women Oral History Project*. OH-31, T-32/Dorothy Ferebee, SL.

100. Merze Tate, telephone interview with the author, April 1984. Merze Tate, interview by Theresa Danley, April 24, 1978 and January 3, 1979, *Black Women Oral History Project*. OH-31, T-32/Merze Tate, SL.

101. Ibid.

102. Ibid.

103. Rayford Logan Diary, entry of September 3, 1942, Folder 7, Box 3, Library of Congress, Washington, DC.

104. Dublin, "Caroline Ware," 662–64. Also see Perkins, "Merze Tate and the Gender Equity at Howard University," 516–51.

105. Rayford Logan Diary, (September 11, 1942), Box 3, folder 7, Library of Congress, Washington, DC.

106. Quoted in Vitalis, *White World Order, Black Power Politics*, 161.

107. Merze Tate to J. St. Clair Price, Dean of Liberal Arts, Howard University, July 17, 1945, Merze Tate Papers, Folder 19, Box 219-5, Manuscript Division, Moorland-Spingarn Research Center, hereafter MSRC.

108. Transcript of an oral history interview of Dorothy Burnett Porter Wesley, January 28 and February 10, 1993, Howard University Oral Histories, MSRC.

109. Ibid.

110. Ibid.

111. Franklin quoted in Rayford Logan's Diaries, December 23, 1954, Folder 1, Box 6, Library of Congress, Washington, DC.

112. Program of the Faculty Women's Club of Howard University, March 5, 1950, Rankin Memorial Chapel, Howard University, in Merze Tate Papers, Manuscript Division, MSRC.

113. Minutes of the Committee on AAUW Accreditation, March 28, 1961, Merze Tate Papers, Manuscript Division, MSRC.

114. Merze Tate in Dorothy Boulding Ferebee, Interview with Radcliffe College, 1979, *Black Women Oral History Project*, Schlensinger Library, Radcliffe College, 34.

115. Ibid.

116. Tate, Report of the Status of Faculty in College of Liberal Arts by Department, Rank, and Salary, 1953–54.

117. Ibid.

118. Merze Tate to Dean J. St. Clair Price, Dean Liberal Arts, Howard University, October 29, 1951, in Merze Tate Papers, Folder 19, Box 219, Manuscript Division, MSRC.

119. Ibid.

120. Ibid.

121. Ibid.

122. Stewart Nelson to Merze Tate, Merze Tate Papers, October 31, 1956, Folder 17, Box 219-4, MSRC.

123. Black women educators like Nannie Helen Burroughs, Charlotte Hawkins Brown, Lucy Laney, and Mary McLeod Bethune who were school founders and led schools and who were also devoutly religious often bore witness to their religion in their speeches and letters. In a communication with Charlotte Hawkins Brown in 1927, Bethune noted the work they were all doing: "I think of you and Nannie Burroughs and Lucy Laney and myself as being in the most self-sacrificing class of our group of women . . . I have, unselfishly, given my best and I thank God that I have lived long enough to see the fruits from it." "Mary McLeod Bethune to Charlotte Hawkins Brown, Wellesley College, Wellesley, MA," October 29, 1927, Charlotte Hawkins Brown Papers, The Schlesinger Library, Radcliffe College, Cambridge, MA; Bethune wrote to Brown commending her on an award she had received: "God bless our women. They [Black women] are reaching forward speedily. Our seed sowing can never be in vain. They have been sown too earnestly and unselfishly . . . The harvest time is bound to come . . . all of those who were sowing seeds when it cost so much more than it does now, must rejoice in the Glory Land over the great harvest that is now coming to Negro womanhood in America and throughout the World." "Mary McLeod Bethune, Founder-President, National Council of Negro Women, Inc. to Mrs. Charlotte Hawkins Brown, Palmer Memorial Institute, Sedalia, North Carolina," June 12, 1947, Charlotte Hawkins Brown Papers, The Schlesinger Library, Radcliffe College, Cambridge, MA.

124. Eva B. Dykes, *Black Women Oral History Project*, 1979, Radcliffe College Archives, Radcliffe College, Cambridge, MA.

125. Merze Tate. Report of the Status of Faculty in College of Liberal Arts by Department, Rank, and Salary, 1961, Box 1, File 1.

126. Faculty Women—College of Dentistry, 1961, Box 9, File 9, Manuscript Division, Howard University.

127. Dorothy Boulding Ferebee, Interview with Radcliffe College, 34, *Black Women Oral History Project*, Schlesinger Library, Radcliffe College.

128. For more details on the activities of these women on a national level see Perkins, "The National Association of College Women," 65–75.

129. Vitalis, *White World Order, Black Power Politics*, 161.

130. Eulogy of Dr. Dorothy Boulding Ferebee by Patricia Robert Harris, Secretary of Health and Human Services, September 20, 1980, Dorothy Ferebee, in Ferebee Papers Manuscript Division, MSRC.

131. Giylard, *Louise Thompson Patterson*.

132. Ibid.

133. Ibid.

134. Gilyard, *Louise Thompson Patterson*.

135. Perkins, Interview with Thelma Bando, November 4, 1986.

136. Charles S. Johnson, "Faculty," *The Journal of Educational Sociology* 19, no. 8, (April 1946): 471–83.

137. Rayford Logan, "Diary Entry," September 29, 1955, Folder 2, Box 6, personal correspondence, Library of Congress.

138. "Interview with Inabel Burns Lindsay," June 20, 1977, Radcliffe College.

139. Reavis L. Mitchell, Jr., "Mary E. Branch," in *Notable Black American Women*, 101–3.

140. The phrase "we specialize in the holy impossible" is the motto Nannie Helen Burroughs founder and educator of the National Training School for Women and Girls in Washington, DC, gave her school because obtaining funding and support for the education of Black girls was viewed as "holy impossible."

141. Mitchell, "Mary E. Branch," in *Notable Black American Women*, 103.

Chapter 9. Education and Marginality

1. Wall, R. E., "'Shall Our Girls Be Educated,'" *AME Review* Six (July 1889): 45–48; "The Homemaker," *AME Church Review* 8, number 1 (n.d.): 63–65; Johnson, James H.A., "Women's Exalted Station," *AME Church Review* 8, no. 4 (April 1882): 402–6.

2. Cooper, *A Voice from the South*, 44–45.

3. Du Bois, *The College-Bred Negro*.

4. "Lady Plane Mechanic," *Ebony* (January 1948).

5. Johnson, *The Negro College Graduate*; Cuthbert, *Education and Marginality*.

6. Cuthbert, 57.

7. Brown, "Student Problems Encountered Daily."

8. Crocco and Waite, "Education and Marginality."

9. Bolton, "The Problems of Negro College Women Graduates" (diss), 52.

10. Ibid., 3.

11. Interview with Inabeth Lindsay, June 30, 1977, *Black Women Oral History Project*, Schlesinger Library, 1.

12. Ibid., 51.

13. "Lady Lawyers," *Ebony*, 1947.

14. "Lady Plane Mechanic," *Ebony*, January 1948.

15. "Lady Buyer," *Ebony*, 1959.

16. "Negro Girls on Capital Hill: Once Rare, Their Numbers Are Increasing," *Ebony*, December 1959.

17. Ibid.

18. Ibid.

19. Farnham, Marynia, "The Tragic Failure of America's Women," *Coronet*, September 1947.

20. Ann Petry, "What's Wrong With Negro Men?," *Negro Digest*, 1947.

21. Pauli Murray, "Why Negro Girls Stay Single," *Negro Digest*, 1947.

22. Noble, *The Negro Woman's College Education*.

23. Fields and Fields, *Lemon Swamp and Other Places*.

24. Noble, *The Negro Woman's College Education*.

25. Linda Perkins, Interview with Hilda Davis, Newark, Delaware, June 15, 1987.

26. Ibid.

27. Lindsay, 4.

28. Ibid.

29. Ibid.

30. Dorothy Boulding Ferebee, Interview with Radcliffe College, December 28, 1979, *Black Women Oral History Project*, Schlesinger Library, Radcliffe College.

31. Ibid.

32. Ibid.

33. Janker, *Rayford W. Logan and the Dilemma of the African American Intellectual*, 72.

34. Ibid., 72–73.

35. Terrell, *A Colored Woman in a White World*.

36. Ibid.

37. May Edward Chinn, 1979, 23, *Black Women Oral History Project*.

38. Davis, Georgia, "The Healing Hand of Harlem," *New York Times*, April 22, 1979, sec. SM.

39. Pitre, Merline, "At the Crossroads," 129–58.

40. Cuthbert, *Education and Marginality*.

41. Ibid.

42. Johnson, John, "Publisher's Statement," *Ebony*, August 1966.

43. "'For a Better Future'—Editorial," *Ebony*, August 1966.

44. Ibid.

45. Ibid.

46. Ibid.

47. Drake, St. Clair, "Why Men Leave Home," *Negro Digest*, April 1950.

48. Gore, *Radicalism at the Crossroad*.

49. "For a Better Future, Photo Editorial," *Ebony*, 1966.

50. Ibid., 150.

51. "Why They Don't Marry: Doctors Say Real Causes of Altar-Phobia Are Seldom Known by Persons Involved," *Ebony*, January 1958.

52. Garland, Phyl, "'Builders of a New South': Negro Heroines of Dixie Play Major Role in Challenging Racist Traditions," *Ebony*, August 1966.

53. "'Woman Fills Man-Size Union Job': Chicagoan Lillian Roberts Is Efficient Vice President of International Labor Group," *Ebony*, April 1965.

54. "Scientific Couple Find Success in Albuquerque," *Ebony*, June 1965.

55. Ibid.

56. "Interview with Inabel Burns Lindsay," 5.

57. "Class History: 1951," in *The Bison: 1951 Howard University Yearbook*.

58. For more on this topic see Linda M. Perkins, "The Black Female American Missionary Association Teacher in the South, 1861–1870," in *AMA Teachers in the South* (North Carolina: University of North Carolina Press, 1984), 122–36.

59. Anderson, *The Education of Blacks in the South*.

60. Motley, *Equal Justice Under Law*.

61. Linda Perkins Interview with Dr. Ruth Brett, Baltimore, Maryland, June 17, 1987; Linda Perkins Interview with Hilda Davis, "Jean Fairfax, Phoenix, Arizona to Linda M. Perkins, UCLA," September 21, 1987. Linda Perkins interview with Dr. Jeanne Noble, New York City, October 9, 1986.

62. "Jean Fairfax, Phoenix, Arizona, to Linda M. Perkins, UCLA," September 21, 1987; "Ida Louise Jackson: Overcoming Barriers in Education," 1984–85, University of

California Black Alumni Series, Oral History, Bancroft Library, University of California–Berkeley; Gilyard, Keith, *Louise Thompson Patterson: A Life of Struggle for Justice*. Bell, Patricia, "Marion Vera Cuthbert," in *Notable Black American Women,* Jessie Carney Smith, ed. (Detroit, MI: Gale Research Inc., 1992).

63. Synnott, "African American Women Pioneers in Desegregating Higher Education."

64. Ford, *Constance Baker Motley.*

65. Franklin, *Young Crusaders.*

66. Du Bois, *The College-Bred Negro.*

67. Du Bois, W. E. B., "Editorial," *The Crisis* 8 (August 1914): 179.

68. Miller, Kelly, "The Risk of Woman Suffrage," *The Crisis* 11 (November 1915): 37–38.

69. Du Bois, "The Damnation of Women," in *Darkwater.*

70. Ibid., 179.

71. "National Center for Educational Statistics, 2020," https://nces.ed.gov/fastfacts/display.asp?id=667, n.d.; "Black Women Students Far Outnumber Black Men at the Nation's Highest-Ranked Universities," *Journal of Blacks in Higher Education* 51 (2006), 26–28, http://www.jstor.org/stable/25073418.

72. "Black Women Students Far Outnumber Black Men at the Nation's Highest-Ranked Universities."

73. The definitive biography on Lucy Diggs Slowe is Miller and Pruitt-Logan, *Faithful to the Task at Hand.*

Bibliography

Oral Interviews and Histories

**RADCLIFFE BLACK WOMEN ORAL HISTORY PROJECT
SCHLESINGER LIBRARY, RADCLIFFE COLLEGE, CAMBRIDGE, MA**

Abbott, Jessie. October 11, 1977.
Adams, Frankie V. April 20 and 28, 1977.
Albrier, Frances Mary. April 25, 1977–78.
Alexander, Sadie Tanner Mossell. 1977.
Chinn, May Edward. 1979.
Ferebee, Dorothy Boulding. December 28 and 31, 1979.
Jones, Susie. July 11, 1977.
Jones, Virginia Lacy. October 10, 1978.
Kelly, Hattie Simmons. April 1, 1977.
Kittrell, Flemmie P. August 29, 1977.
Lindsay, Inabeth. June 30, 1977.
Tate, Merze. April 24, 1978.
Williams, Frances H. October 30, 1977.

INTERVIEWS WITH THE AUTHOR

Bando, Thelma. Baltimore, Maryland, November 4, 1986.
Barksdale, Mildred. Urbana, Illinois, March 5, 1994.
Brett, Ruth. Baltimore, June 17, 1987.
Davis, Hilda. Newark, Delaware, June 15, 1987.
Edmonds, Helen G. Cambridge, Massachusetts, December 8 and 9, 1986.
Fairfax, Jean. Phoenix, Arizona. October 28, 1987.
Forde, Gladys. Houston, Texas, October 23, 2010.
Hutson, Jean Blackwell. New York, June 5, 1997.

Noble, Jeanne. New York, October 9, 1986.
Scott, Charlotte Hanley. Telephone interview. June 9, 1997.
Tate, Merze. Telephone interview. October 25, 1987.

ADDITIONAL INTERVIEWS

Fletcher, Dr. Winona Lee. Interview with Kathy A. Perkins. Chicago, Illinois. July 26, 1994.
Jackson, Ida Louise. Interviewed 1984–85. University of California Black Alumni Series, Oral History of Ida Louise Jackson: "Overcoming Barriers in Education." Berkeley, California: The Bancroft Library, University of California–Berkeley.
Wesley, Dorothy Burnett Porter. January 28 and February 10, 1993. Howard University Oral Histories.

Manuscript Collections and Archival Sources

Amistad Research Center Archives, New Orleans, LA
    American Missionary Association Papers
    Mary McLeod Bethune Papers
Archives and Special Collections, Mount Holyoke College, South Hadley, MA
    Afro-American Students, Alumnae File
    Helen Calder Papers
    History Department, Course Records for History 265, Fall 1973, Background Materials
    Mary Lyon Collection
    Hortense Parker, Class of 1883, Alumnae File
    Alice Stubb, Class of 1926, Alumnae File
    Frances Williams, Class of 1919, Alumnae File
Barnard College Archives and Special Collections, New York, NY
    Virginia Gildersleeves Papers
    Sherry Suttles Papers, BC20-07
Bryn Mawr College Archives, Bryn Mawr, PA
    Marion Edwards Park Papers
    M. Carey Thomas Papers
Cortland County Historical Society, McGraw, NY
Fisk University Archives, Nashville, TN
    Charles S. Johnson Papers
    Thomas E. Jones Papers
    Thomas Jessie Jones Papers
    Julius Rosenwald Papers
Hunter College Archives
    Annual Reports of the Normal College of the City of New York, 1874–1882
    Registrar's Record Book
Library of Congress, Washington, DC
    Rayford Whittingham Logan Papers

Moorland-Spingarn Research Center, Howard University, Washington, DC
    Maryrose Reeves Allen Papers
    Anna Julia Cooper Papers
    Dorothy Boulding Ferebee Papers
    Flemmie Kittrell Papers
    Lucy Diggs Slowe Papers
    Merze Tate Papers
Oberlin Archives, Oberlin College Library, Oberlin, OH
Rockefeller Archives Center, Sleepy Hollow, NY
    General Education Board Papers
Schlesinger Library, Radcliffe Institute, Harvard University, Cambridge, MA
    Charlotte Hawkins Brown Papers
    Ada Louise Comstock, Record of the Office of the President, Radcliffe College, 1923–43
    Mary Gibson Huntley Papers
    Margaret P. McCane Papers
    Radcliffe College Collection of Biographical Data on African American Students
Schomburg Center for Research on Black Culture, New York Public Library, New York
    Jane Bolin Papers
Smith College Archives, Smith College, Northampton, MA
    Admissions Office Records, Black Students Folder
    Faculty Records Files
    Carrie Lee's Folder, Individuals 1917, Box 1789
University of Pennsylvania Archives, Philadelphia, PA
    Alexander Family Papers
Vassar College Archives, Poughkeepsie, NY
Wellesley College Archives, Wellesley College, MA
    Alumnae Association Records

Dissertations and Theses

Bolton, Ina Alexander. "The Problems of Negro College Women Graduates." PhD dissertation, University of Southern California, 1949.

Breaux, Richard Melvin. "'We Must Fight Race Prejudice Even More Vigorously in the North': Black Higher Education in America's Heartland, 1900–1940." PhD dissertation, University of Iowa, 2003.

Brown, Georgia. "Student Problems Encountered Daily by Deans of Women in Sixteen Colleges for Negroes." Master's thesis, University of Michigan, 1943.

Butcher, Beatrice. "The Evolution of Negro Women's Schools in the United States." Master's thesis, Howard University, 1936.

Carter, Mary. "The Educational Activities of the National Association of College Women, 1923–1960." Master's thesis, Howard University, 1962.

Cobb, Deirdre. "Race and Higher Education at the University of Illinois, 1945 to 1955." PhD dissertation, University of Illinois, 1998.

Cuthbert, Marion Vera. "Education and Marginality: A Study of the Negro College Graduate." PhD dissertation, Teachers College Columbia University, 1942.

Duffy, Jennifer O'Connor. "Radcliffe College, 1940–1970: The Intersection of Gender, Social Class, and Historical Context." PhD dissertation, Boston College, 2006.

Fletcher, Juanita D. "Against the Consensus: Oberlin College and the Education of the American Negroes, 1835–1865." PhD dissertation, American University, 1974.

Flowers, Deidre Bennett. "Education in Action: The Work of Bennett College for Women, 1930–1960." PhD dissertation, Teachers College, Columbia University, 2017.

Grunfeld, Katherine Kroo. "Purpose and Ambiguity: The Feminine World of Hunter College, 1869–1945." EdD dissertation, Teachers College, Columbia University, 1991.

Hoff, Tamara. "The History of African American Women at the University of Illinois, 1901–1939." PhD dissertation, University of Illinois, 2015.

Jenkins, Herbert C. "The Negro Student at the University of Iowa: A Sociological Study." Master's thesis, State University of Iowa, 1933.

Lockwood, Nadine Sherri. "Bennett College for Women, 1926–1966." PhD dissertation, SUNY at Buffalo, 2004.

McCusker, Kristine M. "The Forgotten Years of America's Civil Rights Movement: The University of Kansas, 1939–1961." Master's thesis, Department of History, University of Kansas, 1994.

Noble, Jeanne L. "The Negro Woman's College Education." PhD dissertation, Teachers College, Columbia University, 1955.

Sidhu, Samantha. "The Andersons of Shoreham: Intersections of Race, Class and Vermont Identity in the Progressive Era." Unpublished senior thesis, Middlebury College, 2014.

Newspapers and Journals

The A.M.E. Church Review
American Presbyterians
Baltimore Afro-American
Barnard Alumnae Journal
Barnard Bulletin
Bennett Banner
Bulletin of the American Association of University Professors
Bulletin of Oberlin College
Catalogue of Oberlin College
The Colored American
Coronet magazine
The Crisis magazine
Ebony magazine
Freedom's Journal
Genius of Universal Emancipation
Graduate Magazine of the University of Kansas
History of Education Quarterly
Ivy Leaf Magazine

Journal of Blacks in Higher Education
Journal of College Alumnae Association
Journal of Negro Education
The Journal of Negro History
Journal of Presbyterian History
Journal of Sports History
Journal of the National Association of College Women
The Liberator
Lorain County News
Mademoiselle
The Middlebury Campus
Nashville Tennessean
National Anti-Slavery Standard
Negro Digest
New York Daily Times
Oberlin Alumni Magazine
Oberlin Evangelist
Paedagogica Historica
Quarterly Review of Higher Education Among Negroes
The Register of the Kentucky Historical Society
Rights of All
Time Magazine
Vassar Alumnae Magazine
Vassar Quarterly
The Washington Post Magazine
Weekly Advocate
Wellesley Magazine
The Winston Salem Post
Women's Studies Newsletter

Articles

Bell, John. "Confronting Colorism: Interracial Abolition and the Consequences of Complexion." *Journal of the Early Republic* 39, no. 2 (Summer 2019): 239–65.

Bennett Banner. "Homemaking Institute '49 Features Career and Home." Vol. 18, 6 (March 1949): 1.

Bigglestone, W. E. "Oberlin College and the Negro Student, 1865–1940." *The Journal of Negro History* 56, no. 3 (1971): 198–219.

Brown, Charles I. "The Married Student at Bennett College." *The Journal of Negro Education* 32, no. 2 (Spring 1963): 183–87.

Christmas, June Jackson. "A Historical Overview: The Black Experience at Vassar." *Vassar Quarterly* (Spring, 1988): 4–5.

Coming, E. R., and F. J. Hosford. "The Story of LLS: The First Women's Club in America." *Oberlin Alumni Magazine* 23, no. 2 (March 1927): 10–13.

Crocco, Margaret Smith, and Cally L. Waite. "Education and Marginality: Race and Gender in Higher Education, 1940–1955." *History of Education Quarterly* 47, no. 1 (2007): 69–91.

Derricotte, Juliette. "Schools I Have Seen." *Journal of the National Association of College Women*, no. 13–15 (April 8–10, 1926).

Dublin, Thomas, ed. "Caroline Ware," In *Notable American Women: A Biographical Dictionary, Completing the Twentieth Century*, edited by Edward T. James, Janet Wilson James, and Paul S. Boyer, 662–64. Cambridge, MA: Harvard University Press, 2004.

Du Bois, W. E. B. "The Talented Tenth." In *The Negro Problem: A Series of Articles by Representative Negroes of Today.* New York: J. Pott & Co., 1903.

Eells, Walter Crosby. "Earned Doctorates for Women in the Nineteenth Century," *Bulletin of the American Association of University Professors* 42 (1956): 648.

Eisenmann, Linda. "A Time of Quiet Activism: Research, Practice, and Policy in American Women's Higher Education, 1945–1965." *History of Education Quarterly* 45, no. 1 (2005): 1–17.

———. "Educating the Female Citizen in a Post-War World: Competing Ideologies for American Women, 1945–1965." *Educational Review* 54, no. 2 (2002): 133–41.

Franklin, V. P. "In Pursuit of Freedom: The Educational Activities of Social Organizations in Philadelphia, 1900–1930." In *New Perspectives on Black Educational History,* edited by Vincent P. Franklin and James D. Anderson. Boston: G. K. Hall, 1978.

Franklin, V. P., and Bettye Collier-Thomas. "Vindicating the Race: Contributions to African-American Intellectual History." *Journal of Negro History* 81, nos. 1–4. Washington, 1996.

Gasman, Marybeth. "Instilling an Ethic of Leadership at Fisk University in the 1950s." *Journal of College and Character* 2, no. 2 (2001). https://doi.org/10.2202/1940-1639.1286.

Geiger, Roger L. "Higher Education in the 1950s." In *American Higher Education since World War II: A History*. Princeton, NJ: Princeton University Press, 2019. https://doi.org/10.1515/9780691190648.

Graham, Patricia Albjerg. "Expansion and Exclusion: A History of Women in American Higher Education." *Signs* 3, no. 4 (1978): 759–73. https://doi.org/10.1086/493536.

Grundy, Pamela. "From Amazons to Glamazons: The Rise and Fall of North Carolina Women's Basketball, 1920–1960." *The Journal of American History* 87, no. 1 (2000): 112–46.

Guitar, Mary Anne. "Bennett's Proper Pickets: Negro College Girls Must Be Tough Fighters on the Picket Line, Young Ladies at Home." *Mademoiselle* (June 1965).

Henle, Ellen, and Marlene Merrill. "Antebellum Black Coeds at Oberlin College." In *Women's Studies Newsletter* 7, no. 2 (Spring, 1979): 10.

Herbold, Hilary. "Never a Level Playing Field: Blacks and the GI Bill." *The Journal of Blacks in Higher Education*, no. 6 (1994): 104–8.

Hughes, Langston. "Cowards from the Colleges." *The Crisis* 41 (1934): 226–28.

Jenkins, Martin D. "Enrollment in Institutions of Higher Education of Negroes, 1953–54." *The Journal of Negro Education* 23, no. 2 (1954): 139–51.

Jenkins, R. L. "The Black Land-Grant College in their Formative Years, 1890–1920." In *The 1890 Land-Grant Colleges: A Centennial View*, edited by Barbara Cotton. Vol. 65 no. 2 of Agricultural History series, Durham, NC: Duke University Press, 1991.

Johnson, Charles S. "The Faculty," *The Journal of Educational Sociology* 19, no. 8 (1946): 471–83.

Jones, David D. "The War and the Higher Education of Negro Women." *The Journal of Negro Education* 11, no. 3 (July 1942): 329–37.

Kittrell, Femmie P. "Current Problems and Programs in the Higher Education of Negro Women." *Quarterly Review of Higher Education Among Negroes* 12, no. 1 (January 1944): 13–15.

Lawson, Ellen, and Marlene Merrill. "The Antebellum Talented Thousandth: Black College Students at Oberlin before the Civil War." *Journal of Negro Education*, 52, no. 2 (Spring 1983): 143–44.

Lawson, Ellen McKenzie, and Marlene Merrill. "The Three Sarahs: Documents of Antebellum Black College Women." *Studies in Women and Religion*, vol. 13. New York: E. Mellen Press, 1984.

Liberti, Rita. "We Were Ladies, We Just Played Basketball Like Boys: African American Womanhood and Competitive Basketball at Bennett College, 1928–1942," *Journal of Sports History*, 26 (1999): 567–584.

McCuistion, Fred. "The South's Negro Teaching Force." *Journal of Negro Education* 1, no. 1 (1932): 21.

Miller, Patrick B. "Holding Center Stage: Race Pride and the Extracurriculum at Historically Black Colleges and Universities." In *Affect and Power: Essays on Sex, Slavery, Race and Religion*, edited by David Libby, Paul L. Spickerd, and Susan Ditto, 152. Jackson, MS: University Press of Mississippi, 2005.

MIT Institute for Work and Employment Research. "Phyllis A. Wallace: A Tribute." Cambridge, MA: MIT IWER, 1993.

Nashville Tennessean. "Fisk Has Record Enrollment of 600." September 28, 1944.

National Association of Deans of Women and Advisers to Girls in Negro Schools. *Findings of a Conference on Current Problems and Programs in the Higher Education of Negro Women* 12, no. 4 (October 1944).

Nelson, Paul David. "Experiment in Interracial Education at Berea College, 1858–1908." *The Journal of Negro History*, 59, no. 1 (January 1974): 13–27.

Null, Druscilla J. "Myrtilla Miner's 'School for Colored Girls': A Mirror on Antebellum Washington." *Records of the Columbia Historical Society*, Washington, DC, 52 (1989): 254–68.

O'Brien, Patrick. "Lois Irwin, Barber College and Christian Altruism in Alabama, 1926–1927." *Journal of Presbyterian History (1962–1985)* 62 no. 4 (1984): 322–38.

Pearce, Larry M. "Colored Students and Graduates of the University of Kansas." *Graduate Magazine of the University of Kansas* 7, no. 8 (May 1909): 294.

Perkins, Linda M. "Black Women and Racial 'Uplift' Prior to Emancipation." In *The Black Women Cross-Culturally*, edited by Filomina Chioma Steady, 317–34. Rochester, VT: Dean C. Schield, 1981.

———. "For the Good of the Race: Married African-American Academics—A Historical Perspective." In *Academic Couples: Problems and Promises*, edited by Marianne Ferber and Jane Loeb, 80–103. Urbana, IL: University of Illinois Press, 1997.

———. "Lucy Diggs Slowe: Champion of the Self-Determination of African-American Women in Higher Education." *The Journal of Negro History* 81, no. 1/4 (1996): 89–104.

———. "The History of Black Women Graduate Students, 1921–1948." In *The Sage Handbook of African American Education*, 53–67. Thousand Oaks, CA: Sage Publications, 2009.

———. "The Impact of the 'Cult of True Womanhood' on the Education of Black Women." *Journal of Social Issues* 39, no. 3 (1983): 17–28. https://doi.org/10.1111/j.1540-4560.1983.tb00152.x.

———. "Merze Tate and the Quest for Gender Equity at Howard University: 1942–1977." *History of Education Quarterly* 54, no. 4 (2014): 516–51.

———. "The National Association of College Women: Vanguard of Black Women's Leadership and Education, 1923–1954." *The Journal of Education* 172, no. 3 (1990): 65–75.

———. "Women's Education in the United States, 1780–1840 by Margaret Nash." *History of Education Quarterly* 47, no. 2 (2007): 254–56.

Perkins, Linda M. "The Black Female Professoriate at Howard University, 1926–1988." In *Women's Higher Education in the United States: New Historical Perspective*, edited by Margaret A. Nash, 117–37. New York: Palgrave Macmillan, 2017.

Pinkard, Nancy. "Bertha Diggs, Labor Secretary, Attributes Success to Hard Work," *Bennett Banner* vol. 15, no. 6 (April 1946), 1, 4.

Pitre, Merline, "At the Crossroads: Black Texas Women, 1930–1954." In *Black Women in Texas History*, edited by Bruce A. Glasrud and Merline Pitre, 129–58. College Station, TX: Texas A&M University Press, 2008.

Sartorius, Kelly C. "A Coeducational Pathway to Political and Economic Citizenship: Women's Student Government and a Philosophy and Practice of Women's US Higher Coeducation Between 1890 and 1945." In *Women's Higher Education in the United States: New Historical Perspective,* edited by Margaret A. Nash, 161–83. New York: Palgrave Macmillan, 2018.

———. "Counseling US Women for Economic Citizenship: Deans of Women and the Beginnings of Vocational Guidance." *Paedagogica Historica* 56, no. 6 (2020): 831–42.

Scott, Patricia Bell. "To Keep My Self-Respect: Dean Lucy Diggs Slowe's 1927 Memorandum on the Sexual Harassment of Black Women." *National Women's Studies Association Journal—Sexual Harassment Issue* 9, no. 2 (1997): 70–76.

Slowe, Lucy Diggs. "The Dormitory—A Cultural Influence." *Journal of the National Association of College Women* (1931–32): 11–14.

———. "Higher Education of Negro Woman." *Journal of Negro Education* 2, no. 3 (July 1933): 352–58.

Spelman College. "Conference on Negro Women's Problems in Higher Education." *Spelman Messenger* 60, no. 4 (August 1944): 10–11, 24.

Strayhorn, Terrell L. "Alice Carlotta Jackson: She was the First Black Applicant to the University of Virginia." *Journal of Blacks in Higher Education* vol. 51 (Spring, 2006): 19.

Synnott, Marcia G. "African American Women Pioneers in Desegregating Higher Education." In *Higher Education and the Civil Rights Movement: White Supremacy, Black Southerners, and College Campuses*, edited by Peter Wallenstein. Gainesville, FL: University of Florida Press, 2008.

Tate, Merze. "Justification for the Women's College." *Journal of College Alumnae Association* 14 (1938).

Welter, Barbara. "The Cult of True Womanhood: 1820–1860." *American Quarterly* 18, no. 2 (1966): 151–74.

Williams-Burns, Winona. "Jane Ellen McAllister: Pioneer for Excellence in Teacher Education." *Journal of Negro Education* 51, no. 3 (1982): 342–57.

Wormley, G. Smith. "Myrtilla Miner." *The Journal of Negro History* 5, no. 4 (1920): 448–57.

Books

Adams, Beatrice, Shauni Armstead, Miya Carey, Tracey Johnson, Brenann Sutter, Pamela N. Walker, Meagan Wierda, et al. *Scarlet and Black, Volume 2: Constructing Race and Gender at Rutgers, 1865–1945*. New Brunswick, NJ: Rutgers University Press, 2020.

Anderson, James D. *The Education of Blacks in the South, 1860–1935*. Chapel Hill: University of North Carolina Press, 1988.

Antler, Joyce. *Lucy Sprague Mitchell: The Making of a Modern Woman*. New Haven, CT: Yale University Press, 1987.

Attaway, Doris, and Marjorie Rabe Barritt, eds. *Women's Voice : Early Years at the University of Michigan. Bulletin*. Vol. 47. Ann Arbor: Bentley Historical Library, University of Michigan, 2000.

Baumann, Roland M. *Constructing Black Education at Oberlin College: A Documentary History*. 1 online resource (xx, 418 pages): illustrations. Athens: Ohio University Press, 2010.

Baumgartner, Kabria. *In Pursuit of Knowledge*. Vol. 5. New York: NYU Press, 2019. http://www.jstor.org.ccl.idm.oclc.org/stable/j.ctv1f885b0.

Bell, John. *Degrees of Equality: Abolitionist Colleges and the Politics of Race*. Baton Rouge, Louisiana: LSU Press, 2022.

Bond, Horace Mann. *Education for Freedom: A History of Lincoln University*. Lincoln, PA: Lincoln University Press, 1976.

———. *Education for Freedom : A History of Lincoln University*, Lincoln, PA: Lincoln University Press, 2014.

Bordin, Ruth. *Women at Michigan: The "Dangerous Experiment," 1870s to the Present*. Ann Arbor: University of Michigan Press, 1999.

Boyd, Kendra, Marisa J. Fuentos, Deborah Gray White, eds. *Scarlet and Black, Volume 2: Constructing Race and Gender at Rutgers, 1865–1945*. New Brunswick, NJ: Rutgers University Press, 2020.

Browne, Rose Butler, and James W. English. *Love My Children: An Autobiography*. [1st ed.]. New York: Meredith Press, 1969.

Buick, Kirsten Pai. *Child of the Fire: Mary Edmonia Lewis and the Problem of Art History's Black and Indian Subject*. E-Duke Books Scholarly Collection. Durham, NC: Duke University Press, 2010.

Campbell, Stanley W. *The Slave Catchers: Enforcement of the Fugitive Slave Law, 1850–1860*. Chapel Hill, NC: University of North Carolina Press, 1970.

Cansler, Charles. *Three Generations: Story of a Colored Family in Eastern Tennessee*. Privately published, 1939.

Carey, Miya, and Pamela Walker. "Profiles in Courage: Breaking the Color Line at Douglass College." In *Scarlet and Black, Volume 2: Constructing Race and Gender at Rutgers, 1865–1945*, edited by Kendra Boyd, Marisa J. Fuentos, and Deborah Gray White, 106–31. New Brunswick, NJ: Rutgers University Press, 2020.

Carson, Clayborne. *In Struggle: SNCC and the Black Awakening of the 1960s*. 1 online resource (viii, 359 pages): illustrations. Cambridge, MA: Harvard University Press, 1995. http://hdl.handle.net/2027/heb.00590.

Cayton, Horace R. (Horace Roscoe). *Long Old Road*. Seattle: University of Washington Press, 1970.

Chambers-Schiller, Lee Virginia. *Liberty, A Better Husband: Single Women in America: The Generations of 1780–1840*. New Haven, CT: Yale University Press, 1984.

Collier-Thomas, Bettye. *Jesus, Jobs, and Justice: African American Women and Religion*. 1st ed. New York: Alfred A. Knopf, 2010.

Cooper, Anna J. (Anna Julia). *A Voice from the South: By a Black Woman of the South*. 1 online resource (159 pages). Chapel Hill: University of North Carolina at Chapel Hill Library, 2017.

Cooper, Brittney C. *Beyond Respectability: The Intellectual Thought of Race Women*. 1 online resource. Women, Gender, and Sexuality in American History series. Urbana: University of Illinois Press, 2017.

Coppin, Frances Jackson. *Reminiscences of School Life, and Hints on Teaching*. 1 online resource (191 pages): illustrations. Philadelphia: A.M.E. Book Concern, 1913.

Cromwell, Adelaide M. *The Other Brahmins: Boston's Black Upper Class, 1750–1950*. 1 online resource (xii, 284 pages): illustrations, map vols. Fayetteville: University of Arkansas Press, 1994.

Crow, Jeffrey J., and Flora J. Hatley Wadelington. *Black Americans in North Carolina and the South*. Chapel Hill: University of North Carolina Press, 1984.

Cuthbert, Marion Vera. *Education and Marginality: A Study of the Negro College Graduate*. New York: Teacher's College, 1942.

Dowst, Henry Payson, and John Albert Seaford. *Radcliffe College*. Boston: H. B. Humphrey Company, 1913.

Du Bois, W. E. B. *The College-Bred Negro American*. Atlanta: Atlanta University Press, 1910.

———. *Darkwater: Voices from within the Veil*. 1 online resource (viii, 276 pages) vols. Social Theory. New York: Harcourt, Brace and Howe, 1920.

———. *The Talented Tenth*. J. Potts and Company, 1903.

Durr, Virginia Foster, and Hollinger F. Barnard. *Outside the Magic Circle: The Autobiography of Virginia Foster Durr*. 1 online resource (xix, 360 pages): illustrations, portraits vols. Tuscaloosa: University of Alabama Press, 1985.

Eisenmann, Linda. *Higher Education for Women in Postwar America, 1945–1965*. 1 online resource (viii, 280 pages) vols. UPCC Book Collections on Project MUSE. Baltimore, MD: Johns Hopkins University Press, 2006.

Evans, Stephanie Y. *Black Women in the Ivory Tower, 1850–1954: An Intellectual History*. 1 online resource (222 pages) vols. Gainesville: University Press of Florida, 2016.

Fields, Mamie Garvin, and Karen Elise Fields. *Lemon Swamp and Other Places: A Carolina Memoir*. New York: Free Press, 1983.

Fletcher, Robert Samuel. *A History of Oberlin College from Its Foundation through the Civil War*. Vols. 1 and 2. Oberlin, OH: Oberlin College, 1943.

Flexner, Eleanor. *Century of Struggle: The Woman's Rights Movement in the United States*. Revised ed. Cambridge, MA: Belknap Press of Harvard University Press, 1975.

Foner, Philip Sheldon, and Josephine F. Pacheco. *Three Who Dared: Prudence Crandall, Margaret Douglass, Myrtilla Miner: Champions of Antebellum Black Education*. Contributions in Women's Studies series, no. 47. Westport, CT: Greenwood Press, 1984.

Foote, Thelma Wills. *Black and White Manhattan: The History of Racial Formation in Colonial New York City*. New York: Oxford University Press, 2004.

Ford, Gary L., Jr. *Constance Baker Motley: One Woman's Fight for Civil Rights and Equal Justice under Law*. 1 online resource (viii, 164 pages): illustrations, black and white portraits. Tuscaloosa: The University of Alabama Press, 2017.

Franklin, John Hope. *From Slavery to Freedom: A History of Negro Americans*. 3rd ed. New York: Random House, 1969.

Franklin, John Hope, and Loren Schweninger. *Runaway Slaves: Rebels on the Plantation*. New York: Oxford University Press, 1999.

Franklin, V. P. *Black Self-Determination: A Cultural History of African-American Resistance*. 2nd ed. Brooklyn, NY: Lawrence Hill Books, 1992.

———. *Young Crusaders: The Untold Story of the Children and Teenagers Who Galvanized the Civil Rights Movement*. Boston: Beacon, 2022.

Gaines, Kevin Kelly. *Uplifting the Race: Black Leadership, Politics, and Culture in the Twentieth Century*. Chapel Hill: University of North Carolina Press, 1996.

Gatewood, Willard B., Jr. *Aristocrats of Color: The Black Elite, 1880–1920*. Bloomington: Indiana University Press, 1990.

Geiger, Roger. *American Higher Education Since World War II*. Princeton, NJ: Princeton University Press, 2019.

Giddings, Paula. *Ida: A Sword among Lions: Ida B. Wells and the Campaign against Lynching*. 1st ed. New York: Amistad, 2008.

Giddings, Paula. *In Search of Sisterhood: Delta Sigma Theta and the Challenge of the Black Sorority Movement*. First edition. New York: William Morrow and Company, 1988.

Gilyard, Keith. *Louise Thompson Patterson: A Life of Struggle for Justice*. Durham, NC: Duke University Press, 2017.

Glasrud, Bruce A., Merline Pitre, and Angela Boswell. *Black Women in Texas History*. 1st ed. 1 online resource (viii, 248 pages). Centennial Series of the Association of Former Students, Texas A&M University, No. 108. College Station: Texas A&M University Press, 2008.

Gore, Dayo F. *Radicalism at the Crossroads: African American Women Activists in the Cold War*. New York: New York University Press, 2011.

Greene, Harry W. *Holders of Doctorates among American Negroes; an Educational and Social Study of Negroes Who Have Earned Doctoral Degrees in Course 1876–1943.* Boston: Meador, 1946.

Guy-Sheftall, Beverly, and Jo Moore Stewart, eds. *Spelman: A Centennial Celebration 1881–1981.* Atlanta, Ga.: Spelman College, 1981.

Hall, Raymond L. *Black Separatism in the United States.* Hanover, NH: Published for Dartmouth College by the University Press of New England, 1978.

Harlan, Louis R. *Separate and Unequal: Public School Campaigns and Racism in the Southern Seaboard States, 1901–1915.* New York: Atheneum, 1968.

Height, Dorothy I. *Open Wide the Freedom Gates: A Memoir.* 1st ed. New York: Public Affairs, 2003.

Hendricks, Wanda A. *Fannie Barrier Williams: Crossing the Borders of Region and Race.* 1 online resource. The New Black Studies Series. Urbana: University of Illinois Press, 2014.

Higginbotham, Evelyn Brooks. *Righteous Discontent: The Women's Movement in the Black Baptist Church, 1880–1920.* Cambridge, MA: Harvard University Press, 1994.

Hill, Lena M., and Michael D. Hill. *Invisible Hawkeyes: African Americans at the University of Iowa during the Long Civil Rights Era.* 1 online resource. Iowa City: University of Iowa Press, 2016.

Hine, Darlene Clark. *Black Women in White: Racial Conflict and Cooperation in the Nursing Profession, 1890–1950.* 1 online resource (xxiii, 264 pages): illustrations. Blacks in the Diaspora series. Bloomington: Indiana University Press, 1989.

Holloway, Jonathan Scott. *Confronting the Veil: Abram Harris, Jr., E. Franklin Frazier, and Ralph Bunche, 1919–1941.* Chapel Hill: University of North Carolina Press, 2002.

Horowitz, Helen Lefkowitz. *The Power and Passion of M. Carey Thomas.* 1st edition. New York: Alfred A. Knopf, 1994.

Hurston, Zora Neale. *Dust Tracks on the Road: An Autobiography.* Urbana: University of Illinois Press, 1984.

Hylton, Raymond. *Virginia Union University.* The Campus History Series. Charleston, SC: Arcadia Publishing, 2014.

James, Edward T., Janet Wilson James, and Paul S. Boyer. *Notable American Women, 1607–1950: A Biographical Dictionary.* Volume 3, P-Z. 1 online resource (735 pages). Cambridge, MA: Belknap Press of Harvard University Press, 1971.

Janken, Kenneth Robert. *Rayford W. Logan and the Dilemma of the African-American Intellectual.* 1 online resource (xv, 319 pages): illustrations. Amherst: University of Massachusetts Press, 1993.

Johnson, Charles Spurgeon. *The Negro College Graduate.* Chapel Hill: University of North Carolina Press, 1938.

Johnson, Joan Marie. *Southern Women at the Seven Sister Colleges: Feminist Values and Social Activism, 1875–1915.* Athens: University of Georgia Press, 2008.

Jones, Edward A. *A Candle in the Dark: A History of Morehouse College.* Valley Forge, PA: Judson Press, 1967.

Jordan, Vernon E., and Annette Gordon-Reed. *Vernon Can Read! A Memoir.* New York: Public Affairs, 2008.

Jordan, Winthrop D. *White Over Black*. Chapel Hill, North Carolina: University of North Carolina Press, 1968.

Lawrence-Lightfoot, Sara. *Balm in Gilead: Journey of a Healer*. Radcliffe Biography Series. Reading, MA: Addison-Wesley, 1988.

Lefever, Harry G. *Undaunted by the Fight: Spelman College and the Civil Rights Movement, 1957/1967*. 1st ed. Macon, Ga.: Mercer University Press, 2005.

Libby, David J., Paul. Spickard, and Susan Ditto. *Affect and Power: Essays on Sex, Slavery, Race, and Religion*. 1 online resource (256 pages). Jackson: University Press of Mississippi, 2005.

Litwack, Leon. *North of Slavery: The Negro Prior in the Free States, 1790–1860*. Chicago: University of Chicago Press, 1961.

Logan, Rayford Whittingham. *Howard University: The First Hundred Years, 1867–1967*. New York: New York University Press, 1969.

Mack, Kenneth Walter. *Representing the Race: The Creation of the Civil Rights Lawyer*. 1 online resource (330 pages, 12 unnumbered pages of plates): illustrations. Cambridge, MA: Harvard University Press, 2012. https://doi.org/10.4159/harvard.9780674065307.

Manning, Kenneth R. *Black Apollo of Science: The Life of Ernest Everett Just*. 1 online resource (397 pages): illustrations, portraits. ACLS Humanities E-Book (Series). New York: Oxford University Press, 1984.

May, Samuel J. (Samuel Joseph). *Some Recollections of Our Antislavery Conflict*. Boston: Fields, Osgood, 1869.

May, Vivian M., and Anna Julia Cooper. *Visionary Black Feminist: A Critical Introduction*. New York: Routledge, 2007.

McCluskey, Audrey Thomas. *A Forgotten Sisterhood: Pioneering Black Women Educators and Activists in the Jim Crow South*. 1 online resource (x, 181 pages): illustrations, portraits. Lanham, MD: Rowman & Littlefield, 2014.

McGinnis, Frederick A. *A History and Interpretation of Wilberforce University*. Blanchester, OH: Brown, 1941.

McLeod, Jacqueline. *Daughter of the Empire State: The Life of Judge Jane Bolin*. 1 online resource. Urbana: University of Illinois Press, 2011.

Miller, Carroll L. L., and Anne S. Pruitt-Logan. *Faithful to the Task at Hand: The Life of Lucy Diggs Slowe*. 1 online resource (xvii, 448 pages): illustrations. Albany: State University of New York Press, 2012.

Monteith, Sharon. *SNCC's Stories: The African American Freedom Movement in the Civil Rights South*. Athens: University of Georgia Press, 2020.

Moss, Hilary J. *Schooling Citizens: The Struggle for African American Education in Antebellum America*. 1 online resource (xv, 274 pages): illustrations, maps. Chicago: University of Chicago Press, 2009. http://chicago.universitypressscholarship.com/view/10.7208/chicago/9780226542515.001.0001/upso-9780226542492.

Motley, Constance Baker. *Equal Justice Under Law: An Autobiography*. 1st ed. New York: Farrar, Straus, and Giroux, 1998.

Murray, Pauli. *Song in a Weary Throat: An American Pilgrimage*. 1st ed. New York: Harper & Row, 1987.

Nash, Margaret A. *Women's Education in the United States, 1780–1840*. New York: Palgrave Macmillan, 2005.

Neverdon-Morton, Cynthia. *Afro-American Women of the South and the Advancement of the Race, 1895–1925*. Knoxville: University of Tennessee Press, 1991.

Noble, Jeanne L. *The Negro Woman's College Education*. TC Studies in Education. New York: Teachers College, Columbia University, 1956.

Northrup, Solomon. *Twelve Years a Slave*. New York: Community Press, 2013.

Pacheco, Josephine F. *The Pearl: A Failed Slave Escape on the Potomac*. 1 online resource (x, 307 pages): illustrations. Chapel Hill: University of North Carolina Press, 2005.

Painter, Nell Irvin. *Exodusters: Black Migration to Kansas after Reconstruction*. New York: W.W. Norton, 1992.

———. *Sojourner Truth: A Life, a Symbol*. New York: W.W. Norton, 1997.

Palmieri, Patricia. *In Adamless Eden: The Community of Women Faculty at Wellesley*. New Haven, CT: Yale University Press, 1995.

Parker, Marjorie H. *Alpha Kappa Alpha through the Years 1908–1988*. Chicago: Mobium Press, 1990.

Perkins, Linda M. *Fanny Jackson Coppin and the Institute for Colored Youth, 1865–1902*. New York: Garland, 1987.

Quarles, Benjamin. *Black Abolitionists*. New York: Oxford University Press, 1969.

Ransby, Barbara. *Eslanda: The Large and Unconventional Life of Mrs. Paul Robeson*. 1 online resource (xiii, 373 pages, 35 unnumbered pages of plates): illustrations, map. New Haven, CT: Yale University Press, 2013.

Richardson, Joe Martin. *A History of Fisk University, 1865–1946*. Tuscaloosa: University of Alabama Press, 1980.

Ricks, Mary Kay. *Escape on the Pearl: The Heroic Bid for Freedom on the Underground Railroad*. 1st ed. New York: William Morrow, 2007.

Rogers, John A. R. (John Almanza Rowley). *Birth of Berea College a Story of Providence*. 1 online resource (174 pages) illustrations (including portraits). Slavery, Abolition & Social Justice. Philadelphia: H.T. Coates, 1903.

Rosenberg, Rosalind. *Jane Crow: The Life of Pauli Murray*. New York: Oxford University Press, 2017.

Sartorius, Kelly C. *Deans of Women and the Feminist Movement: Emily Taylor's Activism*. Historical Studies in Education. New York: Palgrave Macmillan, 2014.

Shaw, Stephanie J. *What a Woman Ought to Be and to Do: Black Professional Women Workers during the Jim Crow Era*. 1 online resource (xvi, 347 pages). Women in Culture and Society. Chicago: University of Chicago Press, 1996.

Sherwood, Grace H. *The Oblates' Hundred and One Years*. New York: Macmillan 1931.

Smith, Jessie Carney, ed. *Notable Black American Women*. New York: Gale Research, 1996.

Solomon, Barbara. *In the Company of Educated Women: A History of Women and Higher Education in America*. New Haven, CT: Yale University Press, 1985.

Sterling, Dorothy, ed. *We Are Your Sisters: Black Women in the Nineteenth Century*. 1st ed. New York: W. W. Norton, 1984.

Talbert, Horace. *Sons of Allen*. Xenia, OH: The Aldine Press, 1906. Fort Worth, TX: Nyree Press Publishing, 2016.

Terrell, Mary Church. *A Colored Woman in a White World*. New York: Arno Press, 1980.

United States Office of Education and Moses B. Goodwin. *History of Schools for the Colored Population. The American Negro, His History and Literature*. New York: Arno Press, 1969.

Verbrugge, Martha H. *Active Bodies: A History of Women's Physical Education in Twentieth-Century America*. 1 online resource (xi, 391 pages): illustrations. New York: Oxford University Press, 2012.

Vitalis, Robert. *White World Order, Black Power Politics: The Birth of American International Relations*. 1 online resource. The United States in the World. Ithaca: Cornell University Press, 2015.

Waite, Cally L. *Permission to Remain among Us: Education for Blacks in Oberlin, Ohio, 1880–1914*. Westport, CT: Praeger, 2002.

Walker, David. *Walker's Appeal, in Four Articles*. Chapel Hill: University of North Carolina Press, 2011. https://doi.org/10.5149/9780807869482_walker.

Wallenstein, Peter. *Higher Education and the Civil Rights Movement: White Supremacy, Black Southerners, and College Campuses*. 1 online resource (xv, 298 pages). Southern Dissent. Gainesville: University Press of Florida, 2008.

Walton, Andrea. *Women at Indiana University: 150 Years of Experiences and Contributions*. Bloomington: Indiana University Press, 2022.

Washington, Booker T. *The Negro Problem*. 1 online resource (87 pages). Dinslaken, Germany: Anboco, 2016.

Washington, Margaret. *Sojourner Truth's America*. 1 online resource vols. ACLS Humanities E-Book. Urbana: University of Illinois Press, 2009. http://hdl.handle.net/2027/heb.09319.

White, Walter. *A Man Called White: The Autobiography of Walter White*. 1 online resource (viii, 382 pages). Black Thought and Culture. New York: Viking Press, 1987.

Williams, Zachery R. *In Search of the Talented Tenth: Howard University Public Intellectuals and the Dilemmas of Race, 1926–1970*. 1 online resource (xi, 250 pages): illustrations. Columbia: University of Missouri Press, 2009. http://site.ebrary.com/id/10575418.

Wilson, Shannon H. *Berea College: An Illustrated History*. 1 online resource (xi, 246 pages): illustrations. Lexington: University Press of Kentucky, 2006.

Wolters, Raymond. *The New Negro on Campus: Black College Rebellions of the 1920s*. Princeton, NJ: Princeton University Press, 1975.

Woodson, Carter G. *The Education of the Negro Prior to 1861*. New York: Arson Publishing, 1918.

Wright, Richard R. *The Negro in Pennsylvania: A Study in Economic History*. Arno Press and The New York Times, 1969.

Documentaries, Proceedings, and Reports

American Baptist Free Mission Society. "American Baptist Free Mission Society Report on the New York Central College, McGrawville, NY." 1850.

Hanchett, Catherine M. "The Later Careers of Some African American Students from New York Central College," presented before the Cortland Historical Society, February 26, 1992. Cortland Historical Society, Manuscript 678, number 272.

Institute for Colored Youth, the Officers and Students and the Annual Report, 1861.

New York Central College A Beacon on the Hill (1849–1860). McGraw Historical Society, McGraw, New York, 2016. Documentary Film https://vimeo.com/197516592.

New York Central College List of Students, compiled by Catherine M. Hanchett, Manuscript 258 in Cortland County Historical Society, McGraw, New York.

Tate, Merze. *Report of the Status of Faculty in College of Liberal Arts by Department, Rank and Salary, 1953–54.* Washington, DC: Howard University, 1987.

Index

Page numbers in italic indicate illustrations.

Abbott, Cleve, 187–88
Abbott, Jesse, 187–88
abolitionist colleges, 29–33, 307; Berea College as, 2, 52–60; Institute for Colored Youth, Philadelphia, 29, 30–31; New York Central College (NYCC), 2, 30–31, 32, 33; Oberlin College as, 33–41; women and men working at, 32–33
abolitionists, 1–2; escape of slaves assisted by, 18; public universities and, 106–7; religious groups and, 18–19; single sex schools for Black girls established by, 27
academia, Black women in: academic couples, 244–50, 295–97; Black scholarly journals and, 290–91; under Charles S. Johnson, 258–63; colleges offering doctorates and, 237–38; doctoral degree requirements and, 234–35; as faculty at HBCUs, 156–57, 242–44; fellowships and, 241–43, 247, 249; funding for graduate studies and, 238–40; legal challenges against discrimination and, 238–40; quest for gender equity at Howard University and, 263–71; at risk, 250–57; Women's Faculty Club, Howard University, and, 271–80. *See also* marginality of Black women college graduates; individual scholars
academic couples, 244–50, 295–97. *See also* marriage and Black women
Adams, Frankie V., 138
African Benevolent Society, 19
African Methodist Episcopal Church (AME), 132, 279
Afro-American, The, 150
Afro-American Female Intelligence Society, 24
"Ain't I a Woman?," 4, 45
Albrier, Frances Mary, 140–41, 142
Alexander, Harriette, 122
Alexander, Raymond Pace, 157, 250–51
Alexander, Sadie Tanner Mossell, 156–58, 167, 233, 242–43, 250, 264
Allen, Forrest, 120–21
Allen, Julia, 167
Allen, William Grant, 30
all-male and coeducational HBCUs, 132–36
Alpha Kappa Alpha (AKA), 112–13, *115–17*, 120, 124, 142, 168, 169, 264, 295, 305, 311; sports and, 123
Alpha Phi Alpha, 113
AME Review, 284
American Association of University Women (AAUW), 155, 165
American Baptist Home Mission Society, 128
American Colonization Society, 33
American Council of Education (ACE), 155
American Council on Race Relations, 258
American Missionary, The, 38
American Missionary Association, 37, 52–54, 127, 137, 142, 154, 255
American Negro Academy, 5
Amos, Thrysa, 149, 162

Anderson, James D., 71
Anderson, Mary Annette, 63–64
Angell, James, 108
antebellum period, 1
antislavery organizations, 26–27
Antler, Joyce, 167
Appeal to the Coloured Citizens of the World, An, 1
Armstrong, Samuel Chapman, 136
Associated Women's Students (AWS), 186–87
Association of American Colleges and Universities, 8
Association of the Collegiate Alumnae (ACA), 165
Atlanta Baptist Female Seminary, 130–31
Atlanta Constitution, 205
Avery, Charles, 38

Baker, Ella, 301
Baldwin, Ruth, 81
Baltimore Afro-American, 205
Bando, Thelma, 142, 151–52, 214–15, 217, 278–79; on marriage, 294; mentored by Lucy Diggs Slowe, 149–51
Barksdale, Mildred, 139, 248
Barksdale, Richard, 248
Barnard Bulletin, 98
Barnard College, 72, 95–101
Barnett, Ferdinand, 106
Barnett, Ida B. Wells, 5
Bates, Daisy, 301
Baumgartner, Kabria, 3
beauty and phenotype, 31–32
Beecher, Henry Ward, 32, 33
Beecher, Lyman, 33
Benezet, Anthony, 18–19
Bennett Banner, The, 204
Bennett College, 131–32, 180–81, 192–95; Home Making Institute at, 196–200, 221, 223–24, 226; women's curriculum at, 206–7, 210; women's sports at, 204
Berea College, 2, 167; American Missionary Association and, 53–54; Black and white students at, 57–58; department names at, 55–56; faculty at, 56–57, 59–60; first Black students to enroll at, 54–55; founding of, 52–53; interracial dating at, 59; interracial education barred in Kentucky and, 60; mandatory attendance at religious events at, 58–59
Bethune, Mary McLeod, 131, 132, 195
Black, Beatrice Yvonne, 241

Black Greek organizations, 112–22; Alpha Kappa Alpha (AKA), 112–13, *115–17,* 120, 123, 124, 142, 168, 169, 264, 295, 305, 311; Delta Sigma Theta, *118–19, 118–19,* 142, 169, 305, 311
Blackwell, Jeanne, 97, 98
Black Women in America, 282
Bluford, Lucile Harris, 225
boarding schools, 26
Bolin, Charles, 73
Bolin, Jane, 73–75, 100
Bolton, Ina, 288–89, 301
Bond, Horace Mann, 218, 220
Bontemps, Arne, 257
Bordin, Ruth, 107–8
Bousfield, Maudelle Brown, 169
Bowles, Frank, 102
Boyd, Evelyn, 101, 241, 262
Brady, St. Elmo, 251
Branch, Mary E., 280–82
Brandeis, Louis, 102
Brandeis, Susan, 102
Breaux, Richard Melvin, 109, 114, 117, 122, 124
Brett, Ruth, 180, 188–90, 194, 206–7, 213, 216, 249–50, 294
Britton, Julia, 56
Brown, Charles I., 215–16
Brown, Charlotte Hawkins, 131, 132, 154
Brown, Charlotte Leverett Smith, 76–77
Brown, Emma V., 29
Brown, Georgia C., 287
Brown, John, 39–40
Brown, Rose Butler, 239
Brown, Ruth, 73
Brown, Sterling, 263
Brown v. Board of Education, 60, 102, 200, 225
Bryn Mawr College, 72, 84–86; housing at, 91–93; Jewish students at, 86–88
Bunche, Ralph, 263, 270
Bureau for Intercultural Education, 258
Burke, Beulah, 112
Burroughs, Nannie Helen, 131, 132
Burton, Marion, 80
Butcher, Beatrice B., 23, 26–27
Butler, Gwendolyn, 122–23

Caldwell, Julia S., 143
Caliver, Ambrose, 251, 255
Callahan, Virginia Woods, 275
Calvert, George Henry, 41–43
Carman, Harry, 102
Carnegie Corporation, 258
Carney, Mabel, 252

362   Index

Carter, Eunice Hunter, 100
Cashin, Lillian, 251, 255, 257
Caverno, Julia, 79
Cayton, Horace, 185
Chambers-Schiller, Lee Virginia, 22–23
Chicago Conservator, The, 106
Chicago Defender, 153
Chinn, May Edward, 297
Christian schools: Atlanta Baptist Female Seminary, 130–31; Bennett College, 131–32; Hartshorn Memorial College, 128–29; Scotia Seminary, 129–30; white religious denominations and founding of HBCUs, 134–35
Christian Science, 91
Christmas, June Jackson, 95
Churchill, Charles Henry, 48
Civil Rights Act, 1964, 2, 298
civil rights movement, 225–26, 298–301, 305–10
Clark, Kenneth B., 102, 103
classism, 4
Clay, Cassius M., 52–53
Coachman, Alice, 205
Cole, Joan E., 105
College Bred Negro, The, 110, 136, 285
College of New Jersey for Women, 70
Columbia College, 95
Comstock, Ada, 82
Cook, Annie Bailey, 161–62
Cook, Enid, 87–88, 101
Cooke, Anne M., 272
Coolidge, Mary Lowell, 92
Cooper, Anna Julia, 5, 243, 284
Cooper, Brittany, 3
Coppin, Fanny Jackson. *See* Jackson, Fanny
Cornely, Paul, 216
Cowles, Henry, 51
Crandall, Prudence, 20–22
Crawford, Katherine, 108–9
Crawford, Lorraine, 122
The Crisis magazine, 2–3, 75, 80, 93–94, 101, 111, 148, 290; on Black students in Greek organizations, 120, 121; Langston Hughes in, 182; on marginality of Black women college graduates, 307–8; on religious life at Howard University, 160
Cromwell, Adelaide, 223
Cromwell, John, Jr., 234
Cromwell, John Wesley, 79, 234
Cromwell, Otelia, 79–80, 81, 83, 100, 257; doctorate obtained by, 234
Crummell, Alexander, 22

curriculum, 205–9
Cuthbert, Marion, 258–60, 285–87, 289, 293, 298, 301, 304

Daniels, Sadie, 255–56
Davis, Christine, 291
Davis, Hilda, 149, 151, 166, 189, 304, 305; on marginality of Black women college graduates, 294
Davis, Jackson, 211
Davis, John W., 249
Day, Carl, 60
Daytona Education and Industrial School for Girls, 132, 195
deans of women, white, 165–70
deans of women, HBCU: Alice Freeman Palmer, 132, 148, 165, 167; Bennett College, 192–95; challenges and quest for refinement and femininity, 170–76; credentials of, 176–79; home economics and, 193, 195, 196–200; housing issues and, 167–69; Lucy Diggs Slowe, 265, 270 (*see* Slowe, Lucy Diggs); National Association of Women's Deans and Advisors of Women in Colored Schools (NAWDACS) and, 6, 161–64, 213–17; Tuskegee Institute, 181–92; women's sports and, 200–205
Deans of Women and the Feminist Movement: Emily Taylor's Activism, 165
Delta Sigma Theta, 118–19, 142, 169, 305, 311
Derricotte, Juliette, 163–64, 255, 258
Devine, Annie, 301
Dictionary of American Negro Biography, 282
Diggs, Bertha, 221–22
Diggs, Mary Huff, 260–61
doctorates. *See* academia, Black women in
Douglas, Aaron, 257
Douglas, Sarah Mapps, 31
Douglass, Frederick, 32
Drake, St. Clair, 300
Dribble, Clarice, 105
Du Bois, W. E. B., 5, 52, 80, 90; *The College-Bred Negro*, 110, 136, 285; on difficulty for Black women to gain admission to white institutions, 68, 69, 70, 71, 101, 121; on enrollment of Black students in the South, 127; on enrollment of Black women at Vassar, 93, 95; on future of Black women, 308–9; on HBCUs, 137, 164; as staunch supporter of Black women's rights, 307–8; tracking of accomplishments and challenges of Black students in white institutions, 75; on women's suffrage, 308

Du Bois, Yolanda, 164
Duncan, Catherine, 141
Durkee, J. Stanley, 145
Durr, Clifford, 89
Durr, Virginia Foster, 89, 90
Dust Tracks on a Road, 96
Dykes, Eva, 156, 229, 264, 274–75

Earlham College, 257
Ebony, 290, 291, 300, 303, 308, 309–10
Economic Status of University Women in the USA, 167
Edmond, Helen G., 278–79
Edmonson, Emily, 31, 32, 33
Edmonson, Mary, 31, 32, 33
Education and Marginality: A Study of the Negro Woman College Graduate, 285–87
education of African Americans: in abolitionist colleges (*see* abolitionist colleges); antislavery organizations and, 26–27; barred in the South before Emancipation, 18; Black elite communities and, 28–29; Civil Rights Movement and, 225–26, 298–301; compared to whites in the 1940s-1950s, 8; differences between men and women in, 283–84, 293–94, 309–10; doctoral level, 234–35; efforts to deny, in the North, 20; equity in, 8; as essential for freedom and advancement, 2, 17, 25–26; gender ideologies and, 5–6, 283–84; GI Bill and, 7, 227–28, 261; housing and, 90–93; increase in, 2–4, 36, 197–98, 210, 285; Jim Crow laws and, 4, 128; National Scholarship Service and Fund for Negro Students (NSSFNF) and, 101–5; in the northern states, 18–19, 22–23; *Plessy v. Ferguson* and, 4, 34, 71, 94, 121–22, 238; post–Civil War increase in, 127–28; at public universities (*see* public universities); recommendations for antebellum, 1, 283; religious institutions and, 4; secondary level, 26; self-determination and, 23–24; slave-led rebellions and, 1; as teachers, 19–20; for teaching, 11–12, 19–20, 66, 189, 194, 238, 240, 249, 251–52, 258, 285, 292, 297, 303–4; at white institutions (*see* white institutions, Black women at). *See also* women, Black
Eisenmann, Linda, 228
elitism, 4
Emancipation, 1, 18
escapes, slave, 18
Evans, Elizabeth, 41

Evans, Stephanie Y., 3
Exoduster Movement, 109–10

faculty, Black women: in academic couples, 244–50; colleges offering doctorates and, 237–38; doctoral degree requirements and, 234–35; fellowships and, 241–43, 247; funding for graduate studies and, 238–40; at HBCUs, 156–57, 242–44; Jane Ellen McAllister, 251–55; legal challenges against discrimination and, 238–40; quest for gender equity at Howard University and, 263–71; at risk, 250–57; Women's Faculty Club, Howard University and, 271–80. *See also* individual scholars
Fairchild, E. Henry, 56, 59
Fairfax, Jean, 182–84, 186, 190–91, 304–5
Farnham, Marynia Z., 223, 292
Fauset, Jessie, 85
Favrot, Leo, 252
Fee, John G., 52–53, 56, 60
fellowships, 241–43, 247, 249
Female Literary Association of Philadelphia, 24
Feminine Mystique, The, 228
feminism, 165, 194, 228–29
feminist deans, 165
Ferebee, Claude, 295–96
Ferebee, Dorothy Boulding, 264, 267, 272, 277, 295–96
Fields, Mamie, 293
Fieser, Louis, 242
Fifteenth Amendment, 4, 283
Finney, Charles G., 34
Fisher, Ada Lois Sipuel, 225
Fisk University, 137, 140, 142, 172–73, 214; Black women faculty and administrators at, 250–56; Charles S. Johnson years at, 258–63; David D. Jones years at (*see* Jones, David D.); Race Relations Institute at, 258, 259; recruitment of men to, 261–62; resignation of David Jones from, 257
Fitch, Florence, 167–68
Fletcher, Joseph Grant, 247–48
Fletcher, Juanita, 51
Fletcher, Robert, 35, 37
Flexner, Abraham, 198
Flexner, Eleanor, 43, 229
Flood, J. Julius, 189
Flowers, Deirdre Bennett, 196
Ford, Gary, Jr., 306
Forde, Adelaide Fullmighter, 138

Forde, Dorothy, 138
Forde, Gladys, 138–39, 141
Ford Foundation, 103
Foreman, Madeline Clarke, 256, 262
Foster, Mayme, 172, 215
Franklin, John Hope, 263, 270–71
Franklin, V. P., 22, 306–7
Frazier, E. Franklin, 160, 185, 226, 251, 263
Freedman's Bureau, 142
Freedom's Journal, 25
Friedan, Betty, 228
Frost, William G., 59
Fugitive Slave Act, 1850, 18
Furman, Bess, 223

Gaines v. University of Missouri Law School, 239
Garett, Naomi Mill, 240–41
Garland, Phyl, 301, 303
Garrison, William Lloyd, 24
Gatewood, Willard B., 72
Geiger, Roger, 228
gender ideologies, 5–6
General Education Board (GEB), 211–12, 220–21, 235, 238, 247, 258
GI Bill, 7, 227–28, 261
Giddings, Paula, 3
Gildersleeves, Virginia, 97–98
Giles, Harriet E., 131
Goins, Viola, 242, 245
Golightly, Catherine Cater, 245
Golightly, Cornelius Lacy, 245
Gore, Dayo F., 300
graduate study. *See* academia, Black women in
Graham, Mary Henrietta, 106
Graham, Patricia A., 200
Graham, Shirley, 243–44
Gray, Ida, 107–8
Great Society legislation, 2
Green, Harry, 237
Green, Leila Smith, 241–42
Greene, Harry Washington, 3
Grener, Richard T., 49
Groves, Gladys H., 214
Gubbs, Ethel Harris, 305
Guzman, Jessie P., 182, 213

Haines Normal and Industrial School, 131–32
Hall, Primus, 19
Hall, Prince, 19
Hamer, Fannie Lou, 301

Hampton Normal and Industrial Institute, 136, 201, 214, 235–36
Hanley, Charlotte, 99, 307
Harlem Renaissance, 95
Harlow, Ralph, 101
Harris, Abram, Jr., 270
Harris, Blanche V., 35
Harris, Patricia Roberts, 264, 277
Harris, Sarah, 20–21
Hart, Bill, 36
Hartshorn Memorial College, 128–29
Harvard College, 43, 78, 93
Hathaway, James S., 59–60
Hayden, Robert Earl, 257
Hayes, Harriet, 149
Height, Dorothy, 98–99, 239–40
Hemmings, Anita Florence, 93
Hendricks, Derosette, 102
Higginbotham, Evelyn, 20, 154
Higher Education Act, 1965, 2
Higher Education for Women in Postwar America, 1945–1965, 228
Highland, Henry, 22
Hilltop, 147, 153
Hine, Darlene Clark, 3, 282
Historically Black Colleges and Universities (HBCUs), 4, 6, 7, 8, 103, 107; all-male and coeducational, 132–36; Atlanta Baptist Female Seminary, 130–31; Bennett College, 131–32, 180–81, 192–95, 204, 206–7, 210, 221, 223–24; Black women faculty at (*see* faculty, Black women); Civil Rights Movement and, 226; conservative religion and, 128; deans of women at (*see* deans of women, HBCU); founded by white religious denominations, *134–35*; Hartshorn Memorial College, 128–29; institutional diversity among Black women at, 136–40; marginality of Black women college graduates and, 304–6; Morehouse College, 131, 133, 257, 270; Morrill Act, 1890, and, *135*; National Association of Women's Deans and Advisors of Women in Colored Schools (NAWDACS) and, 6, 161–64; Scotia Seminary, 129–30; single-sex institutions for Black women and girls, 128–32; Spelman College, 107, 130–31, 137, 138, 189, 217–29; Tillotson's College, 280–82; Tuskegee Institute, 64, 136, 140–41, 180, 181–92; veterans at, 227–28, 261; women's sports at, 200–205. *See also* Fisk University; Howard University

History of Black Education Prior to 1861, 52
Hoff, Tamara Lynette, 109
Holders of Doctorate Among American Negroes, 3
home economics and homemaking, 8, 193, 195, 196–200, 207, 210, 221–23, 235–36, 289; feminism and, 228–29
Home Making Institute, 196–200, 221, 223–24, 226
homosexuality, 297, 311
Hoover, Herbert, 255
Horowitz, Helen, 84
housing, college, 90–93, 167–69
Houston, Charles Hamilton, 263
Houston, G. David, 185
Houston, Joanna, 171, 173
Howard Record, 148
Howard University, 6, 64–65, 137, 140–43; alumni clubs, 154–55; Black women faculty and administrators at, 250–51, 256, 263–71; Lucy Diggs Slowe as dean of women at, 145–61, 265, 270; missionary funding of, 147; quest for gender equity at, 263–71; religious life at, 160; social life at, 147; Teacher's College, 148–49; Women's Faculty Club at, 271–80
Howland, Emily, 29
Hughes, Langston, 182, 214, 226
Hunter, Charlayne Alberta, 226
Hunter College, 7, 65–70, 69, 137
Huntley, Mary Gibson, 76
Hurston, Zora Neale, 95–96
Hutchins, Grace, 87
Hutchins, Robert, 168

ideal womanhood, 22
Imes, Elmer S., 251
In Pursuit of Knowledge: Black Women and Educational Activism in Antebellum America, 3
Institute for Colored Youth, Philadelphia, 29, 30–31
interracial dating, 59
Irvin, Lois, 130
Ivy Leaf, 112, 120, 123, 124

Jackson, Fanny, 5, 137; George Henry Calvert and, 41–43; graduation from Oberlin, 49; Ladies Literary Society and, 44–45; living situation at Oberlin, 48; at Oberlin College, 41–42, 43–45; at Rhode Island State Normal School, 43; support for Oberlin, 49–50; teaching by, 45–47

Jackson, Ida Louise, 169–70, 181–84, 186, 188, 295
Jackson, John H., 60
Jane Crow, 3, 144, 311
Janken, Kenneth, 296
Jenkins, Herbert, 124
Jenkins, Martin, 250
Jesus, Jobs and Justice: African American Women and Religion, 154
Jet, 290
Jewish students: housing of, 90–93; question of Black and, 86–90
Jim Crow laws, 4, 128, 311
Johnson, Alice Carlotte, 239
Johnson, Charles S., 3, 142, 198, 286, 289; Black women faculty under, 258–63, 279; at Fisk University, 250–51, 295; *The Negro College Graduate* by, 197–98, 209–10, 285
Johnson, Hallie Tanner, 233
Johnson, James Weldon, 257
Johnson, Joan Marie, 89–90
Johnson, Lyndon B., 2
Johnson, Marie, 89
Johnson, Mordecai, 142, 160–61, 263, 265, 267, 270
Jones, David D., 181, 192, 224; Adelaide Fullmighter Forde and, 138–39; at Earlham College, 257; Jane Ellen McAllister and, 252–55; Sadie Daniels and, 255–56; Spelman College conference, 1944, and, 220–21; Susie Williams Jones and, 248–49; "The War and the Higher Education of Negro Women" by, 209–10
Jones, Edward, 36, 246
Jones, Frances, 224
Jones, James Monroe, 106–7
Jones, Sophia Bethena, 106, 108
Jones, Susie Williams, 195, 248–49
Jones, Thomas E., 250
Jonson, J. Hugo, 211
Jordan, Vernon, 104–5
Joseph, Vera, 96–97, 99, 100–101
Journal of Blacks in Higher Education, 310
Journal of Negro Education, 209, 290
Julian, Percy, 270
Just, Ernest, 238, 263, 270

Kelly, Hattie Simmons, 184–91
King, Francis Monroe, 100
King, Martin Luther, Jr., 2
Kinson, Margu, 37–38
Kittrell, Flemmie, 193–95, 198, 213, 264–65, 271, 272; "Current Problems and Pro-

grams in Higher Education" by, 216–17; laboratory school established by, 224; proposal for conference on higher education of Black women, 210–11
Ku Klux Klan, 53, 109

Lacy, Virginia, 246–47
LaGuardia, Fiorello, 74
land-grant colleges. *See* public universities
Lane Seminary, 33–34
Laney, Lucy Craft, 131–32
Lange, Elizabeth, 26
Langley, Joretha, 105
Langston, John Mercer, 48
Lawrence, Charles, 246
Lawrence, Margaret, 246
Lawrence, Paul F., 103, 104–5
Lawson, Kathereyn, 306
Lee, Carrie, 80, 82
Lee, Winona, 247
Leece, Barbara Jeanne, 105
Lever Act, 1914, 133
Lewis, Mary Edmonia, 31
Liberator, The, 24
Lightfoot, Sara Lawrence, 246
Lincoln, C. Eric, 300
Lincoln University, 133
Lindsay, Inabel Burns, 264, 265–67, 269, 290, 294–95, 303
literary and educational societies, 24–26; at Oberlin College, 40, 44
Little Rock nine, 226
Lloyd-Jones, Esther, 149
Locke, Alain, 263
Logan, Rayford, 144, 263, 267, 268–69, 270, 279, 282, 296
Logan, Ruth, 296
Love, Ellen Park, 93
Luce, Henry C., 102
Lucy, Autherine Juanita, 225
Lucy Sprague Mitchell: The Making of a Modern Woman, 167
Lyon, Mary, 81–82

MacCracken, Henry, 94
Mack, Kenneth, 127
Mademoiselle, 226
Mahan, Asa, 34
Malone, Vivian Juanita, 225
manhood rights, 17
Manley, Albert, 226
Manning, Kenneth, 238
Mapp, Grace A., 30–31, 41

March on Washington, 1963, 306–7
marginality of Black women college graduates: Black scholarly journals on, 290–91; Civil Rights Movement and, 298–301, 305–10; HBCUs and, 304–6; Inabel Lindsay on, 290, 301; Ina Bolton on, 288–89; Jane Crow and, 3, 144, 311; Marion V. Cuthbert on, 285–87, 301, 304; marriage and, 292–97, 300–302; political advantages of Black men and, 283–84; W. E. B. Du Bois on, 307–9; Willa Player on, 287–88; women's suffrage and, 308; working in politics, 291–92
marriage and Black women, 215–16, 222–23, 228, 244–50, 292–97, 300–301; in academic couples, 244–50, 295–97; in dual career couples, 301–3
Marshall, Thurgood, 226
Mathis, Corine, 122
May, Samuel J., 20, 22
Mays, Benjamin E., 226, 248, 263, 270
Mays, Sadie Gray, 248
McAllister, Jane Ellen, 251–55, 257
McCane, Margaret Perea, 76
McCarn, Ruth, 168
McCleary, Beatrix, 94–95, 101
McCluskey, Audrey Thomas, 131
McCrorey, H. L., 176
McCuistion, Fred, 197
McGhee, Ethel, 249
McGhee, Sarah, 122
McKenzie, Fayette Avery, 250
Mead, Margaret, 215–16, 226
Methodist Women's Home Mission Society, 196
Meyer, Annie Nathan, 95
Meyerowitz, Joanne, 228, 229
Middlebury College, 63–64
Middleton, George, 19
Miller, Fannie, 58, 59
Miller, Kelly, 308
Miller, Loren, 120–21
Mills College, 70
Miner, Myrtilla, 27–29, 33
Miner Teachers College, 257
Mirror to America, 270
Mitchell, Belle, 53–54
Mitchell, Lucy Sprague, 166–67
Mitchem, Georgiana, 40
Modern Woman: The Lost Sex, 223
Moe, Henry, 242
Monro, John, 102
Monteith, Henrie Dobbins, 226

Index   367

Moore, Cassandra, 111
Moore, Louis Baxter, 233
Moore, Ruth Ella, 271–72, 275–76
Moors, John F., 77–78
moral uplift, 128
Morehouse, Henry, 5
Morehouse College, 131, 133, 257, 270
Morrill Act: 1862, 106, 133; 1890, 133, *135,* 229
Morris, Margaret, 211
Moss, Hillary, 20
Mossell, Aaron, 233
Mossell, Sadie. *See* Alexander, Sadie Tanner Mossell
Motley, Constance Baker, 5, 304, 306
Moton, Robert, 183, 185, 188
Mount Holyoke College, 72, 81–84, 100–101; Jewish students at, 92
Moynihan, Daniel Patrick, 298–99
Murphy, Franklin, 121
Murray, Pauli, 3, 5, 66–67, 69, 71, 144, 225, 292, 293, 300, 311

National Association for the Advancement of Colored People (NAACP), 2, 93, 96, 161, 297; Barnard College and, 99; housing policy at Smith College and, 80–81; legal battles against discrimination, 97, 102, 225, 238–40; *Plessy v. Ferguson* and, 94, 121–22
National Association of College Women (NACW), 6, 154–55, 173–79, 180, 304–5; on curriculum, 206; home economics and, 196–97; women's sports and, 205
National Association of Colored Women's Club, 5, 127, 132
National Association of Women's Deans and Advisors of Women in Colored Schools (NAWDACS), 6, 161–64, 288; 1944 conference, 213–17; challenges and quest for refinement and femininity, 170–76; on curriculum, 206; study of women students at Spelman College, 217–29; white deans and, 165, 166; women's sports and, 201–2, 205
National Conference of Social Work, 258
National Council of Negro Women, 264, 311
National Organization of Women (NOW), 3
National Scholarship Service and Fund for Negro Students (NSSFNS), 101–5
National Training School, 132
National Urban League, 237, 259, 295, 307
National Women's Suffrage Association, 308
Neau, Elias, 18

Negro College Graduate, The, 197–98, 210, 285
Negro Common School, 127
Negro Digest, 290, 292, 300
Neilson, William Allan, 81, 90–91
Nelson, James Sanford, 107
Nelson, William Stuart, 188–89
nepotism, 303
Neverdon-Morton, Cynthia, 3
Newman, Stephen, 144
New York Central College (NYCC), 2, 30–33
New York Times, 205, 222, 223
Nichols, Matilda Adams, 143
Nixon, E. D., 89
Noble, Jeanne, 292–94, 304
Norris, Frances J., 41, 50
Northrup, Solomon, 18
North Star, 32
Noyes Academy, 20

Oberlin College, 2, 7, 29, 30, 33, 63; admission requirements at, 43–44; African students at, 37–38; antislavery activities at, pre–Civil War, 34–35; Black citizens in town of Oberlin and, 35; Black student activism at, 47–48; and decision to become interracial institution, 34–35; early Black, female students at, 39–41; early Black students at, 35–36; Fanny Jackson Coppin and, 41–52; founding of, 33–34; housing at, 168; Ladies Literary Society at, 40, 44–45; Mary Jane Patterson and, 50–51; population of Black students at, pre–Civil War, 37; progressiveness of, 46–47; sense of community and purpose at, 43; tuition and scholarships at, 38–39
Oberlin Evangelist, 40, 50
Opportunity: A Journal of Negro Life, 290
Opportunity News, 105

Packard, Sophia B., 131
Palmer, Alice Freeman, 132, 148, 165, 167
Palmer, Edward N., 245
Palmer Memorial Institute (PMI), 132
Park, Marion Edwards, 86–88, 91, 92
Parker, Hortense, 82
Parker, Mary, 123
Parks, Rosa, 89, 301
Past Is Behind Us, The, 299
Patterson, Frederick, 181, 184, 186–89
Patterson, Inez Robie, 123–24
Patterson, Louise Thompson, 277–78

Patterson, Mary Jane, 35, *36,* 40–41, 50–51
Payne, Daniel, 43
Peace, Larry, 110
Peck, Henry, 48
Petry, Ann, 292, 294, 296, 300
PhD programs. *See* academia, Black women in
Phelps-Stokes Fund, 96, 258
phenotype, 31–32
physical education major, 122–24
Pitre, Merline, 297–98
Pittsburgh Courier, 222
Player, Willa Beatrice, 194, 195, 287–88
Plessy v. Ferguson, 4, 34, 71, 94, 121–22, 238
political advantage of Black men over Black women, 283–84
politics of responsibility, 4, 20
Porter, Dorothy, 264
Powell, Eunice, 236
professorate. *See* academia, Black women in; faculty, Black women
Prosser, Gabriel, 1, 18
prostitution, 32
public universities: Black Greek organizations at, 112–22; Black women and sports at, 122–24; curriculum at, 206; Morrill Acts and, 106, 133; University of Kansas, 110–11; University of Michigan, 97, 106–9, 138–39
Purington, Florence, 82–83

Quakers, 19, 26, 29, 84, 250; abolitionist colleges and, 29, 31
Quarles, Benjamin, 249–50
Quarterly Review of Higher Education Among Negroes, 216, 220

Race Relations Institute, Fisk University, 258, 259
race uplift, 4, 20, 24–25, 109, 127–28, 155–56, 264, 293, 306
Radcliffe College, 72, 75–78
Ralston, Martha, 82
Randolph-Macon Women's College, 69–70
Ray, Charlotte, 143
Read, Florence, 84, 206–7, 210, 240
Reason, Charles, 30–31
Rice, Harriett Alleynce, 72–73, 100
Richardson, Gloria, 301
Richardson, Joseph, 257
Roberts, Deidre Cobb, 109
Roberts, Josie Wilhelmina, 236–37
Roberts, Lilian, 301–2

Roberts, Ordie, 204
Robinson, James, 94, 97–99
Robinson, Ruby, 301
Rockefeller, John D., 211
Rockefeller Foundation, 6, 207
Rogers, J. A. R., 54
Roosevelt, Eleanor, 226
Roosevelt, Franklin D., 244, 255
Rosenwald, Julius, 198, 258
Rosenwald Foundation, 6, 235–36, 238, 240–41, 242, 245–46, 258; fellowships, 249
Russell, Lillian, 88
Russwurm, John, 36

Sadler, Juanita, 172
Sartorius, Kelly C., 165, 166, 168, 192
Scarlet and Black: Volume Two, Constructing Race and Gender at Rutgers, 1865–1945, 4
Schomburg Center for Research in Black Culture, New York Public Library, 97
Schooling Citizens: The Struggle for African American Education in Antebellum America, 20
Schwartz, Felice Nierenberg, 101–2, 105
Scotia Seminary, 129–30
Scott, Alberta, 75–76
Scott, Charlotte Hanley, 100
self-determination, 23–24
Seven Sisters colleges, 7, 9, 63, 68, 96–97, 98, 100, 101, 155, 240; individual colleges of, 70–72; Jewish and Black question at, 86–90
sexual orientation, 297, 311
Shadd, Harriett, 144
Shaw, Stephanie, 3
Shipherd, John Jay, 34
Sidney, Thomas, 22
Simpson, Georgiana, 85, 156, 233, 234, 264
Sims, Alice, 122–23
single-sex schools for Black women and girls, 26–28; Atlanta Baptist Female Seminary, 130–31; Bennett College, 131–32; Hartshorn Memorial College, 128–29; Scotia Seminary, 129–30
slave-led rebellions, 1, 18, 53
Sloan, Ruth, 223
Slowe, Lucy Diggs, 5, 6, 142, 167, 169, 176, 178, 188, 189, 210, 270, 305; appointment and salary of, 145–46; Black women's leadership developed by, 149–52; campus presence at Howard, 147–48; curriculum recommendations of, 160–61; as dean of women at Howard University, 145–61, 265;

Slowe, Lucy Diggs (*continued*): goals for shaping Black women, 148, 152, 171–72, 193, 311; National Association of College Women (NACW) and, 173–79, 180; National Association of Women's Deans and Advisors of Women in Colored Schools (NAWDACS) and, 6, 161–64, 170–76; on racial uplift, 155–56; rules for social events and conduct, 153–54, 159–60; students expelled by, 152–53; Teacher's College and, 148–49; as woman of faith, 178–79
Smith, Bessie, 147
Smith, Carrie Lee, 82
Smith, Charlotte, 242
Smith, Johnson C., 176
Smith, Sophia, 78–79
Smith, Walter Lucius, 64
Smith, W. R., 32
Smith College, 72, 78–81; Jewish students at, 92
Smith-Hughes Act, 1917, 133
Smythe, Hugh, 245
Smythe, Mabel, 245
Snowden, Frank, 263
Snyder, Franklyn Bliss, 168
Society for Relief of Free Negroes Unlawfully Held in Bondage, 19
Society of Friends. *See* Quakers
Solomon, Barbara, 7, 65
Southern Clubs, 90
Southern Project, 103–5
Spelman College, 107, 130–31, 137, 138, 189; study group on women students at, 1944, 217–29
Spelman Messenger, 220
Spencer, Lyle, 102
Spingarn, Joel E., 80
sports and Black women, 122–24, 200–205
Stamps, James, 222
Stanley, Ollie Mae, 102
Stannard, Julia, 108
Stanton, Lucy, 39–40, 44
Stebbins, Lucy, 169
Sterling, Dorothy, 28–29
Stewart, Maria W., 24–25, 45
Stewart, William, 59
St. Frances Academy for Colored Girls, 26
Stinnett, Mabel Myers, 235–36
Stone, Lucy, 40
Stone, Sadie, 111
Storey, Moorfield, 80–81

Stowe, Catherine Beecher, 32–33
Straight University, 64
Stuart, Mary, 41
Student Nonviolent Coordinating Committee (SNCC), 226, 311
Sturtevant, Sarah W., 149
Sullivan, Grace Mae, 236
Synnott, Marcia G., 225, 306

Taft, Jonathan, 107
Taft, William, 107
Talbot, Marion, 165
Tate, Merze, 193–95, 198–200, 264–65, 268–69, 305, 311; Women's Faculty Club at Howard University and, 271, 272–76
Taylor, Alrutheus Ambush, 251
Taylor, Emily, 165
teachers, African American, 19–20, 303–4
Teachers College, Columbia University, 11–12, 66, 189, 194, 238, 240, 249, 251–52, 258, 285, 292, 297
Terrell, Mary Church, 5, 65, 127, 154, 156, 296–97
Thomas, Better Collier, 154
Thomas, M. Carey, 84–86, 88, 90
Thompson, Charles, 261, 269
Thurman, Howard, 263, 270
Tiffany, Charles, 297
Tillotson's College, 280–82
Tobias, Belle, 96, 99
Tobias, Channing, 96, 102
Topeka Plaindealer, The, 112
Truth, Sojourner, 4, 45
Tubman, Harriet, 18
Turner, Nat, 1, 18
Turpin, Josephine, 143
Tuskegee Institute, 64, 136, 140–41, 180; Associated Women's Students (AWS) at, 186–87; deans of women at, 181–92
Twilight, Lucius, 36

Uncle Tom's Cabin, 32
Undaunted by the Fight: Spelman College and the Civil Rights Movement, 1957–1967, 226
Underground Railroad, 18, 48
Unitarianism, 91
United Council of Church Women, 259
United Negro College Fund (UNCF), 103
University of Kansas, 110–11; Black Greek organizations at, 112
University of Michigan, 97, 106–9, 138–39, 190–91

Valien, Bonita, 245
Valien, Preston, 245
Van Dusen, Henry, 102
Vashon, George, 30
Vassar College, 72, 73, 93–95; Jewish students at, 92
Vesey, Denmark, 1, 18
veterans, Black, 7, 227–28, 261
Victorian womanhood, 5
Vitalis, Robert, 276
Voice for the South, A, 284
voting rights, 4, 17, 226, 283

Walden, Edmonia Louise, 249
Walker, David, 1, 17, 18
Walker, Madame CJ, 157
Wallace, Phyllis, 307
Walsh, Stella, 205
Walton, Andrea, 4
Ware, Caroline, 269, 271
Washington, Bernadine Carrickett, 291
Washington, Booker T., 64, 76, 136, 141, 181, 183–84
Waters, Phyllis W., 123
Watkins, Charlotte, 272
Weaver, Robert C., 102, 103
Wellesley College, 72; Jewish students at, 92
Wells, Ida B., 106
Welter, Barbara, 22
Wesley, Dorothy Porter, 264, 269–70, 275
White, Jane, 81
White, Mary Esther, 102
White, Walter, 81
white institutions, Black women at, 60; Barnard College, 72, 95–101; Bryn Mawr College, 72, 84–88, 91–93; College of New Jersey for Women, 70; discrimination against, 68–70; housing and, 90–93, 167–69; Hunter College, 7, 65–70, 137; Jewish and Black question at, 86–90; Middlebury College, 63–64; Mount Holyoke College, 72, 81–84, 92, 100–101; National Scholarship Service and Fund for Negro Students (NSSFNF) and, 101–5; *Plessy v. Ferguson* and, 4, 34, 71, 94; Radcliffe College, 72, 75–78; Seven Sisters colleges, 7, 9, 63, 68, 70–72, 96–97, 98, 100, 101, 155, 240; Smith College, 72, 78–81, 92; Vassar College, 72, 73, 92, 93–95; Wellesley College, 72–75, 92; white deans of women and, 165–70
White Shield League, 129
Wilberforce University, 132–33
Williams, Emily Harper, 107, 108
Williams, Fanny Barrier, 5
Williams, Frances, 83–84
Winston, Michael, 282
Wolters, Raymond, 133, 136
women, Black: in abolitionist colleges (*see* abolitionist colleges); antebellum recommendations for education of, 1; Civil Rights Movement and, 225–26, 298–301, 305–10; as deans (*see* deans of women, HBCU); deciding to stay single, 22–23; denied voting rights, 4; dissertations on higher education by, 3; educated in the North, 23; educational attainment of, 229, 233, 283, 293–94, 309–10; in faculty positions, 156–57; feminism and, 165, 228–29; gender ideologies and, 5–6; graduating as physicians and research scientists, 100–101, 107–9, 110–11, 138–40, 142, 143–44, 242, 246; graduating from law schools, 67, 73–74, 94, 100, 102, 105, 122, 143, 144, 157, 234, 251, 291, 297, 304; Greek organizations and, 112–22; in higher education, 2–3; in Historically Black Colleges and Universities (HBCUs) (*see* Historically Black Colleges and Universities (HBCUs)); home economics and, 193, 195, 196–200, 235–36, 289; as homemakers, 8, 193, 195, 196–200, 207, 210, 221–23, 228–29; housing of, 90–93, 167–69; ideal womanhood and, 22; Jane Crow and, 3, 144, 311; in leadership positions in academia, 51–52; literary and educational societies and, 24–26, 40, 44–45; marginality of college educated (*see* marginality of Black women college graduates); marriage and motherhood among, 215–16, 222–23, 228, 244–50, 292–97, 300–302; phenotype and white perceptions of, 31–32; poverty among, 284; in predominantly white institutions, 7; Prudence Crandall school for, 21–22; at public universities (*see* public universities); religions institutions and, 4–5; respect and chivalry not afforded to, 4, 20–21; salaries of, 297–98; secondary education for, 26; sexual orientation and, 297, 311; in single-sex schools, 26–28; sports and, 122–24, 200–205; studies on higher education and, 3–4; Victorian womanhood and, 5; at white institutions, post–Civil War (*see* white institutions, Black women at); working in politics, 291–92

Women at Indiana University, 4
Wood, Marie, 268
Woodson, Carter G., 52
Woolley, Mary Emma, 92
Works Progress Administration, 244
Wright Edelman, Marion, 301
Wyatt, Donald, 103

Young Crusaders: the Untold story of the Children and Teenagers Who Galvanized the Civil Rights Movement, The, 306–7

Young Men's Christian Association (YMCA), 96
Young Women's Christian Association (YWCA), 84, 94, 123, 124, 138, 224–25; Black women employed by, 257; deans of women and, 149, 153, 161, 163, 183

Zinn, Howard, 201

LINDA PERKINS is a professor and the director of Applied Gender Studies Department at Claremont Graduate University. She is the author of *Fanny Jackson Coppin and the Institute for Colored Youth, 1865–1902.*

The University of Illinois Press
is a founding member of the
Association of University Presses.

———————————————

University of Illinois Press
1325 South Oak Street
Champaign, IL 61820-6903
www.press.uillinois.edu